ADOLESCENT PSYCHOLOGY 98/99

Second Edition

Editors

Anita M. Meehan
Kutztown University of Pennsylvania

Anita M. Meehan is professor of psychology at Kutztown University of Pennsylvania. She received a B.A. from Wilkes College with majors in psychology and elementary education and an M.A. and Ph.D. in developmental psychology from Temple University. Her research interests have focused on cognitive and social development. Most recently, she has published and presented work on gender schemas and sex-role development.

Eileen Astor-Stetson
Bloomsburg University of Pennsylvania

Eileen Astor-Stetson is a professor of psychology at Bloomsburg University. She received an A.B. in psychology from Douglass College, Rutgers–The State University of New Jersey, and a Ph.D. in psychology from Vanderbilt University. She has two general areas of research. One involves age-related changes in perception. The other focuses on predictors of safer sex behaviors in adolescents and young adults, including risk taking, alcohol use, and knowledge about HIV. Dr. Astor-Stetson has also presented work on techniques for teaching students about safer sex.

Annual Editions
A Library of Information from the Public Press
Dushkin/McGraw·Hill
Sluice Dock, Guilford, Connecticut 06437

Visit us on the Internet—http://www.dushkin.com/

The Annual Editions Series

ANNUAL EDITIONS, including GLOBAL STUDIES, consist of over 70 volumes designed to provide the reader with convenient, low-cost access to a wide range of current, carefully selected articles from some of the most important magazines, newspapers, and journals published today. ANNUAL EDITIONS are updated on an annual basis through a continuous monitoring of over 300 periodical sources. All ANNUAL EDITIONS have a number of features that are designed to make them particularly useful, including topic guides, annotated tables of contents, unit overviews, and indexes. For the teacher using ANNUAL EDITIONS in the classroom, an Instructor's Resource Guide with test questions is available for each volume. GLOBAL STUDIES titles provide comprehensive background information and selected world press articles on the regions and countries of the world.

VOLUMES AVAILABLE

ANNUAL EDITIONS
Abnormal Psychology
Accounting
Adolescent Psychology
Aging
American Foreign Policy
American Government
American History, Pre-Civil War
American History, Post-Civil War
American Public Policy
Anthropology
Archaeology
Astronomy
Biopsychology
Business Ethics
Child Growth and Development
Comparative Politics
Computers in Education
Computers in Society
Criminal Justice
Criminology
Developing World
Deviant Behavior
Drugs, Society, and Behavior
Dying, Death, and Bereavement
Early Childhood Education

Economics
Educating Exceptional Children
Education
Educational Psychology
Environment
Geography
Geology
Global Issues
Health
Human Development
Human Resources
Human Sexuality
International Business
Macroeconomics
Management
Marketing
Marriage and Family
Mass Media
Microeconomics
Multicultural Education
Nutrition
Personal Growth and Behavior
Physical Anthropology
Psychology
Public Administration
Race and Ethnic Relations

Social Problems
Social Psychology
Sociology
State and Local Government
Teaching English as a Second
    Language
Urban Society
Violence and Terrorism
Western Civilization,
    Pre-Reformation
Western Civilization,
    Post-Reformation
Women's Health
World History, Pre-Modern
World History, Modern
World Politics
GLOBAL STUDIES
Africa
China
India and South Asia
Japan and the Pacific Rim
Latin America
Middle East
Russia, the Eurasian Republics,
    and Central/Eastern Europe
Western Europe

Cataloging in Publication Data
Main entry under title: Annual Editions: Adolescent Psychology. 1998/99.
        1. Psychology—Periodicals. I. Meehan, Anita, comp.II. Astor-Stetson, Eileen, comp. III. Title: Adolescent Psychology.
    155.5'05   ISBN 0–697–39128–0   82–646006

Second Edition

Cover image © 1997 PhotoDisc, Inc.

Printed in the United States of America

Printed on Recycled Paper

Editors/Advisory Board

Members of the Advisory Board are instrumental in the final selection of articles for each edition of ANNUAL EDITIONS. Their review of articles for content, level, currentness, and appropriateness provides critical direction to the editor and staff. We think that you will find their careful consideration well reflected in this volume.

EDITORS

Anita M. Meehan
Kutztown University of Pennsylvania

Eileen Astor-Stetson
Bloomsburg University of Pennsylvania

ADVISORY BOARD

Lee Abbott
Cayuga Community College

Paul J. Berghoff
Pembroke State University

Christy Buchanan
Wake Forest University

John S. Dacey
Boston College

Florence L. Denmark
Pace University

Gene V. Elliott
Rowan University of New Jersey

Gregory T. Fouts
University of Calgary

Wyndol Furman
University of Denver

Emily J. Johnson
*University of Wisconsin
La Crosse*

Maureen E. Kenny
Boston College

Daniel K. Lapsley
Ball State University

John Mirich
Metropolitan State College of Denver

John Mitchell
University of Alberta

Alinde J. Moore
Ashland University

George Muugi
Kutztown University

Elizabeth B. Newell
*California State University
Fresno*

Joycelyn G. Parish
Kansas State University

John W. Santrock
*University of Texas
Dallas*

Gail Scott
Briar Cliff College

Michael Shaughnessy
Eastern New Mexico University

Margaret B. Spencer
University of Pennsylvania

Staff

Ian A. Nielsen, Publisher

To the Reader

In publishing ANNUAL EDITIONS we recognize the enormous role played by the magazines, newspapers, and journals of the *public press* in providing current, first-rate educational information in a broad spectrum of interest areas. Many of these articles are appropriate for students, researchers, and professionals seeking accurate, current material to help bridge the gap between principles and theories and the real world. These articles, however, become more useful for study when those of lasting value are carefully *collected, organized, indexed,* and *reproduced* in a *low-cost format,* which provides easy and permanent access when the material is needed. That is the role played by ANNUAL EDITIONS. Under the direction of each volume's *academic editor,* who is an expert in the subject area, and with the guidance of an *Advisory Board,* each year we seek to provide in each ANNUAL EDITION a current, well-balanced, carefully selected collection of the best of the public press for your study and enjoyment. We think that you will find this volume useful, and we hope that you will take a moment to let us know what you think.

No longer a child and not yet an adult, adolescents find themselves caught in the middle. Popular culture often depicts adolescence as a period of raging hormones, emotional upheaval, rejection of parents, and blind conformity to peers. One goal of this anthology is to present a more balanced picture of adolescence, including both positive and negative aspects of this developmental transition. In *Annual Editions: Adolescent Psychology 98/99,* we chose articles that address timeless adolescent issues such as puberty, the identity crisis, and establishing independence from parents. We also chose articles that discuss contemporary issues affecting adolescents, parents, and professionals who interact with adolescents. For example, articles examine tracking in schools, AIDS, nonnuclear families, working adolescents, and steroid use. We made an effort to include readings that focus on effective strategies and interventions for helping adolescents through this transition period, particularly at-risk adolescents.

We have organized this anthology into eight units. The units cover issues related to the fundamental biological, cognitive, and socioemotional changes of adolescence as well as the contexts of adolescent development (family, school, peers, work). In keeping with this perspective that the ecological context of adolescent development is crucial to understanding, we also incorporated articles that examine the impact of socioeconomic, gender, ethnic, and cultural influences on adolescent development. Unit 1 looks at adolescence in historical and contemporary perspectives. Unit 2 examines the biological and psychological impact of puberty. Unit 3 explores issues related to cognitive growth and education. Unit 4 addresses identity and socioemotional development. Unit 5 covers family relationships during adolescence, while unit 6 focuses on peers and youth culture. Teen sexuality issues are examined in unit 7. Problem behaviors like teen violence, eating disorders, drug use, and suicide are included in unit 8.

Many readings present controversial topics that we hope will spur classroom debate. For example, should condoms be distributed in schools? Should growth hormones be administered to increase height? Are mandatory exit exams a good solution to ensure that high school students have met educational standards? Should the drinking age be lowered? Are classrooms gender-biased?

We hope that the articles in this second edition of *Annual Editions: Adolescent Psychology* will be thought-provoking and interesting for the reader and that the readings will result in a deeper understanding of adolescent development. We would like to thank the reviewers who made comments on the first edition and we would also like to know what you think. Please take a few minutes to complete and return the postage-paid article rating form in the back of this volume. Anything can be improved, and we need your help to improve future editions of *Annual Editions: Adolescent Psychology.*

Anita M. Meehan

Eileen Astor-Stetson
Editors

Contents

UNIT 1

Perspectives on Adolescence

Three articles in this section examine what defines adolescence.

UNIT 2

Biological and Psychological Aspects of Puberty

Seven selections in this section consider what impact puberty has on the maturing adolescent.

The concepts in bold italics are developed in the article. For further expansion please refer to the Topic Guide and the Index.

UNIT 3

Cognitive Growth and Education

The dynamics encountered by adolescents as they learn to cope with society and educational experiences are discussed in the 10 articles in this section.

The concepts in bold italics are developed in the article. For further expansion please refer to the Topic Guide and the Index.

vi

UNIT 4

Identity and Socioemotional Development

Five articles in this section look at how an adolescent copes with self-esteem, establishing a sense of identity, emotional development, and emotional intelligence.

The concepts in bold italics are developed in the article. For further expansion please refer to the Topic Guide and the Index.

UNIT 5

Family Relationships

In this section, seven articles examine how much influence family life has on adolescent development.

UNIT 6

Peers and Youth Culture

Eight articles in this section consider the extent that gender roles, peer group pressure, drugs, and mass media influence the socialization of an adolescent.

The concepts in bold italics are developed in the article. For further expansion please refer to the Topic Guide and the Index.

viii

UNIT 7

Teenage Sexuality

Eleven articles in this section discuss how adolescents view sexual behavior and the importance of sex education.

The concepts in bold italics are developed in the article. For further expansion please refer to the Topic Guide and the Index.

The concepts in bold italics are developed in the article. For further expansion please refer to the Topic Guide and the Index.

UNIT 8

Problem Behaviors and Interventions

In this section, seven articles address some of the problems faced by today's adolescents. These include: drug abuse, violence, ethnicity, eating disorders, steroid use, and suicide.

The concepts in bold italics are developed in the article. For further expansion please refer to the Topic Guide and the Index.

Topic Guide

This topic guide suggests how the selections in this book relate to topics of traditional concern to psychology students and professionals. It is useful for locating articles that relate to each other for reading and research. The guide is arranged alphabetically according to topic. Articles may, of course, treat topics that do not appear in the topic guide. In turn, entries in the topic guide do not necessarily constitute a comprehensive listing of all the contents of each selection. In addition, relevant Web sites, which are annotated on the next two pages, are noted in **bold italics** under the topic articles.

TOPIC AREA	TREATED IN	TOPIC AREA	TREATED IN
Achievement	12. Program Helps Kids Map Realistic Goals 15. At-Risk Students and Resiliency 19. International Differences in Mathematical Achievement 20. Gender Gap in Math Scores Is Closing *(12, 13, 14)*	**Early Adolescence (cont'd)**	11. Developmentally Appropriate Middle Level Schools 17. Schools the Source of Rough Transitions 29. "Don't Talk Back!" 41. Too Young to Date? *(6, 7, 9, 10, 11, 24, 31, 33)*
Autonomy/ Independence	1. Teenage Wasteland? 28. Enjoying Your Child's Teenage Years 35. Too Old, Too Fast? *(6, 7, 8, 20, 23, 24, 25)*	**Eating Disorders**	5. "My Body Is So Ugly" 6. I'm Okay! 7. Body of the Beholder 56. A's and B's of Eating Disorders *(9, 10, 11, 36, 37, 41)*
Body Image/ Attractiveness	4. Age of Embarrassment 5. "My Body Is So Ugly" 6. I'm Okay! 7. Body of the Beholder 57. Biceps in a Bottle *(6, 9, 10, 11, 28)*	**Extra-curricular Activities**	13. Mommy, What's a Classroom? 15. At-Risk Students and Resiliency 33. Football, Fast Cars, and Cheerleading 35. Too Old, Too Fast? 36. Why Working Teens Get into Trouble *(12, 13, 15, 20, 24)*
College Students	22. College Kids' Parents Should "Keep Cool" 51. Young Adults and AIDS *(22, 25, 33)*	**Fathers**	31. Bringing Up Father *(21, 23, 25)*
Dating	21. There's a First Time for Everything 41. Too Young to Date? *(16, 17, 18, 29, 31, 32, 33)*	**Gender Differences**	14. Boys' Schools Reconsidered 20. Gender Gap in Math Scores Is Closing 34. Football, Fast Cars, and Cheerleading 35. Friendship and Friends' Influence in Adolescence *(15, 18, 23, 28, 29, 36, 37)*
Defining Adolescence	1. Teenage Wasteland? 2. Way We Weren't 21. There's a First Time for Everything 26. Adolescence: Whose Hell Is It? *(6, 7, 8, 9, 18, 19, 39)*	**Homosexuality**	30. Gay Families Come Out 42. Clack of Tiny Sparks 50. Will Schools Risk Teaching about the Risk of AIDS? 51. Young Adults and AIDS *(24, 28, 29, 30, 31, 32, 33, 39, 41)*
Discipline	31. Bringing Up Father *(21, 23, 25)*	**Identity**	6. I'm Okay! 21. There's a First Time for Everything 22. College Kids' Parents Should "Keep Cool" 23. Ethnicity, Identity Formation, and Risk Behavior among Adolescents of Mexican Descent 24. "I'm Just Who I Am" 55. Clinical Assessment of Adolescents Involved in Satanism *(6, 7, 8, 9, 17, 18, 19, 21, 29)*
Divorce	27. How Teens Strain the Family 32. Longitudinal Effects of Divorce on Children in Great Britain and the United States *(21, 23, 24, 25, 35)*		
Drugs and Alcohol	37. Perils of Prohibition 38. Surge in Teen-Age Smoking 39. New Pot Culture 52. Programs Go Beyond "Just Saying No" 55. Clinical Assessment of Adolescents Involved in Satanism 57. Biceps in a Bottle *(2, 26, 27, 28, 29, 38, 41)*	**Media Influences**	6. I'm Okay! 38. Surge in Teen-Age Smoking 39. New Pot Culture 40. Chips Ahoy 44. Virgin Cool *(26, 28, 29, 30, 31, 32, 33)*
Early Adolescence	1. Teenage Wasteland? 4. Age of Embarrassment 5. "My Body Is So Ugly" 8. Study of White Middle-Class Adolescent Boys' Responses to "Semenarche"		

TOPIC AREA	TREATED IN	TOPIC AREA	TREATED IN
Mentoring	16. Good Mentoring Keeps At-Risk Youth in School *(12, 13)*	**Puberty**	4. Age of Embarrassment 5. "My Body Is So Ugly" 8. Study of White Middle-Class Adolescent Boys' Responses to "Semenarche" 10. Long and Short of It 17. Schools the Source of Rough Transitions *(6, 9, 10, 11, 17, 18, 19, 30)*
Middle Schools	11. Developmentally Appropriate Middle Level Schools 12. Program Helps Kids Map Realistic Goals 17. Schools the Source of Rough Transitions *(12, 13)*	**Rape**	46. Sexual Correctness *(30, 31, 32, 33, 38, 41)*
Moral Development	25. EQ Factor 45. Neglected Heart 48. How Should We Teach Our Children about Sex *(18, 19, 30, 31, 32, 33)*	**Rites of Passage**	8. Study of White Middle-Class Adolescent Boys' Responses to "Semenarche" 9. Dangerous Rite of Passage *(28, 29, 30, 31, 32, 33)*
Multicultural Issues	2. Way We Weren't 7. Body of the Beholder 9. Dangerous Rite of Passage 14. Boys' Schools Reconsidered 18. Test of Their Lives 19. International Differences in Mathematical Achievement 23. Ethnicity, Identity Formation, and Risk Behavior among Adolescents of Mexican Descent 24. "I'm Just Who I Am" 51. Young Adults and AIDS *(6, 10, 11, 12, 13, 16, 18, 19, 29, 33)*	**School**	1. Teenage Wasteland? 11. Developmentally Appropriate Middle Level Schools 12. Program Helps Kids Map Realistic Goals 13. Mommy, What's a Classroom? 14. Boys' Schools Reconsidered 15. At Risk Students and Resiliency 16. Good Mentoring Keeps At-Risk Youth in School 17. Schools the Source of Rough Transitions 20. Gender Gap in Math Scores Is Closing 50. Will Schools Risk Teaching about the Risk of AIDS? 52. Programs Go Beyond "Just Saying No" 53. Youngest Ex-Cons *(6, 12, 13, 14, 15, 19, 20)*
Nature vs. Nurture Issues	14. Boys' Schools Reconsidered 19. International Differences in Mathematical Achievement 20. Gender Gap in Math Scores Is Closing 53. Seeking the Criminal Element *(12, 15, 19, 24, 25, 28, 29, 38)*	**Self-Esteem**	4. Age of Embarrassment 6. I'm Okay! 55. Clinical Assessment of Adolescents Involved in Satanism *(6, 7, 8, 9, 10, 11, 17, 18, 19, 21)*
Parenting	1. Teenage Wasteland? 2. Way We Weren't 3. Waaah! Why Kids Have A Lot To Cry About 22. College Kids' Parents Should "Keep Cool" 26. Adolescence: Whose Hell Is It? 27. How Teens Strain the Family 28. Enjoying Your Child's Teenage Years 29. "Don't Talk Back!" 30. Gay Families Come Out 40. Chips Ahoy 43. Learning to Love *(1, 6, 7, 12, 18, 20, 21, 22, 23, 24)*	**Single Parents**	27. How Teens Strain the Family 47. In Defense of Teenaged Mothers *(20, 22, 24)*
		Suicide	58. Adolescent Suicide *(40, 41, 42)*
		Teen Parents/Pregnancy	43. Learning to Love 45. Neglected Heart 47. In Defense of Teenaged Mothers 49. Key Skill for Teen Parents *(30, 31, 32, 33)*
Peers	21. There's a First Time for Everything 33. Football, Fast Cars, and Cheerleading 34. Friendship and Friends' Influence in Adolescence *(6, 16, 28, 29, 31)*	**Theories of Intelligence/Testing**	18. Test of Their Lives 25. EQ Factor
		Violence	40. Chips Ahoy 53. Seeking the Criminal Element 54. Youngest Ex-Cons *(28, 29, 38, 41)*
Physical Health	5. "My Body Is So Ugly" 9. Dangerous Rite of Passage 10. Long and Short of It 36. Why Working Teens Get into Trouble 38. Surge in Teen-Age Smoking 39. New Pot Culture *(2, 6, 9, 10, 11, 21, 28, 33)*	**Work**	12. Program Helps Kids Map Realistic Goals 14. Boys' Schools Reconsidered 35. Too Old, Too Fast? 36. Why Working Teens Get into Trouble *(13, 26, 28)*

Selected World Wide Web Sites for *Annual Editions: Adolescent Psychology*

All of these Web sites are hot-linked through the *Annual Editions* home page: *http://www.dushkin.com/annualeditions* (just click on a book). In addition, these sites are referenced by number and appear where relevant in the Topic Guide on the previous two pages.

Some Web sites are continually changing their structure and content, so the information listed may not always be available.

General Sources

1. Ask NOAH About: Mental Health—*http://www.noah.cuny.edu/ illness/mentalhealth/mental.html*—This enormous resource contains information about child and adolescent family problems, mental conditions and disorders, suicide prevention, and much more.

2. Health Information Resources—*http://nhic-nt.health.org/Scripts/ Tollfree.cfm*—Here is a long list of toll-free numbers that provide health-related information.

3. Knowledge Exchange Network (KEN)—*http://www.mentalhealth. org/about/index.htm*—The CMHS National Mental Health Services Exchange Network (KEN) provides information about mental health via toll-free telephone services, an electronic bulletin board, and publications.

4. Mental Health Net—*http://www.cmhc.com/*—Comprehensive guide to mental health online, featuring 6,300 individual resources.

5. Psychnet—*http://www.apa.org/psychnet/*—Access APA Monitor, the American Psychological Association newspaper, APA Books on a wide range of topics, PsychINFO, an electronic database of abstracts on over 1,350 scholarly journals, and HelpCenter.

Perspectives on Adolescence

6. Adolescence: Change and Continuity—*http://www.personal.psu.edu/ faculty/n/x/nxd10/adolesce.htm#top*—At this site, students who took a course, *The Transition to Adulthood*, at Pennsylvania State University, offer an excellent series of areas to explore concerning basic domains, such as biological, cognitive, and social changes; contexts, such as family changes during adolescence, family influences, school, and work; and issues, such as identity development, intimacy, psychosocial problems, and more.

7. Facts for Families—*http://www.aacap.org/web/aacap/factsFam/*—The American Academy of Child and Adolescent Psychiatry here provides concise, up-to-date information on issues that affect teenagers and their families. Fifty-six fact sheets include teenagers issues, such as coping with life, sad feelings, inability to sleep, or not getting along with family and friends.

8. The Opportunity of Adolescence—*http://www.winternet.com/ ~webpage/adolescencepaper.html*—This paper calls adolescence the turning point, after which the future is redirected and confirmed, and goes on to discuss the opportunities and problems of this period to the individual and society, using quotations from Erik Erikson, Jean Piaget, and others.

Biological and Psychological Aspects of Puberty

9. Adolescence—Age of Change—*http://www.getnet.com/~davidp/ article2. html*—Here is an interesting article on the psychological and biological changes that occur in the transition from childhood to adolescence.

10. Biological Changes in Adolescence—*http://www.personal.psu.edu/ faculty/n/x/nxd10/biologic2.htm*—This site offers a discussion of puberty, sexuality, and biological changes, cross-cultural differences, and nutrition for adolescents.

11. Seven Developmental Needs of Young Adolescents—*http://sunsite. unc.edu/youthlink/needs.html*—This article discusses the developmental diversity of early adolescence, and the wide range of differences encountered within the group of 13- or 14-year-olds.

Cognitive Growth and Education

12. At-Risk Children and Youth—*http://www.ncrel.org/sdrs/areas/ at0cont. htm*—North Central Regional Educational Laboratory (NCREL) offers this list of resources. Critical issues include rethinking learning for students at risk, linking at-risk students to integrated services, providing effective schooling for students at risk, and using technology to enhance engaged learning.

13. Carnegie Council's A Matter of Time—*http://sunsite.unc.edu/ youthlink/carnybp.html*—This summary by the Carnegie Council on Adolescent Development discusses "A Matter of Time: Risk and Opportunity in the Nonschool Hours."

14. Cognitive Changes in Adolescence—*http://www.personal.psu.edu/ faculty/n/x/nxd10/cognitiv.htm#top*—Helpful articles, with related Web addresses, are available at this site. The first is "Adolescents: What Are They Thinking?" The second is "How Do Cognitive Changes during Adolescence Affect the Parent/Child Relationship?"

Identity and Socioemotional Development

15. AAUW's Initial Research—*http://www.aauw.org/2000/resinit. html#J1*— The American Association of University Women shares its research online. Abstracts include "Shortchanging Girls, Shortchanging America" and other reports that can be ordered.

16. ADOL: Adolescence Directory On-Line—*http://education.indiana. edu/cas/adol/adol.html*—This is an electronic guide to information on adolescent issues. Some of the issues concern conflict and violence, peer mediation, mental health problems, and health issues.

17. Adolescent Self-Esteem Depends on Attractiveness—*http://www. geisinger.edu/ghs/pubtips/A/AdolescentSelf-Esteem.htm*—Physicians of the Penn State Geisinger Health System discuss adolescent self-esteem in this article.

18. CYFERNET-Youth Development—*http://www.cyfernet.mes.umn. edu/youthdev.html*—Excellent source of many articles on youth development, including impediments to healthy development.

19. Socioemotional Development—*http://www.valdosta.peachnet.edu/ ~whuitt/psy702/affsys/erikson.html*—Erik Erikson's concepts are outlined here, followed by examples for the use of secondary school teachers in encouraging identity formation in their students.

Family Relationships

20. CYFERNET: Cooperative Extension System's Children, Youth, and Family Information Service—*http://www.cyfernet.org/*—CYFERNET provides hundreds of complete online publications featuring practical, research-based information in six major areas.

21. Family Traits of Adolescents Who Do Well—*http://prpd.netrom.com/ traits.html*—Evidence strongly suggests that family closeness plays a key role in promoting positive health behaviors in adolescents.

22. Help for Parents of Teenagers—*http://www.bygpub.com/parents/*—In addition to discussing the book, *The Teenager's Guide to the Real World,* and how it can help parents also, this site lists other good book sources and Web sites for parents as well as teens.

23. Mental Health Net: Facts for Families Index—*http://www.cmhc.com/ factsfam.htm*—The American Academy of Child and Adolescent Psychiatry publishes informational brochures that provide concise and up-to-date material on issues such as teen suicide, stepfamily problems, teen eating disorders, and manic-depressive illness.

24. NORC Report—*http://www.norc.uchicago.edu/newnhsda.htm*—The National Opinion Research Center released this Family Structure Report. The sample (22,000 respondents) of 12- to 17-year-olds was larger than any analyzed in previous studies, and resulted in a wealth of interesting information.

25. Research Update: Family Type and Adolescent Adjustment—*http://www.stepfam.org/features/research.htm*—David H. Demo discusses the behavior and adjustment of adolescents based on the type of family in which they live.

Peers and Youth Culture

26. Higher Education Center for Alcohol and Other Drug Prevention—*http://www.edc.org/hec/*—This U.S. Department of Education site has interactive discussion forums and a Just for Students section.

27. Justice Information Center (NCJRS): Drug Policy Information—*http://www.ncjrs.org/drgswww.htm*—This is a list of national and international World Wide Web sites on drug policy information.

28. National Clearinghouse for Alcohol and Drug Information—*http://www.health.org/*—This is an excellent general site for information on drug and alcohol facts that might relate to adolescence and the issues of peer pressure and youth culture.

29. Peers—*http://www.personal.psu.edu/faculty/n/x/nxd10/peers2. htm#top*—This paper discusses all aspects of peer relationships, including cliques and crowds, problem behavior and gangs, popularity and rejection, and issues in dating.

Teenage Sexuality

30. Adolescents and Abstinence—*http://www.noah.cuny.edu/sexuality/ siecus/fact2.html*—SIECUS, the Sexuality Information and Education Council of the United States, here produces data on teenage sexual behavior and includes a bibliography.

31. American Sexual Behavior—*http://www.norc.uchicago.edu/ sextrend.htm*—This article, "American Sexual Behavior," discusses trends, sociodemographics, and risky behavior.

32. CDC National AIDS Clearinghouse—*http://www.cdcnac.org/*—This complete source on AIDS includes "Respect Yourself, Protect Yourself," which are public service announcements that target youth.

33. Welcome to About Health—*http://www.abouthealth.com/*—This health site includes information about sexuality, HIV and AIDS, peer pressure, and other information to help adolescents. Sites include In Our Own Words: Teens & Aids, Risky Times, and links to other sites.

Problem Behaviors and Interventions

34. Anxiety Disorders in Children and Adolescents—*http://www.adaa. org/4_info/4i_child/4i_01.htm*—The Anxiety Disorders Association of America (ADAA) discusses anxiety disorders in children and adolescents under seven headings on this page. Included is a glossary and self-test.

35. Connection between Anorexia Nervosa and Achievement in Modern Society: A Review—*http://www.pgi.edu/hagopian.htm*—This is an abstract of an article by Nancy Sondon-Hagopian. It includes a lengthy description of causes of anorexia, a discussion by the author, recommendations, and a good bibliography for further study.

36. Mental Health Net: Eating Disorder Resources—*http://www.cmhc. com/guide/eating.htm*—A very complete list of Web references on eating disorders, including anorexia, bulimia, and obesity.

37. Mental Health Risk Factors for Adolescents—*http://education.indiana. edu/cas/adol/mental.html*—This collection of Web resources is useful for parents, educators, researchers, health practitioners, and teens. It covers abuse, conduct disorders, stress, and support.

38. Questions & Answers about Child & Adolescent Psychiatry—*http://www.aacap.org/aacap/q&a.htm#TOP*—These pages are the product of the American Academy of Child & Adolescent Psychiatry and attempt to answer the questions related to feelings and behaviors that cause disruption in the lives of children and young adults and the people around them.

39. Suicide Awareness: Voices of Education—*http://www.save.org/*—This is the most popular suicide site on the Internet. It is very thorough, with information on dealing with suicide along with material from the organization's many education sessions.

40. Teenage Problems—*http://www.bygpub.com/books/tg2rw/problems. htm*—This extract on the Web from *The Teenager's Guide to the Real World* offers an abstract on teenage problems, which include teenage depression, suicide, eating disorders, and other diseases. It is especially useful for its list of hotline phone numbers.

41. Youth Suicide League—*http://www.unicef.org/pon96/insuicid.htm*—This UNESCO Web site provides international suicide rates of young adults in selected countries.

We highly recommend that you review our Web site for expanded information and our other product lines. We are continually updating and adding links to our Web site in order to offer you the most usable and useful information that will support and expand the value of your Annual Editions. You can reach us at: *http://www.dushkin.com/annualeditions/*.

Perspectives on Adolescence

Meagan applies her lipstick expertly without a mirror, wears the acceptable fashions to school, and clutches her new stuffed bear as she worries that a friend may give her a Barbie doll for her birthday when she clearly has outgrown them. This 12-year old is not a young child, but neither is she an adult. She is in that stage between childhood and adulthood: adolescence.

Just when adolescence begins or ends, and just what characterizes adolescence, is not clearly established. G. Stanley Hall, who is credited with founding the scientific study of adolescence in the early part of the 1900s, saw adolescence as corresponding roughly to the teen years. He believed individuals of this age had great potential, but also experienced extreme mood swings. He labeled this a period of "storm and stress." Because of their labile emotions, he believed that adolescents were typically psychologically maladjusted. What did he believe was the cause of this storm and stress? Basically, he believed that it was biological. Hall's views had a profound effect on the subsequent study of adolescence. Biological factors that underlie adolescence and direct the transition from childhood to adulthood were studied and questioned. More modern researchers took very different views on the causes and characteristics of adolescence than those of Hall.

Erik Erikson (1902–1994), a psychologist interested in how people formed normal or abnormal personalities, believed that adolescence was a key period in development. He felt that it was during adolescence that individuals developed their identity. Like Hall, he believed that there was a biological component underlying development; unlike Hall, Erikson emphasized the role society played in the formation of the individual. Erikson proposed that adolescents must confront a number of conflicts (for example, understanding sex roles and oneself as male or female) in order to develop an identity. The form of these conflicts, and the problems the adolescent faced addressing them, were influenced by the individual's culture. If adolescents were successful in meeting the conflicts, they would develop a healthy identity; if unsuccessful, they would suffer role diffusion or a negative identity. Similar to Hall, Erikson saw adolescence as a period where the individual's sense of self is disrupted, and so it was typical for adolescents to be disturbed. Today, Erikson's ideas on identity formation are still influential. However, his stereotype of adolescents as all suffering from psychological problems has been called into question.

Margaret Mead, an anthropologist who started studying adolescents in the 1920s, presented a perspective on adolescence that differed from both Hall's and Erikson's. She concluded that culture, rather than biology, was the underlying cause of a transitional stage between childhood and adulthood. In cultures that held the same expectations for children as for adults, the transition from childhood to adulthood was smooth; there was no need for a clearly demarcated period where one was neither child nor adult. In addition, adolescence did not have to be a period of storm and stress or of psychological problems. Although some of Mead's work has since been criticized, many of her ideas remain influential. Today's psychologists concur with Mead in that adolescence should not be a time of psychological maladjustment. Modern anthropologists agree that biology alone did not define adolescence. Rather, the sociocultural environment in which an individual is raised will affect how adolescence is manifested and what characterizes it.

What social and cultural factors lead to the development of adolescence in our society? Modern scholars believe that adolescence as we know it did not even exist until the end of the 1800s. During the end of the nineteenth century and the beginning of the twentieth century, societal changes caused the stage of adolescence to be invented. In this period the job opportunities for young people doing either farm labor or apprenticeships in factories were decreasing. For middle-class children, the value of staying in school in order to get a good job was stressed. Since there were fewer job opportunities, young people were less likely to be financially independent and had to rely on their families. They could not assume the economic role of an adult. By the beginning of the twentieth century, legislation ensuring that adolescents could not assume adult status was passed; child labor laws restricted how much time young people could work, and compulsory education laws required adolescents to stay in school. These laws forced adolescents into a position of dependence. They were physically mature people who were dependent on their parents—they were neither children nor adults.

The articles in this unit focus on the emergence of adolescence in our culture, and the characteristics of adolescents in our society. In the first essay, the emotional needs of young adolescents and how parents and schools may respond to these needs are discussed. Stephanie Coontz, in the second article, describes the various forms American families have taken from colonial times to the present, concluding with a discussion of society's influence on families and children. The final article in this section focuses on issues that are faced by adolescents in our society. David Elkind describes how society can help adolescents effectively meet the challenges they face or how society may exacerbate the problems faced by adolescents. He proposes that adolescence in today's society is more stressful and riskier than adolescence has been in times past.

Looking Ahead: Challenge Questions

What issues are faced by adolescents that may cause them to yearn for increased adult guidance? How may schools or parents respond to this need? How may the problems faced by boys and girls differ?

How diverse were families throughout the history of the United States? How have families changed since colonial times? Why is it misleading and counterproductive to assume that there has been a "traditional" American family?

How have changes in society since the 1940s caused changes in the American family?

What are the differences between the "modern family" and the "postmodern" family? How have these changes affected the problems faced by adolescents?

Teenage wasteland?

The passage from age 10 to 14 is very tricky, but it need not be the pits

Leslie Flowers's 13th year was filled with disappointment, change and tumult—all the messiness that makes early adolescence such a dreaded time of life. But Flowers had a blast. For sure, moving to California last November to get to know her adored, divorced dad didn't work out. He was gone a lot; she trimmed the Christmas tree by herself. School was dull, and, yeah, it freaked her out that along with fire drills they practiced drive-by-shooting drills in suburban Los Angeles. She missed her mom and older sister, too. So when she moved back to Pennsylvania, she in effect was starting eighth grade again for the third time in four months. But there, she had seven great girlfriends. They called themselves "the Clique" and shared the same lunch period. They could talk about anything and did everything together. It was, she says, "my greatest year ever."

Without question, for Flowers and the 19 million other 10-to-14-year-olds in America, early adolescence is one of life's trickiest transitions. Kids can seem simultaneously childlike and adult. (Best thing about "the Clique": food fights in the cafeteria and quite mature discussions about boys.) And in a troubled, media-saturated society, they deal ever earlier with tough issues like sex, drugs, divorce and gun violence. But a growing body of research brings a surprising new view of early adolescence:

It is a crucial period in human development, equaled only by infancy.

In the years between 10 and 14, kids search for the roles and values that will guide them all their lives. Last week, the

ON PARENTS

> "I'm trying to be independent, but I need her. If I do anything wrong, she listens and doesn't hold it against me forever."
>
> LESLIE FLOWERS, 14

Carnegie Council on Adolescent Development released "Great Transitions," an important study suggesting that this is the best, and perhaps last, chance to reach kids. Yet, notes David Hamburg of the Carnegie Corp., early adolescence remains the least understood and "most neglected phase of the life span from conception to senescence."

Adolescence is a distinctly American and 20th-century notion. It was psychologist G. Stanley Hall who, in 1904, first proposed that there was a stage to life other than childhood or adulthood. But Hall painted a gloomy picture of adolescence, particularly early adolescence. He called it a time of *sturm und drang,* or storm and stress, for hormone-roiled kids. The best thing adults could do was to get out of the way and let kids' rebellion pass. Today, this "disease theory" dominates popular thinking.

Yet Flowers, now 14, and most young adolescents crave the involvement of adults—particularly parents—in their lives. Flowers says she confides first in her friends, but for something "big or serious" she turns to her mom. In rural Hillsboro, Ind., 14-year-old Reagan DeFlorio (named for the president who was inaugurated the year she was born) goes even further. She wants her junior-senior high school to keep one night a week free of athletic games and other events, and maybe even support a curfew, so that kids would be sure to spend an evening with their parents. She got the idea after seeing how some friends as young as 14 slept overnight in the doorways of downtown businesses in a nearby town.

The total time that American children spend with their parents has de-

From *U.S. News & World Report,* October 23, 1995, pp. 84-87. © 1995 by U.S. News & World Report. Reprinted by permission.

creased by at least one third in the past 30 years. And today slightly more than half of all adolescents will have spent at least part of their lives in a single-parent family, notes the Carnegie study. "Kids need their parents," says DeFlorio. "That's where they get morals and values." When young adolescents are polled, they consistently agree: Most have positive feelings about their parents and want them more involved in their lives.

One reason they covet adult guidance is that they want help with tough decisions. Among eighth graders, marijuana use doubled between 1991 and 1994. Two thirds have tried alcohol, and a quarter say they are current drinkers.

ON PEER PRESSURE

"I do face peer pressure about things like drugs, but that's from people I don't know well. My real peers are right behind me. They back me up."

MELISSA MCCARTER, 14

Nearly 20 percent of 13- and 14-year-olds now report being sometime smokers. About a third of teens have had sex by the time they turn 15. Injury, homicide and suicide account for most adolescent deaths.

Even the physical changes that mark adolescence are coming sooner. Puberty occurs two years earlier than it did a century ago, apparently the result of better nutrition. Young teens' mental and physical growth is enor-

---

I'M DYSFUNCTIONAL, YOU'RE DYSFUNCTIONAL

Unhappy girls and boys

Many have bought the notion that society's ideals for womanhood play havoc with adolescent girls' self-esteem—thanks to a field of research pioneered by Harvard psychologist Carol Gilligan and sometimes oversold by feminist advocates. Now, academics specializing in men's psychology say puberty is no picnic for them, either. Far more teenage boys than girls drop out of school, commit crimes or kill themselves.

The new-masculinity researchers say they are inspired by feminist scholars to take a closer look at the ways in which males are warped by unrealistic and unhealthy models of manhood. Just as a girl who tries to live up to conventions of femininity may fail to fulfill her potential in the workplace, they argue, a boy trained to be a "real man" is more likely to end up a lousy husband and father.

Socialization woes. In fact, they think problems ranging from addiction to violence all have roots in the "male-role socialization process" and that the best solution to such plagues is to redefine what an ideal man should be. To that end, Harvard Medical School lecturer Ronald Levant, author of *Masculinity Reconstucted,* has founded the Society for the Psychological Study of Men and Masculinity. And colleague William Pollack, Harvard psychology professor and author of *In a Time of Fallen Heroes,* directs the Center for

Men, a think tank and clinic, at Mc-Clean Hospital in Belmont, Mass.

They argue that while the worst excesses of macho manhood are ending, it is still a confusing time to be growing up male. Levant points to the mixed cultural messages that leave boys in a damned-if-you-do, damned-if-you-don't position in everything from fighting to crying to joining the theater group to paying for a date.

The contradictions show up in studies of today's young males. Levant polled college men and found that they reject five of the seven most often cited mandates for traditional manhood, such as achieving high status and squelching emotions. Yet, when Pollack asked similar students what they would most like to know from women, two top answers were: "Why do they think we should love them to have sex with them?" and "Why do they get so upset when we forget little things like birthdays and anniversaries?"

The psychologists warn that younger boys may tend to seek refuge from the contradictions by thinking stereotypically. That's a notion supported by a recent *New York Times*/CBS News poll, which found that far more teenage boys than girls support traditional gender roles. Just 58 percent of boys expect their future wives to work outside the home, while 86 percent of girls plan to do so.

Absent fathers undoubtedly add to boys' confusion over what their role should be as men. But many of the fathers who *are* at home are themselves products of an upbringing so limiting that they are not much good at guiding their sons, say the researchers. Levant teaches fathering workshops at Harvard to men who lament that they have no connection with their children or that they cannot control angry outbursts that scare off their kids.

There is no easy prescription for creating a healthier generation of men, nor is there a cookie-cutter version of what a new and improved man will look like. "We're not trying to make all little boys into Alan Alda," jokes Pollack. But researchers insist that certain measures—like training boys to be more "emotionally intelligent" and to resolve conflict without violence—will go a long way toward creating healthier men.

Most likely, the success or failure of attempts to revamp manhood will show up in relations between the sexes. "We live on a fault line of gender," says Pollack, who points to the fact that wives are now twice as likely to be the ones who initiate divorce as evidence that women are fed up. "If men don't get their act together, we will have a civil war on our hands."

BY JOANNIE M. SCHROF

mous. There is a reason young teens can't sit still: A growth spurt makes muscles ache.

Young adolescents develop abstract reasoning, giving them their first adult skills for decision making. As a result, experts say, they need more freedom at school to test their reasoning. But most middle-grade teachers incorrectly believe their students need stricter discipline according to one survey. A major problem, says Peter Scales of the Minneapolis-based Search Institute, is that

ON LEARNING

"You learn best when you have a sense that what you are studying is all connected. Classes make sense when you start off in, and come back to, one place."

JOE LAJTER, 13

just one fifth of teachers get training in what makes middle school students different—and most of them say the training is not very good.

Cultural norms. Raging hormones get blamed for adolescent moodiness. But one study, in which kids were given beepers and asked during the day to note their feelings, found that those going through puberty were no more moody than preadolescents. The hardest part of becoming a teen, it turns out, is simply measuring up to cultural expectations. If waiflike model Kate Moss and muscle-bound actor Arnold Schwarzenegger represent ideal body types, then girls at puberty get further away from the ideal while boys get closer. Indeed, 53 percent of girls say they worry about their body weight, compared with just 16 percent of boys.

"Something dramatic happens to girls in early adolescence," writes psy-

chologist Mary Pipher in her current bestselling book, *Reviving Ophelia: Saving the Selves of Adolescent Girls.* Because girls live in a society obsessed with looks and hostile to females, she argues, they are highly vulnerable to depression, suicide, eating disorders and addictions. Their energy, curiosity and spirit get crushed. Pipher echoes the work of Harvard Prof. Carol Gilligan (*see box,* "Unhappy girls and boys") and studies by the American Association of University Women that claim because schools and society favor boys, adolescent girls suffer a crisis of self-esteem.

Yet boys may have it just as hard, or even harder. Working on a federal grant to help girls catch up with boys in career and life planning, Indiana State University Prof. Lawrence Beymer discovered it was boys who most needed help. Girls, he found, were more ambitious and optimistic about their futures. Further, Beymer notes, boys make up 85 percent of special-education students with often subjective diagnoses such as learning disabled or behavior disordered. They get lower grades and more punishment.

Still, frequent claims of an epidemic of depression among early adolescents are misleading. While their rates of depression have increased, and are certainly higher among girls than boys, depression is slightly less prevalent among early adolescents than among adults. Northwestern University psychiatrist Daniel Offer notes that the overwhelming majority of young adolescents—80 percent—get through adolescence with no such problems. Too often, however, the 20 percent of kids who do need help get ignored because it is considered "normal" to be unhappy during adolescence. There is something particularly tragic when a teen commits suicide. But contrary to common perception, suicide rates are actually lower among teens than among older groups.

Too much self-esteem may even be harmful. That is the argument of Martin Seligman, author of *The Optimistic Child,* who challenges the child-rearing advice commonly given to baby boomer parents. When kids get unconditional positive feedback designed to make sure they feel good about themselves, they do not learn from their failures and do not recognize when they truly have achieved something worthwhile, argues

the University of Pennsylvania psychologist. Kids end up feeling confused and helpless.

Seligman teaches optimism. At several Philadelphia-area schools, kids use role-playing and other exercises to cope with the everyday slights and setbacks

ON GOOD TEACHERS

"The best teachers respect kids. They talk to you on your level. They don't just act superior. It's more fun when they're approachable."

LAURA MORRISON, 12

that can throw young teens for a loop. Both Flowers and Bonnie Harding, who participated at Wissahickon Middle School, say they no longer automatically fear that a group of whispering kids must be gossiping about them. Most important, says Seligman, optimistic thinkers feel empowered to change things.

Redesigning school. One of the best ways to create confident kids is to restructure schools. The beige-brick Batavia Middle School in Batavia, Ill., looks like a typical suburban school. But the program inside is helping to revolutionize middle school teaching. The two-story building has separate wings for its sixth, seventh and eighth graders. Even within these classes, kids are divided into pods of 90 students who take most of their classes together with a team of teachers. The result: An impersonal 1,100-student junior high school is transformed into a comfortable middle school where students are confident that their teachers know them. As Joe Lajter, 13, puts it: "Teachers here can see a problem on your face."

The middle school reform movement is built on the belief that learning and personal growth are accelerated in small communities where kids have stable and close relationships with adults and peers. Students at these schools are less likely to say they feel alienated, fearful or depressed, says Robert Felner of the University of Illinois. Most important, Felner has found significant increases in reading and math test scores. "It's hard not to make at least one friend here," says Laura Morrison, 12, who moved from Ohio last month. Her mother, Sue, a teacher herself, is impressed that Laura's classes are all within doors of each other, that teachers ask parents to write an essay describing how their kids learn best and that kids are encouraged to explore foreign languages, computers and extracurricular activities—including team sports for boys and girls—in search of things in which they excel. Sometimes, however, the effort to include all can seem to go too far: There are 110 seventh- and eighth-grade cheerleaders.

Still, that this is a caring place is clear from the bulletin board outside the counselors' offices. Kids pin notes about their everyday problems. Among recent ones: "I can't get my work done and the teacher has called my mom" or the scrawled "EMERGENCY!!!! People are spreading rumors about me." Counselors meet with each note writer, get him or her thinking about how to solve the problem and then check on how the student follows through. That kind of response made it easy for Melissa McCarter, 14, to ask a counselor to intervene when one of her girlfriends went a week without eating. The school encourages such student involvement, knowing that peer pressure can be used as a force for good.

Adolescents, of course, are a heterogeneous group. A new body of social science research focuses on why even most kids from the poorest neighborhoods sidestep dangers. For all teens, it turns out, the steady presence of an adult to provide support and positive values is the best guarantor of a happy, successful passage to adulthood.

BY JOSEPH P. SHAPIRO WITH
MISSY DANIEL IN BATAVIA

The Way We Weren't

The Myth and Reality of the "Traditional" Family

Stephanie Coontz

Families face serious problems today, but proposals to solve them by reviving "traditional" family forms and values miss two points. First, no single traditional family existed to which we could return, and none of the many varieties of families in our past has had any magic formula for protecting its members from the vicissitudes of socioeconomic change, the inequities of class, race, and gender, or the consequences of interpersonal conflict. Violence, child abuse, poverty, and the unequal distribution of resources to women and children have occurred in every period and every type of family.

Second, the strengths that we also find in many families of the past were rooted in different social, cultural, and economic circumstances from those that prevail today. Attempts to reproduce any type of family outside of its original socioeconomic context are doomed to fail.

Colonial Families

American families always have been diverse, and the male breadwinner-female homemaker, nuclear ideal that most people associate with "the" traditional family has predominated for only a small portion of our history. In colonial America, several types of families coexisted or competed. Native American kinship systems subordinated the nuclear family to a much larger network of marital alliances and kin obligations, ensuring that no single family was forced to go it alone. Wealthy settler families from Europe, by contrast, formed inde-pendent households that pulled in labor from poorer neighbors and relatives, building their extended family solidarities on the backs of truncated families among indentured servants, slaves, and the poor. Even wealthy families, though, often were disrupted by death; a majority of colonial Americans probably spent some time in a step-family. Meanwhile, African Americans, denied the legal protection of marriage and parenthood, built extensive kinship networks and obligations through fictive kin ties, ritual co-parenting or godparenting, adoption of orphans, and complex naming patterns designed to preserve family links across space and time.

The dominant family values of colonial days left no room for senti-mentalizing childhood. Colonial mothers, for example, spent far less time doing child care than do modern working women, typically delegating this task to servants or older siblings. Among white families, pa-triarchal authority was so absolute

From *National Forum: The Phi Kappa Phi Journal*, Summer 1995, pp. 11-14. © 1995 by Stephanie Coontz. Reprinted by permission of the publisher.

that disobedience by wife or child was seen as a small form of treason, theoretically punishable by death, and family relations were based on power, not love.

The Nineteenth-Century Family

With the emergence of a wage-labor system and a national market in the first third of the nineteenth century, white middle-class families became less patriarchal and more child-centered. The ideal of the male breadwinner and the nurturing mother now appeared. But the emergence of domesticity for middle-class women and children depended on its absence among the immigrant, working class, and African American women or children who worked as servants, grew the cotton, or toiled in the textile mills to free middle-class wives from the chores that had occupied their time previously.

Even in the minority of nineteenth-century families who could afford domesticity, though, emotional arrangements were quite different from nostalgic images of "traditional" families. Rigid insistence on separate spheres for men and women made male-female relations extremely stilted, so that women commonly turned to other women, not their husbands, for their most intimate relations. The idea that all of one's passionate feelings should go toward a member of the opposite sex was a twentieth-century invention — closely associated with the emergence of a mass consumer society and promulgated by the very film industry that "traditionalists" now blame for undermining such values.

Early Twentieth-Century Families

Throughout the nineteenth century, at least as much divergence and disruption in the experience of family life existed as does today, even though divorce and unwed motherhood were less common. Indeed, couples who marry today have a better chance of celebrating a fortieth wedding anniversary than at any previous time in history. The life cycles of nineteenth-century youth (in job entry, completion of schooling, age at marriage, and establishment of separate residence) were far more diverse than they became in the early twentieth-century. At the turn of the century a higher proportion of people remained single for their entire lives than at any period since. Not until the 1920s did a bare majority of children come to live in a male breadwinner-female homemaker family, and even at the height of this family form in the 1950s, only 60 percent of American children spent their entire childhoods in such a family.

years as unhealthy. From this family we get the idea that women are sexual, that youth is attractive, and that marriage should be the center of our emotional fulfillment.

Even aside from its lack of relevance to the lives of most immigrants, Mexican Americans, African Americans, rural families, and the urban poor, big contradictions existed between image and reality in the middle-class family ideal of the early twentieth century. This is the period when many Americans first accepted the idea that the family should be sacred from outside intervention; yet the development of the private, self-sufficient family depended on state intervention in the economy, government regulation of parent-child relations, and state-directed destruction of class and community institutions that hindered the development of family privacy.

Not until the 1920s did a bare majority of children come to live in a male breadwinner-female homemaker family . . . .

From about 1900 to the 1920s, the growth of mass production and emergence of a public policy aimed at establishing a family wage led to new ideas about family self-sufficiency, especially in the white middle class and a privileged sector of the working class. The resulting families lost their organic connection to intermediary units in society such as local shops, neighborhood work cultures and churches, ethnic associations, and mutual-aid organizations.

As families related more directly to the state, the market, and the mass media, they also developed a new cult of privacy, along with heightened expectations about the family's role in fostering individual fulfillment. New family values stressed the early independence of children and the romantic coupling of husband and wife, repudiating the intense same-sex ties and mother-infant bonding of earlier

Acceptance of a youth and leisure culture sanctioned early marriage and raised expectations about the quality of married life, but also introduced new tensions between the generations and new conflicts between husband and wife over what were adequate levels of financial and emotional support.

The nineteenth-century middle-class ideal of the family as a refuge from the world of work was surprisingly modest compared with emerging twentieth-century demands that the family provide a whole alternative world of satisfaction and intimacy to that of work and neighborhood. Where a family succeeded in doing so, people might find pleasures in the home never before imagined. But the new ideals also increased the possibilities for failure: America has had the highest divorce rate in the world since the turn of the century.

In the 1920s, these contradictions created a sense of foreboding about "the future of the family" that was every bit as widespread and intense as today's. Social scientists and popular commentators of the time hearkened back to the "good old days," bemoaning the sexual revolution, the fragility of nuclear family ties, the cult of youthful romance, the decline of respect for grandparents, and the threat of the "New Woman." But such criticism was sidetracked by the stock-market crash, the Great Depression of the 1930s, and the advent of World War II.

Domestic violence escalated during the Depression, while murder rates were as high in the 1930s as in the 1980s. Divorce rates fell, but desertion increased and fertility plummeted. The war stimulated a marriage boom, but by the late 1940s one in every three marriages was ending in divorce.

The 1950s Family

At the end of the 1940s, after the hardships of the Depression and war, many Americans revived the nuclear family ideals that had so disturbed commentators during the 1920s. The unprecedented postwar prosperity allowed young families to achieve consumer satisfactions and socioeconomic mobility that would have been inconceivable in earlier days. The 1950s family that resulted from these economic and cultural trends, however, was hardly "traditional." Indeed it is best seen as a historical aberration. For the first time in 100 years, divorce rates dropped, fertility soared, the gap between men's and women's job and educational prospects widened (making middle-class women more dependent on marriage), and the age of marriage fell—to the point that teenage birth rates were almost double what they are today.

Admirers of these very *nontraditional* 1950s family forms and values point out that household arrangements and gender roles were less diverse in the 1950s than today, and marriages more stable. But this was partly because diversity was ruthlessly suppressed and partly because economic and political support systems for socially-sanctioned families were far more generous than they are today. Real wages rose more in any single year of the 1950s than they did in the entire decade of the 1980s; the average thirty-year-old man could buy a median-priced home on 15 to 18 percent of his income. The government funded public investment, home ownership, and job creation at a rate more than triple that of the past two decades, while 40 percent of young men were eligible for veteran's benefits. Forming and maintaining families was far easier than it is today.

Yet the stability of these 1950s families did not guarantee good outcomes for their members. Even though most births occurred within wedlock, almost a third of American children lived in poverty during the 1950s, a higher figure than today. More than 50 percent of black married-couple families were poor. Women were often refused the right to serve on juries, sign contracts, take out credit cards in their own names, or establish legal residence. Wife-battering rates were low, but that was because wife-beating was seldom counted as a crime. Most victims of incest, such as Miss America of 1958, kept the secret of their fathers' abuse until the 1970s or 1980s, when the women's movement became powerful enough to offer them the support denied them in the 1950s.

The Post-1950s Family

In the 1960s, the civil rights, antiwar, and women's liberation movements exposed the racial, economic, and sexual injustices that had been papered over by the Ozzie and Harriet images on television. Their activism made older kinds of public and private oppression unacceptable and helped create the incomplete, flawed, but much-needed reforms of the Great Society. Contrary to the big lie of the past decade that such programs caused our current family dilemmas, those antipoverty and social justice reforms helped overcome many of the family problems that prevailed in the 1950s.

In 1964, after fourteen years of unrivaled family stability and economic prosperity, the poverty rate was still 19 percent; in 1969, after five years of civil rights activism, the rebirth of feminism, and the institution of nontraditional if relatively modest government welfare programs, it was down to 12 percent, a low that has not been seen again since the social welfare cutbacks began in the late 1970s. In 1965, 20 percent of American children still lived in poverty; within five years, that had fallen to 15 percent. Infant mortality was cut in half between 1965 and 1980. The gap in nutrition between low-income Americans and other Americans narrowed significantly, as a direct result of food stamp and school lunch programs. In 1963, 20 percent of Americans living below the poverty line had *never* been examined by a physician; by 1970 this was true of only 8 percent of the poor.

Since 1973, however, real wages have been falling for most Americans. Attempts to counter this through tax revolts and spending freezes have led to drastic cutbacks in government investment programs. Corporations also spend far less on research and job creation than they did in the 1950s and 1960s, though the average compensation to executives has soared. The gap between rich and poor, according to the April 17, 1995, *New York Times*, is higher in the United

States than in any other industrial nation.

Family Stress

These inequities are *not* driven by changes in family forms, contrary to ideologues who persist

tain families. According to an Associated Press report of April 25, 1995, the median income of men aged twenty-five to thirty-four fell by 26 percent between 1972 and 1994, while the proportion of such men with earnings below the poverty level for a family of four more than doubled to 32 percent. The fig-

America needs more than a revival of the narrow family obligations of the 1950s, whose (greatly exaggerated) protection for white, middle-class children was achieved only at tremendous cost to the women in those families and to all those who could not or would not aspire to the Ozzie and Harriet ideal. We need a concern for children that goes beyond the question of whether a mother is waiting with cookies when her kids come home from school. We need a moral language that allows us to address something besides people's sexual habits. We need to build values and social institutions that can reconcile people's needs for independence with their equally important rights to dependence, and surely we must reject older solutions that involved balancing these needs on the backs of women. We will not find our answers in nostalgia for a mythical "traditional family."

. . . romanticizing "traditional" families and gender roles will not produce the changes . . . that would permit families to develop moral and ethical systems relevant to 1990s realities.

in confusing correlations with causes; but they certainly exacerbate such changes, and they tend to bring out the worst in *all* families. The result has been an accumulation of stresses on families, alongside some important expansions of personal options. Working couples with children try to balance three full-time jobs, as employers and schools cling to policies that assume every employee has a "wife" at home to take care of family matters. Divorce and remarriage have allowed many adults and children to escape from toxic family environments, yet our lack of social support networks and failure to forge new values for sustaining intergenerational obligations have let many children fall through the cracks in the process.

Meanwhile, young people find it harder and harder to form or sus-

ures are even worse for African American and Latino men. Poor individuals are twice as likely to divorce as more affluent ones, three to four times less likely to marry in the first place, and five to seven times more likely to have a child out of wedlock.

As conservatives insist, there is a moral crisis as well as an economic one in modern America: a pervasive sense of social alienation, new levels of violence, and a decreasing willingness to make sacrifices for others. But romanticizing "traditional" families and gender roles will not produce the changes in job structures, work policies, child care, medical practice, educational preparation, political discourse, and gender inequities that would permit families to develop moral and ethical systems relevant to 1990s realities.

Stephanie Coontz teaches history and family studies at The Evergreen State College in Olympia, Washington. Her publications include *The Way We Never Were: American Families and the Nostalgia Trap* **and** *The Way We Really Are: Coming to Terms with America's Changing Families* **(both published by Basic Books). She is a recipient of the Washington Governor's Writer's Award and the Dale Richmond Award of the American Academy of Pediatrics.**

Why kids have a lot to cry about

David Elkind, Ph.D.

David Elkind, Ph.D., professor of child study at Tufts University, is the author of more than 400 articles. He is perhaps best known for his books The Hurried Child; All Grown Up and No Place to Go *and* Ties That Stress: Childrearing in a Postmodern Society. *He is an active consultant to government agencies, private foundations, clinics, and mental-health centers.*

"Mommy," the five-year-old girl asked her mother, "why don't you get divorced again?" Her thrice-married mother was taken aback and said in return, "Honey, why in the world should I do that?" To which her daughter replied, "Well, I haven't seen you in love for such a long time."

This young girl perceives family life and the adult world in a very different way than did her counterpart less than half a century ago. Likewise, the mother perceives her daughter quite differently than did a mother raising a child in the 1940s. Although this mother was surprised at her daughter's question, she was not surprised at her understanding of divorce, nor at her familiarity with the symptoms of romance.

As this anecdote suggests, there has been a remarkable transformation over the last 50 years in our children's perceptions of us, and in our perceptions of our children. These altered perceptions are a very small part of a much larger tectonic shift in our society in general and in our families in particular. This shift is nothing less than a transformation of the basic framework, or paradigm, within which we think about and thus perceive our world. To understand the changes in the family, the perceptions of family members, and of parenting that have been brought about, we first have to look at this broader "paradigm shift" and what it has meant for family sentiments, values, and perceptions.

FROM MODERN TO POSTMODERN

Without fully realizing it perhaps, we have been transported into the postmodern era. Although this era has been called "postindustrial" and, alternatively, "information age," neither of these phrases is broad enough to encompass the breadth and depth of the changes that have occurred. The terms modern and postmodern, in contrast, encompass all aspects of society and speak to the changes in science, philosophy, architecture, literature, and the arts—as well as in industry and technology—that have marked our society since mid-century.

THE MODERN AND THE NUCLEAR FAMILY

The modern era, which began with the Renaissance and spanned the Industrial Revolution, was based upon three related assumptions. One was the idea of *human progress*—the notion that the natural direction of human and societal development is toward a more equitable, peaceful, and harmonious world in which every individual would be entitled to life, liberty, and the pursuit of happiness. A second assumption is *universality*. There were, it was taken as given, universal laws of nature of art, science, economics, and so on that transcended time and culture. The third basic assumption was that of *regularity*—the belief that the world is an orderly place, that animals and plants, geological layers and chemical elements could be classified in an orderly hierarchy. As Einstein put it, "God does not play dice with the universe!"

These assumptions gave a unique character and distinctiveness to modern life. Modern science, literature, architecture, philosophy, and industry all embodied these premises. And they were enshrined in the Modern Family as well. The modern nuclear family, for example, was seen as the end result of a progressive evolution of family forms. Two parents, two or three children, one parent working and one staying home to rear the children and maintain the home was thought to be the ideal family form toward which all prior, "primitive" forms were merely preliminary stages.

SENTIMENTS OF THE NUCLEAR FAMILY

The Modern Family was shaped by three sentiments that also reflected the underlying assumptions of modernity. One of these was Romantic Love. In premodern times, couples married by familial and community dictates. Considerations of property and social position were paramount. This community influence declined in the modern era, and couples increasingly came to choose one another on the basis of mutual attraction. This attraction became idealized into the notion that "Some enchanted evening, you will meet a stranger" for whom you and only you were destined ("You were meant for me, I was meant for you"), and that couples would stay together for the rest of their lives, happily "foreveraftering."

A second sentiment of the Modern Family was that of Maternal Love—the idea that women have a maternal "instinct" and a need to care for children, particularly when they are small. The idea of a maternal instinct was a thoroughly modern invention that emerged only after modern medicine and nutrition reduced infant mortality. In premodern times, infant mortality was so high that the young were not even named until they were two years old and stood a good chance of surviving. It was also not uncommon for urban parents to have their infants "wet-nursed" in the country. Often these

infants died because the wet-nurse fed her own child before she fed the stranger, and there was little nourishment left. Such practices could hardly be engaged in by a mother with a "maternal instinct."

The third sentiment of the Modern Family was Domesticity, a belief that relationships within the family are always more powerful and binding than are those outside it. The family was, as Christopher Lasch wrote, "a haven in a heartless world." As a haven, the nuclear family shielded and protected its members from the evils and temptations of the outside world. This sentiment also extended to the family's religious, ethnic, and social-class affiliations. Those individuals who shared these affiliations were to be preferred, as friends and spouses, over those with different affiliations.

PARENTING THE INNOCENT

The modern perceptions of parenting, children, and teenagers grew out of these family sentiments. Modern parents, for example, were seen as intuitively or instinctively knowledgeable about child-rearing. Professional help was needed only to encourage parents to do "what comes naturally." In keeping with this view of parenting was the perception of children as innocent and in need of parental nurturance and protection. Teenagers, in turn, were seen as immature and requiring adult guidance and direction. Adolescence, regarded as the age of preparation for adulthood, brought with it the inevitable "storm and stress," as young people broke from the tight nuclear family bonds and became socially and financially independent.

These modern perceptions of parenting and of children and youth were reinforced by the social mirror of the media, the law and the health professions. Motion pictures such as the Andy Hardy series (starring Mickey Rooney) depicted a teenage boy getting into youthful scrapes at school and with friends from which he was extricated by his guardian the judge, played by Harlan Stone. Fiction similarly portrayed teenagers as immature young people struggling to find themselves. Mark Twain's Huck Finn was an early version of the modern immature adolescent, while J. D. Salinger's Holden Caulfield is a modern version.

Modern laws, such as the child-labor laws and compulsory-education statutes were enacted to protect both children and

adolescents. And the health professions attributed the mental-health problems of children and youth to conflicts arising from the tight emotional bonds of the nuclear family.

POSTMODERNITY AND THE POSTMODERN FAMILY

The postmodern view has largely grown out of the failure of modern assumptions about progress, universality, and regularity. Many of the events of this century have made the idea of progress difficult to maintain. Germany, one of the most educationally, scientifically, and culturally advanced countries of the world, engaged in the most heinous genocide. Modern science gave birth to the atomic bomb that was dropped on Hiroshima and Nagasaki. Environmental degradation, pollution, population explosions, and widespread famine can hardly be reconciled with the notion of progress.

Secondly, the belief in universal principles has been challenged as the "grand" theories of the modern era—such as those of Marx, Darwin, and Freud—are now recognized as limited by the social and historical contexts in which they were elaborated. Modern theorists believed that they could transcend social-historical boundaries; the postmodern worker recognizes that he or she is constrained by the particular discourse of narrative in play at the time. Likewise, the search for abiding ethical, moral, and religious universals is giving way to a recognition that there are many different ethics, moralities, and religions, each of which has a claim to legitimacy.

Finally, the belief in regularity has given way to a recognition of the importance of irregularity, indeterminacy, chaos, and fuzzy logic. There is much in nature, such as the weather, that remains unpredictable—not because it is perverse, but only because the weather is affected by non-regular events. Sure regularity appears, but irregularity is now seen as a genuine phenomenon in its own right. It is no longer seen, as it was in the modern era, as the result of some failure to discover an underlying regularity.

In place of these modern assumptions, a new, postmodern paradigm with its own basic premises has been invented. The assumption of progress, to illustrate, has given way to the presumption of *difference*. There are many different forms and types of progress, and not all progressions are necessarily for the better. Likewise, the belief in universals has moved aside for the belief in *particulars*. Different phenomena may have different rules and principles that are not necessarily generalizable. For example, a particular family or a particular class of children is a non-replicable event that can never be exactly duplicated and to which universal principles do not apply. Finally, the assumption of regularity moved aside to make room for the principle of *irregularity*. The world is not as orderly and as logically organized as we had imagined.

As the societal paradigm has shifted, so has the structure of the family. The ideal nuclear family, thought to be the product of progressive social evolution, has given way to what might be called the *Permeable Family* of the postmodern era. The Permeable Family encompasses many different family forms: traditional or nuclear, two-parent working, single-parent, blended, adopted child, test-tube, surrogate mother, and co-parent families. Each of these is valuable and a potentially successful family form.

The family is permeable in other ways as well. It is no longer isolated from the larger community. Thanks to personal computers, fax and answering machines, the workplace has moved into the home-place. The homeplace, in turn, thanks to childcare facilities in office buildings and factories, has moved into the workplace. The home is also permeated by television, which brings the outside world into the living room and bedrooms. And an ever-expanding number of TV shows (*Oprah, Donahue, Geraldo, and Sally Jessy Raphael*), all detailing the variety of family problems, brings the living room and the bedroom into the outside world.

Quite different sentiments animate the postmodern Permeable Family than animated the modern nuclear family. The transformation of family sentiments came about in a variety of ways, from the civil-rights movement, the women's movement, changes in media, and laws that were part of the postmodern revolution. Because there is a constant interaction between the family and the larger society, it is impossible to say whether changes in the family were brought about by changes in society or vice versa. Things moved in both directions.

For a number of reasons, the Modern Family sentiment of Romantic Love has been transformed in the Postmodern era into the sentiment of *Consensual Love*. In contrast to the idealism and perfectionism of Romantic Love, consensual love is re-alistic and practical. It recognizes the legitimacy of premarital relations and is not premised on long-term commitment. Consensual Love is an agreement or contract between the partners; as an agreement it can be broken. The difference between Romantic Love and Consensual Love is summed up in the prenuptial agreement, which acknowledges the possible rupture of a marriage—before the marriage actually occurs. The current emphasis upon safe sex is likewise a symptom of consensual, not romantic, love.

The Modern Family sentiment of maternal love has yielded to other changes. Today, more than 50 percent of women are in the workforce, and some 60 percent of these women have children under the age of six. These figures make it clear that non-maternal and non-parental figures are now playing a major role in child-rearing. As part of this revision of child-rearing responsibilities, a new sentiment has emerged that might be called *shared parenting*. What this sentiment entails is the understanding that not only mothers, but fathers and professional caregivers are a necessary part of the child-rearing process. Child-rearing and childcare are no longer looked upon as the sole or primary responsibility of the mother.

The permeability of the Postmodern Family has also largely done away with the Modern Family sentiment of domesticity. The family can no longer protect individuals from the pressures of the outside world. Indeed, the impulse of the Permeable Family is to move in the other direction. Permeable Families tend to thrust children and teenagers forward to deal with realities of the outside world at ever earlier ages. This has resulted in what I have called the "hurrying" of children to grow up fast. Much of the hurrying of children and youth is a well-intentioned effort on the part of parents to help prepare children and youth for the onrush of information, challenges, and temptations coming at them through the now-permeable boundaries of family life.

POSTMODERN PARENTS OF KIDS WITHOUT INNOCENCE

These new, postmodern sentiments have given rise to new perceptions of parenting, of children, and of adolescents. Now that parenting is an activity shared with non-parental figures, we no longer regard it as an instinct that emerges once we have become parents; it is now regarded as a matter of learned *technique*.

Postmodern parents understand that doing "what comes naturally" may not be good for children. There are ways to say things to children that are less stressful than others. There are ways of disciplining that do not damage the child's sense of self esteem. The problem for parents today is to choose from the hundreds of books and other media sources bombarding them with advice on child-rearing. As one mother said to me, "I've read your books and they sound okay, but what if you're wrong?"

With respect to children, the perception of childhood innocence has given way to the perception of childhood competence. Now that children are living in Permeable Families with—thanks to television—a steady diet of overt violence, sexuality, substance abuse, and environmental degradation, we can no longer assume they are innocent. Rather, perhaps to cover our own inability to control what our children are seeing, we perceive them as competent to deal with all of this material. Indeed, we get so caught up in this perception of competence that we teach four- and five-year-olds about AIDS and child abuse and provide "toys" that simulate pregnancy or the dismemberment that accidents can cause unbuckled-up occupants. And the media reinforce this competence perception with films such as *Look Who's Talking* and *Home Alone*.

If children are seen as competent, teenagers can no longer be seen as immature. Rather they are now seen as sophisticated in the ways of the world, knowledgeable about sex, drugs, crime, and much more. This is a convenient fiction for parents suffering a time-famine. Such parents can take the perception of teenage sophistication as a rationale to abrogate their responsibility to provide young people with limits, guidance, and supervision. Increasingly, teenagers are on their own. Even junior and senior high schools no longer provide the social programs and clubs they once did.

This new perception of teenagers is also reflected in the social mirror of media, school and law. Postmodern films like *Risky Business* (in which teenager runs a bordello in the parents' home) and *Angel* (demure high school student by day, avenging hooker by night) are a far cry from the Andy Hardy films. Postmodern TV sitcoms such as *Married with Children* and *Roseanne* present images of teenage sophistication hardly reconcilable with the teenagers portrayed in modern

TV shows such as *My Three Sons* or *Ozzie and Harriet*. Postmodern legal thinking is concerned with protecting the *rights* of children and teenagers, rather than protecting children themselves. Children and teenagers can now sue their parents for divorce, visitation rights, and for remaining in the United States when the family travels overseas.

REALITY IS HERE TO STAY

The postmodern perceptions of children as competent and of teenagers as sophisticated did not grow out of any injustices nor harm visited upon children and youth. Rather they grew out of a golden era for young people that lasted from the end of the last century to the middle of this one. Society as a whole was geared to regard children as innocent and teenagers as immature, and sought to protect children and gradually inculcate teenagers into the ways of the world.

In contrast, the perceptions of childhood competence and teenage sophistication have had detrimental effects upon children and youth. Indeed, these perceptions have placed children and teenagers under inordinate stress. And it shows. On every measure that we have, children and adolescents are doing less well today than they did a quarter century ago, when the new postmodern perceptions were coming into play. While it would be unwise to attribute all of these negative effects to changed perceptions alone—economics and government policy clearly played a role—it is also true that government policy and economics are affected by the way young people are perceived.

The statistics speak for themselves. There has been a 50-percent increase in obesity in children and youth over the past two decades. We lose some ten thousand teenagers a year in substance-related accidents, not including injured and maimed. One in four teenagers drinks to excess every two weeks, and we have two million alcoholic teenagers.

Teenage girls in America get pregnant at the rate of one million per year, twice the rate of the next Western country, England. Suicide has tripled among teenagers in the last 20 years, and between five and six thousand teenagers take their own lives each year. It is estimated that one out of four teenage girls manifests at least one symptom of an eating disorder, most commonly severe dieting. The 14- to 19-year-old age group has the second-highest homicide rate of any age group.

These are frightening statistics. Yet they are not necessarily an indictment of the postmodern world, nor of our changed perceptions of children and youth. We have gone through enormous social changes in a very brief period of time. No other society on Earth changes, or can change, as rapidly as we do. That is both our strength and our weakness. It has made us, and will keep us, the leading industrial nation in the world because we are more flexible than any other society, including Japan.

But rapid social change is a catastrophe for children and youth, who require stability and security for healthy growth and development. Fortunately, we are now moving toward a more stable society. A whole generation of parents was caught in the transition between Modern and Postmodern Family sentiments; among them, divorce, open marriage, and remarriage became at least as commonplace as the permanent nuclear family. The current generation of parents have, however, grown up with the new family sentiments and are not as conflicted as their own parents were.

As a result, we are slowly moving back to a more realistic perception of both children and teenagers, as well as toward a family structure that is supportive of all family members. We are moving towards what might be called the *Vital Family*. In the Vital Family, the modern value of togetherness is given equal weight with the Postmodern Family value of autonomy. Children are seen as *growing into competence* and as still needing the help and support of parents. Likewise, teenagers are increasingly seen as *maturing into sophistication*, and able to benefit from adult guidance, limits, and direction.

These new perceptions pop up in the media. Increasingly, newspapers and magazines feature articles on the negative effects pressures for early achievement have upon children. We are also beginning to see articles about the negative effects the demands for sophistication place upon teenagers. A number of recent TV shows (such as *Beverly Hills 90210*) have begun to portray children and youth as sophisticated, but also as responsible and accepting of adult guidance and supervision. There is still much too much gratuitous sex and violence, but at least there are signs of greater responsibility and recognition that children and adolescents may not really be prepared for everything we would like to throw at them.

After 10 years of traveling and lecturing all over the country, I have an impression that the American family is alive and well. It has changed dramatically, and we are still accommodating to the changes. And, as always happens, children and youths are more harmed by change than are adults. But our basic value system remains intact. We do have a strong Judeo-Christian heritage; we believe in hard work, democracy, and autonomy. But our sense of social and parental responsibility, however, was temporarily deadened by the pace of social change. Now that we are getting comfortable in our new Permeable Family sentiments and perceptions, we are once again becoming concerned with those who are young and those who are less fortunate.

As human beings we all have a need to become the best that we can be. But we also have a need to love and to be loved, to care and to be cared for. The Modern Family spoke to our need to belong at the expense, particularly for women, of the need to become.

The Permeable Family, in contrast, celebrates the need to become at the expense of the need to belong, and this has been particularly hard on children and youth. Now we are moving towards a Vital Family that ensures both our need to become and our need to belong. We are not there yet, but the good news is, we are on our way.

Biological and Psychological Aspects of Puberty

Randy, a 14-year-old, is sulking in his room after arguing with his parents. They are upset because he refuses to work on the oral report he is supposed to give in English class tomorrow. He cannot tell them the real reason why he does not want to do the assignment. He just told his parents that the report was on a stupid topic, and he refused to do it. In reality, Randy is worried that his voice will crack, and, worse yet, that he will get an erection while standing up in front of the whole class and everyone will notice.

The physical changes accompanying the onset of puberty are usually the first clear indicators that a child is entering the period of adolescence. The changes are a source of both pride and embarrassment for the developing adolescent. The physiological changes are regulated by a structure in the brain known as the hypothalamus. The hypothalamus is responsible for stimulating the increased production of hormones that control development of the primary and secondary sex characteristics. Primary sex characteristics are physical differences in the reproductive system itself. Examples include growth of the ovaries and testicles. Secondary sex characteristics are physical differences not directly involved in reproduction. Examples include voice changes, height increases, facial hair in males, and breast development in females.

The hypothalamus signals the pituitary gland, which in turn stimulates the gonads to produce sex hormones (androgens and estrogens). The hypothalamus then detects the level of sex hormones present in the bloodstream and either calls for less or more hormone production. During childhood, the hypothalamus is very sensitive to sex hormones and keeps production at a low level. For some reason that is not completely known yet, the hypothalamus changes its sensitivity to the sex hormones. Significantly greater quantities of sex hormones are needed before the hypothalamus signals the pituitary to shut down production. The thyroid and adrenal glands also play a role in the development of secondary sex characteristics.

The physiological changes themselves occur over a 5–6 year span. Girls generally start to undergo puberty 18–24 months before boys, with a typical onset at age 10 or 11. The earliest signs of pubertal changes in girls are breast budding, height spurt, and sparse pubic hair. Experiencing a first menstrual cycle is a mid-pubertal event, with the average age of menarche in the United States being 12 years old. For boys, initial signs are that testicles begin to increase in size, a small amount of pubic hair appears, and the height spurt begins. Facial hair, deepening voice, and first ejaculation occur later.

The sequence of pubertal changes is fairly constant across individuals; however, the timing of puberty varies greatly from one person to the next. Some adolescents are out of step with their peers because they mature early, whereas others are late maturers. The advantages and disadvantages of early vs. late maturation have been the subject of research and several readings touch on this topic. One conclusion is that early maturation is correlated with earlier involvement in risk-taking behaviors like alcohol use and sexual activity. In extreme cases, biological disorders result in delayed or precocious puberty, but there are new medications for treating these conditions.

The onset of puberty is affected by diet, exercise, and genetic history. Largely due to improved nutrition and control of illnesses, puberty occurs 3 to 4 years earlier today than 150 years ago. Adolescents today also grow several inches taller and weigh more. A visit to historical homes will show that the doorways and beds were much smaller in previous centuries. This trend toward earlier maturation is a worldwide phenomenon that has presumably reached a leveling-off point.

As Randy's story illustrates, adolescents experience psychological and social challenges related to puberty. Sexual arousal increases and the teenager must learn how to handle sexual situations. Gender typical behavior is more expected. The adolescent must also incorporate bodily changes into his or her self-image. Concerns about physical appearance become a major preoccupation and play a significant role in self-esteem at this time. Several articles address this issue. In particular, the readings examine body image concerns as they relate to males vs. females, early vs. late maturers, and whites vs. blacks.

Parents and other adults are often less than forthcoming in their talks with adolescents about the changes they will be experiencing. This contributes to adolescents' anxiety about their body and how "normal" they are. One reading looks at boys' experience of their first ejaculation. Girls today are often prepared for their first menstrual cycle and discuss its appearance with mothers and friends. In contrast, boys' first ejaculation is largely a nonevent. Some cultures employ rites of passage to mark entrance into manhood or womanhood. Many such rites of passage involve physical markings of the adolescent. Readers may be familiar with male rites of passage involving circumcision and less familiar with female circumcision, which is discussed in Stephanie Welsh's article, "A Dangerous Rite of Passage."

Looking Ahead: Challenge Questions

What physical changes can parents and teenagers expect at adolescence? Do we adequately prepare teenagers for the physical changes of puberty? How can parents and other adults help teenagers cope with puberty?

How does the timing of puberty (early vs. on time vs. late) affect adolescents? Should hormones be administered to teenagers who want to be taller?

How does body image relate to self-esteem? Why do body image concerns affect girls more than boys? Is body weight more of an issue for whites than for blacks? Why are eating disorders more common in white females?

What puberty rites exist in U.S. culture and subcultures?

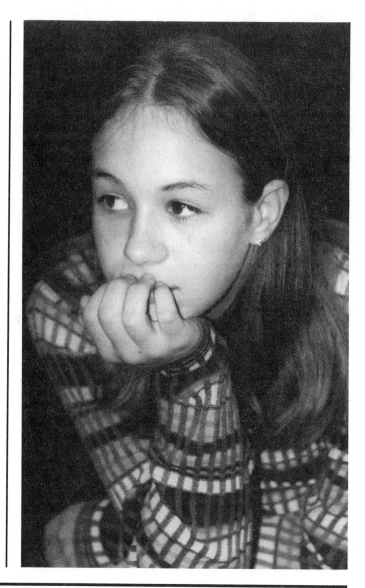

The Age of Embarrassment

When hormones surge, self-image plummets.
Help your child survive puberty.

Anne C. Bernstein, Ph.D.

Anne C. Bernstein, Ph.D., is a professor of psychology at Wright Institute, in Berkeley, California. She is also a practicing psychologist and the author of Flight of the Stork: How Children Think (and When) About Sex and Family Building *(Perspectives Press).*

Preteens have long ago relegated that venerable childhood board game Chutes and Ladders to the attic, along with the Winnie-the-Pooh books and the wading pool. But if you think back to how the game is played, you might just find that Chute and Ladders has a lot in common with preadolescence.

In the game, the players' slow but steady progress toward the final goal is punctuated by swift ascents and precipitous falls, all triggered by random throws of the dice. In the same way, children in the preteen years begin to understand that they, too, are moving toward a goal: adulthood. The journey begins with the onset of puberty. A girl's first period or a boy's first chest hair signals the beginning of a transformation—from a child's body into an adult's.

The sudden, seemingly random highs and lows come not from dice but from preteens' emotions. That's because, as they approach the threshold of adolescence, they often have very mixed feelings about leaving childhood behind. Therefore, 13-year-old Rebecca goes to a friend's sleep-over party wearing makeup on her face and carrying a large purse—which secretly contains her teddy bear. Likewise, 11-year-old John now spends extended periods of time in front of the mirror combing his hair just so (a year ago, it was impossible to get him to comb it at all), while still demanding that the night-light in his room be kept on when he sleeps, "just in case."

And the emotional upheavals of puberty are absolutely the reason 12-year-old Megan, whose breasts are developing earlier than most of her classmates', dissolves into tears in her room after having spent a day at the beach. Why? Because two boys she knows whistled at her, then burst into laughter as she passed them in her new bathing suit.

The uncertainty that accompanies puberty's onset explains a lot about the behavior of preadolescents: their intense, quickly shifting moods; their frequent inability to explain why they are feeling down, or their tendency to fix blame on a single aspect of their lives; their zigzagging between impressive displays of a new responsibility—getting themselves to school on time or caring for siblings—and shows of bad judgment and impulsiveness.

It's easy to chalk up the emotional highs and lows of these years to mere hormonal changes—one mother I know says of her 11-year-old daughter, "She hasn't even had her first period yet, but it's as if she's premenstrual all the time." And in fact, a child's bodily changes do disrupt that sense of a consistent, predictable self.

Because your child feels secure in your love, he can vent frustrations on you.

However, what matters most of all is the meaning preteens attach to these physical changes. And that's where you come in. The messages your preteen gets from you about what growing up means will go a long way toward helping him or her cope with the immense upheavals puberty brings. How can you do a good job of seeing your child safely through this new game of Chutes and Ladders? Here are some guidelines:

Don't overreact, even when your child does. When your preteen gets moody, blows off steam, or recoils from being seen with you in a public place, try to stay calm, and avoid taking her behavior personally. In fact, her behavior might be an indication of the health of your relationship. Precisely because your child feels secure that your love for her is guaranteed, she may see you as a safe target for her pent-up frustrations.

You might try saying, "I know you're upset. Let's talk about things when you're a little calmer." And when the two of you do eventually talk, avoid being blindly reassuring ("I'm sure those boys just whistled at you because you're so pretty") if she expresses self-doubts. What you child needs at a moment like this is to feel understood; your perspective, however accurate, may not be as helpful as your sympathy ("It can really be embarrassing when boys act that way").

Expect inconsistency.   Recognize that there will be stops and starts to your child's growth. You can't expect a preteen to "act grown-up" all the time. Rather than tease your child about the childish traits he hasn't yet lost ("I can't believe you still won't go to sleep without that silly blanket!"), give him an opportunity to talk about what he's looking forward to—and what he will miss—as he grows into an adult.

Be available.   Sometimes, in seeking a sense of who they are, preteens need to get some distance from their parents—but paradoxically, they can only do so if they feel sure you'll be there if they need you. So don't feel rejected if your child retreats into her room for hours on end, or tells you that she'd rather not confide in you when something is obviously bothering her. Encourage your child to talk to you, but don't insist. Make clear that while you're available, you respect her privacy.

Don't push public displays of affection.   Remember that a preteen's well-known aversion to anyone seeing you hug or kiss him does not mean that he no longer needs an encouraging arm around his shoulder from time to time. In most cases, however, you'd be wise to offer it in private. Also, some kinds of affection—sitting in your lap, for example—may no longer appeal to your child. Respect his wishes.

Ask yourself how you feel about your child's maturing.
You're no doubt happy to see signs of newfound responsibility and independence. However, are you also saddened to think of your baby growing up and becoming more distant, less affectionate? Most parents have some mixed feelings about watching their children turn into teenagers. Knowing your own feelings—including the ambivalent ones—allows you to respond appropriately.

Do set limits on rudeness and outbursts of temper.   You can have sympathy for the stresses and emotional vulnerability of puberty, but that doesn't require you to tolerate disrespect. It is appropriate to let your child know when her behavior is out of bounds. When she lashes out at you, the most effective way to set a limit without detouring into mutual blame is to talk about how *you* feel. You can say, "I made a simple request, and I don't like to be yelled at. If it's not a good time for you to straighten up your desk, just say so. I can understand that, and we can talk about finding a better time. But I don't deserve your anger."

As they grow • 11 to 13

"My Body Is So Ugly!"

*Preteens always think they're too heavy or too short or too **something.** How can you give your child some perspective?*

Richard M. Lerner, PhD., and Cheryl K. Olson

Richard M. Lerner, Ph.D., is director of the Institute for Children, Youth, and Families at Michigan State University. Cheryl K. Olson is a specialist in youth and health communications.

With the bathroom door locked, 12-year-old Anya carefully examines her still shower-damp body. She pokes disgustedly at her stomach. A year ago, her body felt comfortable and familiar. But the one in the mirror has new curves, and hair she isn't sure she likes. Maybe she should try that diet Becky told her about. Sighing, Anya pulls on her oversize black sweatshirt.

To their parents, it often seems as if young teenagers and preteens such as Anya are obsessed with their bodies, and that they are determined that their weight, height, and shape be regarded as desirable, or at least acceptable, to their peers. In fact, by age 7—if not sooner—children know which body shapes are considered best. By the early teens, the forms that children's bodies take become crucial to their sense of who they are.

All children this age will complain from time to time about being the wrong size or shape, even when they seemingly fit well within the norm for their peer group or their family. When a child becomes obsessed with appearance, however, there is genuine cause for concern. This is particularly true for young girls; because of the pressure they feel to remain slim in order to be considered attractive, they suffer from body-image problems more often than boys do.

In general, your best response to these complaints is to listen and then to reassure your child that everyone's body goes through awkward changes around this age. Make sure, though, that you don't supply your child with so much sympathy that you make the problem bigger than it is. For example, if your daughter is upset because she looks "dumpy" in a dress she likes, you can commiserate with her briefly by saying, "I remember how frustrating it was when my body was changing. We all grow out of it, though, thank goodness. In the meantime, let's try to find a dress that is better suited to your figure."

Girls' Early Maturity Can Cause Anxieties

Much of the confusion preteens feel about their bodies has its origins, unsurprisingly, in puberty. On average, the first period for a girl arrives when she is between 11½ and 12 years old, with changes in body hair and shape, including breast development, starting even earlier. Because girls typically reach puberty two years earlier than boys, most 10- or 11-year-old girls are bigger and taller than their male counterparts—ironically enough, just at the time when boys begin really wanting to be taller, and girls trimmer.

"I'm So Fat!"

What you should say—and what you shouldn't

Children often go through periods of being heavier than average. Here are two effective ways to respond to a child's complaints about weight—and two common responses that often backfire.

DON'T say, "Well, no wonder you have a weight problem—you keep stuffing yourself with junk food!" Doing so may foster a self-image as "fat" that she may well have trouble shaking off in years to come.

DO say, "At your age, when you're growing and doing so much, you need a lot of calories. But for health reasons, we need to pay more attention to the source of those calories. It would help *me* look and feel better, too, so let's all try to eat better as a family."

DON'T insist, "You look fine!" when your child is going through a period where he's carrying a little extra weight. Although you want to protect and soothe him, he may end up feeling that you don't understand him.

DO say, something like, "You've got years of growing ahead of you. Instead of worrying about your weight, why don't we concentrate on exercising so you feel better?"

—R.M.L. and C.K.O.

While the changes that come with puberty often make life difficult for girls, with boys the reverse is frequently true. Puberty, for them, means more weight and bigger muscles, in addition to sexual development—all physical qualities that we are taught to admire. Therefore, boys who mature early tend to be popular and are more likely to be seen as leaders by peers and adults.

Although these social advantages may last throughout life, it is also often the case that early maturers, by the time they've finished growing, are no bigger or stronger than the late bloomers; the seventh-grade sports hero isn't necessarily destined for the major leagues.

But how can you prepare your early-blooming athlete for a more competitive future without deflating his pride at his accomplishments? You might try saying something along the lines of, "I'm very proud of what a good football player you are. But you know, other boys are going to catch up to you in size eventually, so if you want to continue to be a strong competitor, you have to keep practicing."

Late-Blooming Boys Need Your Reassurance

If your son is distressed because—for the time being, at least—he's shorter and less muscular than his peers, you can help him in several ways. First of all, you might tell him something like, "You know, it's normal for some boys to mature more slowly than others. I realize that it's hard to be patient sometimes, but your time will come, and if you practice and exercise now, it will really pay off later on."

Meanwhile, build your son's self-confidence by encouraging activities that set his intellectual or artistic abilities to good advantage while also promoting sports that are appropriate to his body build. Gymnastics and soccer are often well suited to shorter boys, whereas tall, slim boys often excel at track and field or basketball.

While puberty is often at the root of differences in body build among children this age, other factors such as obesity can play a harmful role. Research shows that preteens see being fat as a greater obstacle to popularity even than missing an arm or a leg. In one landmark study, subjects were shown drawings of children who were disabled along with children who were obese; subjects consistently chose the fat children as the ones they would least like to be, or to be friends with.

Unfortunately, although researchers aren't exactly sure why, a majority of preteen girls want their weight to be below average, and therefore are often unhappy with themselves for having what medical experts consider a normal, healthy weight. A University of Vermont study of 1,500 teenagers found that at any given time, two thirds of girls between the ages of 13 and 18 were trying to lose weight. Most of these girls were considered to be of normal weight. (By contrast, many of the boys were trying to beef up.)

Diet-Conscious Girls Need Your Attention

If your daughter is constantly dieting, chances are good that she's not getting the nutrients she needs for a body that is still growing. She may also be forming a pattern of dieting and bingeing that will carry into adulthood, with adverse long-term health consequences. Should she frequently complain of being overweight when she clearly is not, or should there be a sudden, unexplained shift in her eating habits accompanied by changes in her mood, then she may be having problems accepting her weight.

How can you help her? Start by examining your own attitudes and habits. Do you often complain of feeling fat, or compare your figure unfavorably with those of models in magazines or on television? Do you fluctuate between restricting your diet and indulging yourself? If so, without realizing it, you may be encouraging your child to dislike her postpuberty body. (For tips on what to say, and what *not* to say, when a child frets about her weight, see " 'I'm So Fat!' What You Should Say—and What You Shouldn't.")

Whether your child imagines that she is heavy or is genuinely overweight, you can best address the problem by focusing not on her eating habits but on your family's. Stick to a sensible, nutritious meal plan, and keep the emphasis on health rather than weight so that your daughter can think of changing her body in positive terms rather than negative ones. If you criticize her eating choices too often, or forbid her to eat certain foods, you'll only create power struggles that won't do either of you any good.

Finally, keep reminding your preteen that her body is still working toward its eventual shape, and that while her body's shape and size are hard to control at this time in her life, she still has control over something that's much more important—her good health.

I'M OKAY!

Body-image and self-esteem go hand-in-hand. Learn to accept how you look and who you are.

Michelle Murphy

Fortunately, most people do not suffer from an eating disorder. But it's safe to say that most people do think about the way they look, and about how they can change the way they look. Experts agree that how you view yourself physically affects how you feel about yourself emotionally and mentally. Oftentimes, people begin thinking that a less-than-perfect body means a less-than-perfect person.

"In a culture as appearance-conscious as ours, preoccupation with one's looks has almost become a national pastime," confirms Thomas F. Cash, Ph.D., a professor at Old Dominion University and the author of "What Do You See When You Look in the Mirror?"

To some extent, it's human nature to care about one's appearance, and who doesn't feel better about themselves when they feel that they look their best?

"Body image and self-esteem are part and parcel of the same thing," says Robert White, M.D., medical director of the Hospital of Saint Raphael's psychiatric outpatient clinic. "It's hard to divorce how we think of ourselves as people from how we think of ourselves as bodies. This is important because at the root of self-esteem is self-love. It seems if we can't love ourselves, we can't love others."

Like her mother, Melinda Montovani is petite and small-boned, and has always been known as "the skinny one" in her family — an image she relished. So when her body started to change at puberty, she became worried. "I'd always felt invisible, like I was nobody inside, so I grasped at this skinny identity," says Montovani, 26, who today is 5'4" and 110 pounds, but at the time was two inches shorter and 20 pounds lighter.

While a high school sophomore in West Hartford, Montovani decided to lose weight. "My goal was to reach 75 pounds. I figured that if I could do that, I was a success and in control. I remember when I stepped on the scale and saw that 75 — I was really proud of myself." That was the beginning of a 10-year battle with anorexia nervosa, an eating disorder in which people starve themselves. Anorexia afflicts people who suffer from, among other things, shaky self-esteem and a longing for something they can control.

To outsiders, Montovani looked like she had it all: good grades; captain of the cross-country and track teams; even broke the school record with her 5:23 mile. Yet none of that counted. "I felt like no one liked me. The only thing I was good at was losing weight," she says. "And no matter what weight I got to, it wasn't enough. Inside, I hated myself."

Adds Cash, "If you cannot accept your appearance, you probably also assume others think less of you because of what you look like. This can cause you to feel self-conscious, uncomfortable and inadequate in your social interactions. As a result, you may at times avoid certain social situations and miss out on many of the joys of everyday human relations."

Until recently, and except for the 1920s, "plumpness was considered an attribute. It was a sign of wealth and beauty," says Daniel C. Moore, M.D., a Hamden psychiatrist who specializes in eating disorders and is an associate clinical professor of psychiatry at Yale University School of Medicine. That view has changed in the past three decades, even as the average American woman has been gaining weight (according to the Metropolitan Life height and weight tables). In movies, television, advertisements, even toys like the Barbie doll, the "ideal" woman is the one with huge breasts and tiny waist and hips—"genetic anomalies," as Moore calls them. In the mid-1960s, Barbie came equipped with her own scale set at 110 and a book that advised: "How to Lose Weight: Don't Eat."

Now, it seems, girls want to look almost like boys. Kate Moss, the waif model who carries 110 to 115 pounds on her 5'7" frame, represents perfection for many white teenage girls, reports a University of Arizona study. Judging from the females she knows, Montovani says this rings true. "Some people have said to me, 'you're so lucky — you had anorexia,'" she says. They admired her, she adds, even when she was "ugly-skinny." "They'd say, 'How do you stay so skinny?' It meant I had such great willpower, that I was such a great person. All they saw was skinny," Montovani says.

Females are more likely to subconsciously make judgments that the more attractive person is the "better" person, experts say. The result? "Women's self-esteem fluctuates with the number on the scale," says Lisa G. Berzins, Ph.D., a clinical psychologist in West Hartford.

Many media images reinforce this message. "If you look at television commercials, newscasters or movies, you'll find only very appealing women

of a certain age and certain look," says Abagail Feder, a Bridgeport resident who examined modern media during doctoral studies at Northwestern University. "There's very little latitude — you see very few women of larger size and very few older women. These media images tell us that to have a certain body type is to be good, to be virtuous, to be loved and lovely. And now it's not just the pressure to be thin, but they have to be perfectly toned and perfectly shaped, too."

Studies show that even *Playboy* centerfolds and Miss Americas have been getting thinner over the past few decades, says Berzins. But "only about 5 percent of women age 20 to 29 are as thin as these women," she adds. "A woman has about as much chance of

looking like one of these women as she does of being born with Barbie's high-heeled feet."

That doesn't stop people from trying. Consider these statistics:

• Americans spent $1.75 billion on cosmetic surgery in 1992. Of course,

not all cosmetic surgery cases are elective procedures; in some cases, cosmetic surgery is often required for medical reasons, as well.

• The dieting industry takes in a whopping $35 billion per year—and that doesn't include low-fat foods, exercise equipment or memberships in health clubs. In 1970, the figure was $10 billion.

• At any point in time, nearly half of American women are trying to lose weight—and among young women, the proportions are even higher. Studies show, in the past year, females dieted like crazy: 62 percent of white teenage girls; 76 percent of college women; and 56 percent of women aged 25 to 44. Even more disturbing, 30 percent to 40

percent of nine-year-old girls and 80 percent of 10-year-olds had already dieted, as well.

Yet most of this is for naught, because 95 percent of those who lose weight on a diet regain two-thirds of it

---

"Even if you think you're saying the right things to your kids, your actions speak louder than your words," says Margo Maine, from the Institute of Living in Hartford. "They pick up on it if they see you dieting, talking about not liking your body, not wanting to wear a bathing suit." And that could create another generation of people who believe, perhaps without even realizing it, that someone with a less-than-perfect body may be a less than perfect person. The idea that "image is everything" can be a damaging part of a child's developing value system. Giving children unconditional love is the most important ingredient in the development of healthy self-esteem, the experts say.

---

within a year. For many habitual dieters, the battle to stay thin is an emotional roller coaster that leads nowhere. "Bodies have their own internal gauges, which are pretty fixed," says Berzins. "Your weight is preprogrammed, just as your height is. And the more you diet, the more your metabolism slows down."

A new attitude can alter your self-image more effectively than the weight room or a diet plan.

Why, then, do people keep at it?

"Our culture breeds body-hatred," says Margo Maine, Ph.D., director of the Eating Disorders Program at the Institute of Living in Hartford. "The messages women get from ads and from what we call the body-change industry put pressure on them to feel that they have to do something else to be better than they are. Ads send the message that 'if I just lost weight, exercised more, had smaller breasts, bigger breasts, whatever, then I would be happy.' They make women feel they aren't good enough."

Of course, not everyone buys into this. The Arizona study of teenage girls revealed African-Americans were generally happier than whites with the way they looked: About 70 percent of the African-American girls said they were satisfied with their bodies, compared with only 10 percent of whites. What's more, while the white girls worshipped Kate Moss, the African-American girls aspired to thick thighs, full hips, and "the right attitude."

While boys and men do worry about how muscular they are or about how much hair they have, they are generally not as preoccupied with their weight. Some argue society lets males get away with an extra 25 pounds much more easily than it does females. "You don't find weight-loss articles in *Sports Illustrated*," notes

Maine. That's because men are valued primarily for things other than their looks: "intellect, power, strength," she adds. "Women still have a lot of ambivalence about what role they should have in our culture. But they know they'll be valued by keeping themselves thin and young looking."

That's not to say boys and men aren't concerned about their looks. The boom of men's health and fitness magazines is a clear indication of the pressure men face to achieve physical perfection. Ten years ago, most of the current self-help publications for men didn't exist. Today, journals like *GQ, Men's Health,* and *Men's Journal* consistently attract readers with supposed secrets to a firm, flat belly; the quickest ways to build muscle; or the latest news in cosmetic advances.

Image-conscious males are also taking the surgical route to achieving the perfect look. Hair transplants for men, for instance, represent the fastest growing area in all of cosmetic surgery. The pressure to build a muscular body drives some young men and boys to use harmful steroids. Like any woman, a man's perceived body image can influence how he feels about himself.

What can we do now to feel good about ourselves and help our children develop positive self esteem? The experts say it boils down to maintaining a sense of perspective by putting the way you feel about the way you look into a manageable context within the rest of your life.

Also, while it's important to learn to accept who you are, that doesn't preclude making realistic and reasonable changes in your life. Setting attainable goals is vital to improve self-image.

"Take an inventory of yourself and decide what's realistic to try to change," says White. "Many people try for too much, fail, and become angry. Be honest about what you can do. There are plenty of things you can't change — you can't change your inborn personality or your body type."

One thing you can change, however, is your own self-esteem. Often a new attitude can alter your self-image more effectively than the weight room or a diet plan.

"Self-esteem is a learned behavior; it's not the way you were born think-

ing," says Denise Coryea, a health education instructor who leads workshops in self-esteem and other topics at the Hospital of Saint Raphael and other area hospitals. "Something happens on the way from childhood to adulthood that changes the way we think about ourselves. Much of our sense of self-esteem we lose because we don't get to our goals. If it's not perfection, it's not good enough. We need to let go of perfect and learn to accept ourselves, warts and all." Self-acceptance and maintaining a positive attitude are important factors in developing a healthy self-image, she says.

Otherwise, you may pass your physical appearance anxieties on to your children — even unwittingly.

"Even if you think you're saying the right things to your kids, your actions speak louder than your words," says Maine. "They pick up on it if they see you dieting, talking about not liking your body or not wanting to wear a bathing suit."

"Daughters who perceive their mothers as being critical of their bodies have particularly poor body images, engage in stringent dieting, and are at a greater risk of developing an eating disorder," says Berzins, who has formed a group called PLEASE, or Promoting Legislation and Education About Self-Esteem.

The most important ingredient in the development of healthy self-esteem in a child is unconditional love.

"Both normal weight and overweight grade-school children describe obese silhouettes as stupid, dirty, lazy, sloppy, mean, ugly and sad," she says. "And when 24 children, some just three and four years old, were asked to pick a friend from pictures of handicapped, disfigured, and fat children, only five picked the fat one. One little boy said he rejected the fat child because 'he looks just like me!'"

But, as with everything else in life, there is the possibility of changing this culture — starting with the children.

"Talk to kids about diversity, about differences between people," says Maine. "Teach them that what you like about a person isn't their great hair, it's what kind of person they are inside. You can't give this message too much to kids, because they're getting the opposite (message) all the time." And practice what you preach. "It's so easy to focus on appearance all the time — telling a little girl how cute she looks in her bow and dress, or that boys look so handsome. It's okay to say these things, as long as you follow up with a compliment about something they've done — 'that was a nice thing you did for your brother,' 'you played so well in that game,' 'I'm glad to hear you helped your mother.'"

Says Moore, "Praise them for the real capacities they have. Don't always emphasize how they look or what their weight is. Also, watch how you tease them, such as telling a pubescent girl she's getting chubby, for instance, when all she's doing is going through normal female development."

Most important, the experts say, is to give children unconditional love — the most important ingredient in the development of healthy self-esteem.

"Make the child feel he's wanted, loved, cherished, no matter what he does," says Coryea. "Beware of the hurtful things parents say to kids: 'You're stupid, dumb, unable to do something.' Do you withhold affection from your child when you're angry? Ever say you wish he wasn't born? Can you hug your child — and mean it — when you're angry with the child?

"When you do make a mistake, as we all do, go to the child and admit it. You don't have to take them to the toy store; take them on your lap and hug them," she says. Let children know their appearance or behavior "doesn't earn them the love and acceptance of the adults in their life," adds Coryea.

"Those who are loved no matter what as children are those who feel good about themselves as adults, because they learn to feel good about themselves from within."

The Body of the Beholder

Mind: White girls dislike their bodies, but black girls are proud of theirs, a new study shows. Why is fat to some fit to others?

MICHELE INGRASSIA

WHEN YOU'RE A TEENAGE GIRL, there's no place to hide. Certainly not in gym class, where the shorts are short, the T shirts revealing and the adolescent critics eager to dissect every flaw. Yet out on the hardwood gym floors at Morgan Park High, a largely African-American school on Chicago's Southwest Side, the girls aren't talking about how bad their bodies are, but how good. Sure, all of them compete to see how many sit-ups they can do—Janet Jackson's washboard stomach is their model. But ask Diane Howard about weight, and the African-American senior, who carries 133 pounds on her 5-foot, 7½-inch frame, says she'd happily add 15 pounds—if she could ensure they'd land on her hips. Or La'Taria Stokes, a stoutly built junior who takes it as high praise when boys remark, "Your hips are screaming for twins!" "I know I'm fat," La'Taria says. "I don't care."

In a society that worships at the altar of supermodels like Claudia, Christy and Kate, white teenagers are obsessed with staying thin. But there's growing evidence that black and white girls view their bodies in dramatically different ways. The latest findings come in a study to be published in the journal Human Organization this spring by a team of black and white researchers at the University of Arizona. While 90 percent of the white junior-high and high-school girls studied voiced dissatisfaction with their weight, 70 percent of African-American teens were satisfied with their bodies.

In fact, even significantly overweight black teens described themselves as happy. That confidence may not carry over to other areas of black teens' lives, but the study suggests that, at least here, it's a lifelong source of pride. Asked to describe women as they age, two thirds of the black teens said they get more beautiful, and many cited their mothers as examples. White girls responded that their mothers may have been beautiful—back in their youth. Says anthropologist Mimi Nichter, one of the study's coauthors, "In white culture, the window of beauty is so small."

Moss: What is beauty? White teens defined perfection as 5 feet 7 and 100 to 110 pounds—superwaif Kate Moss's vital stats. African-American girls described the perfect size in more attainable terms—full hips, thick thighs, the sort of proportions about which Hammer ("Pumps and a Bump") and Sir Mix-Alot ("Baby Got Back") rap poetic. But they said that true beauty—"looking good"—is about more than size. Almost two thirds of the black teens defined beauty as "the right attitude."

The disparity in body images isn't just in kids' heads. It's reflected in fashion magazines, in ads, and it's out there, on TV, every Thursday night. On NBC, the sitcom "Friends" stars Courteney Cox, Jennifer Aniston and Lisa Kudrow, all of them white and twentysomething, classically beautiful and reed thin. Meanwhile, Fox Television's "Living Single," aimed at an African-American audience, projects a less Hollywood ideal—its stars are four twentysomething black women whose bodies are, well, *real*. Especially the big-boned, bronze-haired rapper Queen Latifah, whose size only adds to her magnetism. During a break at the Lite Nites program at the Harlem YMCA, over the squeal of sneakers on the basketball court, Brandy Wood, 14, describes Queen Latifah's appeal: "What I like about

her is the way she wears her hair and the color in it and the clothes she wears."

Underlying the beauty gap are 200 years of cultural differences. "In white, middle-class America, part of the great American Dream of making it is to be able to make yourself over," says Nichter. "In the black community, there is the reality that you might not move up the ladder as easily. As one girl put it, you have to be realistic—if you think negatively about yourself, you won't get anywhere." It's no accident that Barbie has long embodied a white-adolescent ideal—in the early days, she came with her own scale (set at 110) and her own diet guide ("How to Lose Weight: Don't Eat"). Even in this postfeminist era, Barbie's tight-is-right message is stronger than ever. Before kindergarten, researchers say, white girls know that Daddy eats and Mommy diets. By high school, many have split the world into physical haves and have-nots, rivals across the beauty line. "It's not that you hate them [perfect girls]," says Sarah Immel, a junior at Evanston Township High School north of Chicago. "It's that you're kind of jealous that they have it so easy, that they're so perfect-looking."

In the black community, size isn't debated, it's taken for granted—a sign, some say, that after decades of preaching black-is-beautiful, black parents and educators have gotten across the message of self-respect. Indeed, black teens grow up equating a full figure with health and fertility. Black women's magazines tend to tout NOT TRYING TO BE SIZE 8, not TEN TIPS FOR THIN THIGHS. And even girls who fit the white ideal aren't necessarily comfortable there. Supermodel Tyra Banks recalls how, in high school in Los Angeles, she was the

---

WHITE GIRLS
- 90% are dissatisfied with their bodies.
- 62% dieted in the last year. They define the perfect body as 5 feet 7, 100 to 110 pounds.

BLACK GIRLS
- 70% are satisfied with their bodies.
- 64% say it's better to be a little overweight than underweight.
- 65% say women get more beautiful as they age.

---

envy of her white girlfriends. "They would tell me, 'Oh, Tyra, you look so good'," says Banks. "But I was like, 'I want a booty and thighs like my black girlfriends'."

Men send some of the strongest signals. What's fat? "You got to be *real* fat for me to notice," says Muhammad Latif, a Harlem 15-year-old. White girls follow what they *think* guys want, whether guys want it or not. Sprawled across the well-worn sofas and hard-back chairs of the student lounge, boys at Evanston High scoff at the girls' idealization of Kate Moss. "Sickly," they say, "gross." Sixteen-year-old Trevis Milton, a blond swimmer, has no interest in dating Kate wanna-bes. "I don't want to feel like I'm going to break them." Here, perfection is a hardbody, like Linda Hamilton in "Terminator II." "It's not so much about eating broccoli and water as running," says senior Kevin Mack.

And if hardbodies are hot, girls often need to diet to achieve them, too. According to the Arizona study, which was funded by the National Institute of Child Health and Human Development, 62 percent of the white girls reported dieting at least once in the past year. Even those who say they'd rather be fit than thin get caught up. Sarah Martin, 16, a junior at Evanston, confesses she's tried forcing herself to throw up but couldn't. She's still frustrated: ". . . have a big appetite, and I feel so guilty when I eat."

Black teens don't usually go to such extremes. Anorexia and bulimia are relatively minor problems among African-American girls. And though 51 percent of the black teens in the study said they'd dieted in the last year, follow-up interviews showed that far fewer were on sustained weight-and-exercise programs. Indeed, 64 percent of the black girls thought it was

better to be "a little" overweight than underweight. And while they agreed that "very overweight" girls should diet, they defined that as someone who "takes up two seats on the bus."

The black image of beauty may seem saner, but it's not necessarily healthy. Black women don't obsess on size, but they do worry about other white cultural ideals that black men value. "We look at Heather Locklear and see the long hair and the fair, pure skin," says Essence magazine senior editor Pamela Johnson. More troubling, the acceptance of fat means many girls ignore the real dangers of obesity. Dieting costs money—even if it's not a fancy commercial program; fruits, vegetables and lean meats are pricier than high-fat foods. Exercise? Only one state—Illinois—requires daily physical education for every kid. Anyway, as black teenagers complain, exercise can ruin your hair—and, if you're plunking down $35 a week at the hairdresser, you don't want to sweat out your 'do in the gym. "I don't think we should obsess about weight and fitness, but there is a middle ground," says the well-toned black actress Jada Pinkett. Maybe that's where Queen Latifah meets Kate Moss.

With KAREN SPRINGEN *in Chicago and* ALLISON SAMUELS *in New York*

A Study of White Middle-Class Adolescent Boys' Responses to "Semenarche" (The First Ejaculation)

James H. Stein and Lynn Whisnant Reiser

James H. Stein, Instructor, Department of Medicine, Rush–Presbyterian–St. Luke's Medical Center, Chicago, Illinois. Received M.D. from Yale School of Medicine.

Lynn Whisnant Reiser, Clinical Professor, Department of Psychiatry, Yale University School of Medicine, New Haven, Connecticut. Received M.D. from Yale School of Medicine.

Received September 4, 1992; accepted August 18, 1993

Few empirical studies focus on how boys respond to puberty. This paper presents the results of a questionnaire and interview survey of 36 white middle-class adolescent male camp counselors (mean age, 18.4 years) that addressed pubertal changes and first ejaculation ("semenarche"). It is a descriptive and hypothesis-generating study. The first ejaculation, biologically significant in sexual and reproductive functioning, was found to be psychological meaningful but socially invisible. The mean age at semenarche was 12.9 years. All of the boys in the group had sex education in school, yet many felt unprepared for their first ejaculation, which occurred earlier than they expected and before formal education. Those who felt prepared expressed more positive feelings and coped better. Common responses to semenarche included surprise, curiosity, pleasure, and confusion. Most subjects did not tell anyone that this event occurred and many boys initially confused ejaculation and urination. The association of the first ejaculation with sexuality makes it a charged event. Psychosocial and developmental difficulties in sexual education for young males are noted.

INTRODUCTION

The male experience of the first ejaculation has received little research attention. This invisibility is reflected in the lack of a generally accepted term in the English language for the event. "Semenarche"—a word meaning the beginning of semen—is a logical term for the first ejaculation (Sarrel, personal communication, 1987).[1] This paper uses this designation and suggests the common adoption of this term as a name for the first ejaculation.

Research interest in male puberty and the significance of the first ejaculation has focused on biology (Kinsey, 1948; Tanner, 1971; Richardson and Short, 1978; Hirsch, 1988)—the psychological and social components of this phenomena have not been adequately addressed. This deficiency is found both in standard textbooks of psychiatry (Kaplan and Saddock, 1989) and pediatrics (Behrman, 1992) and in the psychoanalytic literature. Yet there are indications that semenarche is an important event.

Kinsey *et al.* (1948) concluded from his retrospective study of 4590 men that the first ejaculation was "the most significant of all adolescent developments" and stated that "the newly adolescent boy's capacity to ejaculate, [and] his newly acquired physical characteristics of other sorts, do something to him which brings child play to an end and leaves him awkward about making further socio-sexual contacts." A questionnaire study of 146 male college students (Shipman, 1968) suggested that semenarche was an important and frightening experience because sex education for boys was inadequate. In contrast, Gaddis and Brooks-Gunn (1985) concluded from a small interview study of 13 adolescent boys that the first ejaculation was not as traumatic as previously reported.

This paper presents a descriptive and hypothesis-generating study of adolescent male camp counselors to determine how they remembered the experience of semenarche and other changes of puberty, and how their education and interaction with family and peers contributed to their understanding pubertal changes.

METHOD

Thirty-six white, middle-class, Jewish male camp counselors ranging in age from 15.7 to 21.5 years (average age of 18.4 years) enrolled in this study. This corresponds to 98% participation by the male counseling staff at this private camp. A written questionnaire was followed by a 45 minute audiotaped semistructured interview (with JS). The questionnaire served as an introduction to the topics that were more explicitly discussed in the interview. Using both research tools provided a measure of intrasubject reliability—questions in the questionnaire and interview were parallel and responses were consistent when compared (except for one exception described below). The research tools included questions regarding physical changes that accompanied puberty, education and sources of information about puberty, and psychological and social responses to these changes. Fearing that parents might consider this an explicit introduction of sexual topics, camp officials excluded campers age 10–14 years from the study. Subjects were informed about the study by the camp director who presented it as a survey study of how boys experience the changes of puberty. They were interviewed individually in a private setting by a researcher who had been a former camper and counselor at the camp. Each discussant signed a release assuring confidentially.

RESULTS

Age at Semenarche

When asked how old they were when they had their first ejaculation, most subjects initially claimed not to remember (responded "don't know" on the questionnaire, or answered "I don't know" in the interview). Five subjects left the question blank on the questionnaire. When restated in the interview as "What grade were you in?" and when more specific questions about context were asked, *all* remembered the circumstances of this event (although 2 still did not remember their age). The average age was 12.9 ± 1.5 years.

Context of Semenarche

Semenarche occurs in a number of different contexts—such as during sleep (nocturnal emission), masturbation, or in sexual activity with another person. In interview data, a wet dream was the most common context for semenarche (20 boys) and masturbation was the next (13 boys). In contrast to the agreement on other questions, there was a discrepancy between 4 subjects' answers to this in the interview and on the questionnaire. These subjects reported on the questionnaire that semenarche occurred during masturbation, but in the interview as a nocturnal emission. These subjects' discomfort during the interview was rated high by self-report and by the interviewer, and these subjects provided few descriptive details. This suggests that masturbation may be a more common context for semenarche than is reflected in the interview data. Three subjects experienced semenarche during heterosexual activity—2 having intercourse, one engaging in petting. No subjects reported that their first ejaculation occurred during homosexual activity.

Response to Semenarche

Subjects were asked to rate the extent to which they experienced 22 feelings at semenarche (Table 1). A 4-point scale (*not at all, a little, somewhat, a lot*) was adapted from Gaddis and Brooks-Gunn (1985). The final two categories (*somewhat* and *a lot*) were reported as "a lot" to facilitate comparison with Gaddis and Brooks-Gunn, who did the same. In the interview, subjects were encouraged to elaborate on any strong feelings that they may have had. Representative and interesting anecdotes are presented below. Many reported having had strong feelings (rarely negative) at their first ejaculation. The qualitative aspect of their response and conflict was more evident in the interviews:

> My wet dream was kind of an experience that I *didn't experience.* It had nothing to do with my mental attitude. I was sound asleep, I woke up the next morning and my sheets were pasty—I slept through it—After you wake up your mind is kind of happy and then you realize 'oh my god, this is my wet dream.' (Emphasis added)

Seventy-five percent of the subjects reported feeling surprised that they were so young when their first ejaculation took place and at the physical intensity of the first ejaculation. The extent to which a subject felt "surprised" was strongly correlated with feeling confused (Pearson $r > 0.60$, $p < .001$), embarrassed ($r > 0.52$, $p < 0.001$), scared ($r > 0.61$,

Table I. Experience of Positive and Negative Feelings at Semenarche (Interview Data)[a]

Feeling	Percentage			
	Mean	Not at all	A little	A lot
Positive feeling				
Positive	2.4	28	14	58
Prepared	2.6	17	25	58
Pleasurable	2.4	36	8	56
Grown up	2.2	39	17	45
Excited	2.1	33	31	36
Glad	2.0	39	28	34
Relieved	1.9	42	25	34
Happy	1.8	44	33	22
Proud	1.5	61	28	11
Negative feeling				
Surprised	3.0	14	11	75
Confused	2.4	33	14	52
Embarrassed	2.0	47	25	27
Out of control	1.7	64	14	22
Upset	1.4	75	11	14
Dirty	1.4	81	6	14
Scared	1.5	64	25	12
Disgusted	1.5	67	22	12
Unhappy	1.3	78	17	6
Painful	1.1	92	6	3
Angry	1.1	94	6	0
Ripped off	1.0	97	3	0
Neutral feeling				
Curious	2.9	8	25	67

[a]$N = 36$. A 4-point scale was used, including (1) *not at all*, (2) *a little*, (3) *somewhat*, and (4) *a lot*. The percentage of subjects who responded "somewhat" are included above in "a lot."

$p < 0.001$), and out of control ($r > 0.68$, $p > 0.001$). Many of those who felt "surprised" also felt unprepared ($r > 0.52$, $p < 0.001$). "Surprised" did not correlate with "pleasure" or "happiness."

Subjects whose semenarche was a wet dream were more likely to initially confuse semen with urine. Eleven subjects (31%) reported that their first ejaculation reminded them of "urinating" or "wetting the bed."

It took kind of awhile to click in—later in the day I finally figured out what the hell was going on. I thought I had pissed in my pants at first!
It reminded me of peeing in my pants—that was my first reaction even thought I'd never done it.

Subjects whose first ejaculation was during masturbation remembered more pleasure (two-tailed $t = 3.71$, $df = 31$, $p < 0.05$) and happiness (two-tailed $t = 2.08$, $df = 31$, $p < 0.05$) than did subjects whose first ejaculation was during a nocturnal emission. The latter, however, did not express more negative feelings. The data suggest that the source of difference was the conscious experience of an orgasm that accompanied masturbation.

Boys who experienced their first ejaculation while masturbating commented:

My parents had these videotapes. I knew they were X-rated and I really wanted to see them. My parents were out of town. I knew they were hidden in their closet. I threw them in. I thought 'this is very interesting' and the next thing I knew—Bam!—I honestly didn't know what I was doing.
I think I was trying to masturbate—I didn't really—it was—the actual ejaculation came as a surprise—I knew what I was doing but didn't know what would happen—I—I remember—I remember—realizing what had happened but not really knowing exactly until later.

The only common negative feeling was confused (50%):

I was in my bed—I really didn't know what I was doing—just touching myself. I was at the point where I knew it would happen but I was confused—I really didn't know what was going on and was embarrassed because of it.

A boy who woke up after a nocturnal emission remembered:

I didn't know what it was so I blew off, since the rest of the mornings I woke up normal. I thought I was just nervous or something.

Sixty-seven percent of the subjects remembered feeling curious, wondering how they could make the ejaculation happen again, when it would happen again, and if it would be different with a girl. This boy expresses that sense of wonder:

I was curious to see—I wasn't expecting to have sex or anything. It was just generally—I didn't know exactly how—would it happen again? It had never happened before.

In interviews, the strongest negative responses were related to embarrassment and feeling out of control, especially to less prepared subjects.

I was alone but I was very embarrassed because I was *out of control.* That was my major feeling—I was worried it would happen again. I put it together about a week later when I did it again. Then I figured it out. (Emphasis added)

The association with urination may also contribute to the sense of being out of control—some boys had expected ejaculation, like urination to be under voluntary sphincter control. "I thought it was just like peeing."

I thought it would happen when I wanted it to, that I'd have control over it. I was scared about the *loss of control.* (Emphasis added)

The most stressful experience of semenarche, and the only one that was described as "painful," was that of a boy whose first ejaculation (at age 17) was with a woman. He was embarrassed about not having control over his body in the presence of another person.

It was a lot painful. It hurt. I don't know why. That's what I remember. It was enjoyable to have it done, not physically. I was just glad I got it over. The pain was indescribable.

In contrast to that subject's experience, many of the subjects described the experience as pleasurable:

Well at first I felt really—like it was weird cuz I had never felt that way before. But after a little bit it was—pleasurable. It was good—It felt good—You just have to feel it for yourself."

Some subjects, however, reported feeling uncomfortable with the unexpected intensity of the pleasure that they felt at the first ejaculation.

Education

Classes at school were the most common source of information about puberty in general. Nearly all of the subjects completed "health education" courses in fifth or sixth grade, and continued their education about physical development and human sexuality well into high school. In spite of having an extensive health and sex education curriculum, more than one-quarter of the boys recalled that classes failed to explain ejaculation. In the classes that did discuss ejaculation, the topic was postponed until the eighth grade, after many boys had already experienced their first ejaculation. The boys remembered that teachers put emphasis on informing students that pubertal changes were "normal" and "healthy." The subjects' responses reflected this focus, as many subjects described their first pubertal changes as a signal that they were "normal."

One boy whose semenarche was during masturbation at age 12 expressed these complicated feelings:

It didn't make me feel proud. It made me feel guilty, like I'd done something wrong. Those kind of feelings—The class didn't say anything. I still think it's something I shouldn't do—My only relief was that I was *normal.* (emphasis added)

Another boy whose semenarche was a nocturnal emission described a predominant sense of relief at being normal:

I woke up the next morning and noticed the wetness. I felt relieved. I expected it. I mean, people talked about it and the classes—sex ed—told about what happens and it happened. *It's a normal thing*—I didn't have much emotion attached to it. I felt prepared for it, but I never expected it—I didn't want anyone to know—I was glad that it happened. (emphasis added)

The only late-maturer in the study expressed this sentiment (relief at being normal) most strongly.

Forty-two percent of the subjects felt unprepared for semenarche. "Prepared" subject reported feeling more "proud" and "positive" (two-tailed $t = 3.02$, $df = 34$, $p < 0.005$); "Unprepared" subjects, stronger negative feelings—more "confused" (3.87, 34, $p < .001$), "upset" (4.87, 34, $p < 0.001$), "scared" (3.18, 34, $p < 0.005$), "disgusted" (3.34, 34, $p < 0.002$), "out of control" (2.70, 34, $p < 0.02$).

For example, one boy stated:

I'm almost positive that it was a wet dream. The problem was that I didn't know what it was. It was just so—I never knew what it was. I was surprised I wet my bed—what did I do? I only found out a year later what it was.

Only one-third of the boys considered parents important sources of information about ejaculation. For those, this topic was usually discussed by a father alone or both parents together—in one case information about ejaculation was provided by a mother alone. Conversations about semenarche *after* it happened were rare. Only 2 subjects told their mother or father that their first ejaculation had occurred. Most boys were very secretive:

For the first time I knew something that they [parents] didn't—it was a private thing that nobody else knew.

Boys often hid the evidence of a nocturnal emission by changing the sheets themselves (some even performed midnight laundering). Others assumed their parents knew but did not mention it directly:

My mom, she knew I had them. It was all over my sheets, and bedspread and stuff, but she didn't say anything, didn't tease me and stuff. I was kind of glad. She never asked if I wanted to talk about it—I'm glad. I never could have said anything to my mom.
I don't remember when it happened or how old I was, but I didn't tell anyone. My friends, we didn't talk about it, but if it came up, you know we always played these games—'So have you done this, so have you done this, so have you done this'—I would say I had. But I didn't say 'By the way mom, my bed is wet.' I mean, I knew what an ejaculation was, and I knew that I hadn't wet my bed.

When a boy did tell someone, it was usually a friend. The boys' descriptions reveal more about the fragmentary quality of this kind of discussion with friends:

Before it I remember being in the boy's locker room at school and my friend telling me about having a wet dream and he said 'Oh, everyone has it' and I remember thinking and I remember lying and I remember experimenting with masturbation after that.
While it was going on no one wanted to say anything about it. We all kind of left it alone—After it happened and we knew what was going on, we laughed about it with friends. Laughed at guys' penises, you know.
I had no idea what—I had no ides what was happening—It just hurt and I said 'I gotta go,' so I found my friend and said 'I gotta talk to you' and it just went from there. He made me feel better—I was embarrassed about telling my friend—it just really hit me. I just told him. I didn't hold back cuz I wanted to know what was happening. I said 'I wanna know what happened.' He said 'Oh yeah, you came,' and I felt happy after that, glad it happened.

Pubertal Events

Seventy-eight percent of the subjects stated that the appearance of pubic hair was a memorable signal that puberty had started.[2] However, as a group they felt that neither this biological change nor any other was in itself a symbol for their change in status and self-perception. A few boys like this one did assert the importance of the first ejaculation:

The next morning I felt really gross—I knew what it was. I don't think it was pleasurable—I was embarrassed. I don't know, I just remember being in my bed and feeling that I had just—I knew I didn't wet my bed. I mean, I felt weird that this change had just happened—*it was pretty major.* (Emphasis added)

Less than 40% felt that the first ejaculation was important. More often they asserted, like this boy, that

The things that I really remember are the things that I did sexually.

The events (Table II) that were most meaningful for this group were social—"making out" was very meaningful for 89%, "dating" for 83%, and "Bar Mitzvah" for 72%.

Only 10 subjects (28%) felt it was noteworthy that after the first ejaculation they were physically able to "get a girl pregnant." Most reported that they rarely considered the possibility that they could father a child. Their confusion is evident in their words:

I never thought about getting a girl pregnant. I knew biologically that I could father a child.

DISCUSSION

The subjects comprised a homogeneous sample of boys with similar religious, educational, and socioeconomic backgrounds. They were socially well adjusted enough to be chosen as camp counselors. Because participation was high, this well-defined population can be *compared* to others, but cannot be used to generalize about other demographic groups. As in all retrospective studies, experiences subsequent to target events may have influenced memories of the event in an unquantifiable manner (recall bias). The average time since semenarche for our subjects was 5.5 ± 0.9 years, so it relied more on memory than the study of young adolescent boys conducted by Gaddis and Brooks-Gunn (1985). Although both of these study samples were small, the higher participation rate (90%) and larger sample size (36) suggest that this study had less selection bias than the study by Gaddis and Brooks-Gunn (1985, 62% participation, 13 subjects). Given these limitations, the study is meant to be descriptive and hypothesis-generating.

The results were consistent with the descriptions of the events that signaled pubertal onset in the populations studied by Kinsey *et al.* (1948) and Tanner (1971). The average age of semenarche in Kinsey's study was about a year older, 13.88 years. Adolescent boys experience strong, but rarely negative feelings at semenarche, including surprise, confusion, curiosity, and pleasure. The conscious experience of orgasm allows those who experience

Table II. The Significance of Social and Physical Events (Interview Data)[a]

Feeling	Mean	Percentage		
		Not at all	A little	A lot
Physical event				
Develop pubic hair	2.9	8	14	78
Growth spurt	2.8	8	31	61
Growth of penis	2.5	11	28	61
Develop facial hair	2.5	19	25	56
Develop acne	2.3	33	22	45
Voice change	2.3	25	33	42
First ejaculation	*2.3*	*19*	*42*	*39*
Develop axillary hair	2.1	22	44	34
Growth of testes	1.9	31	44	25
Social event				
Making out	3.3	8	3	89
Dating	3.2	6	11	83
Bar Mitzvah	3.0	14	14	72
Shaving	2.7	17	17	66
Using cologne	2.2	25	39	36
Change nudity practice	2.1	31	36	33
Showering	1.9	44	28	28
Using deodorant	1.9	39	36	25
Wearing jockstrap	1.8	50	28	22

[a]$N = 36$. A 4-point scale was used, such that (1) *not at all*, (2) *a little*, (3) *somewhat*, and (4) *a lot*. The percentage of subjects who responded "somewhat" are included above in "a lot."

their first ejaculation by masturbation to feel more "pleasure" and "happiness." Although boys whose first ejaculation is during a wet dream do not report more negative feelings, they more often confuse semen with urine, at least initially. Boys rarely discuss their first ejaculation and usually hide the evidence. Semenarche is not a socially recognized event and adolescent boys deny attaching much significance to it, especially in light of later sexual experiences.

The first ejaculation, biologically significant in sexual and reproductive functioning, is socially invisible. Thus, semenarche is not comparable to menarche as a significant symbolic developmental milestone. The lack of a name for the first ejaculation contributes to making this an invisible event and parallels the failure to label adequately the female external genitalia (especially sexual structures) in the education of girls (Lerner, 1976). The connection of the first ejaculation with sexuality makes it a charged event.

Despite sex education and hygiene classes at school and some parental input, many of the boys in this group felt unprepared for their first ejaculation, which occurred earlier than they expected. Education, including a specific discussion about ejaculation before semenarche occurs, can positively influence how boys experience pubertal transformation. Those who were prepared coped better, in contrast to the subjects interviewed by Gaddis and Brooks-Gunn (1985) and in agreement with Shipman's study (1968).

In view of the current crisis in the prevention of AIDS and unwanted pregnancies, the data from this study raise many questions about how best to educate boys about puberty and when to provide information. Education regarding semenarche frequently occurred *after* the boys had already experienced the event, so earlier sex education is clearly needed. In addition, emphasis should be placed on the fact that many boys are fertile at or before semenarche (Richardson and Short, 1978; Hirsch, 1988).

The difficulties in sexual education for preadolescents are many:

Frequently, newly provided sexual information seems to be promptly forgotten. At times this rather amazing phenomenon may be due to a feigned ignorance in the service of secrecy, out of uneasiness with the subject matter or compliance with the cultural double standard. Frequently, thought, it represents a genuine, unconscious denial of anxiety-producing knowledge. ("Normal Adolescence," 1968, p. 792).

In addition, a boy's ability to understand the physical changes of puberty is limited by his cognitive ability, which is usually still at the concrete or early formal operations stage (Piaget, 1972) when he experiences his first ejaculation. Sigmund Freud (1895/1959a, 1895/1959b) pointed out how persistently adults, particularly parents, avoided acknowledging childhood (and adolescent) sexuality. This observation is still accurate and is reflected in the boy's reports and in the paucity of empirical studies of childhood sexuality.

One boy suggested an approach to this problem in terms of a favorite series of childhood picture books:

I would describe it [puberty] as 'Curious George.'[3] *Because you really don't know what's going on unless you really get it explained by somebody who doesn't have a bias on it.* I always really liked Curious George—he always wants to find out more about things he shouldn't, and that's what puberty is. (Emphasis added)

This empirical survey study of a well-defined population of normal adolescent boys suggests that although the first ejaculation is not traumatic for the majority of boys, it is a memorable, highly charged event that is less anxiety producing if there has been prior education. There is a need for both prospective and retrospective studies documenting the experience of semenarche in other ethnic and socioeconomic groups in order to delineate the impact of this event upon subsequent psychosocial development and to clarify how best to respond to boys' curiosity in preparing them for puberty.

REFERENCES

Behrman, R. E. (1992). *Nelson's Textbook of Pediatrics* (14th ed.). W. B. Saunders, Philadelphia, PA.

Freud, S. (1959a). The Sexual Enlightenment of Children—an Open Letter to Dr. M. Furst, 1907. In *Standard Edition* (Vol. 9). London: Hogarth Press. (Originally published 1895).

Freud, S. (1959b). On the Sexual Theories of Children, 1908. In *Standard Edition* (Vol. 9). London: Hogarth Press. (Originally published 1895.)

Gaddis, A., and Brooks-Gunn, J. (1985). The male experience of pubertal change. *J. Youth Adolesc.* 14: 61-69.

Hirsch, M., Lunenfeld, B., Modan, M., Ovadia, J., and Shemesh, J. (1988). Spermarche-The age of onset of sperm emission. *Sex. Active Teen.* 2: 34–38.

Kaplan, H., and Saddock, B. J. (1989). *Comprehensive Textbook of Psychiatry* (5th ed.). Williams & Wilkins, Baltimore, MD.

Kinsey, A. C., Pomeroy, W. B., and Martin, C. E. (1948), *Sexual Behavior in the Human Male*. W. B. Saunders, Philadelphia, PA.

Lerner, H. (1976). Parental mislabeling of female genitals as a determinant of penis envy and learning inhibitions in women. In *Female Psychology—Contemporary Psychoanalytic View*, ed. H. Blum. International Universities Press, New York.

Normal Adolescence: Its dynamics and impact. (1968). In Group for the Advancement of Psychiatry (Volume VI, Report No. 68).

Piaget, P. (1972). *The Child's Conception of the World.* Littlefield Adams, Totowa, NJ.

Rey, H. A. (1941). *Curious George.* Houghton Mifflin, Boston.

Richardson, D. W., and Short, R. V. (9178). Time of onset of sperm production in boys. *J. Biosocial Sci. Suppl.* 5, 15–25.

Sarrel, P. M. (1987). Personal communication.

Shipman, G. (1968), The psychodyamics of sex education. *Family Coord.* 7, 3–12.

Tanner, J. M. (1971), Sequence, tempo, and individual variation in growth and development of boys and girls aged twelve to sixteen. *Daedalus* 100, 907–930.

NOTES

1. Shipman (1968) proposed that the first ejaculation be named either "primus ejaculatus" from the Latin or "spermarche" from the Greek. The latter term is used most commonly but is inaccurate, since "spermarche"—the appearance of sperm (using spermaturia as a marker)—occurs *before* the first ejaculation (Richardson and Short, 1978; Hirsch *et al.*, 1988).
2. This is in accordance with Tanner's Developmental Stage 2, when pubic hair first appears (Tanner, 1971). Reddening of the scrotum and enlargement of testes and scrotum, also occurring in Stage 2, were not mentioned by any subject.
3. *Curious George* refers to a series of children's picture books (Rey, 1941) that recount the adventures of a "good little monkey" who is "always very curious."

A Dangerous Rite of Passage

Daily NATION

Penina, a 13-year-old Masai girl, sits on a sheepskin laid at the door of her mother's hut. Her legs are held open by her aunts while an elderly circumciser makes rapid cuts to her genitals. Without any anesthesia and forbidden to cry out or show fear, the girl bites on a cloth during the 10-minute operation until the circumciser is through.

Toward the end of the operation, Penina passes out from pain and blood loss. The wound is cleansed with cow urine and smothered in goat fat to stop the bleeding, and the girl is put in bed until she regains consciousness. Her proud husband-to-be, waiting outside, is congratulated by elders. Many relatives and friends have come, bringing gifts of goats and money for Penina's father.

The next initiate, Penina's 11-year-old sister Enkarsis, is not so brave. As the circumciser makes the first cut to the clitoris, the child howls in pain: "Why are you killing me? Leave me alone. Why do you want to kill me?" The circumciser cackles with laughter. "Mom, why can't you save me?" pleads Enkarsis.

Her mother reprimands her sternly, "Keep quiet! You should be able to withstand this thing. You are not a coward."

When asked why she laughed throughout the operation, the circumciser answered, "The pain doesn't kill. We laugh because it is our culture, and we have all passed through this stage . . . . She is so beautiful because she is a clean woman now. She is a grown-up."

Despite repeated denunciations of female genital mutilation by humanitarian and women's organizations and even a presidential ban on the practice, mutilations continue. Many ask why. The answer is deeply rooted in tradition, and the stark brutality of the act is readily justified through culture.

"Circumcision is meant to reduce a woman's sexual desire so that she won't go looking for extramarital affairs," says women's health advocate Lois Towon. Ironically, the result may be the reverse. The headmistress of a girls' boarding school in Kajiado, Priscilla Nangurai, says the school loses 10 to 20 young girls a year who become pregnant after being circumcised. "A girl is free to have sex with any man after she is circumcised, and men take advantage of that," says Nangurai. "It is not in our culture to refuse a man."

Unlike Somali and other Muslim cultures that circumcise to preserve virginity around the age of seven, the Masai circumcise girls at puberty as an important initiation into the tribe.

Circumcision is considered the most significant rite of passage to adulthood. It is said to enhance tribal and social cohesion, increase a girl's marriage opportunities, and increase a father's status within the community. "Parents are not out to hurt their daughters," says Charity Mailutha, program officer for the Family Planning Association of Kenya. "But to prepare them for marriage, to prepare them to be women who can be accepted in society; circumcision is the only way they know. It is a passage from childhood to adulthood."

But how far must a woman go to feel that she belongs to her society and culture? According to World Health Organization estimates, at least 100 million women in 26 countries in Africa have had to pay a high price for their identity. And even in its mildest forms, female genital mutilation poses serious health risks.

"Female circumcision deals with the most sensitive part of the body, [and] the wound left behind is both physical and psychological," says Mailutha. The type of genital mutilation most common among the Masai and Samburu tribes is excision, where the clitoris and the adjacent parts of the labia minora are removed. Many Samburus also practice infibulation, which involves sewing together the two sides of the vulva. The girl is required to hold her legs together for up to a month, allowing scar tissues to grow together and leaving only a small opening for urine and menstrual flow.

Besides blood loss, which can be fatal, genital mutilation can have severe long-term side effects including urinary tract infections, chronic vaginal infections, excessive growth of scar tissue, and stones in the urethra and bladder caused by the obstruction of menstrual flow. The mutilation often leads to reproductive tract infections and infertility.

By far the most critical complications arising from genital mutilation come during pregnancy. Prolonged labor, which is life-threatening to both mother and child, is a common result.

> *"What could be more important than the health of thousands of women?"*

Most people say that the practice of female genital mutilation is dying out, especially in Nairobi and other urban centers. But there is little hope of eradication in the near future. "We have more important things to worry about," such as the poor and unemployed, says Minister William ole Ntimama, one of the most influential Masai leaders.

"What can be more important than the health of thousands of women in Kenya?" asks women's health activist Leah Muuya. About 70 percent of the food produced in Africa is the work of women. Women also carry the burden of raising children and running the household. "Without women, African society would fall apart," she adds.

In 1982, President Daniel arap Moi officially banned female genital mutilation, but 13 years later, the ban seems to have had little effect. Some circumcisers were arrested, Mailutha says, "but when they went to court, the cases were thrown out because there is no law that makes circumcision illegal."

—*Stephanie Welsh, "Daily Nation" (independent), Nairobi, May 7, 1995.*

The Long and Short of It
New Medications for Growth Disorders

Margie Patlak

Margie Patlak is a freelance writer in Elkins Park, Pa.

Many homes have pencilled lines on a wall that chart the rapidly rising height of children, and often even the most picky pint-size eaters will be inspired to chow down if they are told the food will make them "big and strong."

When a child's growth or development goes awry, it often dismays parents and prompts them to seek medical help. Whether or not there is actually a physical abnormality when a child's growth varies greatly from the average, social and emotional problems may result. A child who is significantly shorter than his or her friends or one who has delayed or precocious (early) puberty, for example, may be shunned or ridiculed by other children.

Several new drugs can set a child's abnormal growth back on track. In the late 1980s, the Food and Drug Administration approved Protropin and Humatrope two synthetic forms of human growth hormone, to treat children with small stature. These drugs can boost the growth rate of children deficient in the hormone, preventing extremely sort adult stature.

(Growth hormone extracted from cadaver pituitaries was used to treat such children before the development of synthetic human growth hormone. But the discovery in April 1985 that some of the natural growth hormone was contaminated by a microbe that causes a fatal brain illness known as Creutzfeldt-Jakob disease prompted officials to stop its use.)

In delayed puberty, it is development of sexual characteristics rather than final height that is impeded. Physicians use sex hormones and their chemical cousins experimentally to boost the growth and development of these "late bloomers." (See box, "Late Bloomers.")

At the opposite extreme, some children develop adolescent sexual characteristics at a very young age and stop growing much earlier than normal so that they grow up to be short adults. To treat this condition, known as precocious puberty, two synthetic hormones called histrelin acetate (Supprelin) and nafarelin acetate (Synarel), were approved by FDA in the past two years.

Ethical Dilemmas

Although these treatments may benefit children with extreme cases of short stature, or delayed or precocious puberty, their use in borderline children—those on the short end of the measuring stick, for example, but not rack bottom on the charts—is raising some thorny ethical issues.

Short stature doesn't always stem from a disease, for example, but often is part of the normal variation in height and is inherited from short parents.

Physicians are wary of treating normal short children with growth hormone for merely cosmetic or social reasons, especially since the benefits and adverse effects of the hormone treatments on these children are not fully known. The decision of which children to treat rests with physicians and parents. It cannot wait until the child matures to adulthood and is able to make his or her own decision, since growth hormone is not thought to be effective in full-grown adults.

"Often it isn't the kids who are worried about being short, but their parents," points out pediatric endocrinologist Gilbert August, M.D., of George Washington University. "These parents, who are short themselves, vicariously relive through the child their own failures in high school about not being able to make the team, etc. I've often joked that if you could just do a 'parentectomy' these kids would be fine."

But even without parental pressures, short stature can be costly in our society, which values height. Some scientists cite studies showing success is tied to inches, with taller people making more money or having more prestigious jobs on average than shorter individuals.

Drawing the line between normal growth and development and medical disorder is not always clear-cut. Growth disorder can be difficult to diagnose because of the wide variation in normal growth rates, and researchers are just beginning to tease apart the various hormones and other factors that govern a child's growth and entrance into puberty.

Growth Hormone Deficiency

One of the more challenging growth disorders to diagnose is a growth hormone deficiency. It affects only 15,000 to 20,000 children in this country. Some children with a growth hormone deficiency have normal growth rates the first few years of life. This growth abnormality is suspected if a child is between 3 and 12 years of age and growing less than 2 inches a year for an extended period.

But before diagnosing growth hormone deficiency, physicians first rule out several more common conditions that can temporarily slow growth, including a deficient diet, abnormal digestion, stress, hypothyroidism, diabetes, brain tumor or injury, and chronic illness, such as severe asthma or a kidney disorder.

An inherited tendency to be on the short side of normal, as evidenced by a child's sort parents, can also explain a slow growth rate. Children may have delayed puberty, in addition, which can temporarily retard growth. (See box, "Late Bloomers.")

Once these factors are ruled out, using various blood, cell and urine tests and x-rays, standard growth hormone stimulation tests are usually done. Growth hormone levels are measured in the blood after the child is given certain drugs known to prompt growth hormone secretion.

Low levels of growth hormone in these tests signal a classic growth hormone deficiency. Children's growth hormone levels many hover around the somewhat arbitrary "normal" cutoff point in these tests, however. Whether these children have a true growth hormone deficiency can't be known for certain, especially because growth hormone stimulation tests are not considered precise or sensitive.

Other children may "pass" growth hormone stimulation tests even though they may have a growth hormone disorder. For example, growth hormone stimulation tests can't detect children

From *FDA Consumer*, October 1992, pp. 30-34. Reprinted by permission of *FDA Consumer*, the magazine of the U.S. Food and Drug Administration.

Late Bloomers

Children with delayed puberty are exceptionally short for their age, and have no need for the bras or shavers that are standard equipment for their adolescent peers.

Girls are considered delayed if they don't show any signs of puberty by age 12 or 13, boys by age 14 or 15. At the age when most children experience a pubertal growth spurt, delayed children continue growing at the same slower rate, making them short for their age. Once late bloomers complete puberty, however, their height catches up to that of their peers. About 1 out of every 100 children has delayed puberty.

A red flag for such late bloomers is x-ray evidence that bone maturation lags behind what is expected for the child's age. The degree of bone maturation is appropriate for the child's height, however. Rarely, puberty is delayed or never occurs because of a central nervous system disorder such as hypopituitarism or because of abnormalities in the sex chromosomes. Chronic illness, malnutrition, or emotional stress can also delay puberty. But usually doctors are unable to detect a cause for delayed puberty. Children with delayed puberty often have a parent who was a late bloomer and the condition is neither a physical abnormality nor a sign of disease, but nevertheless can have social and psychological ramifications.

Adolescents with delayed puberty, like children with precocious puberty, are often teased or sometimes even ostracized by their peers. A major source of anxiety for these children, especially boys, is short stature.

In several studies, an experimental drug known as oxandrolone—a synthetic compound similar to the male hormone testosterone—boosted growth rates of boys with delayed puberty. Given daily in low doses by mouth, oxandrolone doesn't usually prompt puberty, studies suggest, nor does it appear to affect final height, although more studies are needed to firmly establish this. It mainly accelerates children's growth so their heights reach those of their peers already undergoing puberty. Several studies found no short-term side effects tied to oxandrolone therapy.

To boost sexual development, doctors may treat late bloomers with sex hormones, though this use is experimental. Testosterone given monthly by injection to boys usually induces sprouting of pubic and facial hair and the enlargement of the penis. The therapy sometimes makes boys more aggressive and may have other side effects. Girls given female hormones—estrogen or estrogen and progestin combinations—often develop breasts and start to menstruate. Potential side effects of this therapy include nausea, fluid retention, depression, and circulatory disorders.

There is concern that sex hormone treatments might limit final height, as they do in precocious puberty. But recent research suggests that low doses of these hormones do not rob late bloomers of inches.

Oxandrolone, testosterone, estrogen, and progestin are usually only given for about six months to a year to children with delayed puberty. At this point, studies show, most children have entered puberty and no longer need the drugs.

—M.P.

---

who secrete adequate quantities of an abnormal form of growth hormone that is unable to prompt normal growth. Also, some children may secrete normal amounts of growth hormone when stimulated by the tests, but don't make enough of the hormone under normal circumstances. Both types of children may benefit from growth hormone therapy.

It is known that radiation therapy or brain tumors can cause growth hormone deficiency, but in most cases the causes are not known. Decades of experience with growth hormone therapy have shown, however, that it works in nearly all children accurately diagnosed with the condition even if the cause cannot be pinpointed.

Growth hormone therapy is given by injection, either daily or several times per week. Parents are trained to give these injections unless the children feel comfortable doing it themselves. Therapy continues until the end of puberty, when bone growth stops, or sooner, if both family and doctor feel the child has reached an acceptable height.

The sooner before puberty therapy begins, the greater the height that can be achieved. There is no firm evidence tying growth hormone therapy to any significant side effects when it is used properly. Reports that the therapy can boost the likelihood of developing leukemia or other disorders have not been confirmed, although long term studies are addressing this.

Giants in the Making

Even less common than growth hormone deficiency is growth hormone excess, which can cause gigantism. One such person with this condition in the 1930s was nicknamed the "Alton Giant," after his Illinois hometown. He reached a height of nearly 9 feet and a 37 shoe size according to the . . . book *Growth*.

Fewer than 50 such "giants" have been reported in the medical literature. Most owed their amazing growth to pituitary tumors that prompted excessive production of growth hormone. Other symptoms that often accompany pituitary tumors are headaches, dizziness, vomiting, and vision disturbances such as double vision.

Nearly all pituitary tumors can be detected with CT (computerized tomography) scans or magnetic resonance imaging (MRI) scans. Patients with these tumors are treated with surgery, radiation, or an experimental drug that mimics the natural compound somatostatin, which inhibits the release of growth hormone. These treatments can sometimes stem excess growth hormone production and return a child's growth rate to normal.

Excess growth hormone production should be suspected if a child is exceptionally tall and growing unusually fast. The vast majority of such children, however, do not have abnormal growth hormone production, but are merely following in their tall parents footsteps.

Precocious Puberty

Some children are tall for their age and grow faster than expected because they are undergoing precocious puberty. Although the onset of puberty varies considerably, sexual development before age 8 in girls and age 9 in boys is generally considered precocious puberty. This condition can occur as early as in infancy. About one child of every 10,000 in the United States starts puberty prematurely, according to the National Institute of Child Health and Human Development.

The hormonal changes responsible for early puberty are usually the same ones that trigger normal puberty. The brain secretes pulses of a hormone called lutemizing hormone releasing hormone (LHRH), which prompts the pituitary gland to release hormones called gonadortopins. These hormones in turn stimulate the ovaries and testes to make sex hormones that cause the development of sexual characteristics as well as trigger a growth spurt.

Consequently, children who start puberty prematurely are initially tall for their age. But the sex hormones also cause growth to stop earlier than normal so the children may not achieve their full height potential. Boys may not grow taller than 5 feet 2 inches, and half of the girls do not exceed 5 feet.

The cause of precocious puberty in girls with the condition often is not known. Rarely, early puberty in girls is prompted by tumors, brain disorders, injuries, or infections. Also, in rare cases, girls have hormone, secreting tumors or cysts in the ovaries or adrenal glands that prompt what is known as pseudo-precocious puberty. (Unlike children undergoing true precocious puberty, girls with psedoprecocious puberty don't ovulate, and boys with the condition don't generate sperm.) Precocious puberty in boys, in contrast, is often caused by brain tumors. The rare boys who undergo pseudoprecocious puberty, in addition, often have tumors in the adrenal glands or the testicles.

Doctors can determine what type of precocious puberty a child has from blood hormone levels and CT or MRI scans of the head, adrenal glands or sex organs.

Early puberty is inherited in nearly 1 out of 10 boys with the condition. The tendency to start puberty prematurely can be passed directly from father to son, or indirectly from the maternal grandfather through the mother (who does not start puberty early herself) to her son. Premature puberty is inherited in fewer than 1 in 100 girls with the condition.

"Precocious puberty is a problem," points out FDA pediatric endocrinologist Saul Malozowski, M.D., "because a child who experiences it has the sex drive of someone with [adolescent levels of] sex hormones, but lacks the emotional maturity to deal with it."

Because precocious puberty often limits height, and is accompanied by teasing by a child's peers, doctors usually recommend treating the condition. Such treatment aims to halt or even reverse the condition.

If puberty is being prompted by tumors, radiation treatment or surgical removal of such tumors may be recommended. But often such removal—especially of brain tumors—is not feasible. Moreover, even when surgery is performed, it may not successfully stop sexual development.

Consequently, most doctors prefer to treat children with precocious puberty with drugs that restore the normal hormonal balance in the body. The two newly approved drugs Suppreline and Synarel can stop the accelerated growth and stem or sometimes reverse sexual development in children with true precocious puberty. Supprelin injections can be given at home by a parent. Synarel is given via a nose spray.

These drugs mimic LHRH. Daily doses apparently stem the pituitary gland's responsiveness to the natural hormone. The child's own secretion of LHRH, consequently, no longer triggers sex hormone production. Within weeks of beginning treatment, menstruation and ovulation, or sperm production, usually stop. After several months, many girls' develop breasts shrink and their pubic hair may fall out. The penis and testicles usually shrink back to normal size in boys, and pubic and facial hair often disappear.

The most frequent side effects of these drug therapies are light vaginal bleeding within the first month of treatment in girls, and in both sexes, redness, swelling, and itching at the injection site for Supprelin. Therapy is stopped when a child reaches the appropriate age for the onset of puberty.

Psychological Boosts Needed, Too

Most children on the fringes of what's considered "normal" for growth and development need to be reassured that their unique way of growing up is worthwhile, according to pediatric endocrinologist Leona Cuttler, M.D., of Case Western Reserve University in Cleveland.

"The need to be like everybody else is so strong in children," she says. "It's important to emphasize to them the wide range of what's considered normal for height and development."

In her clinic, she adds, social workers and psychologists assess and help improve, if necessary, the psychological well-being of children with short stature or delayed or precocious puberty. How well these children adjust to their height and development enters into her decision on whether to treat them.

As FDA's Malozowski points out, "the more time you spend with a patient, the less medicine you have to use."

Cognitive Growth and Education

Social Issues (Articles 11–16)
Cognitive Performance (Articles 17–20)

Adolescence entails changes in cognitive capacities that are just as monumental as the biological changes. Whereas the thinking of children tends to be more literal, more tied to reality and to what is familiar, the thought processes of adolescents are more abstract, systematic, and logical. Adolescents can appreciate metaphor and sarcasm, they can easily think about things that do not exist, they can test ideas against reality, and they can readily conceive of multiple possibilities. Many of these improvements in thinking abilities contribute to conflict with adults as adolescents become much better able to argue a point or take a stand. They are better at planning out their case and at anticipating counterarguments. They are also more likely to question the way things are because they can now conceive of other possibilities.

Study of the cognitive changes that occur in adolescence has largely been based on the work of the Swiss psychologist Jean Piaget and his colleague Bärbel Inhelder. Piaget and Inhelder described the adolescent as reasoning at what they called the "formal operational" stage. Children from the approximate ages of 7 to 11 years old were described as being in the "concrete operational" stage. Although not all researchers agree with Piaget and Inhelder that these adolescent cognitive abilities represent true stage-like changes, all agree that adolescent thought is characteristically more logical, abstract, and hypothetical than the thought of children. Having certain mental capacities does not mean that adolescents, or even adults for that matter, will always reason at their rational best!

Indeed, building on the work of Piaget and Inhelder, David Elkind has argued that the newly emerging formal operational cognitive abilities lead to some troublesome consequences for adolescents. For one thing, adolescents tend to overintellectualize. They often make things too complex and fail to see the obvious, a phenomenon that Elkind calls pseudostupidity. Teachers often experience this as adolescents overanalyze every word of a multiple-choice question. Elkind also maintains that much of the extreme self-consciousness of adolescents occurs because they construct an imaginary audience. Formal operations make it possible for adolescents to think about other people's thoughts. Adolescents lose perspective and think that others are constantly watching them and thinking about them. A related mistake is that adolescents are likely to believe that everyone shares their concerns and knows their thoughts. This belief that one is at the center of attention further leads to the development of what Elkind calls the personal fable. Namely: If everyone is paying so much attention to me I must be special and invulnerable. Bad things won't happen to me. I won't get in a car crash. I won't get pregnant. Pseudostupidity, the imaginary audience, and the personal fable diminish as adolescents' cognitive abilities mature and as they develop friendships in which intimacies are shared. Peer interaction helps adolescents see that they are not as unique as they thought, nor are they such a focus of everyone else's attention.

Piaget's views on cognitive development have been quite influential, particularly in the field of education. The general philosophy is that learning must be active and that the curriculum needs to be tied to the student's cognitive level. Also, as Elkind points out, awareness of the cognitive abilities and shortcomings of adolescents can make their behaviors more comprehensible to parents, teachers, counselors, and other professionals who work with adolescents.

While developmentalists in the Piagetian tradition focus on the ways in which the thought processes of children and adolescents differ, other researchers have taken a different turn. In the psychometric approach the emphasis is on quantifying cognitive abilities such as verbal ability, mathematical ability, and performance on general intelligence (IQ) tests. Adolescents clearly have more vocabulary, more mathematical knowledge, more spatial ability, etc., than children. Their memories are better as they process information more efficiently and use memory strategies more effectively. They have a greater knowledge base, which enables them to link new concepts to existing ideas. Psychometric intelligence, in other words, increases with age. Because of comparison to age peers, though, relative performance on aptitude tests remains fairly stable. A 9-year-old child's performance on an IQ test, for example, is fairly predictive of that same adolescent's IQ score at age 15. Performance on standardized tests is often used to place junior high and high school students in ability tracks, a practice that is increasingly being questioned.

The measurement of intelligence, as well as the very definition of intelligence, has been controversial for de-

cades. A classic question is whether intelligence is best conceptualized as a general capacity that underlies many diverse abilities or as a set of specific abilities. Traditional IQ tests focus on abilities that relate to success in school and ignore abilities such as those that tap creativity, mechanical aptitude, or practical intelligence. The role of genetic vs. environmental contributions to intelligence has been hotly debated. At the turn of the century, the predominant view was that intelligence was essentially inherited and little influenced by experience. Today, the consensus is that an individual's intelligence is very much a product of both nature and nurture. Greater controversy centers on the role that heredity vs. the environment plays in explaining racial, ethnic, and gender differences in performance on various cognitive tests. A subsection of this unit explores current issues in measuring and explaining cognitive performance.

Issues about cognitive abilities are important for education. Schools need to take the developmental abilities and needs of adolescents into account in planning programs. Moreover, we have a high dropout rate and need to examine alternatives for keeping youth in school. Several articles discuss ideas for improving the educational climate and experience for all students, including women and minorities.

Looking Ahead: Challenge Questions

Who benefits from tracking by ability? What are the alternatives to tracking and ability-grouping?

How does the school environment impact the academic and social development of boys and girls? Are single sex schools a better environment for development than co-ed schools? Do adolescents who are schooled at home have sufficient opportunities to interact with peers?

How can we decrease the high school dropout rate? What makes some at-risk students academically successful while others are not? Should high schools institute exit exams for graduation? Why or why not?

What role does heredity and environment play in intelligence? Why does it matter? What about racial and cultural differences in mathematics achievement?

Developmentally Appropriate Middle Level Schools

M. Lee Manning

M. Lee Manning is Assistant Professor, Department of Educational Curriculum and Instruction, Darden College of Education, Old Dominion University, Norfolk, Virginia

Education theorists have suggested that learners' developmental levels should provide the basis for school curricular, instructional and organizational practices, as well as the overall teaching/learning environment. While insightful theories have been offered regarding physical, psychosocial and cognitive development, the process of translating theories into practice has been somewhat slow, especially beyond the elementary school years.

Recognition of early adolescence as a legitimate developmental period is a hopeful sign. The 1990s have ushered in a new emphasis on improving schools for young adolescents. The growing middle level school movement represents a commitment to base school practices on the developmental needs of 10- to 14-year-olds. To support this effort, ACEI's *Developmentally Appropriate Middle Level Schools* examines young adolescents' physical, psychosocial and cognitive characteristics and suggests develop-mentally appropriate educational experiences. An abstract of this forthcoming book follows.

Time for Appropriate and Decisive Action

For decades, the role of schools for 10- to 14-year-olds remained unclear. The problem may have resulted from the mindset that elementary school should address the education needs of the childhood years and secondary school focus upon the adolescent years. Except for serving as a transition between the two, the middle level school lacked a clear rationale.

Several factors have contributed to the increased emphasis on developmentally responsive middle level schools. First, early adolescence has now been accepted as a legitimate developmental period (Thornburg, 1983). Second, the middle level school has progressed beyond its infancy and has developed to a stage where genuine improvements are possible. Third, the contemporary emphasis on reforming middle level schools to be more responsive to the needs of young adolescents can be seen in many forms: *Turning Points* (Carnegie Council on Adolescent Development, 1989), *Making the Middle Grades Work* (Children's Defense Fund, 1988), *Caught in the Middle* (California State Department of Education, 1987) and *What Matters in the Middle Grades* (Maryland State Department of Education, 1989). Fourth, the formation of ACEI's Division for Later Childhood/Early Adolescence demonstrates a commitment to young adolescents and their education.

Young Adolescents' Developmental Characteristics

Young adolescents' developmental characteristics have been clearly defined. Physical characteristics include a marked increase in body growth, readily apparent skeletal and structural changes (bones growing more rapidly than muscles), widely varying developmental rates, onset of puberty, faster development in girls than boys and increases in physical endurance. Psychosocial characteristics include increased social interactions and concern with friendships, shifting allegiance from parents and teachers to peers, constant examination of development and the overall "self," quests for freedom and independence and fluctuating self-concept. Cognitive characteristics include increased abilities to think hypothetically, abstractly, reflectively and critically and to make reasoned moral and ethical choices. Some young adolescents develop from Piaget's concrete operations stage to the formal operations stage.

From *Childhood Education*, Annual Theme Issue, 1992, pp. 305-307. © 1992 by the Association for Childhood Education International, 17904 Georgia Avenue, Suite 215, Olney, MD 20832. Reprinted by permission.

Educators basing teaching/learning experiences on these and other developmental characteristics should not assume all young adolescents develop at a similar rate. As Thornburg (1982) suggested, diversity is the hallmark characteristic of young adolescents. Considerable differences exist between early and late maturers and shy students and the socially outgoing. In addition, learners may be functioning at various stages of development, from the concrete to the formal operations stage.

Providing Developmentally Appropriate Practices

Once educators commit to developmentally appropriate instruction, actual experiences, methods and materials can be planned. The forthcoming book discusses the "why, how and what" of practices that reflect physical, psychosocial and cognitive development of middle level children.

Physical characteristics of 10- to 14-year-olds suggest the need to provide learning opportunities to master physical skills; develop positive attitudes toward health, fitness and nutrition; and understand drug and tobacco use and abuse. Likewise, activities that stress size, strength, stamina and competition among early and late maturers should be avoided.

Educational experiences that involve social interaction and friendships and develop appropriate sex-role identification address the psychosocial needs of middle level students. Strategies include cooperative learning, teacher and student teams, adviser-advisee programs, cross-cultural grouping and the school-within-a-school organizational model.

Cognitive needs may be met by integrating subject matter across disciplines and providing communities of learning. Strategies include cooperative and experiential learning, proper academic counseling, exploratory programs for studying areas of interest and

working in small groups. As middle level school educators plan group instruction, whether large or small, grouping students by ability should be avoided at all costs. Equating ability or achievement levels with development can result in dire consequences for academic achievement, self-concept, multicultural concerns and teacher behaviors (Manning & Lucking, 1990).

Concerns and Issues

The book also addresses several relevant issues and concerns, such as the many differences that distinguish young adolescents from their peers, the need to teach young adolescents about their constantly changing bodies and minds and last, the pressing need to re-engage parents and families in the education of their 10- to 14-year-olds.

Developmentally Appropriate Middle Level Schools staunchly maintains that young adolescents' individual development should be the basis for curricular, organizational and managerial decisions. Reaching these decisions, however, should include consideration of learners' individual, gender, class and cultural differences. Cultural and social class differences may be seen in friendship patterns, identity development, social expectations, learning styles and self-esteem. Similarly, gender differences can be identified in health concerns, social networks, sex-role attitudes and relationship between self-image and school achievement.

Teaching young adolescents about themselves and their development can be one of the greatest contributions a middle level school can make. Subjects to consider are: developmental changes, growing arms and legs, increased hair, deepening voices, rapidly changing friendships, shifts from being parent-centered to peer-centered, feelings of anonymity, effects of peer pressure, perceptions of morals and values, differ-

ing levels of thought and varying levels of test-taking abilities. Sometimes, young adolescents feel uncomfortable talking with their parents and often receive inaccurate information from friends. Through curricular content, adviser-advisee sessions, exploratory programs and counseling sessions, educators can explain the normalcy of development and distinguish between false and genuine concerns.

A recent survey of 8th-graders and their parents revealed two-thirds of the students never or rarely discussed classes or school programs with parents and half of the parents had never talked to school officials about academic programs ("Parents Key," 1991). The developmental changes being experienced by 10- to 14-year-olds, the current outcry to improve middle level education and the long overdue recognition that middle level school students need developmentally appropriate educational experiences all point to the acute need to re-engage parents in educational efforts. Parents and teachers working together can enhance the education of learners. Teachers can provide parents with opportunities to play crucial roles in children's health and safety. In addition, teachers can help parents to create a home environment that contributes to school achievement and overall development. Students benefit in their school work, attitudes and aspirations for continued schooling when parents remain knowledgeable partners with the schools in their children's education (Children's Defense Fund, 1988).

Closing Remarks

Developmentally Appropriate Middle Level Schools, to be published by ACEI in 1993, examines young adolescent development and developmentally appropriate educational practices in middle level schools. While providing a preview of the book, this abstract cannot comprehensively explain the entire contents. In addition to ideas discussed, readers will find information such as: putting assessment in its proper perspective, the dangers of ability grouping, the concept of multiple intelligences and re-engaging parents in schools' efforts. Likewise, the book will include a detailed, annotated bibliography and checklist to evaluate educators' responses to young adolescent development.

A major goal of middle level educators during the 1990s and 21st century will be to improve the lives of young adolescents. ACEI's contribution to the improvement of middle level schools can be seen in its decision to publish *Developmentally Appropriate Middle Level Schools* and also in its commitment to be a powerful advocate for all children, infancy through early adolescence.

References

California State Department of Education. (1987). *Caught in the middle.* Sacramento, CA: Author.

Carnegie Council on Adolescent Development. (1989). *Turning points.* Washington, DC: Author.

Children's Defense Fund. (1988). *Making the middle grades work.* Washington, DC: Author.

Manning, M. L., & Lucking, R. (1990). Ability grouping: Realities and alternatives. *Childhood Education, 66,* 254-258.

Maryland State Department of Education. (1989). *What matters in the middle grades.* Baltimore, MD: Author.

Parents key to classroom experience. (1991). *Middle Ground, 18*(4), 1-2.

Thornburg, H. (1982). The total early adolescent in contemporary society. *The High School Journal, 65,* 272-278.

Thornburg, H. (1983). Is early adolescence really a stage of development? *Theory into Practice, 22,* 79-84.

Note to readers: The book *Developmentally Appropriate Middle Level Schools* was published in 1993. If you wish information, please write to: Marilyn Gardner, Director of Marketing, Association for Childhood Education International, 11501 Georgia Avenue, Suite 315, Wheaton, Maryland 20902.

Program Helps Kids Map Realistic Goals

An experimental school program encourages children to find their true talents and channel them into career goals.

Bridget Murray

Monitor staff

Sixth-graders Jon, Cheri and Almira are making "employee badges" that reflect the careers of their dreams: Jon wants to play baseball for the big leagues, Cheri hopes to be a famous rhythm-and-blues singer and Almira aims to be a pediatrician.

Smiling widely, Cheri proudly hangs the badge around her neck and points to the made-up name of the singing company that will employ her: "Hill Entertainment Association." A few tables away, Almira writes the word "doctor" on her badge with quiet determination. Meanwhile Jon seems to hesitate. Squinting down at the blank cardboard before him, he agonizes over the glamorous choice of baseball player or the more realistic one of managing an auto-repair shop.

His deliberations please his teacher, Vernita Harris, who means for the activity to spur thinking about choices and feasible alternatives.

Unlike many kids their age, Jon and his classmates at Central East Middle School in Philadelphia understand the realities of reaching their goals. Even Cheri, with her passion for singing, has practical plans to go to nursing school. And Jon realizes that vocational training in auto repair and business management is a surer path than baseball stardom.

The source of their practical outlook is an experimental curriculum that helps inner-city children develop their talents, identify their career wishes and cultivate basic academic skills to achieve those goals.

Help for Inner-City Children

Psychologists, educators and social scientists at Johns Hopkins University created the talent-building model to replace the present system of tracking or "sorting" students into higher- and lower-level classes according to ability. While the old system taught students in lower tracks remedial material, the talent model exposes them to challenging material, increasing their chances of higher-level mastery, according to its creators.

Psychologists have long warned that tracking serves privileged children at the expense of the disadvantaged, and talent development may be a viable alternative, the Hopkins researchers say.

"Inner-city kids often have high aspirations for college, but many times their schools don't offer them the necessary learning opportunities," says psychologist Douglas MacIver, PhD, who oversees the Central East project for Hopkins. "We're selecting specific types of curricula that put them in a strong trajectory for college."

To help MacIver and his colleagues in their quest, the U.S. Department of Education's Office of Educational Research and Improvement has funded a five-year collaboration between Johns Hopkins and Howard University researchers to develop and test the talent development model in area middle schools and high schools.

In middle schools the program includes a scheduling and curriculum overhaul and the addition of 45-minute weekly career classes, like the one Vernita Harris is teaching to sixth-graders. Last year, Central East teachers voted to make their school one of the first talent-development sites. Peterson High School in Baltimore is the only other site thus far.

Central East teachers believed a strong skills-building program would boost prospects for the school's highly diverse student body, which is 39 percent Hispanic, 26 percent African-American, 13 percent Asian and 12 percent white. More than half the students speak a language besides English at home and many of their parents are immigrants with no high school degree.

Career Curricula

Both the middle school and high school talent programs emphasize teamwork, goal setting, self-exploration and career guidance, says MacIver. Teachers teach two different subjects to the same groups of students instead of teaching one subject to several different classes, as is typical of most middle schools.

Every student receives the same curriculum, rather than being assigned to a certain level based on their perceived ability. Students sacrifice electives to take tutorial classes if they need help in the core areas of math, reading and writing.

Johns Hopkins researchers and instructional aids trained Central East teachers for the new model last February, and installment began in September with changes in curricula and classroom format. Building students' career skills is a new experience for Harris, who will track her sixth-graders' career interests over the next two years, serving as their career guide and "helping to keep their dreams alive," MacIver says.

Before making badges, Harris's students picked their careers using the "Self-Directed Search Career Explorer," developed by psychologist John Holland, PhD. Now they'll make timelines that map out how to meet those goals.

For instance, Almira has figured out that she needs to take advanced mathematics and science courses in high school and spend eight years in college to be a pediatrician. Students will also fill out applications for competitive college preparatory programs at area high schools and practice completing college applications to develop practical career skills.

Teamwork

A major thrust of talent development is team teaching and learning. Groups of two or three educators teach the same 99 students over three years and weave common themes, such as Puerto Rican or African-American culture, into their teaching.

All seventh-graders are currently reading the novel "Going Home" by Nicholas Mohr, which describes the clash between Puerto Rican and American culture. The cultural themes are meant to sensitize students to differences in heritage. Each instructor teaches a combined curriculum called RELA—reading, English and language arts—and a subject in which they specialize to 33 students at a time, and then sends the children on to other teachers on their "team."

Cindy Engst teaches RELA and her specialty, math. She sends her stu-

dents to Miguel Rivera-Diaz, who teaches science and Jonathan Grayson, who teaches social studies. Spending more time with fewer students allows the teachers to compare notes and keep closer tabs on their pupils.

The talent project also provides teachers with team-building curricula, such as a sentence-building exercise Engst uses to spice up her vocabulary teaching. Students in groups of four cluster around tables, heads bent in concentration over large sheets of paper as they try to fit words like "absolutely" and "clique" into meaningful sentences.

"TRACKING IS AN OUTMODED MODEL AND AN INSUFFICIENT SUPPORT SYSTEM FOR STUDENTS. TALENT DEVELOPMENT TURNS THAT AROUND BY CAPITALIZING ON KIDS' ASSETS."
WADE BOYKIN, PhD
HOWARD UNIVERSITY

Writing vivid sentences, or "mind movies" tunes students in the deeper meaning of words, say Engst and MacIver. One group, looking for a creative way to define "circumference," writes: "For the track tryouts they had to run the circumference of the field because the inner part was too grassy."

Acceleration for All

A fundamental tenet of talent development is helping students in areas where they're struggling, instead of assigning them to remedial classes where they fall behind, says MacIver.

Students who have trouble in math and reading forfeit electives in Span-

ish, gym, art and music for a double-dose of math or reading instruction. Those who need help in arithmetic spend an extra 45 minutes a day brushing up their math skills in the computer laboratory.

During lab time, students run math programs on the computer in teams of four and take weekly quizzes. Teams are recognized for excellence when all their members do well on the quizzes. This encourages team members to help each other learn, says their teacher Cheryl Kanyok. Students don't seem to feel short-changed by missing electives, she added.

"I'm missing gym class but I don't mind," says Rosa, a seventh-grader who comes to the lab from Engst's language-arts class. "It really helps my algebra."

To assess the program's success, MacIver plans to compare Central East to another school with a similar population. He and his Johns Hopkins colleagues will survey students, teachers and parents for their reactions to the program. They'll also use students' scores on standardized testing and track their grades through high school.

More talent-development sites are planned for both high schools and middle schools. Psychologist Wade Boykin, PhD, and his colleagues at Howard University are scouting out potential talent-development sites in Washington, D.C.

"Tracking is an outmoded model and an insufficient support system for students," Boykin says. "Talent development turns that around by capitalizing on kids' assets."

After just a few months with the model, teacher Vernita Harris has seen improvements in her students' work, Cheri's in particular. Cheri receives little academic help at home and was reading and writing far below grade level at the beginning of the school year, Harris says. Classmates are boosting her writing skills by giving her needed feedback on her writing— the sort of leg up MacIver and his colleagues hope students will give one another.

"With this program, even the weakest students are given the tools, training and support they need to succeed," MacIver says.

Mommy, What's a Classroom?

It's not only Christian fundamentalists anymore: now hundreds of thousands of parents are teaching their own kids at home. Just what the unschooled are learning—or aren't—is a subject of much debate.

By Bill Roorbach

I LOVED GRADE SCHOOL. I MEAN, EVERY SEPtember I just loved getting back to it. I loved sharpening those pencils and putting grocery-bag covers on my textbooks. I loved my teachers unquestioningly—those towering, unbenign presences—and shrank before them. I loved the games at recess, the bullying danger of the blacktop, the qualmy allure of the off-limits forest at the far end of the playground. I loved the checker games in the back of the classroom when recess got rained out. I loved snow days, because then there was time to play at home and time to read whatever grown-up book I wanted to read. Best of all, I loved staring out the schoolroom windows in spring, watching the maples bud and leaf and fill out. And man, come to think of it, there was nothing—nothing—like the last day of school when you roared off the bus and leapt on your bike and rode away into summer. Even if you loved school, there was nothing better than not going, nothing better in the world.

THIS AFTERNOON, THE PLAN IS A FIELD TRIP TO THE science museum downtown, so Janet Rhodes is going easy—no need for a highly structured morning. There's always tomorrow,

Bill Roorbach teaches in the graduate writing program at Ohio State University. He is the author of "Summers With Juliet," a memoir.

or the day after, plenty of time for the formal stuff when you're teaching at home. Her husband, Kevin, a lawyer, is already on his way to the upscale firm in Columbus where he works.

Janet is in the kitchen of the family's modest town house in suburban Powell, Ohio, sipping coffee, making plans for the rest of the week: Darcy's first Girl Scout outing, Hilary's choir rehearsals, Gillian's skating lessons. A little math every day for each, a lot of quiet reading, essays for Darcy and Hilary, handwriting practice for all. On Thursday, it's the library, then over to see Connie, a good old friend, to borrow a book of science experiments and make plans for group Spanish and French lessons with Connie's kids, who are also taught at home.

"Where's my book!" Hilary shouts. She's 8 and imperious, and expects that book to appear, right now. No mystery why a book might go missing in this house, though. Books are everywhere: in the bedrooms, in the bathroom, stacked under Mom's desk, piled around the armchair Hilly regally occupies, her fingerprinted eyeglasses high on her nose.

Gillian, 6, springs downstairs from the bedroom, hesitates long enough to see what her sisters are up to, blitzes the basement playroom and the jazzy new computer: math drills from CD shareware.

"Your book is in Mom and Dad's room," she calls up. Hilary groans, but deigns to rise.

The oldest daughter, Darcy, 10, sits at the dining-room table, ignoring all the bustle around her; she hasn't once looked

From *The New York Times Magazine,* February 2, 1997, pp. 30-37. © 1997 by Bill Roorbach. Reprinted by permission of International Creative Management, Inc.

'Until recently, I was also paranoid about the level of education I was receiving,' says Peter Kowalke, 17, home-schooled his entire life. 'I mean, I thought I was smart, but what was really going on behind the doors of the school? Was I missing anything?'

up from her book about Harriet Tubman. She has books to read, essays to write.

Not much after 9, Mom comes into the living room, drying her hands. Her voice is a bell: "Who wants to sing?" She sits easily on the floor in front of the natty little couch. Gillian pops up the stairs, somersaults dramatically across the living-room carpet, arranges herself between Mom's outstretched legs. Darcy marks her page, rises deep in thought, shuffles over. Hilary, not to be hurried, comes to sit at last. She and Darcy each throw an arm around Mom's neck.

"Yankee Doodle," says Janet Rhodes. She opens "Hear the Wind Blow: American Folksongs Retold," by Scott Russell Sanders, hot from the library. And they begin. Mom's voice is full and strong. Hilary kids around, singing loud like an opera diva. Darcy is very serious, reading along, singing softly. Gillian partly sings and partly listens, rolls her head, pats Mom's knees. They take the song to six obscure verses, then Mom reads Sanders's text, explaining big words, making connections to other lessons. The girls titter at Doodle's feisty independence.

FORGET VOUCHERS AND CHARTER SCHOOLS, forget private or parochial. To a rapidly growing number of parents, school choice means no school at all. This new breed includes not only religious fundamentalists hoping to avoid profane teaching but also all kinds of parents concerned about the method and quality of their children's education. They have done some serious research, found support groups, ransacked libraries, availed themselves of computer and Internet resources and have taken their kids out of school. Or never enrolled them.

Peter Kowalke, 17, lives in a woodsy suburb of Cleveland and hasn't attended a single day of school, at least not until now. He's taking math and science at the local community college, filling in gaps before he applies to a university, getting the first grades of his life: two A's and one B. Peter's father teaches electronics and television production at nearby Mentor High School; his mother used to teach English and is now studying to become a paralegal.

"The highs of home schooling are pretty obvious," Peter says. "Better education, personalized education, strong family influence, better understanding of self, an ardent desire to learn, exposure to the possibilities. Some of the lows? Alienation, horrible spelling, horrible handwriting. The most negative thing is the life style. Personally, I often feel separated from others. Until recently, I was also paranoid about the level of

education I was receiving. I mean, I thought I was smart, but what was really going on behind the doors of the school? Was I missing anything?"

The decision to home-school is problematic, not often supported by family and friends and only recently finding any approval at all from the culture at large. The very mention of home schooling excites distrust: What about the kids' socialization? Are parents competent to teach? Does home schooling even work?

A spoof by three home-schooling mothers from Lexington, N.C. (to the tune of "The Twelve Days of Christmas"), asks the rest:

"On the 12th day of home school my neighbor said to me: 'Can they go to college? What about graduation? They'll miss the prom! I could never do this! Look at what they're missing! How long will you home-school? Why do you do this? [Here comes the "five golden rings" part] You *are* so strange! What about P.E.? Do you give them tests? Are they socialized? And can you home-school legally?' "

The answer to the last question is perhaps the only easy one. After more than two decades of court battles, home schooling is now legal in every state, subject to various restrictions and reporting requirements. For home schoolers in Ohio, like the Rhodeses and the Kowalkes, the regulations are fairly simple. A family must notify the school district superintendent of its intention to home-school and promise to provide 900 hours of instruction per year covering fine arts, language arts, math, science, social studies, geography, fire safety, physical education and health. At the end of the school year, each child must submit to standardized achievement exams or have a portfolio of his or her work evaluated by a certified teacher. If a child's progress doesn't satisfy the evaluator—which is rare—it might be back to school.

Though home schooling clearly means sacrifice for parents (loss of income and the death of free time, for two examples; "You *are* so strange," for a third), thousands are opting in. Their reasons range over an enormous spectrum, from religious to pedagogical, from political to entirely personal. Libertarians see home schooling as a basic gesture of freedom. Deinstitutionalizers think of it as the natural next step after home birthing. Some progressive educators see in home schooling an inexhaustible laboratory in which their ideas can be observed at work. Certain conservatives consider home schooling the last, best hope for the three R's. And of course there's the protective impulse: many parents cite what they call negative socialization—school violence, rampant sex, illegal drugs—as prime incentives for teaching their own kids.

'I wouldn't want my child educated like that,' says a spokeswoman for the National Education Association. 'Or to grow up in a society where the majority were educated like that. Our society is loose enough as it is. The thing that binds us together in this country is public education.'

Because of the diffuse nature of the movement, a dependable count of home schoolers is hard to come by. Patricia Lines, senior research associate with the United States Department of Education in Washington, calculates that 500,000 to 700,000 American children are now taught at home, up from just 10,000 to 15,000 in 1970. Brian Ray, president of the National Home Education Research Institute in Salem, Ore., estimates that 700,000 to 1.15 million kids learn at home; other sources put the number as high as 2.5 million. According to Ray's figures, 50,000 children are taught at home in Ohio, making it the third-largest home-schooling state, after Texas and California (New York is seventh, with about 35,000.)

Ray teaches his own seven children at home, so it may be difficult to see him as a disinterested researcher. But his studies about the efficacy of home schooling seem solid enough to warrant examination. In one, 16,311 home-schooled students from around the country took the nationally calibrated Iowa Test of Basic Skills; their average placed them in the 79th percentile in reading, the 73d in language and math. Ray cites other studies asserting that home-schooled children have "lower problem behavior scores" and "significantly higher self-concepts" than children in public schools.

Ronald Areglado, the associate executive director of programs with the National Association of Elementary School Principals, is not persuaded by Ray's findings. "There's too much emphasis on test scores as the evidence that home schooling is successful," he says. "My worry is that these children become isolated and fragmented; their world is cut up into pieces; there's no interaction with school kids; they may not play as much. If you think about your own elementary school experience, one of the main things was that you hung around with other kids. It's going to take a kid with a lot of resiliency to keep up friendships without school."

Peter Kowalke shrugs off such suggestions. "Last year, I went to two homecoming dances," he says. "Two different girls, two different school systems. Girls? I've met some through the mail, through the Internet, met some at various functions. One time I was volunteering at a senior-citizen's dance, hit it off with another volunteer. You know, you're out and doing things and one friend leads to another and it snowballs. It's the way any adult makes friends."

THE LEADING VOICE OF THE SECULAR HOME-schooling movement continues to be the education theorist John Holt, despite his death in 1985. Holt believed that experts

are of little use, that "credentialism" is at the heart of the sickness of American education. After years spent trying to reform schools, he finally came to believe that school itself was the problem. In "Teach Your Own" (1981), he recommended "unschooling"—child-led, interest-based learning—whose fundamental belief is that kids are great learners and don't need to be told how or when to do it. Holt felt that testing and ranking and sorting, even teachers themselves, are schoolish ideas that are harmful and inhibitive and unnecessary.

Away from schools, especially public schools, Holt's argument goes, kids keep their naturally intense love of learning and get a better, less fractured education. Kids don't learn that adults are the enemy, so they can develop real relationships with the adults around them; kids don't learn to taunt and fear each other, so they can develop real relationships with each other as well. In the end, parents and kids grow closer as education becomes indistinguishable from daily family life, and kids and parents get to know each other as people, even as friends.

"People say to us, 'Oh, I'd never have the patience to home-school,'" Janet Rhodes says. "But it's not patience. You've just got to like your kids. Which isn't so hard. When they're with you all the time, you know them better. They're not coming home stressed out about something that happened at school that you don't know about."

When I described unschooling, or at least my understanding of it, to Kathleen Lyons, a spokeswoman for the National Education Association, she didn't pause. "I wouldn't want my child educated like that," she said. "Or to grow up in a society where the majority were educated like that. Our society is loose enough as it is. The thing that binds us together in this country is public education."

Holt wrote that schools don't really provide that kind of glue, and can't, "Not as long as they also have the job of sorting out the young into winners and losers, and preparing the losers for a lifetime of losing."

At the other end of the vast home-schooling movement from Holt and the unschoolers are what one home-schooling researcher calls "the essentialists," many of them religious, who feel that schools have collapsed from listening to too many ideas like Holt's. For them, it's back to the basics of education, which often include the Bible. This is home schooling with the trappings of the classroom intact: maps and blackboards, tests and grades, corporal punishment and detention,

'In school, a kid like Darcy is road kill,' says Darcy's mother. Kids who are different really get it from other kids. And teachers, even the best teachers, don't have time to protect a more tender child. Sometimes they're as mean as the kids.'

old-fashioned values and school prayer. Mom is called Mrs. Whomever, and it's definitely Mom doing the teaching.

The Home School Legal Defense Association is the primary organization at the Christian end of the spectrum and easily the largest home schooling organization of any kind. Its president, Michael Farris, is a lawyer, a former co-chairman of Pat Buchanan's Presidential campaign and the father of nine children, all of whom have been or will be taught at home. For Farris, home schooling fits into a package of familiar fundamentalist Christian issues, including creationism. But he respects unschoolers, sees them as allies. "I like that the unschoolers reject textbooks and embrace real books," he says. "The thing I don't care to follow myself is the 'let my kid do his own thing' philosophy. I think you need to offer more parenting and leadership, more skills. But the unschoolers' results are really good, and we'll defend them to the hilt. There's not one right way to do it."

BACK WHEN SHE WAS IN COLLEGE, PAULA KOWALKE began thinking she would find an alternative to school for her future children. "I read A. S. Neill's 'Summerhill' and then John Holt," she recalls. "I just got fascinated." And when the other 5-year-olds got on the bus for kindergarten, her son Peter stayed home.

For Kevin and Janet Rhodes, the route to home schooling was different, less planned. During Darcy's first year at a progressive Montessori preschool, her teachers noticed she couldn't concentrate in a roomful of kids. Her parents were unhappy with the changes they saw in her: she was coming home agitated, stressed out. She developed nervous habits and slept poorly. Her parents launched an exhaustive search of alternative schools and private programs, hoping to find schooling that would allow their daughter to learn and concentrate in her own way.

They ran across books by John Holt and other home-schooling advocates. Janet had never seen herself as an education experimenter, but the example of a home-schooling friend convinced her to try it. Kevin was cautious but willing.

"We gave ourselves a year," Janet says. She had already quit her job as the executive secretary to the president of a small oil company (the work that put Kevin through law school), had already decided she would dedicate herself to her kids' lives. Kevin had started his own law practice and was sometimes able to come home at lunchtime and lend a hand. They began.

"We knew home school was working right away as we watched Darcy's agitation diminish," Kevin says. "Suddenly this frustrated child could learn. One by one, her nervous habits dropped away." Kevin and Janet continued their reading and planning, attended the meetings of a home-schooling support group, inspected (and for the most part rejected as too inhibiting) prepackaged curriculums, grew more confident.

"In school, a kid like Darcy is road kill," Janet says. "Kids who are different really get it from other kids. And teachers, even the best teachers, don't have time to protect a more tender child. Sometimes they're as mean as the kids. Darcy is a very deliberate child; she speaks slowly, she learns methodically, she's sensitive. Even her sisters are tough on her."

Hilary and Gillian, Darcy's younger sisters, are pretty standard learners, if there are such things. Why not send them to school, make life easier for Mom?

"We just started to see Hilary engaged in the learning process, Kevin says. "Then Gillian too. Everything was working beautifully. There was no incentive to do anything different—though my older sister, Kathy, is quite skeptical."

Kathy Chase lives in Spokane, Wash., where her own two children go to public school. "I wasn't surprised that Kevin and Janet would home-school," she says. "They're very closely knit, very within themselves. They don't feel the need to have huge social interactions. They're content with the five of them. Very protective. I worry they get a little isolated." Long pause. "But I'm sure their kids are well ahead of mine, just because of the one-on-one time working with them. Home schooling is for a certain kind of parent—not me.

Janet's father, too, is ambivalent. "He thinks they'd be better off in school," Janet says. "I think I've finally convinced him, though. My mom worries about them not getting socialized."

Kevin looks pained. "The 'S' word," he says.

When I ask if he's worried about isolation, it's clear he has heard the question before. "A complete nonissue!" he says, rising in his seat. "Define the context in which you fear there may be isolation. Is the concern that somehow if you home-school you're never going to let your kids go out and play with the neighbors, or attend Brownies, or take skating lessons? Is it that somehow you won't be part of the community, won't go to church or concerts or museums or the mall? Which is more isolating, to be with the same 30 other kids and teacher in a building with 500 kids and other teachers, day after day, month after month, or to be out in the larger community several times every week, nearly every day, with people of all ages and races and socio-economic backgrounds?"

The Rhodeses spend about $700 a year directly on home schooling: museum and historical society memberships, gas money for two or three field trips a week, whatever books they can't get out of the library, models, kits, workbooks, the required yearly evaluation ($45 per child). Last year, they spent an additional $893 on music classes, but the girls have moved on to cheaper pursuits—Girl Scouts and Brownies, history club, choir, swimming lessons, skating, ballet.

"People ask, 'How long are you going to do this?' " Kevin says. "I tell them, 'As long as it's working.' "

But if the Rhodeses object to any form of standardized testing, how do they know it's working?

"It's not a mystery—I compare my kids to other kids, of course," Kevin says. "You know, at a birthday party, I hear someone Gillian's age read her birthday card aloud, and I realize, well, we're doing pretty well here."

Last year, the family even brought in Linda Campbell, their Ohio-certified evaluator, for a voluntary midyear visit. "I was having a confidence crisis," Janet says. "And we got some reassurance. A reality check. When you're home-schooling, the responsibility is on *you*. And you feel it."

Campbell has made a business of advising parents and evaluating home-schooled children, whether by administering achievement tests or, for families who shun testing, assessing portfolios. "Some people come to me all nervous, like I'm going to have my hair in a bun, look down my nose through my glasses at them," Campbell says. "But I just try to guide them through the areas the state requires: math, science, reading, all of it. My standards are high. When I sign on the line, I'm saying the child is learning and growing at an appropriate level. In more than 600 evaluations, I've had to decline only 3—all of them teens. They basically spent their year getting up late, turning on the tube. Then when school gets out, they're out the door to see friends. Sometimes they *want* to do poorly. They *want* to be in school, and it's the only way their parents are going to let it happen."

The Rhodeses say it's up to their girls, one by one, whether or not they go into the public schools for junior high or high school. Janet suspects the girls will opt to stay at home. "From what I hear, the teen years are when home schooling really takes off," Janet says. "It becomes theirs; they begin to own it."

PETER KOWALKE HAS ALWAYS PLANNED ON COLLEGE. "In my family, there's the idea that successful people go to college," he says. "I could do a home-school college thing—there would certainly be benefits—but there are trials to both ways. The way I figure, I'm so tired of the trials of home schooling that I want to sample the trials of college."

He shows me around his house. There's a cozy sunken living room, a spare bedroom made over into a packed computer command post. Peter is at once confident and self-conscious, part boy, part man, awkward yet assured. He is close to his brother, Adam, 15, also 100 percent home-schooled. ("Adam's very sharp, very likely my best friend.") Their bedroom is super tidy, carefully arranged: fancy cantilevered bunks built

by their father for littler boys, two small desks tucked in, a packed shelf of books. Peter's favorites: "How to Win Friends and Influence People," "Awaken the Giant Within" and, of course, "The Teen-Age Liberation Handbook," by Grace Llewellyn, who advises teens not to drop out of high school but to "rise out."

Sitting at the kitchen table, Peter recalls younger days: "When I first started home schooling, people hadn't heard of it. Clerks at stores would comment, 'Aren't you supposed to be at school?' I'd launch into my speech, how I don't go to school. I didn't feel like some weirdo, though I was aware that certain people were thinking, 'This is this really strange kid, he's got all these weird beliefs.'

"Junior-high age was a hard time. I stayed at home a lot more. Young teens are often known for having these delusions of grandeur, and I had the biggest. Because I didn't go to school, a lot of people thought I was this genius, too good for the schools, and I kind of played that up, started to believe it. Not the geek-genius thing. I mean, I was a football player, too. The image I promoted was the football star who walked around reading Shakespeare at practice."

Peter played football in a youth football league until he was 15. He broke both wrists (separately), played anyway, became a kind of local hero. The next step should have been the high-school team, but the Ohio High School Athletic Association wouldn't—and won't—let unenrolled kids play. No classes, no sports. Peter turned down one solution: partial enrollment, in which a class or two gets you on the team. (Nationally, access to sports and other extracurricular activities is shaping up as the next legal battle for home schoolers.)

His mother looked into fighting the ruling, but Peter asked her not to bother. "I decided to bow out at my glory," he says, "rather than go to a mediocre high school to play on a team that wasn't very good and probably have my delusions about my own ability shattered, all after turning my back on home schooling, which I really valued."

The next year he got himself certified as a coach, which kept him in the game. "Coaching lessened the pain of quitting," he says. "But those first few hits as the other kids started the game were always hard on me. And at the banquets, they wouldn't talk about my playing ability or even my coaching ability but about my intellectual ability, how I was always reading."

Peter played softball for a while, then got seriously interested in weight lifting. And more and more he spent his time publishing a desktop zine called Nation ("Not *The* Nation," he says, anticipating a complaint). Nation is filled with the voices of, among others, scores of Peter's pen pals and E-mail friends; he's got 100 subscribers by now and puts out an issue every other month.

One regular contributor is Amy Tavormina, 16, who attends the private Notre Dame Academy in Toledo, several hours from the Kowalkes' Cleveland suburb. She and Peter started as pen pals three years ago, wrote back and forth daily, then actually met. They dated in a long-distance way for a year, but now they are back to being buddies and pen pals. "Peter has as many friends as I do, but not the close personal contact all the time," Tavormina says. "A lot of his communication is via E-mail and letters. But my friendships are face to face. Home-schooled kids miss other stuff, too, the fine moments, like the victory of finishing a paper. And I've got wonderful teachers. That's another person, another adult you can get an opinion from. Me, I need the pressure and the competition. I would hate to home-school."

Peter became obsessed with charting his home-schooling progress, fastidiously documenting his studies for the Clonlara School, a private school based in Ann Arbor, Mich., that also works with home schoolers. The Kowalkes, like many home-schooling families, use Clonlara not only for the academic help (including the company's Compuhigh, which offers high school courses over the Internet) but for the credentials it can supply: transcripts, documentation of study and a functional high-school diploma, which helps home schoolers avoid the stigma of a G.E.D. (General Educational Development) diploma.

"I went from just living to living with a purpose," Peter says. "I took it very literally, that I had to keep all these records for Clonlara. I had the dream of graduating in three years. I had to prove myself, show that I was as good as schooled kids. I worried. There were moments of fear. Those young teen years you don't realize that all kids have these doubts about themselves. You think it's about home schooling.

"So I did five hours of academic work a day. I obsessively kept track to the minute. On reflection, I'm really sad I did that. My mom, of course, was letting me follow my interests. There was this horrible weakness in math and science. I spent my time publishing, writing, weight lifting, thinking about football. At that age, you're pretty stubborn. You know the best way. I should have asked for more help. Finally, I just got into a crisis stage, a panic: 'I'm not going to make the three years! I'm not a super-genius!' It was a big crash. I was the lowest of the low."

As it turns out, Peter's A.C.T., or American College Test, score of 27 puts him in the 91st percentile; he won't tell me his S.A.T. scores, which disappointed him. One of his goals in taking math and science at Lakeland Community College is to complete his Clonlara program; another goal is to get used to classrooms, to ease into an alien world.

His first pick for a university (he'll apply when he finishes up at Lakeland) is Case Western Reserve in Cleveland, a respected private school, comfortably close to home. His second pick is Miami University (known nationally as Miami of Ohio), a less expensive, less selective public university, just a little farther away. His A.C.T. score easily puts him in the running at Case and is well above the mean at Miami.

"We've actually developed a specific policy on home-schooled applicants in the last two or three years," says William T. Conley, the dean of undergraduate admissions at Case. "College admissions is all about the pipeline, and the home schooling numbers are growing rapidly, so we better be ready."

Still, Conley has some personal reservations about home schooling. "My wife and I have said to each other that people must be out of their minds to want to spend that much time with their kids," he says. "And the academics! It's hard enough just worrying that your kid has got his poem written for class

the next day. I'm skeptical, concerned for the kids—there's a lot to be said for suffering the fools in their local high schools."

Eric J. Furda, director of undergraduate admissions at Columbia University (whose nieces, coincidentally, are home-schooled), says that the admissions process for home schoolers isn't unlike that for the graduates of progressive or experimental private schools. But Furda admits that he needs plenty of background information to compare home-schooled applicants with applicants from known high schools: What curriculum was used? How was it decided that the student was ready to move on to the next level in, say, math? How significant are the transcripts when they are provided by parents? "We need some national comparison," Furda says, recommending that home schoolers take five S.A.T.-II subject tests: writing, math, history, science and a language.

How will Peter Kowalke's application to Case be evaluated?

"We are looking at these students in a very specific light," Conley says. "Are they prepared for the intellectual, academic and social environment here at Case Western Reserve? The S.A.T.-II subject tests give us a handle on how much French or calculus or history the home-schooled kid has actually learned. Then, once the kid's in our pool, we look for the subtleties. In some cases, the home schoolers are very limited in nonacademic involvement. There won't be the traditional marching band, tennis 1, 2, 3, 4. One automatically assumes that a home-schooled kid will be limited socially. So we look closely: Do they work at the local McDonald's? Do they volunteer with Habitat for Humanity, have a paper route, work with the town theater company?"

Then there's the interview, required for home schoolers. "We feel that if they've been pursuing their education at 31 Walnut Lane, we need to get them on the academic plant, see if they feel comfortable," Conley says.

When I describe Peter Kowalke—test scores, community involvement, independent projects, college-level math and science—Conley says: "What's his name? Can you tell me his name? He sounds good."

O.K. for Peter, but (assuming they would even be interested in college) what about the purest unschoolers, who often refuse to take tests, refuse to create schoolish transcripts, refuse to use grades?

"I don't think so," Conley says. "We just don't know how to look at that."

I'M A COLLEGE PROFESSOR; I HAVE DEGREES; I'm a product of public schooling from Grade 1 to Grade 12. It's all but impossible for me to see learning in any light but the fluorescent blare of the classroom, with testing and grades and grade levels, with layers of experts in control, with winners and losers, standards, norms, averages against which to judge the efforts and abilities of every kid you send up.

It's tough to let go of all that, maybe impossible. My American sense of the rightness of school, the inevitability of school, the hegemony of school, is akin to my sense of the rightness of the oceans, of rivers, of rain. God made them, right?

Still, there's something noble—if perhaps quixotic—in refusing the culture's assumptions about school, in marching into the fray alone, an individualism distinctly American.

The Rhodeses carry on, cheerfully stressed, caught up in their commitment, intrepidly facing the future and its unknown challenges, alone.

For Peter Kowalke, the deed is done. Twelve years ago, his folks marched him off in his own direction, and there's general agreement—from friends, from teachers, from standardized tests—that he has come out fine. Perhaps it does no good to wonder how it would have been for Peter in school. Would he have starred in sports? Would he have suffered his crisis? Would he have published Nation and made so many friends so far from home? Would he have handled the pressures of the cliques? Or got in with the wrong crowd? Would he have found mentors among his teachers? Or would he have remained too proud to ask for help?

All moot. Now it's off to college. "This is the time when most kids become individuals," he says. "But I've always been an individual. My friends and I are finally all getting on the same wavelength. I've proved I can do well academically. I know I can interact well with the other kids. I can do well in college. I'm O.K."

Peter has become so interested in science that he plans to major in it. And eventually, college behind him, he wants to mix emerging computer technologies with his publishing experience in some way no one has yet dreamed of. "The biggest benefit of home schooling is that it chops away the barriers, opens up all the limits in life. Even with its trials, home schooling shows you there are alternatives. You think: Could I do it a different way? You have confidence."

He looks around his mother's kitchen, shakes his head, gives me a hard look. His assurance seems to flicker, then blazes.

Boys' Schools Reconsidered:

GOOD NEWS IN TROUBLED TIMES

Keeping the sexes separated has been shown to relieve many social tensions that interfere with the prime mission of schools—education.

by Richard Hawley

THE REAL MISSION of independent education is to conceive of good and great schools. Great schools are those that take children as far along their creative, moral, and intellectual range as they can go.

Gender composition must be understood and valued as it promotes this goodness, not for its own sake. Schools are not good because they are composed of boys, but a good boys' school could not be better composed. This is a crucial distinction. If society loses its vision of what good schooling means, and closes its eyes to what the best evidence says is really true of boys and girls, then it is running blind.

It is the relationship between all-boys composition and school excellence that requires attention and understanding. This is where boys' schools, especially strong ones, have been too timid and too lazy over the past two decades of widespread coed conversion.

There are two important jobs ahead for boys' schools, and they are much tougher than they might have been if school heads had taken a longer and deeper view in the

Dr. Hawley, headmaster, University School, Hunting Valley, Ohio, is the author of Boys Will Be Men: Masculinity in Troubled Times.

1970s. The first and easiest of these is to answer the boys' school-as-dinosaur charge. The second, more challenging and also more important in the long run, is demonstrating that boys' schools are a progressive and humane answer to America's, and to some extent the world's, educational malaise.

The charge that boys' schools are cultural dinosaurs rests on a fallacy involving poor causal thinking. Bad social outcomes like misogynist behavior, destructive aggression, and arrogant entitlement are placed at the feet of all male schools. If the gender composition of schools is a causal factor at all in these social outcomes, then the coed schools must be the culprits, since they have educated more than 90% of the nation's school-children since the U.S.'s founding. Today, the percentage is far higher.

In fact, there has been an almost weird reluctance to associate coed schools with gender-related problems and tensions. State coed schools are experiencing crises that have brought many of them to the brink of dissolution. David Tyack and Elizabeth Mansat's exhaustive account of American coeducation, *Learning Together*, concludes with the dispiriting notion that nothing about the nation's coeducational practice has produced superior results for

either sex, but the authors see little chance of revising or altering coeducation, especially in state schools: "Cost, customs, institutional inertia, and now fear of litigation virtually guarantee the survival of coeducation." It is chilling and depressing to think that these are the driving forces in American educational practice. They hardly constitute a ringing endorsement of coeducation or for rushing to convert fine single-sex schools to the dominant model.

Recognizing the dinosaur fallacy allows a compelling point about boys' schools to be made—that they are in an especially good position to lead the way out of, rather than into, social inequities. At the very core of the so-called Milwaukee plan to create all-male schools, primarily for African-American youth, is the notion that, in rigorous and nurturing all-boys' schools, with purposeful, humane goals, and lots of positive male examples, even the most imperiled and disadvantaged boys will thrive. The underlying assumption of the Milwaukee plan—and of many similarly structured private and parochial school initiatives—is that, when male peer identity and strong male modeling are removed from a boy's life, you get trouble. The remedy is putting it back in. This is not an assumption about

From *USA Today Magazine*, January 1996, pp. 77-79. © 1996 by the Society for the Advancement of Education. Reprinted by permission.

just African-American boys, but one about boys in general. The establishment of all-boy academies in American cities may set out to address very specific social concerns, but these schools also may reveal an essential, general truth about child development.

Americans will go a long way in dispelling the dinosaur fallacy if school advocates learn to confront dismissive and mean-minded statements about boys' schooling in an informed manner. Facts, including those of existing schools, sometimes speak for themselves, but school people must be prepared to go further.

There is a radically unexamined, and actually silly, conclusion about boys' schools drawn by some feminists, and it has appeared in print in American, British, and Australian publications: "Single-sex schools are better for girls; coed schools are better for boys." Think about this for a second. If the first premise is true, the second damns the unlucky girls who have to attend coed schools to a fate of mitigating the problematic effect of males. There is a far more harmful premise implied in this position, though—that males are, by their nature, toxic. If you let them express themselves freely, if they band together, they will make trouble. This assumption, sometimes tacit, sometimes not, pervades a good deal of late-20th-century popular culture. It is a false assumption. To propose anything of the kind is straightforward bigotry, however stylish and widely held the position may be. As a barb, or a politically charged gesture of complaint about current gender inequities, it can be taken as one takes other beeps and honks in political traffic, but the assumption of male toxicity is seriously bad for children. No youngster should be made to feel guilty about or ashamed of what may be his most essential dimension. School people can argue forever about school structures and child development, but they must premise these arguments on an almost unreasonable love of and respect for children—of both sexes.

The current educational climate requires that boys' schools get off the defensive and set about making the case for their humanity and social necessity. Here, what schools actually do matters more than winning words. Toward this end, there is some very good news.

Biology, anthropology, and all manner of social science confirm that human beings are deeply gendered: sex runs more deeply than culture. Moreover, the research supporting innate, rather than culturally formed, gender is growing. If gender is turning out to be more than a mere cultural imposition, the futility and arrogance of imposing unisex conventions from toys to bedtime stories to courting protocol are becoming ever clearer. Even well-meaning attempts to neuter male children weaken, demoralize, and confuse them. Sanitizing children's environments

of gender evidence and nuance is in effect a deceptive approach to gendered children. In certain elementary school environments, a boy could not possibly locate himself or his kind. Schools like this, incidentally, have not produced nicer, socially compliant youngsters.

Rampant, unapologetic aggression and misogyny do not stem from intense male culture. Rather, they are sad, sometimes dangerous, overcompensations for the absence of male culture. The much publicized abusive and criminal behavior on the part of suburban California high school boys in 1994 or the infantile vulgarities of an entertainer like Andrew Dice Clay do not derive from patriarchal, chivalric codes. These revered women, decent behavior, and courteous speech. It is the breakdown of standards in the 1970s, 1980s, and 1990s—the era of unisexual marketing and coed conversion—that has produced this current wave of unrepentant misogyny. Skinheads do not derive from the Western heritage, but from a popular culture that has forsaken that heritage. That popular culture has provided plenty of sexual ideology, but precious little sexual understanding.

Because gender is real, it must be understood, valued, and educated respectfully. Gender-based variations in tempo and pattern of learning can be identified from the pre-kindergarten through the high school years. Primary school girls generally demonstrate reading and writing proficiency earlier than boys do. Middle and high school boys' mathematical logical capacities accelerate more rapidly than those of girls. Females reach the peak of their pubertal growth spurt a year or two sooner than males. Each gender-based physiological difference is accompanied by distinctive psychological and social adjustments.

Child psychologist J.M. Tanner has demonstrated that girls' skeletons and nervous systems are more fully developed at birth than those of boys, and the maturational gap increases somewhat through early childhood. From their preschool years through their late teens, boys reveal a number of other sex-specific contours in their skeletal, motor, and neurological development. They develop language skills, the capacity for quantitative analysis, and large- and small-muscle proficiencies at a developmentally different tempo from girls.

If the learning styles or learning tempos of boys and girls are at variance, a homogeneous school program, whether curricular or extracurricular, unavoidably will miss either the masculine or the feminine mark, if not both. This last point, the desirability of pitching instruction to the developmental and gender realities of one's students, is worthy of further inquiry. Neither current science nor honest observation sup-

port the notion that one sex has a moral or intellectual edge over the other. Gender differences are not social entitlements.

The argument that the needs and special features of boys and girls are addressed best in single-sex schools is hard to contest. Even harder to refute is the fact that, from the early middle school years onward, cross-gender preoccupation and distraction bear negatively on learning. This point, however delicately stated, always puts coed school advocates in a terrible mood.

The point actually is as ancient as schooling itself. Throughout that history, until the mid 20th century, all of the demonstrably best schools and colleges in the world were single-sex. A number of those institutions still are.

The concern about cross-gender distractions and preoccupation is not an invention of defensive single-sex schools. It was educator James Coleman who, at the early onset of the postwar baby boom, complained that the social agenda of American schools was threatening the learning agenda. His prophetic book, *The Adolescent Society,* was for and about state coeducational schools, and he wrote it in 1961.

The scholastic toll taken by cross-gender preoccupation is understood best if one simply considers the flow of a child's energy in various school settings. Only some of these energy expenditures are visible—in sexual gestures such as flirting, erotic looking, dressing, grooming, acting out. I contend that even more adolescent energy goes into suppressing sexual interests and urges in school. The flattest adolescent appearances are likely to conceal intense arousal neutralized by equally intense suppression; in other words, even an apparent disinterest or coolness in the proximity of an adolescent's gender opposite comes at a cost of energy and focus. It takes more energy to block a desire than it does to express it. Whether expressed or suppressed, sexual distraction is an undeniable impediment to focused activity and learning. That is why sociologist Alexander Astin attributed the positive effects of single-sex colleges in the 1970s (when there still were single-sex colleges, including most of the leading schools) to "restricted heterosexual activity." This also is why sociologists Valerie Lee and Tony Bryk's 1986 study of single-sex and coeducational parochial schools invited a reconsideration of learning environments where adolescent boys' and girls' "social and learning environments are separated."

Perhaps a key—if not *the* key—factor is the presence of effective females on the faculty and staff, not the presence of adolescent girls in classrooms and at lunch tables. If the mere presence of female counterparts humanized and civilized boys, then the U.S. long ago would have been enjoying a golden age of gender equity and bliss, since the vast majority of American boys and girls have been schooled together for decades.

Cross-gender understanding does not result from mixing school-aged boys and girls together. The experience of seasoned boys' school faculty suggests that there is no better, franker, more comfortable climate in which to examine male and female sexuality and psychology, including gender and gender justice, than in a boys' school.

It is not unreasonable to see boys' schools as laboratories of humanizing social sensitivities. Yet, in current practice, only a few are directing effort and attention to that end. If and when more schools do, what some critics regard as the fatal flaw of boys' schools could emerge, literally, as their saving grace.

In some respects, the National Coalition of Girls' Schools has taken a lead in generating positive research in support of its mission. Yet, even now, the best data schools have are that of their current practices.

Boys' school staff know that theirs is a school culture whereby students really are stimulated enough and secure enough to realize their distinctive selves in all of their astonishing variety. It is in boys' schools that the full range of a youngster's vitality finds expression. In boys' schools, some ancient and traditional patterns unfold, including the heroic pattern of striving, enduring rigor and hardships, and deepening as a result. In such schools, the more tender, more elusive, more creative impulses also are given room and an honored place. Nowhere more than in boys' schools can one feel and appreciate the passing on of what men and older boys have and know to younger ones. Some of what is passed on is challenge, posed in a decidedly virile and robust way; some is conveyed in the kindest, most welcoming way imaginable.

Finally, boys' schools at their best may be an antidote to much of what has gone wrong with Western culture in the aftermath of this century's appallingly destructive wars and dislocations. The sheer scale of the losses and carnage and waste, including the lives of so many millions of young men at the hands of millions of others, has eclipsed the heroic vision of boys and men. In the place of that vision has arisen the anti-hero, the boy who, racked by doubt and despair, refuses to become a man. He is more or less sympathetic, and his brooding image sells products, but he is neither whole nor strong or socially helpful. He is Holden Caulfield, not young Abe Lincoln or Romeo or Alexander the Great or the David who slew Goliath.

The anti-heroic age bespeaks a culture that does not like or trust boys and men enough. Yet, every loving parent and every committed teacher knows the necessity of doing otherwise. To be that kind of school, to recognize and bring forth the best and truest of what is in these boys—what a generous offering to mankind that would be.

At-Risk Students and Resiliency: Factors Contributing to Academic Success

JAMES H. McMILLAN and DAISY F. REED

James H. McMillan is a professor and Daisy F. Reed is an associate professor—both at the School of Education, Virginia Commonwealth University, Richmond, Virginia. Funds to support this research were received from the Metropolitan Educational Research Consortium. The views expressed are those of the authors and do not represent opinions or beliefs of the members of the consortium.

The increasingly high number of at-risk middle and high school students—those in danger of dropping out of school because of academic failure or other problems—is a major concern in education today. At-risk students show persistent patterns of under-achievement and of social maladjustment in school, leading to their failure to finish high school. Indeed, the national dropout rate averages about 25 percent (Sklarz 1989), and for minorities, that rate is higher, with an average of 30 percent leaving school before they graduate (Liontos 1991). In Texas, the dropout rate for Hispanic Americans is 45 percent. Additionally, students in urban schools have much higher dropout rates than those in other areas: in Boston, Chicago, Los Angeles, Detroit, and other major cities, dropout rates range from 40 percent to 60 percent of the total school population (Hahn 1987).

An interesting approach to helping at-risk students succeed is to examine the notion of "resilience." Despite incredible hardships and the presence of at-risk factors, some students have developed characteristics and coping skills that enable them to succeed. They appear to develop stable, healthy personas and are able to recover from or adapt to life's stresses and problems. These students can be termed *resilient* (Winfield 1991).

In one recent large-scale study, approximately 19 percent of students who could be classified as at-risk became individuals who had success in school, with positive goals and plans for the future (Peng, Lee, Wang, and Walberg 1992). What enables these resilient students to succeed

academically? What can educators and other concerned citizens do to foster these qualities in the 81 percent of at-risk students who do not succeed in school? We believe that much can be learned from studying students who may be classified as at-risk but are resilient, that is, doing well in school despite the odds against them. In this article, we integrate existing literature with our own research that examines resiliency, and then suggest a model to explain resiliency that can be used to better understand why these students have been successful and what can be done to help other at-risk students.

The factors that seem to be related to resiliency can be organized into four categories: individual attributes, positive use of time, family, and school (Peng et al. 1992; McMillan and Reed 1993).

Elements of Resiliency

Individual Attributes

Resilient at-risk students possess temperamental characteristics that elicit positive responses from individuals around them. These personality traits begin in early childhood and are manifested in adolescence as students seek out new experiences and become self-reliant. This begins a cycle of positive reciprocity that enables these students to reach out to other people and expect help. Their positive attitudes are usually rewarded with helpful reactions from those around them. Thus, they come to see the world as a positive place in spite of the difficult issues with which they have to deal. Their positive attitudes include respecting others, coming to class prepared, volunteering for in- and out-of-class assignments, and knowing how to play the school game.

High intrinsic motivation and internal locus of control seem to enable resilient at-risk students to succeed. In their study of 17,000 tenth graders from low-income families, Peng et al. (1992) found that locus of control was a significant predictor of academic success—students with higher academic achievement tended to have a more in-

From *The Clearing House*, January/February 1994, pp. 137-140. © 1994 by the Helen Dwight Reid Educational Foundation.
Reprinted by permission of Heldref Publications, 1319 Eighteenth Street, NW, Washington, DC 20036-1802.

ternal locus of control. They also found that successful students had higher educational aspirations than non-resilient students. In a qualitative study of the perceptions of academically successful at-risk students, many students spoke of satisfaction gained from experiencing success in self-fulfilling activities (McMillan and Reed 1993). These students were motivated by a desire to succeed, to be self-starting, and to be personally responsible for their achievements. They attributed poor performance to internal factors such as a lack of effort, not caring, not trying, not studying as much as they needed to, goofing off, and playing around; most respondents thought that poor performing students could do better if they put in more work and got serious about school. A strong sense of self-efficacy is important; students see themselves as being successful because they have chosen to be so and give much credit to themselves.

Resilient students have clear, realistic goals and are optimistic about the future. They have hope, despite all the negative circumstances in their lives, and confidence that they can achieve their long-range goals. For some students a particularly difficult experience, either direct or vicarious, reinforces the importance of getting an education. These might be called "reality checks" because they seem to motivate students toward positive goals (McMillan and Reed 1993). The reality check may have been dropping out of school, becoming pregnant, being in drug rehabilitation, or some other event or circumstance that showed them that without an education their opportunities would be limited. As a result, these resilient students tend to be very mature in their explanations and goals.

Resilient students do not believe that the school, neighborhood, or family is critical in either their successes or failures. They acknowledge that a poor home environment can make things difficult, but they do not blame their performance on these factors.

Positive Use of Time

In the qualitative study conducted by McMillan and Reed (1993), resilient students were asked about their hobbies, activities, and participation in clubs, church, or other organizations and about how they spend their time. It was clear that they used their time positively and were meaningfully involved in school and other activities. With some exceptions, this involvement was not in a special program or group for at-risk students or students with specific problems. This positive involvement did not leave these students with much spare time. Active involvement in extracurricular events at school and in other areas seems to provide a refuge for resilient students. Hobbies, creative interests, and sports help promote the growth of self-esteem. Being recognized and supported for special talents is also important. In addition, simply being involved in an activity considered special appears to increase self-esteem and a belief in one's ability to succeed (Geary 1988; Werner 1984; Coburn and Nelson 1989; McMillan and Reed 1993). Such involvement may provide an important social-psychological support system by connecting the students to others in meaningful ways. Success in these activities may be important in enhancing self-esteem by providing recognition and a sense of accomplishment.

Involvement in "required helpfulness" seems to be a factor in resilient students' experiences. Required helpfulness may mean volunteer work in the community, tutoring or buddying at school, or taking care of siblings or otherwise helping at home. These activities seem to lend purpose to the difficult life of an at-risk student and serve to increase their caring about others. They realize there are people that even they can help (Werner 1984; Philliber 1986).

Family Factors

Most resilient at-risk students have had the opportunity to establish a close bond with at least one caregiver who gives them needed attention and support. A sense of trust is developed that is very important in interactions with teachers and peers. This support may be from people other than parents, such as siblings, aunts, uncles, or grandparents who become positive role models. Resilient children seem to be adept at finding these substitute caregivers, much as they are adept at eliciting positive responses from many people around them (Werner 1984).

Family support seems to be an attribute of successful at-risk students. Parents of resilient students have higher expectations for their children's education. Such expectations exert pressure on the children to remain engaged in school and work toward high achievement. These students are more likely to interact with parents, to have more learning materials in the home, and to be involved in out-of-school educational activities than are non-resilient at-risk students (Peng et al. 1992).

Interestingly, family composition seems to have no significant relationship to at-risk students' success or failure (Peng et al. 1992). Students living with both parents do not necessarily have a higher level of resiliency than students in single-parent families or other configurations. Instead, good parent-child relationships and supportive attachments appear to act as protective factors from the environment. Parents who are committed to their children provide informal counseling, support, and help in achieving success. This parental commitment lends a feeling of coherence to the family unit. Werner (1984) maintains that these strong family ties help at-risk students to believe that life makes sense and that they have some control over their own lives. This sense of meaning becomes a powerful motivation for many resilient at-risk students.

Finally, the educational background of parents is related to student resiliency. Peng et al. (1992) found that less than 11 percent of students whose parents had less than a high school education were classified as resilient students as compared with 23 percent of students whose parents had a high school education or beyond.

School Factors

Resilient students seem to find support outside of the home environment, usually in school. They like school, in general, or at least put up with it. Most attempt to involve themselves in classroom discussions and activities. School is more than academics for these students. Most are involved in at least one extracurricular event that becomes an informal source of support. The extracurricular event not only increases involvement, belonging, and self-esteem, it also provides a network of people who have a common bond and work in cooperation with each other (Werner 1984; Coburn and Nelson 1989). Extracurricular events at school, especially sports, seem to mitigate the powerful and widespread peer pressure not to do well. Many resilient students seem to feel they must be involved with a nonacademic activity in order to "fit in" with the majority of students. This involvement maintains the resilient at-risk student's positive engagement in school (Geary 1988).

Teachers play an important role in the success of resilient students. In three qualitative studies, resilient at-risk students mentioned school staff who had taken a personal interest in them as being important to their success (Geary 1988; Coburn and Nelson 1989; McMillan and Reed 1993). Both interpersonal relations and professional competence are important to at-risk students. They cite the following interpersonal qualities of a teacher as important: being caring, having respect for them as persons and as learners, being able to get along with them, listening without being intrusive, taking them seriously, being available and understanding, helping and providing encouragement, and laughing with them. Professional behavior and competence are also important. Resilient at-risk students look for these qualities: the ability to represent and further the goals of the system and the school, a willingness to listen to the motivations behind inappropriate behavior before they discipline, fairness in grading and instruction, praise and encouragement that they can succeed, high expectations, and a willingness to get to know the students personally as well as academically (Werner 1984). Students feel that they can talk to "good" teachers and counselors about almost anything and that the teacher or counselor will listen without judging the student. These counselors and teachers "push" the students and at the same time are very supportive.

Profile of the Resilient Student

Resilient at-risk students have a set of personality characteristics, dispositions, and beliefs that promote their academic success regardless of their backgrounds or current circumstances. They have an internal locus of control and healthy internal attributions, taking personal responsibility for their successes and failures and showing a strong sense of self-efficacy. They feel that they have been successful because they have *chosen* to be successful and have put forth needed effort. Even though they wel-

come and appreciate the efforts of the significant adults in their lives, they do not see these people as being responsible for their success or failure. They credit themselves. They have positive expectations about their abilities and the future, an optimistic perspective with realistic long-range goals. This strong sense of hope is accompanied by a belief that doing well in school is necessary to doing well in life. These students are very mature in their outlook and attitudes and tend to make positive choices about how to use their time.

To develop these characteristics, resilient students have a psychological support system that provides a safety net and encouragement. This system is evident in the way the students are meaningfully connected to others, in or out of school. They are actively involved in positive activities that provide a sense of support, success, and recognition. Activities such as hobbies give these students a reason to feel proud and provide a solace when other aspects of their lives are troubling. Involvement in both academic and extracurricular activities maintains resilient students' positive engagement in school.

Resilient students have adults—usually a parent (more often mother than father) and someone from the school—with whom they have trusting relationships. These adults have high expectations and provide support and encouragement with firmness. Students respect these adults because they obviously care about their welfare.

Thus, there are important environmental factors that contribute to the strong, resilient personalities and beliefs that are critical to these students. These factors are illustrated with the conceptual model in figure 1. The model shows how significant relationships with adults and positive use of time provide encouragement, high expectations, a psychological suport system, and recognition and accomplishment. These environmental factors influence these students so that they develop self-efficacy, goals, personal responsibility, and so forth. It is these traits that make students resilient. The challenge to schools is to provide the relationships and involvement that can foster this development.

Implications for School Personnel

The model suggests several implications for school personnel. First, instructional strategies and techniques, as well as other dimensions of the school environment, must be developed to promote a sense of internal locus of control, self-efficacy, optimism, and a sense of personal responsibility. Teachers should establish reference points where achievement will be identified, and they must continually relate success to effort and ability. Goal setting is also important, particularly setting long-range goals that demonstrate the need to focus beyond one's immediate interests and activities.

Second, teachers, administrators, and counselors need to be trained and encouraged to provide classroom activities and classroom environments that stress high academic achievement while also building students' self-es-

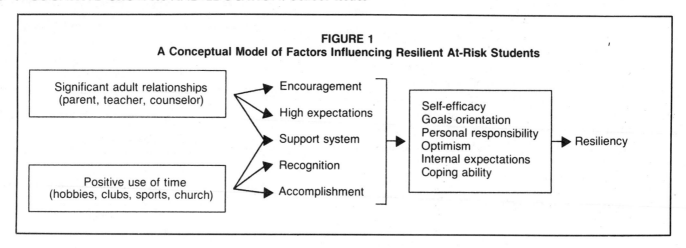

FIGURE 1
A Conceptual Model of Factors Influencing Resilient At-Risk Students

teem and self-confidence. The classroom environment should facilitate time-on-task, student interaction, student success, and positive reinforcement for desired classroom behaviors. Teachers need to be aware of the difference between high expectations and high standards. High expectations involve beliefs about what students are capable of doing and achieving, while high standards do not necessarily suggest that students can reach them. Positive experiences in school help provide students a sense of belonging, bonding, and encouragement.

In addition, extracurricular activities need to be expanded and promoted in schools where there are large populations of at-risk students. As previously mentioned, these activities increase involvement in school. However, many at-risk students will not voluntarily participate in activities because of their general feelings of disconnectedness. Teachers and administrators should develop needed programs and systematically issue personal invitations for at-risk students to join. These programs should include the usual school clubs such as drama, choir, "Future Teachers," "Future Farmers," and others, as well as support groups for various concerns such as adolescent mothers, victims of abuse, children of alcoholic parents, and children of incarcerated parents.

Third, teachers need to be provided with training and encouragement to develop relationships that benefit at-risk children. These students need teachers who are respectful, caring, honest, patient, open-minded, and firm. They also need teachers who understand learning styles, expect positive results, and recognize cultural norms and differences. Perhaps teacher education programs for preservice and inservice teachers need to offer special seminars or classes on working with at-risk populations.

Resilient students give us hope and encouragement, for it is clear that despite unfavorable odds, they have succeeded. We need to learn from them and put into practice what we have learned.

REFERENCES

Coburn, J., and S. Nelson. 1989. *Teachers do make a difference: What Indian graduates say about their school experience* (Report No. RC–017–103). Washington, D.C.: Office of Educational Research and Improvement. (ERIC Document Reproduction Service No. ED 306 071)

Geary, P. A. 1988. *"Defying the odds?": Academic success among at-risk minority teenagers in an urban high school* (Report No. UD-026–258). Paper presented at the annual meeting of the American Educational Research Association, New Orleans, La. (ERIC Document Reproduction Service No. ED 296 055)

Hahn, A. 1987. Reaching out to America's dropouts: What to do? *Phi Delta Kappan* 69(4): 256–63.

Liontos, L. B. 1991. *Trends and issues: Involving families of at-risk youth in the educational process.* ERIC Clearinghouse on Educational Management. Eugene, Oregon: College of Education, University of Oregon. ED 328946

McMillan, J. H., and D. F. Reed. 1993. A qualitative study of resilient at-risk students. Paper presented at the 1993 annual meeting of the American Educational Research Association, Atlanta.

Peng, S. S., R. M. Lee, M. C. Wang, and H. J. Walberg. 1992. Resilient students in urban settings. Paper presented at the 1992 annual meeting of the American Educational Research Association, San Francisco.

Philliber, S. 1986. *Teen outreach: Data from the second year of a national replication.* Paper presented at the 1986 annual national conference of the Children's Defense Fund, Washington, D. C.

Sklarz, D. P. 1989. Keep at-risk students in school by keeping them up to grade level. *The American School Board Journal* 176(9): 33–34.

Werner, E. E. 1984. Resilient children. *Young Children* 40(1): 68–72.

Winfield, L. A. 1991. Resilience, schooling, and development in African-American youth: A conceptual framework. *Education and Urban Society* 24(1): 5–14.

Good Mentoring Keeps At-Risk Youth in School

Psychologists develop mentoring programs that encourage students to stay in school and improve their performance.

Bridget Murray

Monitor staff

Sandra Castellanos, a Houston community activist, wasn't surprised when officials at a local high school expelled Crystal, a young girl she was mentoring. She knew Crystal had been skipping school and blamed her behavior on "a bad crowd" Crystal had become friendly with.

On Castellanos's suggestion, Crystal apologized to the school principal and was allowed back. Now Castellanos is helping Crystal pay more attention to the consequences of her actions, encouraging her to run with a tamer crowd and concentrate on her schoolwork.

Instances like this and research by psychologists prove that mentoring relationships keep kids in school. Mentors give kids a sense of personal connection and encouragement to function well, academically and socially.

As an added bonus, mentors sometimes boost students' academic performance by providing tutoring. In fact, psychologist Ellen Slicker, PhD, of Middle Tennessee State University, found a 100 percent retention rate for well-mentored sophomores in a study she conduced in Houston's Spring High School in the late 1980s. Every student who had a positive mentoring experience returned to school in the fall after the mentoring intervention.

Mentoring programs for 12- to 17-year olds gained popularity after 1990 U.S. Census figures showed a national high school dropout rate averaging 12 percent. Some urban areas battle dropout rates of up to 50 percent.

Dropout prevention is among several objectives in the federal government's National Education Goals. Psychologists have played an important role in coordinating and evaluating mentoring programs that bring these rates down, said Ronda C. Tally, PhD, director of the APA Center for Psychology in School and Education.

A Sense of Belonging

Slicker and her then-colleague at Texas A & M University, Douglas Palmer, PhD, studied how well Spring High School's mentoring program kept its dropout rate in check.

"Kids need to feel a sense of belonging and mentors help give them that," said Slicker. "A good mentor is someone who cares, someone who helps them feel a part of the school."

The relationship needn't be extensive, just consistent, said Rick Short, PhD, head of the APA Education Directorate's Center of Education and Training in Psychology.

"What's important is that the mentor stop by regularly, just to make sure the kid's in school and to see how things are going," said Short,

who helped run mentoring programs in Kentucky schools.

In their study, Slicker and Palmer monitored mentors assigned to 86 students identified as high risk for dropping out due to low skills, bad grades and poor behavior records. Mentors were volunteer school personnel, including teachers, secretaries and teacher aides. They received special training and instructions.

During school, the mentors talked with students at their lockers between classes and met them for lunch. They kept records of the level and consistency of their mentoring activities.

MENTORS GIVE KIDS A SENSE OF PERSONAL CONNECTION AND ENCOURAGEMENT TO FUNCTION WELL, BOTH ACADEMICALLY AND SOCIALLY.

The results indicated that poorly mentored students dropped out more than controls who received no mentoring at all. The poorer mentors failed to keep a stable relationship with their students. They met with the kids irregularly if at all, which caused students to lose faith in them and feel abandoned. The research suggests that at-risk kids want an adult to be available, supportive and trustworthy, said Slicker. The mentor has to keep regular appointments and show confidence in the student's abilities.

'Check and Connect'

The Partnership for School Success, a school dropout prevention project run by the University of Minnesota and the Minneapolis Public Schools, relies heavily on a mentoring component. Funded by the U.S. Department of Education, the program seeks to keep seventh- and eighth- graders with learning and emotional/behavioral disabilities from leaving school.

Using a "check-and-connect" procedure, mentors monitor students regularly for signs of truancy, acting out or academic failure, and work to connect them with services that address risk factors, said school psychologist Sandra Christenson, PhD, one of the program's principal investigators. Mentors solicit teachers, parents, administrators and community outreach workers to provide help to kids. They link students with academic supports, community service projects and recreational activities.

Mentors meet with youth at least once a week. They establish a friendship with the youth, talk to them about the economic costs of dropping out and prepare them to deal with po-

tential challenges through social problem-solving. The mentor works through attendance problems with the child, for instance, using a five-step strategy:

- What are some choices?
- Choose one.
- Do it.
- How did it work?

The project extends traditional mentoring to include checking on students' behaviors consistently over time and immediately connecting students with pertinent interventions, said Christenson.

Nontraditional Models

Some schools, like Canton Middle School in east Baltimore, encourage mentoring relationships among students themselves.

In the early 1990s Canton paired up sixth- and eighth-graders, assigned them to work on arts-and-crafts projects and encouraged them to volunteer for philanthropic activities. Although older eighth-graders played more of a mentor role as they oriented incoming sixth-graders to the school, the general idea was to improve social skills and establish ties across grades, said an investigating psychologist, Kenneth Maton, PhD, of the University of Maryland-Baltimore County.

Other programs pair students with members of the community. Besides

bad grades, a lack of friends and low participation in extracurricular activities predict dropout, Short says. Mentoring programs involve kids in the community to help build their commitment to school.

In Chicago's inner city, for example, psychologist Jean Rhodes, PhD, recruits volunteers to mentor pregnant African-American teenagers at the Simpson Alternative School. Many of the mentors are Simpson graduates who have established careers in the community.

"Mentors show the teens how successful you can be if you finish school and don't get pregnant again," said Rhodes.

A psychology professor at the University of Illinois, Rhodes is principal investigator in the five-year mentoring project, which is partially funded by the National Institute of Children's Health and Human Development.

In Washington, D.C., the Capital Partners for Education program pairs at-risk kids from inner-city schools with community leaders. Local lawyers, government officials and bankers take students to dinners and baseball games, help them with homework and call them regularly to check on their progress.

Whether mentors are parents, teachers, community leaders or older schoolmates, they may provide youths with the best incentive to get an education, Short says.

"There's nothing like a relationship to get someone to do something," he said.

Schools the source of rough transitions

Psychologists study the difficulties children face when they move from elementary school to middle school.

By Beth Azar
Monitor staff

In September, thousands of 10- to 12-year-old children will face one of the most critical transitions of their lives—the move from elementary school to middle school. For some, it sparks a downward spiral that can lead to school failure and withdrawal.

The switch from elementary school to junior high school coincides with several major changes for young adolescents. Most are in the throes of puberty; they're becoming more self-aware and self-conscious, and their thinking is growing more critical and complex. At the same time, parents and junior high teachers and parents complain that their students are flagging both in motivation and performance.

Traditionally, parents, teachers and even researchers blamed puberty alone for what they branded as inevitable declines in academic drive and achievement. But research psychologists are amassing evidence which shows that the environment and philosophy of middle schools often conflict with the needs of young adolescents. Researchers are using developmental theories of motivation to explain this conflict and to show how children can avoid failure in middle school.

ADOLESCENTS

Developmental mismatch

Since the early 1980s, psychologist Jacqueline Eccles, PhD, of the University of Michigan, and her colleagues, have collected data on the transition from elementary school to middle school. They've found that:

• On average, children's grades drop dramatically during the first year of middle school, compared to grades in elementary school.

• After moving to junior high, children become less interested in school and less self-assured about their abilities.

• Compared to elementary schools, middle schools are more controlling, less cognitively challenging, and focus more on competition and comparing students' ability.

The differences between elementary schools and middle schools cause what Eccles and her University of Michigan colleague Carol Midgely, PhD, call "developmental mismatch." They've found that middle school children report fewer opportunities for decision-making and lower levels of cognitive involvement than they had in elementary school, said Eccles' colleague, Eric Anderman, PhD, of the University of Kentucky.

At the same time, children must contend with a more complex social environment. They switch from a single teacher who knows their academic and social strengths to brief contact with many teachers. And they often face larger classes with a new group of peers.

These variables interact to make the transition to middle school challenging, said Anderman. Studies find that decreased motivation and self-assuredness contribute to poor academic performance. They have also found that drops in grades triggered by the transition can alter self-assuredness and motivation.

Goal setting

To better explain how these environmental changes affect students, some researchers have turned to goal-orientation theory, developed by Carol Ames, PhD, and her colleagues at Michigan State University. The theory identifies two types of goals that motivate people to achieve in school.

Task goals encourage learning for learning's sake—people concentrate on mastering a task, rather than striving for an expected grade. Performance goals favor learning for performance's sake—people desire a good grade to prove their competence to others or to achieve a particular end, such as parental approval.

Everyone subscribes to both types of goals, said Midgely. We want to expand our knowledge base *and* get

---

"For the low achievers, the transition to the new environment sparks a downward spiral that they can't seem to recover from."

Eric Anderman, PhD
University of Kentucky

---

good grades. But most people lean more toward one than the other. Transition researchers speculate that elementary schools are more task-focused and middle schools are more performance-focused.

This shift may throw children off balance during the transition. Indeed, several studies find that students become less task-oriented and more performance-oriented as they move from elementary to middle school, and students believe their middle-school teachers focus more on performance than tasks. At the same time, their belief in their own academic ability decreases dramatically, the studies find.

A study by Anderman and Midgely found that grades decreased more for middle-school students who had been low achievers in elementary school than for those who had been high-achieving students at the elementary level. By the year after the transition, high achievers seemed to have bounced back from first-year grade

declines while low achievers failed to rebound.

"For the low achievers, the transition to the new environment sparks a downward spiral that they can't seem to recover from," said Anderman.

These longitudinal studies suggest that changes in a child's goal orientation occur during the transition and these changes correlate with declines in motivation and performance, said Midgely. However, they don't prove that one causes the other. It's important to look beyond mean changes across big groups of students, she admits.

Carole Dweck, PhD, of Columbia University, agrees. She's found that some children thrive after the transition to middle school while others are particularly prone to failure.

The key is how they think about intelligence, she asserts. She found that children who think about intelligence as fixed—known as entity theorists—avoid tasks that challenge their ability or that risk failure. They instead choose to work on problems they know how to solve. Dweck calls this response pattern maladaptive or helpless. She believes it coincides with performance goals because the children prefer performing well to mastering something new.

Children who think about intelligence as malleable—known as incremental theorists—embrace challenging tasks and look at failure as a way to learn and improve. They tend to blame their failures on a lack of effort rather than a lack of ability. Dweck calls this response pattern mastery-oriented and believes it coincides with task goals.

Because elementary schools don't emphasize performance or failure vs. success, the differences between the two types of theorists should not show up until after the transition to junior high school, said Dweck.

In a study of 165 seventh-grade students, one year after the transition to junior high, she found an overall decline in academic achievement, compared with scores from sixth grade.

But not all students' grades declined. Indeed, while confidence in one's ability seemed to predict grades in elementary school—high confidence children had the highest grades—intelligence theory took over in junior high. The grades of high-confidence incremental theorists stayed level but those of high-confidence entity theorists sank. Also, the grades of low-confidence incremental theorists soared while those of low-confidence entity theorists remained as low as in sixth grade.

"These high-confidence kids who think intelligence is fixed, think that you should be able to do well without a lot of effort if you're smart," said Dweck. That strategy didn't work in the more challenging middle school, where teachers judged performance not based on general knowledge but on task performance.

Meanwhile, the low-confidence incremental theorists blossomed in their new environment. They were more willing to face the challenge, said Dweck.

These studies imply that not all children will suffer a drop in academic performance when they enter middle school. However, both the school environment and children's goals and attitudes about learning and intelligence need to be re-evaluated, the researchers agree.

During the school-reform boom of the 1980s, middle schools were largely ignored, according to the final report of the Carnegie Council on Adolescent Development, released last year. That omission needs to be addressed and the research on adolescent motivation and school environment included in reform efforts, the report says.

THE TEST OF THEIR LIVES

Exit exams may whip America's schools into shape, but some good kids pay a heavy price

By JAMES S. KUNEN

COMMENCEMENT IS NOT AN END, it is a beginning, graduates around the country are being assured this spring. But for Catherine Cockrell's dreams and aspirations, her high school graduation ceremonies may have marked the beginning of the end.

Denied the chance to graduate with her classmates at Paris (Texas) High School, she attended the event anyway and bravely joined their celebration. "It's kind of hard," she confessed. "I'm the oddball. Everybody else has a diploma, and I don't."

Cockrell went to all her classes, did all her homework, earned all her credits. But, like just one other of her 162 classmates, she could not pass Texas' statewide high school exit exam. Cockrell had enlisted in the Army, having passed its qualifying test, and was getting ready to ship out the week after graduation. But without passing the Texas Assessment of Academic Skills, she could not get a diploma, and without a diploma, her enlistment was void.

"Some people get testaphobia," she says. "I passed my math classes with flying colors, but I get to that TAAS test and my mind's like blank. I have no idea why." She'll try once more in July, but if she fails, all her plans will have come to nothing.

That's what happened to Lee Hicks, Paris High School should've-been class of '93. Had he lived 14 miles away in Oklahoma, which has no statewide exit test, he'd have received a diploma and would now be serving his country in the Navy. Instead Hicks serves customers in a Paris supermarket; he won management's Aggressive Hospitality Award for 1996. "He's a great employee, a bright young man—extremely hardworking," says store director Larry Legg. "He has the capability to go as far as he wants." But how far can one go without a high school diploma?

More and more young Americans may find themselves in Hicks' and Cockrell's shoes. So-called high-stakes testing is the latest silver bullet designed to cure all that ails public education, and accountability is the vocabulary word of the day. High schools, it is widely believed, are graduating too many kids who haven't mastered basic skills. Solution: all students, even after passing their courses, must also pass a statewide standardized "exit test" to graduate. And the test scores can then be used to gauge how well teachers and school administrators are doing their jobs.

Already 18 states have high school exit tests. National tests, endorsed by Bill Clinton and George Bush before him, will begin in 1999 with fourth-grade reading and eighth-grade math. The tests are supposed to serve only as a benchmark to assess educational progress, but they could one day lead to nationwide graduation standards. Now Wisconsin Governor Tommy Thompson and IBM chairman Louis

LAST HURDLE: TAAS questions like this decide kids' future

The graph shows the percent of compact discs sold for each music category at Mike's Music Store last month.

Compact Disc Sales

Rhythm and Blues
Classical 5% — 14%
Country 32%
Rap 20%
Rock 29%

22 Which is a reasonable conclusion from the information on the graph?

A Mike's Music Store doesn't sell cassette tapes.

B Mike's customers don't like rhythm and blues music.

C Classical compact discs are more popular than rap compact discs at Mike's.

D Rap compact discs are less popular than rock compact discs at Mike's.

E Fewer than 10 customers bought classical compact discs last month.

From *Time*, June 16, 1997, pp. 62-63. © 1997 by Time Inc. Magazine Company. Reprinted by permission.

Gerstner Jr., co-chairs of last year's Education Summit, are adding to the pressure, enlisting companies to pledge that they will look at young applicants' academic records, including exit-test scores, rather than rely on interviews and job-skill tests.

Texas is a national leader in high-stakes testing, having instituted a statewide high school exit exam in 1985 at the urging of a committee chaired by Ross Perot. Since then scores have climbed. In 1993, 51% of Texas 10th-graders passed all three sections of the TAAS—math, reading, writing—on the first try. This year 67% did. (Students get eight tries over three years.)

But low-income and minority students, often trapped in inferior schools, fail at a disproportionate rate. About 9% of the state's black and Hispanic seniors—7,380 last year—fail the exit test; less than 2% of whites do. The Texas N.A.A.C.P. has complained to the U.S. Department of Education's Office of Civil Rights that the TAAS has a discriminatory impact. A ruling may be announced this week. "We're not against testing," says state N.A.A.C.P. president Gary Bledsoe, "but testing should be used as a diagnostic tool, not for punitive purposes."

Cultural bias has been weeded out of most standardized tests—the SATs don't ask questions about chablis—and Texas officials insist that the TAAS is race neutral. But even if a test is fair, it can be put to uses that are not. Low TAAS scores, for example, have not been shown to correlate with the inability to do any particular job, but the lack of a high school diploma does correlate with the inability to find work. Should students poorly educated by substandard teachers be further penalized when they can't pass a test? What about good students who just don't test well? Argues Linda Darling-Hammond of Teachers College at Columbia University: "The use of tests as a sole determinant of high school graduation imposes heavy personal and societal costs without obvious social benefits."

Standardized testing was adopted early in this century, largely in pursuit of what Thomas Jefferson had called an "aristocracy of virtue and talent." Opportunities would be allotted on the basis of what you knew, not whom you knew. Reliance on tests grew, to compensate for the divergent standards in schoolrooms across the country. But tests cannot quantify qualities such as cooperativeness, creativity, or the perseverance a teenager needs to sit down in a two-room shack and do homework every night.

Critics argue that high-stakes tests can have other unfortunate consequences. Because high scores can bring rewards to the school—Texas at one point offered principals $5,000 bonuses for boosting TAAS results—while low scores invite sanctions, high-stakes tests may make it even harder for schools serving disadvantaged students to recruit the best faculty. Some schools inflate their scores by tinkering with the test pool; techniques include pushing low achievers into special education, or making them repeat a grade, which may cause them to fall further behind and ultimately drop out.

What's more, with so much riding on the test results for both students and school, there is a tendency to "teach to the test," emphasizing narrowly focused drills rather than broader—and ultimately more useful—education. "Believing we can improve schooling with tests is like believing we can fatten cattle by weighing them," says Monty Neill of FairTest, a Cambridge, Mass., advocacy group.

Proponents of testing respond that while it may be unfair to deny graduation to a kid who has passed his or her courses, it's also unfair to let a student graduate who can't read or do math. "You've got to start sometime saying to kids that the tests of the real world are going to flunk you anyway," says E.D. Hirsch Jr., author of *Cultural Literacy*. "Tough love is the right kind of fairness. And you have to change the system with shock treatment at some point."

Paris High School principal Randy Wade agrees. Before he took over, the school had been branded "low performing" because of its TAAS scores. "With the low-performance rating, we knew our backs were against the wall," says Wade. He aligned the curriculum to the test and shortened classes by five minutes in order to create a 35-minute, daily TAAS tutorial. "We realized we can identify the individual needs of all learners and do a better job—that's what I like about TAAS," he says. Still, Wade laments the denial of graduation to hardworking students and believes "there ought to be another way" to earn some sort of diploma.

Perhaps one day there will be, but for Catherine Cockrell it may be too late.

International Differences in Mathematical Achievement: Their Nature, Causes, and Consequences

David C. Geary[1]

Department of Psychology, University of Missouri at Columbia, Columbia, Missouri

Every now and then, a spate of popular-press articles reminds us of the poor educational achievement of American children in comparison to their international peers. For many people, concerns about the education of American children likely fade, as these articles are bumped from our memory by a slew of hotter popular-press issues. In this article, the mathematical achievement of American children is first contrasted with that of their cohorts in other industrialized nations, and then sources of these cross-national achievement differences are briefly reviewed. The article closes with a discussion of the potential consequences of the poor mathematical development of American children, consequences that speak to the importance of the associated educational issues and remind us that our concern for the education of American children must continue unabated, even after the popular press has moved on to other issues.

NATURE

In 1964, the International Project for the Evaluation of Education-

al Achievement (IEA) conducted the first large-scale multinational study of mathematical achievement (Husén, 1967). The results of this study, which included 13- and 17-year-olds from 12 industrialized nations, were the first to systematically document the poor mathematical development of American adolescents relative to their international peers.[2] The overall performance of the American 13-year-olds ranked 11th, and their mean scores were below the international mean in every area assessed (i.e., arithmetic, algebra, and geometry). The American 17-year-olds fared worse. The overall mean performance of these largely college-bound seniors was considerably below the international mean (by about 1 standard deviation) and was considerably lower than the mean performance of adolescents from the 11th-ranked nation.[3] In other words, these American seniors not only ranked last overall, but about 4 out of 5 of them scored below the international average.

The second IEA study, conducted in the early 1980s, and more recent assessments have also yielded alarming results (Crosswhite, Dossey, Swafford, McKnight, & Cooney, 1985; Lapointe, Mead, & Askew, 1992). For instance, the second IEA study included a comparison of 17-year-olds enrolled in college-prep math courses (about 13% of American high school seniors) from 22 educational systems. The top 5% of

these elite American students had only average scores in relation to the international standard in algebra and in functions and calculus, and had slightly above average scores in geometry (M.D. Miller & Linn, 1989). This same comparison showed that within this relatively elite group, students who scored at the 95th percentile in the United States would score at about the 30th percentile in Japan and the 50th percentile in England. America's most elite students, the top 1%, consistently scored below the most elite students from most other nations. The gap was especially large for geometry. For instance, fewer than 1 out of 5 and only 1 out of 10 of America's most elite geometry students scored above the average college-prep Hungarian and Japanese student, respectively.

The research of Stevenson, his colleagues, and other investigators has also revealed important differences in the mathematical development of American children and children from East Asian nations, specifically, China, Korea, Japan, and Taiwan (Geary, Fan, & Bow-Thomas, 1992; Song & Ginsburg, 1987; Stevenson, Chen, & Lee, 1993). Differences in the mathematical achievement of American children and East Asian children are consistently found in first grade (sometimes in kindergarten), are evident for nearly every area of mathematical competence that is taught in school, and become greater with each successive year of schooling. Stevenson et al. (1993) found that the top 10% of American 5th and 11th graders had mathematics test scores that were at about the average of Japanese and Taiwanese children of the same age. Moreover, the gap might become even wider in the future, as the mathematical competencies of children from some East Asian nations (e.g., Taiwan) are improving from one generation to the next (Stevenson et al., 1993), while the competencies of American students are static or declining (Geary, Salthouse, Chen, & Fan, 1996).

The results of these studies are clear: American children do not measure up to international standards in mathematical achievement—and have not for many decades. The following sections present an overview of potential causes of the achievement gap between American children and their East Asian and European peers. The focus is primarily on American and East Asian children because the differences between them have been studied more systematically than have the differences between American and European children. Overall, the causes of the gap between American children and European children and between American children and East Asian children are likely similar in many respects (e.g., differences in mathematics curricula) but differ in others (e.g., language differences, described later).

CAUSES

In considering potential causes of cross-national differences in mathematical achievement, it is useful to distinguish between biologically primary and biologically secondary abilities (Geary, 1995). The former are natural abilities that have been shaped by evolutionary processes, whereas the latter are, in a sense, unnatural. Language is an example of a natural, or primary, ability that is found in one form or another throughout the world. Reading is an example of an unnatural, or secondary, ability because learning to read involves the use of language, and other primary systems, in unnatural ways.[4] Language and other pri-

mary abilities emerge largely in the context of children's natural activities, such as play. Reading and other secondary abilities emerge largely in unnatural contexts, primarily school. Moreover, the motivation to acquire primary abilities is likely to be inherent, whereas the motivation to acquire secondary abilities is more strongly influenced by cultural goals than by the inherent interests of children.

A distinction between primary and secondary mathematical domains has important implications for understanding potential biological as well as cultural influences on cross-national differences in mathematical achievement (Geary, 1995).[5] If the source of cross-national differences in mathematical development is largely biological, then these differences should be evident in primary domains and before the onset of formal schooling. If differences in mathematical achievement are largely the result of cultural influences, then these differences should be evident for secondary, but not primary, domains, and the source of the differences should stem largely from schooling and the cultural valuation of mathematical achievement.

Biology and Intelligence

Although the definitive study has yet to be conducted, it does not appear that East Asian and American children differ in primary mathematical abilities, suggesting that it is very unlikely that there is anything like an "Asian math gene" (Song & Ginsburg, 1987). In other words, except for the influence of language on the development of early counting skills (described next), East Asian children do not start school with an advantage over their American peers in fundamental mathematical competencies (K.F. Miller, Smith, Zhu, & Zhang, 1995).

Similarly, it does not appear that potential racial differences in the intelligence (IQ) of American and East Asian children can explain the achievement gap. Although Lynn (1982, 1983) estimated that there was about a 4-point difference in the mean IQs of Japanese and American children, Stevenson and his colleagues (1985) found no evidence for mean IQ differences across groups of Anglo-American, Japanese, and Chinese children. Thus, if the mean IQs of East Asian children are higher than those of Anglo-American children, the differences are likely to be rather small and not sufficient to explain the large cross-national differences in mathematical achievement. Of course, any racial differences in IQ cannot explain the mathematical achievement gap between Anglo-American children and children from most European countries.

Language

In East Asian languages, number words past 10 are translated as "ten one," "ten two," "ten three" (i.e., 11, 12, 13), . . ."two ten one," "two ten two," "two ten three" (i.e., 21, 22, 23), and so on. These number words mirror the underlying base-10 structure of the number system. In European languages, including English, there is no straightforward correspondence between number words from 11 to 100 and the underlying base-10 system. For most American children, "thirteen," for instance, represents a collection of 13 items, not one 10 and three 1s. For East Asian children, it is obvious that the corresponding number word "ten three," represents one 10 and three 1s.

Because of this difference in the structure of number words, East Asian children make fewer counting errors (past 10) and understand some counting, number, and basic arithmetic concepts, such as place value, at a younger age than both their American and their European peers (Miura, Okamoto, Kim, Steere, & Fayol, 1993; K.F. Miller et al., 1995). Nevertheless, the influence of the structure of number words on mathematical competencies is probably limited to certain counting and arithmetical abilities and is not sufficient to explain the more ubiquitous achievement gap between American and East Asian children, or the gap between American children and children from most European countries.

Schooling

Relative to international standards, the mathematics curricula in most American school districts is poorly organized and too easy. For instance, it has been found that many arithmetic topics that are introduced in the fifth or sixth grade in the United States are introduced in the second or third grade in Japan, China, the former Soviet Union, and Taiwan (e.g., Fuson, Stigler, & Bartsch, 1988). Even when the same topics are taught, the materials tend to be more conceptually advanced in many European and East Asian mathematics curricula than in the mathematics curricula in most U.S. school districts.

In comparison to American children, children in East Asian and most European nations do more mathematics homework and receive more mathematics instruction in school; they are on task more often during math lessons and have more math lessons during the school year (Lapointe et al., 1992; Stevenson et al., 1993; Stevenson & Stigler, 1992). The nature of math lessons differs as well (Perry, VanderStoep, & Yu, 1993; Stevenson & Stigler, 1992). For instance, East Asian children spend the majority (74% to 90%) of their math instruction time engaged in activities directed by the teacher, such as discussing a particular problem. American children, in contrast, spend about one half of their time doing seat work or other activities (e.g., socializing) that are not directed by the teacher. On average, mathematics teachers in East Asia tend to foster children's conceptual understanding of the material better than American teachers. For example, East Asian teachers are much more likely than American teachers to ask children to come up with as many different ways as possible to solve the same problem, a method that fosters the conceptual understanding of the problem (Geary, 1994).

Cultural Valuation

Except for the influence of the structure of number words on early counting skills, the first emergence of differences in mathematical achievement between East Asian and American children occurs with the onset of formal schooling and occurs largely for unnatural, or secondary, mathematical domains. This pattern strongly implicates schooling as the primary source of cross-national differences in mathematical achievement (see also Husén, 1967). Differences in the mathematical schooling of East Asian and American children, in turn, reflect deeper and more pervasive cultural differences in the valuation of mathematical achievement (Stevenson & Stigler, 1992). Hatano (1990) suggested that different nations not only develop and emphasize different national sports, they also develop different cognitive-educational emphases. Mathematics is an area of emphasis in East Asia, but is deemphasized in the United States. These cultural differences in the importance of mathematical competencies directly affect the in-school experiences of American and East Asian children. In China, for instance, elementary school mathematics teachers are specialists, teaching only mathematics, much as art teachers are specialists in the United States.

Another cultural factor that almost certainly influences mathematical achievement is the structuring of educational opportunities from one level of schooling to the next (e.g., primary to secondary). Relative to the United States, East Asian nations, and many European nations to a lesser extent, maintain a much stronger relationship between early educational accomplishments and later educational and employment opportunities. In many of these nations, excellent early academic achievement creates opportunities for advanced education (e.g., college) and subsequent improvements in standard of living through better employment. In contrast, America is the land of second chances, based on the belief that an individual's options for success should more or less always be available. There are certainly benefits to this cultural belief, but there are also costs. The most prominent of these costs is the ease with which achievement in primary and to a lesser extent secondary school can be deemphasized, without risking the opportunity to attend college.

When considered in terms of primary and secondary mathematical abilities, the importance of these cultural differences in the value of mathematics becomes clear: Cultural valuation of unnatural, or secondary, abilities is likely to be essential for high levels of development, given that most children, American, East Asian, and European, would prefer to do things other than learn secondary skills. American children are allowed to pursue their inherent interests much more than are East Asian and many European children, reflecting widely accepted cultural beliefs about the importance of "free choice." These cultural values, combined with the structure of educational opportunities, appear to influence children's exposure to mathematics in school and at home and, as a result, might be the ultimate source of differences in mathematical achievement between American children and children in most other industrialized nations.

CONSEQUENCES

The gap in mathematical achievement between American children and children from East Asian and most European nations highlights lost educational opportunities within this country. Consider the comments of a noted economist: "When the academic achievement of students completing their schooling declines substantially, then economic costs are large and last for generations" (Bishop, 1989, p. 194). For instance, the sharp decline in the literacy and numeracy of American high school graduates from 1967 to 1980 was estimated to cost the U.S. economy $86 billion in 1986. The estimated costs would be considerably higher if international standards were used to gauge the adequacy of academic achievement in the United States.

Even basic arithmetic skills, specifically, the ability to do computations (e.g., 34 + 69) and to use arithmetic to solve "real-world problems" (i.e., word problems), are important. These basic quantitative skills have been found to influence employability, wages, and productivity in the United States as well as in other nations, above and beyond the influence of liter-

acy, years of schooling, and intelligence (e.g., Rivera-Batiz, 1992). Thus, although the national differences summarized in this article might raise concerns about this country's ability to adequately educate enough individuals adequately for entry into math intensive careers (e.g., engineering), perhaps the real concern should be for the rest of us and our children.

SUMMARY AND CONCLUSION

Thirty years of comparative assessments indicate that American children are consistently among the most poorly educated mathematics students in the industrialized world. The differences in the mathematical achievement of American children and their European and East Asian cohorts are evident as early as first grade, widen with successive years of schooling, and are substantial in magnitude. The finding that East Asian and American children do not differ in more primary, or natural, mathematical abilities indicates that East Asian children do not begin school with an advantage over their American peers and that it is very unlikely that the source of the mathematical achievement gap is primarily biological in origin. In fact, except for the influence of number words on certain counting and arithmetic skills, these differences emerge with the onset of formal schooling and are found largely for secondary mathematical domains, those domains most strongly influenced by schooling (Geary, 1995).

Indeed, important differences in the quantity and quality of the mathematics education of American children relative to East Asian and European children point to schooling as the primary source

of cross-national differences in mathematical achievement. These schooling differences, in turn, reflect more pervasive cultural differences in the valuation of mathematical achievement and the relative importance of primary and secondary schooling for later educational and thus employment opportunities. The poor mathematical competence of American children is cause for serious national and, for those of us with children in the public schools, personal concern, as this poor competence bodes long-term social and economic consequences for the United States.

Acknowledgments—Preparation of this article was supported by Grant 1R01-HD27931 from the National Institute of Child Health and Human Development.

Notes

1. Address correspondence to David C. Geary, Department of Psychology, 210 McAlester Hall, University of Missouri at Columbia, Columbia, MO 65211; e-mail: psycorie @mizzou1.missouri.edu.

2. The participating nations were Australia, Belgium, England, Finland, France, Germany, Holland, Israel, Japan, Scotland, Sweden, and the United States.

3. Adolescents from Belgium, Germany, Israel, and Japan consistently scored above the international mean in nearly all mathematical areas.

4. For example, the phonological (i.e., language sound) system that supports language was not designed for reading, but with instruction can be used for this purpose (specifically, for sounding out words).

5. Primary mathematical abilities include, among others, the ability to distinguish sets of small numbers of items without counting (e.g., sets of three vs. four objects), an understanding that adding increases quantity and subtraction decreases quantity (again, for small numbers), and some basic counting skills. Much of mathematics, however, is biologically secondary. Secondary mathematical abilities in-

clude, among others, learning number names (e.g., "one," "two," "three"), complex arithmetic (e.g., 34 + 46 = ?), and most features of more complex mathematical domains (e.g., algebra).

References

Bishop, J.H. (1989). Is the test score decline responsible for the productivity growth decline? *American Economic Review, 79,* 178–197.

Crosswhite, F.J., Dossey, J.A., Swafford, J.O., McKnight, C.C., & Cooney, T.J. (1985). *Second International Mathematics Study summary report for the United States.* Champaign, IL: Stipes.

Fuson, K.C., Stigler, J.W., & Bartsch, K. (1988). Grade placement of addition and subtraction topics in Japan, Mainland China, the Soviet Union, Taiwan, and the United States. *Journal for Research in Mathematics Education, 19,* 449–456.

Geary, D.C. (1994). *Children's mathematical development: Research and practical applications.* Washington, DC: American Psychological Association.

Geary, D.C. (1995). Reflections of evolution and culture in children's cognition: Implications for mathematical development and instruction. *American Psychologist, 50,* 24–37.

Geary, D.C., Fan, L., & Bow-Thomas, C.C. (1992). Numerical cognition: Loci of ability differences comparing children from China and the United States. *Psychological Science, 3,* 180–185.

Geary, D.C., Salthouse, T.A., Chen, G.-P., & Fan, L. (1996). Are East Asian versus American differences in arithmetical ability a recent phenomenon? *Developmental Psychology, 32,* 254–262.

Hatano, G. (1990). Toward the cultural psychology of mathematical cognition. Commentary on Stevenson, H.W., Lee, S.-Y., Chen, C., Stigler, J.W., Hsu, C.C., & Kitamura, S. Context of achievement: A study of American, Chinese, and Japanese children. *Monographs of the Society for Research in Child Development, 55*(1–2, Serial No. 221).

Husén, T. (1967). *International study of achievement in mathematics: A comparison of twelve countries* (Vols. 1 and 2). New York: Wiley.

Lapointe, A.E., Mead, N.A., & Askew, J.M. (1992). *Learning mathematics.* Princeton, NJ: Educational Testing Service.

Lynn, R. (1982). IQ in Japan and the United States shows a growing disparity. *Nature, 297,* 222–223.

Lynn, R. (1983). Reply to Stevenson and Azuma. *Nature, 306,* 292.

Miller, K.F., Smith, C.M., Zhu, J., & Zhang, H. (1995). Preschool origins of cross-national differences in mathematical competence: The role of number-naming systems. *Psychological Science, 6,* 56–60.

Miller, M.D., & Linn, R.L. (1989). Cross-national achievement with differential retention rates. *Journal for Research in Mathematics Education, 20,* 28–40.

Miura, I.T., Okamoto, Y., Kim, C.C., Steere, M., & Fayol, M. (1993). First graders' cognitive representation of number and understanding of place value: Cross-national comparisons—France, Japan, Korea, Sweden, and the United States. *Journal of Educational Psychology, 85,* 24–30.

Perry, M., VanderStoep, S.W., & Yu, S.L. (1993). Asking questions in first-grade mathematics classes: Potential influences on mathematical thought. *Journal of Educational Psychology, 85,* 31–40.

Rivera-Batiz, F.L. (1992). Quantitative literacy and the likelihood of employment among young adults in the United States. *Journal of Human Resources, 27,* 313–328.

Song, M.J., & Ginsburg, H.P. (1987). The development of informal and formal mathematical thinking in Korean and U.S. children. *Child Development, 58,* 1286–1296.

Stevenson, H.W., Chen, C., & Lee, S.Y. (1993). Mathematics achievement of Chinese, Japanese, and American children: Ten years later. *Science, 259,* 53–58.

Stevenson, H.W., & Stigler, J.W. (1992). *The learning gap: Why our schools are failing and what we can learn from Japanese and Chinese education.* New York: Summit Books.

Stevenson, H.W., Stigler, J.W., Lee, S.Y., Lucker, G.W., Kitamura, S., & Hsu, C.C. (1985). Cognitive performance and academic achievement of Japanese, Chinese, and American children. *Child Development, 56,* 718–734.

Gender Gap in Math Scores Is Closing

Girls still avoid math in school, but new research challenges the notion that they have less mathematical ability than boys.

Bridget Murray

Monitor staff

Boys have historically outscored girls on the mathematical sections of national achievement tests, fueling the age-old debate about whether socialization or biology accounts for the performance difference.

But, except at the highest levels of analytical thinking, the gender gap in mathematical performance is narrowing, according to psychologists and testing experts.

Thirteen-year-old girls have practically caught up to boys in their adeptness at intermediate math involving moderately complex procedures and reasoning, such as geometry and simple algebra, according to a recent report from the Educational Testing Service, the nation's largest private educational measurement institution.

In 1992, 59 percent of girls vs. 60 percent of boys had reached that intermediate level, compared with 48 percent of girls vs. 55 percent of boys in 1973.

During the same period, 9-year-old boys and girls exhibited equal ability to solve basic problems.

But at age 17, boys remained ahead of girls in their ability to solve complex algebraic and precalculus problems. Roughly 10 percent of boys reach the most complex level compared with 5 percent of girls.

The findings derive from testing by the government-based National As-

sessment of Educational Progress, also known as America's Report Card, which has tracked trends in students' academic achievement for the National Center for Education Statistics since 1973.

> "GIRLS ARE DOING BETTER AT MATH [THAN BEFORE], BUT BOYS ARE STILL AIMING HIGHER BECAUSE MORE OF THEM WANT TO MAKE A CAREER OF IT. AS A RESULT, WE'RE STILL SEEING A CAREER GAP FOR MEN AND WOMEN."
> INA MULLIS, PHD
> BOSTON COLLEGE

"Girls are doing better at math [than before], but boys are still aiming higher because more of them want to make a career of it," said Ina Mullis, PhD, an education professor at Boston College and a co-author of the ETS report. "As a result, we're

still seeing a career gap for men and women."

A 1990 meta-analysis of gender differences in math performance backs the Report Card findings. Psychologist Janet Hyde, PhD, and math education professor Elizabeth Fennema, PhD, of the University of Wisconsin–Madison, examined 100 studies covering national achievement testing of 3 million people and found that males barely outperformed females at math.

A similar meta-analysis released this year by Larry Hedges, PhD, and his student Amy Nowell, of the University of Chicago, also showed boys with an unremarkable mathematical edge on girls.

Moreover, Hyde's analysis suggests that at all ages and levels, girls and boys showed similar understanding of math concepts, and that girls actually surpass boys in computation before high school. But in high school, boys show more skill at solving complex problems.

"Some people think boys are better at math at all levels," Hyde said. "We found no evidence of that. It's not until high school that boys pull ahead."

In debating reasons for the disparity at the top, psychologists and educators have offered myriad nature-vs.-nurture explanations.

Is It Variability?

Some psychologists propose a score-variability hypothesis. They contend that a greater disparity in math ability among boys compared with girls explains boys' higher scores on complex problems.

They note that more boys score higher as well as lower in math than girls and that there are more male geniuses *and* more males with developmental disabilities in the general population.

More boys than girls consistently show up in the Iowa State precocious youth study, which selects 13- to 15-year-olds with high math SAT scores.

Also, Hedges and Nowell found more male variance in their meta-analysis of six large data sets collected from tests of adolescents' cognitive abilities.

Males generally scored higher than females in all areas except reading comprehension, perceptual speed and associative memory. More males scored lower than females, as well. For instance, on the analytic reasoning section of one national test, almost twice as many males as females were in the bottom 10 percent.

...Or Biology?

Psychologist Doreen Kimura, PhD, at the University of Western Ontario, attributes much of the difference to biology. Men are, on average better at math reasoning, she argues.

Her research suggests a hormonal contribution to math ability, she says. Her 1991 study on 88 college students, for example, suggests that women with high testosterone levels and men with low testosterone levels have higher spatial and mathematical ability than low testosterone women and high testosterone men. She has also found differences in the way men and women think. In a 1993 study of nearly 100 undergraduates' map-route learning, for example, men took more direct routes and made

fewer errors, while women relied more on landmarks and made more errors.

Brainwaves, rather than hormones, could cause men to dominate the higher end of the math spectrum, some speculate. Based on her findings in an ongoing study of mathematically precocious youth, Iowa State University psychologist Camilla Benbow, PhD, suggests that highly intelligent boys and girls differ in the way their brains approach spatial activities.

In the study of 40 youth, researchers asked boys and girls to perform a specified spatial task—judging such facial expressions as happy, sad, angry or perplexed. The researchers found that boys had higher activity in the right hemisphere of their brains than girls. The study results are now in press.

But Hyde discounts both biological and variability hypotheses faulting the biological explanations for being unreplicable, and the variability hypothesis for being purely descriptive and failing to describe the causes of the variability. In keeping with Hyde's meta-analysis, Benbow notes an important distinction between math performance and reasoning: Girls usually *perform* better than boys, often earning higher grades, while boys *reason* better than girls at the highest mathematical levels. Nature and nurture work together to produce this pattern.

"We need to work on nurturing girls' reasoning skills," said Benbow, noting that girls in high school select fewer math course than boys.

...Or Course Choice?

The real issue is gender differences in course choice, not math ability, said Hyde. Girls opt out of tougher high-school math courses, which explains their lower scores on standardized tests, she believes.

While Benbow links girls' math avoidance with a dislike for math, Hyde and other psychologists view gender conditioning by parents, teachers and society as the real culprit.

"Girls hear a message that math won't be as valuable for their futures as boys' and they have lower expectations for success than boys," said Hyde.

Psychologist Jacquelynne Eccles, PhD, has seen strong parental influences as she's tracked students from more than 2,000 families in southeastern Michigan schools. In a 1990 finding, she noted that parents' gender stereotyping influenced kids' own self-perceptions. This in turn influenced students' course selection. By high school, more boys participated in sports, and made honors in math and physics than girls. Some of this sex-typing was even evident by the second and third grades.

Girls are also more likely than boys to view themselves as unskilled at math and, as a result, avoid it, said Eccles, who is based at the University of Michigan Institute for Social Research. Because girls place a low value on math, they avoid optional math courses in high school, she asserted.

Gender stereotypes lead more girls to view English and other verbal courses as more important than math and science courses for their future careers. Schools can help change those preconceived notions, pointing out that even careers in the social sciences require solid math knowledge, Hyde said.

"Schools need to give girls a broader view of the careers they can choose," she said. "Once girls avoid high school math, they close themselves out of fields like engineering and other fields they didn't realize involve math, and it's a shame."

Identity and Socioemotional Development

Each age period is associated with developmental tasks. A major aspect of psychosocial development for adolescents is the formation of a coherent personal identity. Erik Erikson referred to this as the adolescent identity crisis. Identity formation is a normative event, but it represents a turning point in development that will have consequences for later psychosocial tasks.

Children's identities often represent an identification with parents and significant others. Adolescents reflect on their identity and come to some sense of who they are and who they are not. Identity formation involves an examination of personal likes and dislikes, political, religious, and moral values, occupational interests, and gender roles and sexual behaviors. Adolescents must also form an integrated sense of their own personality across the various roles they engage in (e.g., son or daughter, student, boyfriend or girlfriend, part-time worker).

To aid in the identity formation process, Erikson advocated that adolescents be given license to explore alternative roles and values. He believed that such a moratorium period would allow adolescents to make commitments that reflect true personal choices. James Marcia elaborated on Erikson's ideas about identity formation. He described four identity statuses that depend on the degree of exploration an adolescent has engaged in and whether the adolescent has made choices or commitments to certain paths. Adolescents who are actively searching and evaluating options are said to be in moratorium, as Erikson described. An identity-achieved status is expected to follow this moratorium period eventually. Other adolescents adopt values and life roles without experiencing a period of questioning. These adolescents are called identity-foreclosed as they essentially conform to parental expectations for themselves. Conformity to parents is not automatically a sign of identity foreclosure, however. Identity-achieved individuals often make choices that fit parental values and expectations, but they do so after reflection. As a result, they are more invested in their choices and more self-confident. Finally, Marcia describes some adolescents as identity-diffused. These adolescents have not undergone a period of questioning and exploration, nor have they made clear ideological, occupational, or personal commitments. Identity-diffusion is expected for early adolescents, but it is seen as developmentally immature in college-age adolescents.

Formulating his ideas in the 1950s, Erikson proposed some differences in male and female identity development. Females were presumed to delay full identity development until the formation of an intimate relationship (that is, marriage). Interpersonal issues were seen as more paramount in female identity development with the occupational domain being more relevant to male identity development. Recent research indicates that there are fewer gender differences in identity development than may have been true of earlier generations. Carol Gilligan maintains that moral decision making is another area of gender differences. She argues that females' moral values and moral judgments reflect more concern for interpersonal relationships and caring. Males are said to have more of a legalistic outlook that is less compassionate and more focused on the abstract application of rules. Gilligan's ideas have not been well tested to date.

An area that has received recent attention is how identity development may differ for minority individuals. In addition to exploring ideological, occupational, sexual, and interpersonal commitments, ethnicity is a salient component that must be integrated into the person's identity. An adolescent may or may not identify with an ethnic group and may either value or reject their ethnicity. Jean Phinney has articulated several phases characteristic of ethnic identity development. The stages parallel Marcia's identity statuses. Similar to identity foreclosure, some minority adolescents simply adopt the values of the dominant culture and have an unexamined ethnic identity. Others are in moratorium and are wrestling with conflicts between the values of the dominant culture and their own culture. Finally, adolescents with an achieved ethnic identity feel an emotional attachment to their ethnic group and have come to some resolution integrating ethnic group values with the dominant culture's values.

Whether male or female, minority or majority, identity issues have implications for the adolescent's emotional health, self-concept, and self-esteem. Adolescents' self-concepts become more differentiated and abstract as they think of themselves in terms of personality traits. They compare themselves to others in order to evaluate their own characteristics and abilities. They often construct an ideal self that is difficult to live up to. The abstract nature of their self-concept also means that self-evaluation is more removed from concrete, observable behaviors and is, therefore, more subject to distortion. Adolescents who are struggling with identity issues are also likely to undergo fluctuations in their self-concept as they explore alternative roles, values, and personalities.

Self-esteem reflects how good one feels about the self. The essential question is: Am I okay? Self-esteem is at a low point in early adolescence relative to other age periods. More dimensions contribute to adolescent self-esteem than is the case for children. Global self-esteem measures are often less informative as adolescents' self-esteem varies in different domains (e.g., physical attractiveness, peer acceptance, academic competence, athletic competence). Research by Susan Harter and her colleagues indicates that feeling good about one's physical appearance is the number one predictor of overall self-esteem for adolescents. Pubertal changes heighten concerns about body image and appearance. Females are even more concerned about their looks and are much more likely to have a negative body image than males are. Contrary to most expectations, recent studies show that self-esteem in African Americans is comparable to that of Caucasian Americans. Little work on self-esteem has been done in other minority populations.

The articles in this unit elaborate on the concepts discussed in this overview. Readings relate to identity formation, ethnic identity, moral values, self-esteem, and emotional functioning.

Looking Ahead: Challenge Questions

What is your portrait of a "normal" adolescent? What about an "abnormal" adolescent? When you were a teenager, did you worry about whether you were "normal"?

How should parents handle adolescents' identity exploration?

Why is ethnic identity important? Can fostering ethnic identity help reduce risk-taking behavior? Why? How are identity and social development compounded for adolescents from multiracial backgrounds?

How is self-esteem affected at adolescence? Do you think girls have lower self-esteem than boys? Why or why not? How can self-concepts be improved?

How can we encourage prosocial values?

Should we worry more about a child's emotional intelligence and less about academic intelligence? Defend your answer.

THERE'S A FIRST TIME FOR EVERYTHING: UNDERSTANDING ADOLESCENCE

ABSTRACT

Adolescence has been regarded as a stormy, emotionally turbulent time by many. Some have blamed physiological factors; others have pointed to peer pressure and intimacy. This paper examines the phenomenon of the "first time"—the teenager's first date, first job, first sexual experience. Since these "firsts" are embued with an inordinate amount of emotional investment, they offer an alternative understanding for the "storm and stress"—the emotional underpinnings of adolescence.

Janna Siegel and Michael F. Shaughnessy

Much has been written about the phenomenon of adolescence. Erikson developed the idea of the "identity crisis" (1963); Kohlberg (1971) discussed moral development, and Sullivan (1953) examined the place of the "chum" and peer relations in adolescence.

Marcia (1966, 1980) contributed the idea of identity diffusion, moratorium, identity achieved, and other major constructs relative to the adolescent years. Elkind's construct of the personal fable does much to explain the behavior of teenagers. Piaget also discussed the cognitive changes in adolescence, the rise of formal operations, and hypothesis testing. However these theorists have only partially explained the pervasive emotional elements of adolescence.

Adolescence is a time of one's first kiss, first dance, first job, first date, first crush, and first "love." Childhood had been a period of "make believe" with much adult supervision. In adolescence, the teenager is confronted with "the real thing" for the first time.

A common thread that runs throughout these theories is the idea of a new awakening, or a fresh perspective. The "first time" is a crucial time for an adolescent—be it a first handholding, or a first sexual encounter—it is heavily weighted with a flood of feelings never before encountered by the adolescent who may not be emotionally prepared for that first encounter. It is suggested here that the glory and trauma of adolescence is due to the intensity of these events.

Reprint requests to Michael Shaughnessy, Associate Professor, Department of Psychology Station 25, Eastern New Mexico University, Portales, New Mexico 88130.

This is not to say that children under the age of 12 do not have feelings or dreams, but that the cognitive and emotional awareness that accompanies adolescence compounds the effects. The teenager begins to develop a new perspective on interpersonal relationships.

Friendships

An example would be friendships. During this period, peers become of critical importance. Adolescents believe that their friendships will last forever. But as they grow into adulthood, they find that "wedding bells are breaking up that old gang of mine" and that their peer group is leaving for different places including colleges. Sullivan (1953) wrote about the importance of a "chum." The chum is an integral part of adolescence and also lays a foundation for later adult relationships. Berndt (1982, 1986) investigated the phenomenon of friendship during adolescence and the role it plays in the transition to adulthood. The "best friend" becomes critical for many adolescents as the parents' role as confidante diminishes. Peers become the new support system.

Adolescent Views of Time

Prior to adolescence, children do not look extensively toward the future. Usually, they are self- and ego-centered in the present. As adolescents they can perceive a future, but the future they perceive may be identical to the present. How they feel today is how they think they will feel tomorrow. If they are in love, they will be in love forever; their friends will be friends for a lifetime; if their heart is broken, this is how they will always feel. They may not completely understand that their intense passion or pain will pass with time and they may not have developed the skills for coping with the trauma, for example, of a lost love.

One explanation is that for many adolescents it is the first time for these intense feeling[s]. Thus, they cannot understand that others may feel the same way, or that one day they may feel differently.

They are convinced that no one has ever loved as they have, or been hurt as deeply, or felt the same exhilaration or depth of anxiety. There is a desperation to adolescent "first times"—a desperation to engage in the behaviors other adolescents are enjoying. They emulate their peer group in an attempt to be part of it. They are jealous of what other adolescents have—be it a car, a job, girl/boy-friend.

This desperation may also reflect earlier deprivation. If teenagers have not received much love from their parents or have come from a single-parent home, or have not been able to form relationships, there is an inordinate sense of loss.

Adolescents want to submerge themselves in a relationship, which may be why many of them spend so much time on the phone or with their boy/girlfriends. They involve themselves with their peer group because they may, for the first time, receive acceptance from others who "understand them."

Not having experienced these feelings before, they have no evidence that anyone else has ever felt this way, or that they will ever feel any differently.

The ability to understand the euphoria experienced by a teenager in love is difficult for adults, and this makes counseling adolescents so problematic. Each adolescent has his or her own "personal fable" (Elkind, 1974). An adult perspective is much more long range and global for several reasons. Adults realize that deep emotional pain is temporary—that love, for example is not always a lifetime emotion. Adults know that things sometimes get better, and sometimes worse. Mature adults realize that things do change with time.

Impulsiveness

Suicide, risk-taking behaviors and the personal fable of Elkind (1974) are often associated with adolescence—a time of "present orientation." The personal fable and perhaps even more importantly, the "invincibility fable" lead teenagers to act with no thought of the consequences. Students who begin to smoke, do drugs or drive recklessly may be fueled by this phenomenon, and if they receive support from their peer group who validate the experiences. For the first time, adults become less important.

In particular, the reaching out for love is magnified in adolescence, as exemplified in this excerpt from a teenager's diary:

Please don't turn me away
Please don't leave me crying
Loving you without your love

Can't you see I'm dying?!
Good bye my friend if you need help
For me you can always send
Unless it's for a broken heart
I've got my own to mend.

The powerful need for love is one reason adolescents become engaged in premarital sex resulting in pregnancy. Shaughnessy and Shakesby (1992) discussed some of the inherent problems when adolescents try to be emotionally intimate when they do not have the requisite skills. Thus, they rely on physical intimacy.

Further, teenagers are often concerned about being "crazy" as they are bombarded with incomprehensible and powerful feelings. Some of these feelings lead to suicidal ideation, attempts, and actual suicide (Shaughnessy & Shakesby, 1986). Again, an excerpt from a diary exemplifies this phenomenon:

I'm crazy
I need help.
But I am selfish if I ask for it;
And selfish if I don't.
I'm not a very good friend;
I'm not a very good anything
Unfortunately I'm just me.

The following is from another adolescent's diary.

So I'm almost 16—
It seems so old and yet still young
I don't want to get old
because when I am, I want to have had a better child-
    hood.

The adolescent can be overly sensitive to the peer group. Again a diary excerpt exemplifies the degree of sensitivity:

I'm too sensitive
And now I know why.
It is because I believe all the bad things that people
    say to me or kid around with.
But why should I believe them when I know they
    don't mean it?
Because, I feel that I am as horrible as they say, and
I wish I wasn't me.
But I will have to make the best of it and learn to be
    happy with
what I am, since I'll never have a chance to be some-
    one else.

Although using adolescent diary entries is not the most scientific approach to the study of adolescence, diaries do portray the turmoil, stress, and confusion of this period of life. In spite of the fact that not all teenagers are confronted with the same degree of anguish, there is a common theme and pattern to many adolescent concerns.

SUMMARY AND CONCLUSIONS

In studying adolescence, we must bear in mind that for many teenagers, this is a period of "firsts"—and for many of these first experiences, they may not be prepared. But by understanding the amount of emotional energy they invest in jobs, cars, dating and other concerns, we can better comprehend this transitional period. Although this "first time paradigm" obviously needs further study, this paper has reviewed a few salient domains of these first experiences.

REFERENCES

Berndt, T. J. (1982). The features and effects of friendships in early adolescence. *Child Development, 53,* 1447–1460.

Berndt, T. J. (1986). Children's comments about their friendships. In M. Perlmutter (Ed.), *Cognitive perspectives on children's social and behavioral development. Minnesota Symposium on Child Psychology,* Vol. 18). Hillside, NJ: Erlbaum.

Elkind, D. (1940). *Children and adolescents: Interpretive essays on Jean Piaget.* New York: Oxford University Press.

Erikson, E. (1963). *Childhood in society.* New York: Norton.

Kohlberg, L. (1981). Identity in adolescence. In J. Adelson (Ed.), *Handbook of adolescent psychology.* New York: Wiley.

Shaughnessy, M F., & Nystul, M. S. (1985). Preventing the greatest loss—suicide. *Creative Child Quarterly, 10*(3), 164–170.

Shaughnessy, M. F., & Shakesby, P. (1992). Adolescent sexual and emotional intimacy. *Adolescence, 27*(106), 475–480.

Sullivan, H. S. (1953). *The interpersonal theory of psychiatry.* New York: Norton.

College Kids' Parents Should "Keep Cool"

What should parents do if their son comes home from college wearing an earring and quoting Marx? What if your freshman daughter says she wants to switch religions and move to Bolivia? The best advice is to avoid overreacting to the various new ideas and behaviors. "The more vehemently parents react, the more likely their children will become locked into a position in order to demonstrate their independence," cautions Barbara Newman, professor of family relations and human development, and Philip Newman, adjunct professor of human ecology and senior researcher, Ohio State University. The husband-and-wife team are co-authors of *When Kids Go to College: A Parent's Guide to Changing Relationships.*

"Parents should adopt a stance of interested neutrality when their [offspring] bring back unusual plans or ideas. Parents should ask their children where they are learning these ideas, what they think about them. They should try to get their children to think about the issues themselves, to evaluate what it means to them."

The Newmans stress that the college years are a critical time for adolescents to develop their own unique identity. That process involves exploring new roles, values, and ways of thinking. It's important for mothers and fathers to realize that this experimentation is not the same as a lifelong commitment. College students may experiment by changing political parties, switching majors several times, or by seemingly rejecting lifelong values and beliefs. More than likely, many of these will be temporary.

"Adults who have made 25 or 30 years of commitments find it difficult and frightening to see their children experimenting with new ways of thinking. They're understandably afraid that their children will jump into something too quickly or make mistakes they can't change." They should consider college students' search for identity to be somewhat similar to that of preschoolers. Youngsters may pretend to be a fireman, astronaut, or mother, but that doesn't mean that that's how they are going to end up. In some ways, college students have the same attitude when they explore and experiment with roles. Unlike youngsters who usually will admit they are only pretending, however, college students may play out roles as if they were for real.

Parents should feel reassured that, if they have a basically good relationship with their offspring and keep the lines of communication open, their college-age children will end up all right. "Their basic personality isn't going to change. A child who works hard and is loyal to his or her family will continue to be that way. So when you see behavior that is unusual, you just have to learn to let it go."

Although experimentation and role-playing are important for college students, the Newmans maintain it can go too far. Some students experience intense anxiety and confusion about making long-term commitments. As soon as they get close to making a serious decision about their lives, they back away or change their minds. These youths may benefit from counseling. Parents often are the best judge of when their children may need outside help.

For most families, things will turn out well in spite of the inevitable problems. "In a healthy family, there will be a revision of the relationship between children and their parents when the children are off at college. There may be some conflict. But when you keep the dialogue going, it usually comes out positive."

From *USA Today Magazine*, January 1993, p. 5. © 1993 by the Society for the Advancement of Education. Reprinted by permission.

Ethnicity, Identity Formation, and Risk Behavior Among Adolescents of Mexican Descent

Arik V. Marcell

Arik V. Marcell is an MD/Masters in Public Health degree candidate at The University of Illinois College of Medicine, Chicago, and Johns Hopkins University School of Hygiene and Public Health, Baltimore.

PERSONS of Mexican descent, the largest Hispanic group, make up 50 to 63 percent of the U.S. Hispanic population, which, in turn, comprises about 9 percent of the U.S. population and is one of the fastest growing U.S. ethnic minorities. Mexican Americans are at greater risk of mortality and morbidity than the general U.S. population. However, only a few studies have assessed the health of adolescents of Mexican descent.

High levels of problem behavior, such as alcohol use, unsafe sexual behavior, school dropout, and delinquency, have been cited for youth of Mexican descent. Understanding the factors contributing to risk behavior in adolescents of Mexican descent may help improve health care service delivery and use. Various factors influence the involvement of adolescents of Mexican descent in problem behaviors:

Socioeconomic factors. Hispanic adolescents are more likely to fall below poverty level than white adolescents. A higher proportion of Hispanic adolescents are uninsured as compared to white adolescents. Access to care by Mexican American populations is limited due to unfamiliarity with available services, lack of regular health care providers, type of health care facility used, and proximity of facility to residence. Consequently, Mexican Americans are more likely to use public health facilities, hospital outpatient clinics, and emergency rooms than to establish continuity with one primary care physician.

Family factors. Mexican American cultural values traditionally place great importance on family relations and bonds. In the United States, as cultural awareness declines with successive generations, familism may suffer, leading to problems for adolescents in these families. Mexican American adolescents living in single-parent, female-headed households have higher rates of drinking, drug use, overall risk-taking behavior, and earlier sexual activity onset, than adolescents living with both parents. These observations demonstrate that family members engage in risk behavior in the absence of the nuclear family structure in the U.S. It has been argued, however, that quality of the parenting relationship is more significant in predicting social deviance, substance use, and dropping out than the family's composition. Poor parent-child relationships; insufficient bonding, communication, and guidance; and too authoritative or permissive parents may better predict problem behavior than does family structure.

Community factors. The degree to which an ethnic community is organized with religious institutions, welfare organizations, and ethnic businesses determines its ability to foster ethnic identification and preserve ethnic culture among its members. A community lacking cohesiveness and sense of kinship may decrease self-esteem development among its youth, leading to poor impulse control, less developed sense of right and wrong, and greater risk-taking behavior. Living in high-risk urban settings, where most youth of Mexican descent live, may further expose them to acute problem behavior.

School factors. School environment and quality as well as school teachers' attitudes and classroom practices also may lead to school failure and dropout. Dropout rates are higher among students attending segregated schools, public vocational schools, schools with low teacher-to-pupil ratios, large schools with large classes, and in schools which emphasize tracking and testing. Students of Mexican descent living in urban centers attend schools characterized by these factors and hence may be at risk for dropping out.

Problem behavior in minority adolescents appears inversely related to identity formation and ethnic identification and directly related to acculturation.

From *The Education Digest,* April 1995, pp. 58-62. Condensed from *Journal of School Health,* October 1994, pp. 323-327.
Reprinted by permission of Prakken Publications, Inc., Ann Arbor, MI 48107.

Identity formation. Ethnic identity—a component of a more general process of identity formation which occurs during adolescence—is the commitment made to a social grouping of common ancestry characterized by the sharing of common values, behavioral patterns, or symbols different from the larger society's.

For Mexican American immigrant adolescents, carrying out developmental tasks in the context of a new culture—and also in the presence of language barriers, social constraints as members of a devalued minority group, and social class differences—can greatly influence identity formation. Many decisions immigrant adolescents choose to make regarding their sexuality, independence, and future may be distinct from their parents' choices and at odds with their background values. An achieved ethnic identity, leading to increased self-esteem, results from exploration and resolution of these issues, whereas a foreclosed ethnic identity, leading to low self-esteem, poor mental health outcomes, poor educational performance, and alienation, results from failure to do so.

Cultural retention/acculturation. Retention of ethnic culture among immigrants varies due to length of time in the host society, opportunity to practice the culture, degree of cultural incorporation (taking on elements of the mainstream culture), and degree of structural incorporation (acceptance into host society institutions). In addition, ethnic cultural retention depends on one's degree of ethnic identification (ethnic loyalty), acculturation (acceptance of new cultural traits at the loss of old), and social assimilation (integration of an ethnic minority group into mainstream society).

Rate and degree of Mexican American acculturation depend on generational status. First-generation immigrants encounter more difficulties than second- and third-generation counterparts. Age at immigration also is important: the younger the person, the easier to acquire elements of the mainstream culture. As Hispanics become more acculturated, their health status worsens, tobacco and alcohol use increases, diet worsens, risk-taking behavior increases, and morbid-ity and mortality for certain diseases increase.

Whereas acculturation, a prerequisite for assimilation, is strongly linked to generational status, it has been argued that ethnic identification with people of Mexican descent is not. One study shows cultural awareness declining significantly in the study population between the first and second generations and continuing to decline through the fourth generation, whereas ethnic loyalty decreases only slightly between the first and second generations and in fact remained virtually constant through the fourth generation. The authors also suggest that social assimilation, a third related process, contributes to ethnic culture change. This study can help in understanding how Mexican Americans adjust to mainstream society and how ethnicity and culture change affect adolescents of Mexican descent as well as their community.

Ethnic identity. Understanding how Mexican youth identify themselves provides insight into the interaction among ethnic identity, cultural awareness, and risk behavior. A study performed in a California high school examines the interrelatedness of ethnicity and ethnic identity, minority status, and perceptions of adult opportunities in Mexican-descent students.

The students separate themselves into five groups depending on degree of ethnic identification and cultural awareness. Individually perceived ethnic identity has strong implications for success in school, risk of dropping out, and possible involvement in risk-taking behavior.

Recent Mexican immigrant students have limited English proficiency and claim closer ties with Mexico than any other group. *Mexican-oriented students*, maintaining strong bicultural ties with both Mexico and the United States, are bilingual speakers with varying degrees of English proficiency who perform well in school and have lived in the U.S. more than five years. *Mexican American students*, born in the U.S. and proficient in English (speaking little Spanish), describe themselves as totally assimilated and are the most successful of the Mexican-descent student population. *Chicanos* (U.S. native-born students), representing the majority of the student population, alienate themselves from school activities and favor behavior that promotes failure in school (frequent absence, disruptive activities, noncompliance with classroom assignments). Finally, *Cholos* (low riders or rebellious students) are identified by some of the other groups as "students who had lost their Mexican roots" and as most likely to be gang members or "gang sympathizers."

Membership in the Chicano or Cholo group is identified as derogatory by the other three groups, but not by Chicanos or Cholos themselves. However, identification with Chicanos or Cholos does have negative consequences, since school achievement is defined as antithetical to ethnic solidarity. The fact that most in the Chicano or Cholo groups share the same beliefs predisposes them to dropping out and thereby engaging in risk-taking activities. Recent Mexican immigrant students also could be at risk for dropping out secondary to "negative" influences from Chicano and Cholo youth and due to low English proficiency.

These observations do not imply that successful students do not engage in high-risk behavior. Comprehending ethnic identity formation for adolescents of Mexican descent can only help to identify characteristics which most likely predispose to risky activities. Correspondingly, not all school settings will resemble the California high school referred to here. However, similar subgroupings based on degree of ethnic identification and acculturation may exist in different geographic locations and may apply to other ethnic populations as well.

The following are some recommendations for programs:

1. Promote ethnic identity and appropriate level of prevention.
■ Recognize the heterogeneity among Hispanic and Mexican-origin adolescent populations in health care delivery settings.
■ Identify Mexican American adolescents' degree of ethnic identification and acculturation in health care delivery settings.
■ Develop better ways to identify this population's health needs, how it defines its needs regarding problem

behavior, and how it perceives and identifies risk.

■ Learn about the medical conditions for which this population does seek care, and develop better ways and alternative education approaches to increase awareness for services this population does not deem necessary.

■ Develop specifically designed education materials for new immigrant Mexican American adolescents to help them integrate into the school environment and external society.

2. Promote interaction among social workers, schools, families, and communities.

■ Develop education materials to help instruct all persons in the community regarding high-risk behavior and their consequences to increase prevention knowledge.

■ Adolescent clinics, working in concert with social workers and school staff, could become advocates for Mexican American adolescents from deteriorating families.

■ Integrate youth centers into the clinic setting to help encourage youth of Mexican descent to use preventive services.

■ Examine teacher expectations of students, making teachers aware of personal stereotypes and prejudices that may affect student-teacher relations.

3. Adapt program activities.

■ Use same-ethnic and same-gender staff trained to collect information from these youth regarding their backgrounds to help better understand the needs of this population and enhance communication between staff and youth.

■ Use bilingual personnel and appropriately translated literature to help break down language barriers in providing services and help improve the relationship with the community.

■ Include representative youth in program planning to facilitate use of health services and prevention programs.

■ Develop leadership training for adolescents of Mexican descent to help bridge health care providers with their peers.

■ Develop specific risk-factor programs, such as dropout prevention, to target potentially high-risk individuals. Provision of health services, counseling, and self-efficacy/work-study programs may help these individuals remain in school.

■ Establish referral systems with health settings used by this population, such as public health facilities and emergency rooms, to target youth of Mexican descent who are out of school and may not have access to care.

■ Together with the schools, develop communication strategies such as school presentations, one-on-one dialogues, and small-group discussions to encourage these youth to explore their feelings and attitudes regarding ethnicity, family, and community. Identify discrepancies between adolescents of Mexican descent and their parents regarding degree of acculturation and ethnic identification to stimulate changes in health-related behavior and motivate these students to take an active role in their own health education.

■ Develop more qualitative and health status assessment research to address adequately this population's needs and concerns.

□ WHITE □ BLACK □ ASIAN □ OTHER

"I'm just who I am"

Race is no longer as simple as black or white.
So, what does this mean for America?

By **JACK E. WHITE** WASHINGTON

H IS NICKNAME NOTWITHSTAND-ing, professional golfer Frank ("Fuzzy") Zoeller saw Tiger Woods quite clearly. He gazed upon the new king of professional golf, through whose veins runs the blood of four continents, and beheld neither a one-man melting pot nor even a golfing prodigy but a fried-chicken-and-collard-greens-eating Sambo. Zoeller saw Woods, in short, as just another stereotype, condemned by his blackness to the perpetual status of "little boy."

Zoeller soon paid a price for saying openly what many others were thinking secretly. K Mart, the discount chain with a big African-American clientele, unceremoniously dumped him as the sponsor of a line of golf clothing and equipment, and he abjectly withdrew from the Greater Greensboro Open tournament. "People who know me know I'm a jokester. I just didn't deliver the line well," Zoeller tearfully explained. But his real crime was not, as he and his defenders seem to think, merely a distasteful breach of racial etiquette or an inept attempt at humor. The real crime was falling behind the times. The old black-white stereotypes are out of date, and Zoeller is just the latest casualty of America's failure to come to grips with the perplexing and rapidly evolving significance of racial identity in what is fast becoming the most polyglot society in history.

MELDING POT

Children of interracial marriages in millions

Interracial marriages in millions

1970   1980   1990

Percentage of African Americans marrying whites

Women   8.9
Men

3.9
1.9
0.7

1970   1993

If current demographic trends persist, midway through the 21st century whites will no longer make up a majority of the U.S. population. Blacks will have been overtaken as the largest minority group by Hispanics. Asians and Pacific Islanders will more than double their number of 9.3 million in 1995 to 19.6 million by 2020. An explosion of interracial, interethnic and interreligious marriages will swell the ranks of children whose mere existence

makes a mockery of age-old racial categories and attitudes. Since 1970, the number of multi-racial children has quadrupled to more than 2 million, according to the Bureau of the Census. The color line once drawn between blacks and whites—or more precisely between whites and non-whites—is breaking into a polygon of dueling ethnicities, each fighting for its place in the sun.

For many citizens the "browning of America" means a disorienting plunge into an uncharted sea of identity. Zoeller is far from alone in being confused about the complex tangle of genotypes and phenotypes and cultures that now undercut centuries-old verities about race and race relations in the U.S. Like many others, he hasn't got a clue about what to call the growing ranks of people like Woods who inconveniently refuse to be pigeonholed into one of the neat, oversimplified racial classifications used by government agencies—and, let's face it, most people. Are they people of color? Mixed race? Biracial? Whatever they like?

And if we don't know what to call them, how are we supposed to cope with them? Are they a new and distinct category of "real" Americans, due the same respectful recognition—and governmental protections—as more familiar groups? Or should they be lumped into the demeaning catchall category of "minorities" or "other"? How we eventually answer these questions will affect everything from the first Census forms of the 21st century, which will be issued a mere three years from now, to university admissions policies to the way civil rights laws are enforced. Even more important, it may ultimately transform the

From *Time*, May 5, 1997, pp. 32-36. © 1997 by Time Inc. Magazine Company. Reprinted by permission.

way Americans identify themselves and the tribe or tribes they belong to. In one grandiose vision, shared by conservative analyst Douglas Besharov of the American Enterprise Institute and communitarian sociologist Amitai Etzioni of American University, the ambiguous racial identity of mixed-race children may be "the best hope for the future of American race relations," as Besharov puts it. Letting people define themselves as multiracial, Etzioni argues, "has the potential to soften the racial lines that now divide America by rendering them more like economic differences and less like harsh, almost immutable, caste lines." Those who blend many streams of ethnicity within their own bodies, the argument goes, will render race a meaningless concept, providing a biological solution to the problem of racial justice. This idea reflects a deeply pessimistic view of human nature. It suggests that people can get along with each other only if they are all the same, instead of learning to accept and respect differences.

In any event, the way Americans think and talk about race will have to catch up with the new reality. Just how anachronistic our racial vocabulary has become was made clear by Woods in an appearance last week on *The Oprah Winfrey Show*. When asked if it bothered him, the only child of a black American father and a Thai mother, to be called an African American, he replied, "It does. Growing up, I came up with this name: I'm a 'Cablinasian,' " which he explained is a self-crafted acronym that reflects his one-eighth Caucasian, one-fourth black, one-eighth American Indian, one-fourth Thai and one-fourth Chinese roots with a precision that a racial-classifications expert under South African apartheid would admire. He said that when he was asked to check a box for racial background, he couldn't settle on just one. "I checked off 'African American' and 'Asian.' Those are the two I was raised under, and the only two I know."

KERBOOM! A MINI–RACIAL FIRE storm erupted. Woods' remarks infuriated many African Americans who hailed his record-setting triumph at the Masters as a symbol of racial progress but see him as a traitor. To them Woods appeared to be running away from being an African American—a condition, they were quick to point out, that he himself had emphasized when he paid tribute to black golf pioneers Teddy Rhoades, Charlie Sifford and Lee Elder in his graceful victory speech. In a mirror image of Zoeller's constricted views, some blacks saw Woods' assertion of a multiracial identity as a sellout that could touch off an epidemic of "passing." Arthur Fletcher, a black member of the U.S. Com-

"YOU CAN'T BE A FAIRY"

WHEN SHEBA HOWERTON AUDITIONED for a sixth-grade performance of *Sleeping Beauty*, two white girls in the play told her to forget it. "You're black," they said. "You can't be a fairy." But when she tried to mix with a group of African Americans in high school, she got another challenge. "Why is your skin so light?" one demanded. Says Howerton, 15, whose father is of African, Cherokee and Irish descent and whose mother comes from a family of German Jews: "I can't pass for white, and I can't pass for black. But I definitely feel there is a lot of pressure to align myself with one group or another."

Instead Howerton has tried to find a middle ground, choosing friends of all races and switching between ethnic cliques at De Anza High School in Richmond, California. "I flow back and forth," she says. To combat further their alienation, Sheba and her 12-year-old sister Shira have joined Generation Pride, a group of a dozen teenagers of interracial background in the San Francisco Bay Area. The group holds social gatherings and discussions about interracial issues, offering a rare space free from racial pigeonholing. The group is an offshoot of an adult group, Interracial/Intercultural Pride, whose members are of mixed races or in mixed couples. Doug Howerton, Sheba's father, is I-Pride's vice president. "Those that are biracial and multiracial have a unique look" at things, he says. "They see from both sides, and they try to be more just." ∎

mission on Civil Rights, testified at a 1993 congressional hearing devoted to whether a new, "multiracial" category should be added to U.S. Census forms that "I can see a whole host of light-skinned black Americans running for the door the minute they have another choice. All of a sudden they have a way of saying, 'In this discriminatory culture of ours, I am something other than black.' "

In their rush to judgment, the fearful apparently never stopped to consider that Woods was not turning his back on any part of his identity but instead was embracing every aspect of it. As he put it, "I'm just who I am, whoever you see in front of you"—and that includes his Asian side. "The influence of Tiger's mother Kultida in his life is very important," declares a family friend. "He goes to the temple with her occasionally. She's a devout Buddhist. He wears a family heirloom Buddha around his neck. He's a hybrid of a lot of things, and that's how he sees himself. He honestly sees himself as a somewhat separate person from the norm—not in terms of talent but in terms of his makeup."

Woods grew up in a suburb of Los Angeles with mostly white friends. But over the years he has made four visits to Thailand, where locals like to say he's "Asian from the eyes up," and he has also embraced the role model of his father Earl, who was the first black to play baseball in the Big Eight (for Kansas State). Now Tiger seems to be saying that if acknowledging the totality of his genetic and cultural makeup is difficult for many Americans, they will just have to try harder.

If history is any guide, a lot of them won't try at all. "It's very hard for other folks to embrace our philosophy without thinking we are being racist or trying to create a new race," says Nancy G. Brown, a Jewish woman who is married to a black man and is a past president of the 10-year-old advocacy group Multiracial Americans of Southern California. "It's hard for people to believe we are just looking for equality and that we are able to live with the concept of duality. Constantly calling Tiger Woods black is a good example of what we are talking about."

WHO WOULD "SEE THE ASIAN IN ME"?

FAY YARBROUGH, 21, CAN STILL feel the tug of ethnic loyalties from her Korean mother. "In high school," recalls the daughter of an African-American serviceman, "after I cut my hair, my mother looked at me with this really sad expression on her face. She said people would not be able to see the Asian in me, and that was hard for her. I didn't feel I was making some kind of statement, but my mother took it as a rejection of that cultural side of me."

When she was a freshman at Rice University in Texas, she recalls, she walked to a meeting of the Korean Student Association and stunned a fellow student by talking to her in Korean. The schoolmate had just said, "'Oh, no, we couldn't possibly be going to the same place. I am eating with the Korean Student Association.' The other students looked at me the same way, even though I was one of a handful who could speak Korean and who ever had lived in Korea."

Yarbrough now leans toward her black heritage, finding African Americans more receptive. "Blacks come in all shapes and colors," she says. "Koreans are very homogenous. Someone like me is a much bigger issue for them." She is dating a black man. "Asian men don't date women who look like me." ■

Groups like Brown's have lobbied for a multiracial category on government forms, but they also point out that recognizing multiracialism is more than just a matter of "psychic comfort." There are important health issues, for example, such as bone-marrow matching and how such race-specific syndromes as Tay-Sachs manifest themselves and get treated in biracial individuals. And most multiracial Americans have had the experience of being arbitrarily assigned an ethnic identity by a school principal, a caseworker or an employer that may differ from other family members'—or from one form to the next.

THE NOXIOUS PRACTICE OF PIGEONHOLing people in narrow racial classifications is a deeply ingrained American habit that predates independence. It began with a desire to enforce firm distinctions between free citizens and slaves. In 1661, for example, Virginia decreed that the legal status of the mother would determine whether a black child was a slave or free. Three years later, Maryland went a step further, declaring that if either of a child's parents was a slave, the child would also be. The purpose of this law, its authors said, was to deter "divers freeborn English women" from marrying black slaves. But it did nothing to deter white male slave owners from trying to expand their human holdings by impregnating black female slaves.

Eventually, these pioneering efforts at codifying racial distinctions hardened into so-called miscegenation laws, which aimed to preserve the "purity" of the white race by making interracial sex a crime. Though upholding such laws required ever more tortured legal definitions of who was black and who wasn't, 16 states continued to ban interracial marriages until 1967, when the U.S. Supreme Court struck down such laws. In what was perhaps the most ridiculous example of racial pigeonholing, Louisiana ordained that anyone with a "trace" of black ancestry would be classified as black. Then, in an ostensibly "humane" 1970 reform, it enacted the "one thirty-second rule," by which anyone with a single black great-great-great-grandparent and 31 white great-great-great-great-grandparents was legally black. That regulation went unchallenged until Susie Guillory Phipps, the wife of a wealthy seafood importer who had always considered herself white, got a look at her birth certificate when applying for a passport and discovered that according to the state, she was black. In 1982 she sued the state, which hired a genealogist to delve into Phipps' ancestry. He dug up, among other ancestors, Phipps' great-great-great-great-grandmother—the black mistress of an Alabama plantation owner back in 1760—and concluded that Phipps was precisely three thirty-seconds black. The preposterous law stayed on the books until 1983.

For many decades, people on all sides of the color line chafed at these legal restraints on their ability to love and procreate. Even where black-white marriages were legal, these couples had to seek refuge in more tolerant black neighborhoods and raise their children as African Americans. But in the past 20 years, as the number of mixed-race marriages has increased dramatically, to more than 3 million by some estimates, attitudes among all racial groups have evolved. Tracey Mandell, 26, is an English instructor at Loyola Marymount University. Her partner Michael Bartley is a black man from Jamaica, and their son Noah is coming up on his first birthday. Mandell remembers last March, when she and members of her family were taking a get-acquainted tour of the maternity ward at Santa Monica Hospital. "There were about 50 couples on the tour," she says. "At least half of them were multiracial. My cousin, who lives in Minnesota, pointed it out to me. I hadn't even noticed. I think in L.A. there are so many multiracial people you don't even pay attention. But it's different when you leave Los Angeles."

IT IS PRECISELY BECAUSE THEY FEEL under attack and in need of solidarity that many American minorities fear the blurring of racial lines. Congressional black leaders argue that adding a multiracial category to Census forms, which the Office of Management and Budget will be considering through June of this year, would make it much harder to detect and combat racial discrimination. For example, according to a recent article in *Emerge*, the black newsmagazine, in 1991 some 35,000

A MOTHER'S CRY: "MY SON IS THREE RACES"

MELISSA MEYER AND THALLIEUS MASSEY DON'T SIMPLY WANT TO CHECK OFF a box marked "multiracial" for their eight-year-old son Jordan. With light brown skin, golden, wavy hair and light brown eyes, Jordan Massey is clearly the product of several races. Yet when his mother enrolled him in second grade at Coconut Grove Elementary in Dade County, Florida, the school registrar gave her a form that asked her to pick just one of the following: black, white, Hispanic, American Indian/Alaskan Native, or Asian/Pacific Islander. Meyer, 31, who is white and whose husband's ancestors included both Africans and Native Americans, refused to select a box. "My son is three races," she said. "Can I choose all three?"

When the school said no, Meyer contacted the American Civil Liberties Union, and after a lot of wrangling, Dade County public schools agreed in 1995 to add a multiracial option on school-registration forms. But Meyer and Massey are not satisfied, because their son still cannot choose all three races. "We're not saying one race is better than the other," she says. "But he is our child, and we want him to understand exactly who he is." Sitting in his Boy Scout uniform, Jordan proclaims, "I'm American Indian, African American, European, American Indian." ∎

people chose "other" on Home Mortgage Disclosure Act papers meant to track bias in lending. Allowing people to opt out of traditional race categories, says Congressional Black Caucus chairwoman Maxine Waters, a California Democrat, "just blurs everything. [People pushing for a multiracial category] want to be seen for all they are, but I don't think they're making the connection about how it could affect how they're represented, or who's being an advocate for them when they get mistreated." Among the many programs administered on the basis of racial tallies: minority employment on government contracts, court-ordered school desegregation plans and protection of minority voting rights. All would have to be retooled, at great cost, if the categories change.

In the end, however, the impact of multiracialism will be decided not by the content of a Census form but in the hearts of Americans. Tiger Woods can proclaim his personal diversity, but if most people, like Zoeller, just see a "boy," it won't make much difference. Multiracial Americans will not get the right to define themselves as they choose without a fight. —*Reported by Tamala M. Edwards/Washington, Elaine Lafferty and Sylvester Monroe/Los Angeles and Victoria Rainert/New York*

The EQ Factor

New brain research suggests that emotions, not IQ, may be the true measure of human intelligence

NANCY GIBBS

IT TURNS OUT THAT A SCIENTIST can see the future by watching four-year-olds interact with a marshmallow. The researcher invites the children, one by one, into a plain room and begins the gentle torment. You can have this marshmallow right now, he says. But if you wait while I run an errand, you can have two marshmallows when I get back. And then he leaves.

Some children grab for the treat the minute he's out the door. Some last a few minutes before they give in. But others are determined to wait. They cover their eyes; they put their heads down; they sing to themselves; they try to play games or even fall asleep. When the researcher returns, he gives these children their hard-earned marshmallows. And then, science waits for them to grow up.

By the time the children reach high school, something remarkable has happened. A survey of the children's parents and teachers found that those who as four-year-olds had the fortitude to hold out for the second marshmallow generally grew up to be better adjusted, more popular, adventurous, confident and dependable teenagers. The children who gave in to temptation early on were more likely to be lonely, easily frustrated and stubborn. They buckled under stress and shied away from challenges. And when some of the students in the two groups took the Scholastic Aptitude Test, the kids who had held out longer scored an average of 210 points higher.

When we think of brilliance we see Einstein, deep-eyed, woolly haired, a thinking machine with skin and mismatched socks. High achievers, we imagine, were wired for greatness from birth. But then you have to wonder why, over time, natural talent seems to ignite in some people and dim in others. This is where the marshmallows come in. It seems that the ability to delay gratification is a master skill, a triumph of the reasoning brain over the impulsive one. It is a sign, in short, of emotional intelligence. And it doesn't show up on an IQ test.

For most of this century, scientists have worshipped the hardware of the brain and the software of the mind; the messy powers of the heart were left to the poets. But cognitive theory could simply not explain the questions we wonder about most: why some people just seem to have a gift for living well; why the smartest kid in the class will probably not end up the richest; why we like some people virtually on sight and distrust others; why some people remain buoyant in the face of troubles that would sink a less resilient soul. What qualities of the mind or spirit, in short, determine who succeeds?

The phrase "emotional intelligence" was coined by Yale psychologist Peter Salovey and the University of New Hampshire's John Mayer five years ago to describe qualities like understanding one's own feelings, empathy for the feelings of others and "the regulation of emotion in a way that enhances living." Their notion is about to bound into the national conversation, handily shortened to EQ, thanks to a new book, *Emotional Intelligence* (Bantam; $23.95) by Daniel Goleman. Goleman, a Harvard psychology Ph.D. and a New York *Times* science writer with a gift for making even the chewiest scientific theories digestible to lay readers, has brought together a decade's worth of behavioral research into how the mind processes feelings. His goal, he announces on the cover, is to redefine what it means to be smart. His thesis: when it comes to predicting people's success, brainpower as measured by IQ and standardized achievement tests may actually matter less than the qualities of mind once thought of as "character" before the word began to sound quaint.

At first glance, there would seem to be little that's new here to any close reader of fortune cookies. There may be no less original idea than the notion that our hearts hold dominion over our heads. "I was so angry," we say, "I couldn't think straight." Neither is it surprising that "people skills" are useful, which amounts to saying, it's good to be nice. "It's so true it's trivial," says Dr. Paul McHugh, director of psychiatry at Johns Hopkins University School of Medicine. But if it were that simple, the book would not be quite so interesting or its implications so controversial.

This is no abstract investigation. Goleman is looking for antidotes to restore "civility to our streets and caring to our communal life." He sees practical applications everywhere for how companies should decide whom to hire, how couples can increase the odds that their marriages will last, how parents should raise their children and how schools should teach them. When street gangs substitute for families and schoolyard insults end in stabbings, when more than half of marriages end in divorce, when the majority of the children murdered in this country are killed by parents and stepparents, many of whom say they were trying to discipline the child for behavior like blocking the TV or crying too much, it suggests a demand for remedial emotional education. While children are still young, Goleman argues, there is a "neurological window of opportunity" since the brain's prefrontal circuitry, which regulates how we act on what we feel, probably does not mature until mid-adolescence.

And it is here the arguments will break out. Goleman's highly popularized conclusions, says McHugh, "will chill any veteran scholar of psychotherapy and any neuroscientist who worries about how his research may come to be applied." While many researchers in this relatively new field are glad to see emotional issues finally taken seriously, they fear that a notion as handy as EQ invites misuse. Goleman admits the danger of suggesting that you can assign a numerical yardstick to a person's character as well as his intellect; Goleman never even uses the phrase EQ in his book. But he (begrudgingly) approved an "unscientific" EQ test in *USA Today* with choices like "I am aware of even subtle feelings as I have them," and "I can sense the pulse of a group or relationship and state unspoken feelings."

"You don't want to take an average of your emotional skill," argues Harvard psychology professor Jerome Kagan, a pioneer in child-development research. "That's what's wrong with the concept of intelligence for mental skills too. Some people handle anger well but can't handle fear. Some people can't take joy. So each emotion has to be viewed differently."

EQ is not the opposite of IQ. Some people are blessed with a lot of both, some with little of either. What researchers have been trying to understand is how they complement each other; how one's ability to handle stress, for instance, affects the ability to concentrate and put intelligence to use. Among the ingredients for success, researchers now generally agree that IQ counts for about 20%; the rest depends on everything from class to luck to the neural pathways that have developed in the brain over millions of years of human evolution.

It is actually the neuroscientists and evolutionists who do the best job of explaining the reasons behind the most unreasonable behavior. In the past decade or so, scientists have learned enough about the brain to make judgments about where emotion comes from and why we need it. Primitive emotional responses held the keys to survival: fear drives the blood into the large muscles, making it easier to run; surprise triggers the eyebrows to rise, allowing the eyes to widen their view and gather more information about an unexpected event. Disgust wrinkles up the face and closes the nostrils to keep out foul smells.

Emotional life grows out of an area of the brain called the limbic system, specifically the amygdala, whence come delight and disgust and fear and anger. Millions of years ago, the neocortex was added on, enabling humans to plan, learn and remember. Lust grows from the limbic system; love, from the neocortex. Animals like reptiles that have no neocortex cannot experience anything like maternal love; this is why baby snakes have to hide to avoid being eaten by their parents. Humans, with their capacity for love, will protect their offspring, allowing the brains of the young time to develop. The more connections between limbic system and the neocortex, the more emotional responses are possible.

It was scientists like Joseph LeDoux of New York University who uncovered these cerebral pathways. LeDoux's parents owned a meat market. As a boy in Louisiana, he first learned about his future specialty by cutting up cows' brains for sweetbreads. "I found them the most interesting part of the cow's anatomy," he recalls. "They were visually pleasing—lots of folds, convolutions and patterns. The cerebellum was more interesting to look at than steak." The butchers' son became a neuroscientist, and it was he who discovered the short circuit in the brain that lets emotions drive action before the intellect gets a chance to intervene.

A hiker on a mountain path, for example, sees a long, curved shape in the grass out of the corner of his eye. He leaps out of the way before he realizes it is only a stick that looks like a snake. Then he calms down; his cortex gets the message a few milliseconds after his amygdala and "regulates" its primitive response.

Without these emotional reflexes, rarely conscious but often terribly powerful, we would scarcely be able to function. "Most decisions we make have a vast number of possible outcomes, and any attempt to analyze all of them would never end," says University of Iowa neurologist Antonio Damasio, author of *Descartes' Error: Emotion, Reason and the Human Brain*. "I'd ask you to lunch tomorrow, and when the appointed time arrived, you'd still be thinking about whether you should come." What tips the balance, Damasio contends, is our unconscious assigning of emotional values to some of those choices. Whether we experience a somatic response—a gut feeling of dread or a giddy sense of elation— emotions are helping to limit the field in any choice we have to make. If the prospect of lunch with a neurologist is unnerving or distasteful, Damasio suggests, the invitee will conveniently remember a previous engagement.

When Damasio worked with patients in whom the connection between emotional brain and neocortex had been severed because of damage to the brain, he discovered how central that hidden pathway is to how we live our lives. People who had lost that linkage were just as smart and quick to reason, but their lives often fell apart nonetheless. They could not make decisions because they didn't know how they felt about their choices. They couldn't react to warnings or anger in other people. If they made a mistake, like a bad investment, they felt no regret or shame and so were bound to repeat it.

If there is a cornerstone to emotional intelligence on which most other emotional skills depend, it is a sense of self-awareness, of being smart about what we feel. A person whose day starts badly at home may be grouchy all day at work without quite knowing why. Once an emotional response comes into awareness—or, physiologically, is processed through the neocortex—the chances of handling it appropriately improve. Scientists refer to "metamood," the ability to pull back and recognize that "what I'm feeling is anger," or sorrow, or shame.

Metamood is a difficult skill because emotions so often appear in disguise. A person in mourning may know he is sad, but he may not recognize that he is also angry at the person for dying—because this seems somehow inappropriate. A parent who yells at the child who ran into the street is expressing anger at disobedience, but the degree of anger may owe more to the fear the parent feels at what could have happened.

In Goleman's analysis, self-awareness is perhaps the most crucial ability because it allows us to exercise some self-control. The idea is not to repress feeling (the reaction that has made psychoanalysts rich) but rather to do what Aristotle considered the hard work of the will. "Anyone can become angry—that is easy," he wrote in the *Nicomachean Ethics*. "But to be angry with the right person, to the right degree, at the right time, for the right purpose, and in the right way—that is not easy."

Some impulses seem to be easier to control than others. Anger, not surprisingly, is one of the hardest, perhaps because of its evolutionary value in priming people to action. Researchers believe anger usually arises out of a sense of being trespassed against—the belief that one is being robbed of what is rightfully his. The body's first response is a surge of energy, the release of a cascade of neurotransmitters called catecholamines. If a person is already aroused or under stress, the threshold for release is lower, which helps explain why people's tempers shorten during a hard day.

Scientists are not only discovering where anger comes from; they are also exposing myths about how best to handle it. Popular wisdom argues for "letting it all hang out" and having a good cathartic rant. But Goleman cites studies showing that dwelling on anger actually increases its power; the body needs a chance to process the adrenaline through exercise, relaxation techniques, a well-timed intervention or even the old admonition to count to 10.

Anxiety serves a similar useful purpose, so long as it doesn't spin out of control. Worrying is a rehearsal for danger; the act of fretting focuses the mind on a problem so it can search efficiently for solutions. The danger comes when worrying blocks thinking, becoming an end in itself or a path to resignation instead of perseverance. Overworrying about failing increases the likelihood of failure; a salesman so concerned about his falling sales that he can't bring himself to pick up the phone guarantees that his sales will fall even further.

But why are some people better able to "snap out of it" and get on with the task at hand? Again, given sufficient self-awareness, people develop coping mechanisms. Sadness and discouragement, for instance, are "low arousal" states, and the dispirited salesman who goes out for a run is triggering a high arousal state that is incompatible with staying blue. Relaxation works better for high-energy moods like anger or anxiety. Either way, the idea is to shift to a state of arousal that breaks the destructive cycle of the dominant mood.

The idea of being able to predict which salesmen are most likely to prosper was not an abstraction for Metropolitan Life, which in the mid-'80s was hiring 5,000 salespeople a year and training them at a cost of more than $30,000 each. Half quit the first year, and four out of five within four years. The reason: selling life insurance involves having the door slammed in your face over and over again. Was it possible to identify which people would be better at handling frustration and take each refusal as a challenge rather than a setback?

The head of the company approached psychologist Martin Seligman at the University of Pennsylvania and invited him to test some of his theories about the importance of optimism in people's success. When optimists fail, he has found, they attribute the failure to something they can change, not some innate weakness that they are helpless to overcome. And that confidence in their power to effect change is self-reinforcing. Seligman tracked 15,000 new workers who had taken two tests. One was the company's regular screening exam, the other Seligman's test measuring their levels of optimism.

One Way to Test Your EQ

UNLIKE IQ, WHICH IS GAUGED BY THE FAMOUS STANFORD-Binet tests, EQ does not lend itself to any single numerical measure. Nor should it, say experts. Emotional intelligence is by definition a complex, multifaceted quality representing such intangibles as self-awareness, empathy, persistence and social deftness.

Some aspects of emotional intelligence, however, can be quantified. Optimism, for example, is a handy measure of a person's self-worth. According to Martin Seligman, a University of Pennsylvania psychologist, how people respond to setbacks—optimistically or pessimistically—is a fairly accurate indicator of how well they will succeed in school, in sports and in certain kinds of work. To test his theory, Seligman devised a questionnaire to screen insurance salesmen at MetLife.

In Seligman's test, job applicants were asked to imagine a hypothetical event and then choose the response (A or B) that most closely resembled their own. Some samples from his questionnaire:

You forget your spouse's (boyfriend's/girlfriend's) birthday.
A. I'm not good at remembering birthdays.
B. I was preoccupied with other things.

You owe the library $10 for an overdue book.
A. When I am really involved in what I am reading, I often forget when it's due.
B. I was so involved in writing the report, I forgot to return the book.

You lose your temper with a friend.
A. He or she is always nagging me.
B. He or she was in a hostile mood.

You are penalized for returning your income-tax forms late.
A. I always put off doing my taxes.
B. I was lazy about getting my taxes done this year.

You've been feeling run-down.
A. I never get a chance to relax.
B. I was exceptionally busy this week.

A friend says something that hurts your feelings.
A. She always blurts things out without thinking of others.
B. My friend was in a bad mood and took it out on me.

You fall down a great deal while skiing.
A. Skiing is difficult.
B. The trails were icy.

You gain weight over the holidays, and you can't lose it.
A. Diets don't work in the long run.
B. The diet I tried didn't work.

Seligman found that those insurance salesmen who answered with more B's than A's were better able to overcome bad sales days, recovered more easily from rejection and were less likely to quit. People with an optimistic view of life tend to treat obstacles and setbacks as temporary (and therefore surmountable). Pessimists take them personally; what others see as fleeting, localized impediments, they view as pervasive and permanent.

The most dramatic proof of his theory, says Seligman, came at the 1988 Olympic Games in Seoul, South Korea, after U.S. swimmer Matt Biondi turned in two disappointing performances in his first two races. Before the Games, Biondi had been favored to win seven golds—as Mark Spitz had done 16 years earlier. After those first two races, most commentators thought Biondi would be unable to recover from his setback. Not Seligman. He had given some members of the U.S swim team a version of his optimism test before the races; it showed that Biondi possessed an extraordinarily upbeat attitude. Rather than losing heart after turning in a bad time, as others might, Biondi tended to respond by swimming even faster. Sure enough, Biondi bounced right back, winning five gold medals in the next five races.   *—By Alice Park*

Among the new hires was a group who flunked the screening test but scored as "superoptimists" on Seligman's exam. And sure enough, they did the best of all; they outsold the pessimists in the regular group by 21% in the first year and 57% in the second. For years after that, passing Seligman's test was one way to get hired as a MetLife salesperson.

Perhaps the most visible emotional skills, the ones we recognize most readily, are the "people skills" like empathy, graciousness, the ability to read a social situation. Researchers believe that about 90% of emotional communication is nonverbal. Harvard psychologist Robert Rosenthal developed the PONS test (Profile of Nonverbal Sensitivity) to measure people's ability to read emotional cues. He shows subjects a film of a young woman expressing feelings—anger, love, jealousy, gratitude, seduction—edited so that one or another nonverbal cue is blanked out. In some instances the face is visible but not the body, or the woman's eyes are hidden, so that viewers have to judge the feeling by subtle cues. Once again, people with higher PONS scores tend to be more successful in their work and relationships; children who score well are more popular and successful in school, even then their IQs are quite average.

Like other emotional skills, empathy is an innate quality that can be shaped by experience. Infants as young as three months old exhibit empathy when they get upset at the sound of another baby crying. Even very young children learn by imitation; by watching how others act when they see someone in distress, these children acquire a repertoire of sensitive responses. If, on the other hand, the feelings they begin to express are not recognized and reinforced by the adults around them, they not only cease to express those feelings but they also become less able to recognize them in themselves or others.

Empathy too can be seen as a survival skill. Bert Cohler, a University of Chicago psychologist, and Fran Stott, dean of the Erikson Institute for Advanced Study in Child Development in Chicago, have found that children from psychically damaged families frequently become hypervigilant, developing an intense attunement to their parents' moods. One child they studied, Nicholas, had a horrible habit of approaching other kids in his nursery-school class as if he were going to kiss them, then would bite them instead. The scientists went back to study videos of Nicholas at 20 months interacting with his psychotic mother and found that she had responded to his every expression of anger or independence with compulsive kisses. The researchers dubbed them "kisses of death," and their true significance was obvious to Nicholas, who arched his back in horror at

Square Pegs in the Oval Office?

IF A HIGH DEGREE OF EMOTIONAL INTELLIGENCE IS A PREREQUISITE FOR OUTstanding achievement, there ought to be no better place to find it than in the White House. It turns out, however, that not every man who reached the pinnacle of American leadership was a gleaming example of self-awareness, empathy, impulse control and all the other qualities that mark an elevated EQ.

Oliver Wendell Holmes, who knew intelligence when he saw it, judged Franklin Roosevelt "a second-class intellect, but a first-class temperament." Born and educated as an aristocrat, F.D.R. had polio and needed a wheelchair for most of his adult life. Yet, far from becoming a self-pitying wretch, he developed an unbridled optimism that served him and the country well during the Depression and World War II—this despite, or because of, what Princeton professor Fred Greenstein calls Roosevelt's "tendency toward deviousness and duplicity."

Even a first-class temperament, however, is not a sure predictor of a successful presidency. According to Duke University political scientist James David Barber, the most perfect blend of intellect and warmth of personality in a Chief Executive was the brilliant Thomas Jefferson, who "knew the importance of communication and empathy. He never lost the common touch." Richard Ellis, a professor of politics at Oregon's Willamette University who is skeptical of the whole EQ theory, cites two 19th century Presidents who did not fit the mold. "Martin Van Buren was well adjusted, balanced, empathetic and persuasive, but he was not very successful," says Ellis. "Andrew Jackson was less well adjusted, less balanced, less empathetic and was terrible at controlling his own impulses, but he transformed the presidency."

Lyndon Johnson as Senate majority leader was a brilliant practitioner of the art of political persuasion, yet failed utterly to transfer that gift to the White House. In fact, says Princeton's Greenstein, L. B. J. and Richard Nixon would be labeled "worst cases" on any EQ scale of Presidents. Each was touched with political genius, yet each met with disaster. "To some extent," says Greenstein, "this is a function of the extreme aspects of their psyches; they are the political versions of Van Gogh, who does unbelievable paintings and then cuts off his ear."

History professor William Leuchtenburg of the University of North Carolina at Chapel Hill suggests that the 20th century Presidents with perhaps the highest IQs—Wilson, Hoover and Carter—also had the most trouble connecting with their constituents. Woodrow Wilson, he says, "was very high strung [and] arrogant; he was not willing to strike any middle ground. Herbert Hoover was so locked into certain ideas that you could never convince him otherwise. Jimmy Carter is probably the most puzzling of the three. He didn't have a deficiency of temperament; in fact, he was too temperate. There was an excessive rationalization about Carter's approach."

That was never a problem for John Kennedy and Ronald Reagan. Nobody ever accused them of intellectual genius, yet both radiated qualities of leadership with an infectious confidence and openheartedness that endeared them to the nation. Whether President Clinton will be so endeared remains a puzzle. That he is a Rhodes scholar makes him certifiably brainy, but his emotional intelligence is shaky. He obviously has the knack for establishing rapport with people, but he often appears so eager to please that he looks weak. "As for controlling his impulses," says Willamette's Ellis, "Clinton is terrible." —By Jesse Birnbaum.
Reported by James Carney/Washington and Lisa H. Towle/Raleigh

her approaching lips—and passed his own rage on to his classmates years later.

Empathy also acts as a buffer to cruelty, and it is a quality conspicuously lacking in child molesters and psychopaths. Goleman cites some chilling research into brutality by Robert Hare, a psychologist at the University of British Columbia. Hare found that psychopaths, when hooked up to

electrodes and told they are going to receive a shock, show none of the visceral responses that fear of pain typically triggers: rapid heartbeat, sweating and so on. How could the threat of punishment deter such people from committing crimes?

It is easy to draw the obvious lesson from these test results. How much happier would we be, how much more successful as individuals and civil as a society, if we were more alert to the importance of emotional intelligence and more adept at teaching it? From kindergartens to business schools to corporations across the country, people are taking seriously the idea that a little more time spent on the "touchy-feely" skills so often derided may in fact pay rich dividends.

In the corporate world, according to personnel executives, IQ gets you hired, but EQ gets you promoted. Goleman likes to tell of a manager at AT&T's Bell Labs, a think tank for brilliant engineers in New Jersey, who was asked to rank his top performers. They weren't the ones with the highest IQs; they were the ones whose E-mail got answered. Those workers who were good collaborators and networkers and popular with colleagues were more likely to get the cooperation they needed to reach their goals than the socially awkward, lone-wolf geniuses.

When David Campbell and others at the Center for Creative Leadership studied "derailed executives," the rising stars who flamed out, the researchers found that these executives failed most often because of "an interpersonal flaw" rather than a technical inability. Interviews with top executives in the U.S. and Europe turned up nine so-called fatal flaws, many of them classic emotional failings, such as "poor working relations," being "authoritarian" or "too ambitious" and having "conflict with upper management."

At the center's executive-leadership seminars across the country, managers come to get emotionally retooled. "This isn't sensitivity training or Sunday-supplement stuff," says Campbell. "One thing they know when they get through is what other people think of them." And the executives have an incentive to listen. Says Karen Boylston, director of the center's team-leadership group: "Customers are telling businesses, 'I don't care if every member of your staff graduated with honors from Harvard, Stanford and Wharton. I will take my business and go where I am understood and treated with respect.'"

Nowhere is the discussion of emotional intelligence more pressing than in schools, where both the stakes and the opportunities seem greatest. Instead of con-

stant crisis intervention, or declarations of war on drug abuse or teen pregnancy or violence, it is time, Goleman argues, for preventive medicine. "Five years ago, teachers didn't want to think about this," says principal Roberta Kirshbaum of P.S. 75 in New York City. "But when kids are getting killed in high school, we have to deal with it." Five years ago, Kirshbaum's school adopted an emotional literacy program, designed to help children learn to manage anger, frustration, loneliness. Since then, fights at lunchtime have decreased from two or three a day to almost none.

Educators can point to all sorts of data to support this new direction. Students who are depressed or angry literally cannot learn. Children who have trouble being accepted by their classmates are 2 to 8 times as likely to drop out. An inability to distinguish distressing feelings or handle frustration has been linked to eating disorders in girls.

Many school administrators are completely rethinking the weight they have been giving to traditional lessons and standardized tests. Peter Relic, president of the National Association of Independent Schools, would like to junk the SAT completely. "Yes, it may cost a heck of a lot more money to assess someone's EQ rather than using a machine-scored test to measure IQ," he says. "But if we don't, then we're saying that a test score is more important to us than who a child is as a human being. That means an immense loss in terms of human potential because we've defined success too narrowly."

This warm embrace by educators has left some scientists in a bind. On one hand, says Yale psychologist Salovey, "I love the idea that we want to teach people a richer understanding of their emotional life, to help them achieve their goals." But, he adds, "what I would oppose is training conformity to social expectations." The danger is that any campaign to hone emotional skills in children will end up teaching that there is a "right" emotional response for any given situation—laugh at parades, cry at funerals, sit still at church. "You can teach self-control," says Dr. Alvin Poussaint, professor of psychiatry at Harvard Medical School. "You can teach that it's better to talk out your anger and not use violence. But is it good emotional intelligence not to challenge authority?"

SOME PSYCHOLOGISTS GO further and challenge the very idea that emotional skills can or should be taught in any kind of formal, classroom way. Goleman's premise that children can be trained to analyze their feelings strikes Johns Hopkins' McHugh as an effort to reinvent the encounter group: "I consider that an abominable idea, an idea we have seen with adults. That failed, and now he wants to try it with children? Good grief!" He cites the description in Goleman's book of an experimental program at the Nueva Learning Center in San Francisco. In one scene, two fifth-grade boys start to argue over the rules of an exercise, and the teacher breaks in to ask them to talk about what they're feeling. "I appreciate the way you're being assertive in talking with Tucker," she says to one student. "You're not attacking." This strikes McHugh as pure folly. "The author is presuming that someone has the key to the right emotions to be taught to children. We don't even know the right emotions to be taught to adults. Do you really think a child of eight or nine really understands the difference between aggressiveness and assertiveness?"

The problem may be that there is an ingredient missing. Emotional skills, like intellectual ones, are morally neutral. Just as a genius could use his intellect either to cure cancer or engineer a deadly virus, someone with great empathic insight could use it to inspire colleagues or exploit them. Without a moral compass to guide people in how to employ their gifts, emotional intelligence can be used for good or evil. Columbia University psychologist Walter Mischel, who invented the marshmallow test and others like it, observes that the knack for delaying gratification that makes a child one marshmallow richer can help him become a better citizen or—just as easily—an even more brilliant criminal.

Given the passionate arguments that are raging over the state of moral instruction in this country, it is no wonder Goleman chose to focus more on neutral emotional skills than on the values that should govern their use. That's another book—and another debate. —*Reported by Sharon E. Epperson and Lawrence Mondi/New York, James L. Graff/Chicago and Lisa H. Towle/Raleigh*

Family Relationships

When Larry looked over his daughter's shoulder to see if she was doing her math homework correctly, she snapped "I didn't order a Hovercraft." Why would a normally compliant 13-year-old be so rude, impertinent, and, yes, clever? And what would be an appropriate response on Larry's part? Modern psychologists believe that in order to understand the influence of the family on its members, the family needs to be viewed as a system. This means that parents do not simply shape their child; rather, each part of the family influences the other parts. For example, just as parents influence their children's behavior, children influence not only their parents' behavior, but their parents' relationship with each other. A child who complies with parental rules may put less stress on the parents than a child who is consistently in trouble. The compliant child's parents may then argue less with each other over issues like discipline. Similarly, the parents' marital relationship influences how each parent interacts with the children. Parents whose marriage is stressed may have less patience with children or may be less available to help their children.

Because the family is a system, factors that affect one part of the system will have implications for the rest of the system. This can be seen in how changes in the adolescent or in the parent affect the rest of the family. Adolescents may be described as changing in three major areas: biologically, cognitively, and socially. As adolescents enter puberty, parents see their children become sexually mature individuals. How parents react to this may be influenced by a variety of factors, including the parents' view of their own aging. Parents who see their attractiveness or health or sexuality as in decline may react to their child's development very differently than do parents who have a more positive view of themselves.

Adolescents' cognitive development may also stress their relationship with their parents. As adolescents become more cognitively sophisticated, they frequently become more questioning of parental behavior and rules. Although adolescents' demands for reasons underlying parental judgments may reflect their newly developed cognitive skills—a positive development from an intellectual perspective—it may increase conflicts with parents. Parents who expect their rules to be obeyed without question may be more upset by their child's arguments than will parents who expect to discuss rules.

Concurrent with these physical and cognitive changes, adolescents also undergo social changes. These include increased demands for autonomy or independence. Par-

ents whose children were docile and compliant prior to adolescence may feel their authority threatened by these changes. Parents may find it more difficult to discipline children than they had before. This may be especially problematic for families who had difficulty controlling their children earlier in childhood.

Although families may be viewed as a system, there is no one form that this system must take. In the 1950s, the ideal form of the family system was a breadwinner father, a homemaker mother, and their children. Today families take many different forms. About 50 percent of American adolescents will live in single-parent families for some period. This rate is higher for African Americans. About 75 percent of women with school-age children are employed outside the home. About 21 percent of American children live in reconstituted families. It is clear that there is no "typical" family. Does this mean that the family plays a less significant role in the life of the adolescent? The research indicates no: the family is still among the most important influences on an adolescent. How well adolescents resist peer pressure, how successful they are in developing an identity, how capable they become in making independent decisions, and what they strive for in the future all seem to be predominantly influenced by the family. What characteristics of the family predict success in these areas?

Diana Baumrind, a leading researcher on the effects of differing parenting styles on adolescent development, proposed that some styles of parenting result in more competent, independent children than do other styles. She classified parents as either authoritative, authoritarian, or permissive. Authoritative parents encourage their children to discuss rules, rather than expecting children to obey without question. When the rules are broken, parents address this in a nonpunitive manner. That is, they neither ignore the offense nor do they use punitive discipline. Like authoritative parents, authoritarian parents have clear rules and limits. However, authoritarian parents are more likely to expect their children to obey without question. They are also more aloof with their children than are authoritative parents. Permissive parents fall into two categories. Some permissive parents have a warm relationship with their children, but they do not impose many controls on them. Other permissive parents are basically uninvolved in the lives of their children.

Baumrind and others investigated the relationship between parenting styles and social competence in adolescents. Issues such as how well adolescents resisted peer pressure, how well adjusted they were, or how many prob-lems they had with delinquency were investigated. It was found that children from authoritative families, where parents are emotionally warm to their children but have clear rules, limits, and controls, generally scored best. This was found to be the case regardless of family structure.

The articles in this unit demonstrate aspects of the family system. The first two articles emphasize the ways in which crises faced by parents may then affect the way parents interact with their adolescents. The next two articles provide advice on how parents may effectively respond to adolescents' increased demands and arguments. Both suggest parents maintain rules while treating their children as rational individuals. The next article describes gay families, societal attitudes toward these families, and the prejudice the members of these families may face. The conclusion of the article is that children of gay families are at no more psychological risk than are the children of heterosexuals. The final two articles also present optimistic views of the family system. The first, "Bringing Up Father," emphasizes the role fathers may play in caring for their children. The second concludes that divorce per se is not necessarily harmful for children.

Looking Ahead: Challenge Questions

What kinds of crises may parents face when their children reach adolescence? How may each of these crises affect the manner in which parents interact with their children? How may these crises differ for mothers as compared to fathers? For single parents as compared to intact families?

What kinds of demands may adolescents make of their parents that differ from those of childhood? What kinds of arguments may adolescents start presenting to their parents?

What kinds of emotional changes may result from adolescents' attempts to gain independence? How may parents react to these emotional changes? What kinds of reactions may be most adaptive?

Given that adolescents may be moodier or more critical than they were earlier in childhood, how can one tell when these changes are no longer within normal limits?

What are the attitudes of Americans to gay families? What are the major problems face by children in gay families? How has the legal system treated gay families?

How has the role fathers played in the family changed over the last 100 years? Why is it important for fathers to play a more active role with their children today?

How may divorce affect the mental health of children?

Adolescence
Whose Hell Is It?

The image of teenagers as menacing and rebellious is a big fiction that's boomeranging on kids. We've mythologized adolescence to conceal a startling fact: It is indeed a difficult and turbulent time—for parents. The trouble is, kids look like adults much sooner than ever before. Kids wind up feeling abandoned—and angry at the loss of their safety net. If we haven't got adolescence exactly figured out yet, there's some consolation in the fact that it's a brand-new phenomenon in human history.

Virginia Rutter

I recently spent the weekend with a friend's 13-year-old son. In contrast to the tiny tots most of my friends have, Matthew seemed much more like an adult. The time spent with him wasn't so much like baby-sitting; it was like having company. It was impressive to see how self-sufficient he was. Simple matters struck me: he didn't need someone to go to the bathroom with him at the movies; he could help himself to ice cream; he was actually interested in following the O. J. Simpson story, and we discussed it.

He was polite, thoughtful, and interesting. While the intensive caretaking necessary for smaller children has its own rewards (I suppose), Matthew's contrasting autonomy was pleasant to me. And so I imagined it would be for parents of adolescents. But then, I am not a parent. And most parents report not feeling pleasant about their adolescents.

The weekend reminded me of how easy it is to think of these youngsters as adults. Compared to an eight-year-old, an adolescent is a lot like an adult. Can't reason like an adult, but doesn't think like a child anymore, either. Some parents are tempted to cut 'em loose rather than adjust to the new status of their teenager. Others fail to observe their

adolescent's new adultlike status, and continue monitoring them as closely as a child. But it's obvious that adolescents aren't miniature adults. They are individuals on their way to adulthood; their brains and bodies—to say nothing of their sexuality—stretching uneasily toward maturity.

A couple of teachers are my heroes. My history teacher is great because he listens to what everybody has to say and never judges.
—Chelsea, 14, Bakersfield, California

Yet the sight of kids reaching for some form of adult status commonly evokes contempt rather than curiosity. Negative feelings about teenagers have a strong grip on American culture in general, and on surprising numbers of parents in particular. It's not uncommon for parents to anticipate their child's adolescence with fear and trepidation even before they've gotten out of diapers. They expect a war at home.

"It becomes a self-fulfilling prophesy that adolescence is seen as this bizarre, otherworldly period of development, complete with a battleground set for World War III," says Tina Wagers, Psy.D., a psychologist who treats teens and their families at Kaiser Permanente Medical Center in Denver.

We were all once 13, but it seems we can no longer imagine what kind of parenting a 13-year-old needs. Perhaps it's gotten worse with all the outside opportunities for trouble kids have—gangs, guns, drugs. Families used to extend their turf into their children's schools, friends, and athletic activities. But kids now inhabit unknown territory, and it is scary for parents. "I think this fear and lack of understanding makes some parents more likely to back off and neglect teenagers," reports Wagers. "There is an expectation that you can't influence them anyhow."

This skeptical, sometimes hostile view of teens, however, was countered by my experience with Matthew. I found him hardly a "teenager from hell." Like most teens, Matthew prefers to be with his own friends more than with family or other grown-ups. He's not good with time, and music, basketball, and girls are more central to him than achievement, responsibility, and family. (Despite his tastes, he does very well in school.) At home there is more conflict than there has been in the past, though not less love and commitment to his mom, with whom he lives in eastern Washington.

The story of Matthew falls in line with new research on adolescents, and it's causing psychologists to totally revise conventional wisdom on the subject. According to psychologist Laurence Steinberg, Ph.D., of Temple University, the majority of adolescents are not contentious, unpleasant, heartless creatures. They do not hate their parents—although they do fight with them (but not as much as you might think). "In scrutinizing interviews with adolescents and their families, I reaffirmed that adolescence is a relatively peaceful time in the house." Kids report continued high levels of respect for their parents, whether single, divorced, or together, and regardless of economic background.

When fighting does occur, it's in families with younger teenagers, and it has to do at least in part with their burgeoning cognitive abilities. Newly able to grasp abstract ideas, they can become absorbed in pursuing hypocrisy or questioning authority. In time, they learn to deploy relativistic and critical thinking more selectively.

NOT A DISEASE

If adolescents aren't the incorrigibles we think—then what to make of the endless stream of news reports of teen sexism, harassment, drug abuse, depression, delinquency, gangs, guns, and suicide?

Any way you measure it, teens today are in deep trouble. They face increasing rates of depression (now at 20 percent), suicide (12 percent have considered it, 5 percent attempted), substance abuse (20 percent of high school seniors), delinquency (1.5 million juvenile arrests—about 1 percent of teens—in 1992), early sexual activity (29 percent have had sexual relations by age 15), and even an increased rate of health problems (20 percent have conditions that will hamper their health as adults). And kids' problems appear to be getting worse.

How to reconcile the two parts of the story: adolescents aren't so bad, but a growing number are jeopardizing their future through destructive behavior? Though we look upon teenagers as time bombs set to self-destruct at puberty, in fact the problems teens face are not

encoded in their genes. Their natural development, including a surge of hormonal activity during the first few years of adolescence, may make them a little more depressed or aggressive—but how we treat them has much more to do with teenagers' lives today. From the look of it, we aren't treating them very well.

A CRISIS OF ADULTS

If what goes on in adolescence happens largely in the kids, what goes wrong with adolescence happens primarily in the parents. "It wasn't until I turned to the parents' interviews that I really got a sense that something unusual was going on," reports Steinberg of his ongoing studies of over 200 adolescents and their families. As he details in his recent book, *Crossing Paths: How Your Child's Adolescence Triggers Your Own Crisis* (Simon & Schuster), Steinberg finds that adolescence sets off a crisis for parents.

Teenagers say that parents are not understanding and I don't think it is always that way.
—Gabriel, 16, Albuquerque, New Mexico

Parents do not have positive feelings during the time their kids go through adolescence, and it isn't simply because they expect their kids to be bad (although that's part of it). Scientists have studied the behavior and emotions of parents as well as their adolescent children, and found that when children reach puberty, parents experience tremendous changes in themselves. What's more, they shift their attitudes toward their children. It isn't just the kids who are distressed. Parents are too. Consider the following:

- Marital satisfaction, which typically declines over the course of marriage, reaches its all-time low when the oldest child reaches adolescence. Married parents of adolescents have an average of seven minutes alone with each other every day. For the marriages that don't pass the point of no return during their kids' teen years, there is actually an increase in satisfaction after the kids complete adolescence.

- Happily married parents have more positive interactions with their kids than unhappy parents. In single-parent families, parental happiness also influences their response to adolescence.

- In a surprising finding, the marital satisfaction of fathers is directly affected by how actively their adolescents are dating. Especially when sons are busy dating, fathers report a marked decline in interest in their wives. Dads aren't lusting for the girls Johnny brings home, they just miss what now seem like their own good old days.

Adults want kids to learn to take care of themselves. Kids need guides and advice. That is how you help people mature—not by leaving them alone.
—Michelle, 16, Clackamas, Oregon

- In family discussions, parents become increasingly negative toward their adolescents—there's more criticism, whining, frustration, anger, and defensiveness expressed verbally or in grimaces. While the kids are always more negative than their parents (it comes with increasing cognitive ability, in part), the parents are actually increasing the amount of negativity toward their children at a higher rate.

- Working mothers don't spend less time at home with their teenagers than nonworking moms do, but they do risk higher levels of burnout, because they continue to cover the lioness' share of work at home. On the other hand, a mother's employment makes her less vulnerable to the ups and downs of parenting an adolescent. Maternal employment also benefits kids, especially teen daughters, who report higher levels of self-esteem.

- Despite their fulfillment, mothers' self-esteem is actually lower while they are with their adolescents than when they are not. After all, a mother's authority is constantly being challenged, and she is being shunted to the margins of her child's universe.

- Teenagers turn increasingly to their friends, a distancing maneuver that feels like an emotional divorce to parents. Since mothers are generally more emotionally engaged with their children than are fathers, the separation can feel most painful to them. In fact, mothers typically report looking forward to the departure of their kids after high school. After the kids leave, mothers' emotional state improves.

- Fathers emotional states follow a different course. Fathers have more difficulty launching their adolescents, mostly because they feel regret about the time they didn't spend with them. Fathers have more difficulty dealing with their kids growing into adolescence and adulthood; they can't get used to the idea that they no longer have a little playmate who is going to do what daddy wants to do.

Add it all up and you get a bona fide midlife crisis in some parents, according to Steinberg. All along we've thought that a midlife crisis happens to some adults around the age of 40. But it turns out that midlife crisis has nothing to do with the age of the adult—and everything to do with the age of the oldest child in a family. It is set off by the entry of a family's first-born into adolescence.

Once the oldest child hits adolescence, parents are catapulted into a process of life review. "Where have I been, where am I now, where am I going?" These questions gnaw at parents who observe their children at the brink of adulthood.

It hits hardest the parent who is the same sex as the adolescent. Mothers and daughters actually have more difficulty than fathers and sons. In either case, the children tend to serve as a mirror of their younger lost selves, and bear the brunt of parents' regrets as parents distance themselves.

Steinberg tracks the psychological unrest associated with midlife crisis in parents:

- The onset of puberty is unavoidable evidence that their child is growing up.
- Along with puberty comes a child's burgeoning sexuality. For parents, this can raise doubts about their own attractiveness, their current sex life, as well as regrets or nostalgia for their teenage sexual experiences.
- The kids' new independence can make parents feel powerless. For fathers in particular this can remind them of the powerlessness they feel in the office if their careers have hit a plateau.
- Teens also become less concerned with their parents' approval. Their peer

group approval becomes more important. This hits mothers of daughters quite hard, especially single mothers, whose relationship to their daughters most resembles a friendship.

- Finally, de-idealization—kids' often blunt criticism of their parents—is a strong predictor of decline in parental mental health. Parents who used to be the ultimate expert to their kids are now reduced to debating partner for kids who have developed a new cognitive skill called relativism.

A clear picture begins to emerge: parents of a teenager feel depressed about their own life or their own marriage; feel the loss of their child; feel jealous, rejected, and confused about their child's new sexually mature looks, bad moods, withdrawal into privacy at home, and increasing involvement with friends. The kid is tied up in her (or his) own problems and wonders what planet mom and dad are on.

EMOTIONAL DIVORCE

The sad consequence is that parents who experience a midlife crisis begin avoiding their adolescent. Although a small proportion of parents are holding on to their teens too closely—usually they come from traditional families and have fundamentalist religious beliefs—more parents are backing off. The catch is that these teenagers want their parents' guidance. But more and more they just aren't getting it.

Some parents back away not out of their own inner confusion but because they think it's hip to do so. Either way, letting go causes confusion in the kids, not help in making their way into adulthood. Even if they are irritating or irritable, or just more withdrawn than they used to be, teens are seeking guidance.

Adults need to understand that it is very difficult to be a teenager nowadays. It takes a lot of understanding with so many problems like guns, drugs, AIDS, and gangs.
—Melissa, 14, Dallas, Texas

"I have this image of a kid groping through adolescence, kind of by himself" confides therapist Wagers, who sees a lot of parents out of touch with their kids. "The parents swarm around him, but don't actually talk to him, only to other people about him."

The mantra of therapists who work with adolescents and their families is "balance." Parents have to hold on, but not too tightly. They need to stay involved, even when their kids are ignoring them. Roland Montemayor, Ph.D., professor of psychology at Ohio State, finds it is not so different from learning how to deal with a two-year-old. You must stay within earshot, and be available whenever they falter or get themselves into trouble.

With a two-year-old, trouble means experimenting with mud pies or bopping a playmate; with a 14-year-old, it means experimenting with your car keys or sex. The task is the same—keep track of them and let them know what the rules are. Parents unfortunately taken up with their own midlife concerns may not embrace the task. God knows, it isn't easy. But it is vital.

Among parents who have gone through a real divorce, the emotional divorce that occurs between adolescents and their parents can heighten difficulty. It may reawaken feelings of sadness. Parents who don't have many interests outside the family are also vulnerable. Their kids are telling them to "Get a life!"—and that is exactly what they need to do.

DROPOUT PARENTS

As an adolescent reaches age 13, the time she is spending with parents is typically half that before age 10. "Teens come home and go into their bedrooms. They start to feel more comfortable by themselves than with siblings or parents around. They talk on the phone with friends, and their biggest worry usually has to do with a romantic interest," explains Reed Larson, Ph.D., who studies families and adolescents at the University of Illinois, Champaign-Urbana. Larson, coauthor of the recent book, *Divergent Realities: The Emotional Lives of Mothers, Fathers, and Adolescents,* studied 55 families who recorded their feelings and activities for one week, whenever prompted at random intervals by a beeper. He surveyed another 483 adolescents with the beeper method.

The families' reports revealed that a mutual withdrawal occurs. "When kids withdraw, parents get the message. They even feel intimidated. As a result they don't put in the extra effort to maintain contact with their kids," observes Larson. The kids feel abandoned, even though they're the ones retreating to their bedroom. The parents, in effect, cut their kids loose, just when they dip their toes in the waters of autonomy.

I don't think adults understand how complicated kids' minds are today, how much they think; they don't just accept something but wonder why it is.
—Adam, 14, Bethesda, Maryland

Separation is natural among humans as well as in the animal kingdom, Larson notes. Yet humans also need special care during this life transition—and suffer from reduced contact with parents and other adults. They still need to be taught how to do things, how to think about things, but above all they need to know that there is a safety net, a sense that their parents are paying attention and are going to jump in when things go wrong. The kids don't need the direct supervision they received at age two or eight, but they benefit emotionally and intellectually from positive contact with their parents.

Despite the tensions in family life, studies continue to confirm that the family remains one of the most effective vehicles to promote values, school success, even confidence in peer relationships. When it works, family functions as what Larson calls a "comfort zone," a place or a relationship that serves as a home base out of which to operate. Kids feel more secure, calm, and confident than those without a comfort zone. Similarly, Steinberg finds, the one common link among the many successful adolescents in his studies is that they all have positive relationships with their parents. Without positive relationships, the kids are subject to depression and likely to do poorly in school.

Parental withdrawal is a prime characteristic of families where adolescents get into trouble. It often catapults families into therapy. Wagers tells the story of a single parent who wasn't simply withdrawn, her head was in the sand: "I was seeing a mother and her 12-year-old son, who had depression and behavior problems. The mother called me up one time to say she had found all this marijuana paraphernalia in her son's room, in his pocket. She said she wasn't sure what it means. When I said 'it means that he's smoking pot,' she was very reluctant to agree. She didn't want to talk to her son about why he was getting into trouble or smoking pot. She wanted me to fix him." (Eventually, in therapy, the mother learned how to give her son a curfew and other rules, and to enforce them. He's doing much better.)

Teenagers know what is happening around them in school but adults hide things. Parents should shield their kids from some things but not so much that kids are afraid to go out into the world.
—Sarah, 17, Hanover, NH

Marital problems also enter into the distancing equation. Although the marital decline among teens' parents is part of the normal course of marriage, the adolescent can exacerbate the problem. "Here is a new person challenging you in ways that might make you irritable or insecure," explains Steinberg. "That can spill over into the marriage. The standard scenario involves the adolescent and the mother who have been home squabbling all afternoon. Well, the mom isn't exactly going to be in a terrific mood to greet her husband. It resembles the marital problems that occur when a couple first has a new baby." Trouble is, when the parents' marriage declines, so does the quality of the parenting—at a time when more parental energy is needed.

As if there are not enough psychological forces reducing contact between parents and adolescents today, social trends add to the problem, contends Roland Montemayor. Intensified work sched-

ules, increased divorce and single parenthood, and poverty—often a result of divorce and single parenthood—decrease parent–child contact. A fourth of all teenagers live with one parent, usually their mother. Families have fewer ties to the community, so there are fewer other adults with whom teens have nurturing ties. The negative images of teenagers as violent delinquents may even intimidate parents.

ALONE AND ANGRY

Whatever the source, parental distancing doesn't make for happy kids. "The kids I work with at Ohio State are remarkably independent, yet they are resentful of it," says Montemayor. "There is a sense of not being connected somehow." Kids are angry about being left to themselves, being given independence without the kind of mentoring from their parents to learn how to use their independence.

I am insecure about my future. The main view toward people in my generation is that we are all slackers and it's kind of disturbing. We are actually trying to make something of ourselves.
—Jasmine, 16, Brooklyn, New York

Adult contact seems to be on teenagers' minds more than ever before. Sociologist Dale Blythe, Ph.D., is an adolescence researcher who directs Minneapolis' noted Search Institute, which specializes in studies of youth policy issues. He has surveyed teens in 30 communities across the country, and found that when you ask teens, they say that family is not the most important thing in their lives—peers and social activities are. Nevertheless a large proportion of them say that they want more time with adults—they want their attention and leadership. They want more respect from adults and more cues on how to make it in the adult world. What a shift from 25 years ago, when the watchword was "never trust anyone over 30"!

The Invention of Adolescence

Are Romeo and Juliet the Quintessential adolescents? On the yes side, they were rebelling against family traditions, in the throes of first love, prone to melodrama, and engaged in violent and risky behavior. But the truth is that there was no such thing as adolescence in Shakespeare's time (the 16th century). Young people the ages of Romeo and Juliet (around 13) were adults in the eyes of society—even though they were probably prepubescent.

Paradoxically, puberty came later in eras past while departure from parental supervision came earlier than it does today. Romeo and Juliet carried the weight of the world on their shoulders—although it was a far smaller world than today's teens inhabit.

Another way to look at it is that in centuries past, a sexually mature person was never treated as a "growing child." Today sexually mature folk spend perhaps six years—ages 12 to 18—living under the authority of their parents.

Since the mid-1800s, puberty—the advent of sexual maturation and the starting point of adolescence—has inched back one year for every 25 years elapsed. It now occurs on average six years earlier than it did in 1850—age 11 or 12 for girls; age 12 or 13 for boys. Today adolescents make up 17 percent of the U.S. population and about a third of them belong to racial or ethnic minorities.

It's still not clear exactly what triggers puberty, confides Jeanne Brooks-Gunn, Ph.D., of Columbia University Teachers College, an expert on adolescent development. "The onset of puberty has fallen probably due to better nutrition in the prenatal period as well as throughout childhood. Pubertal age—for girls, when their first period occurs—has been lower in the affluent than the nonaffluent classes throughout recorded history. Differences are still found in countries where starvation and malnutrition are common among the poor. In Western countries, no social-class differences are found." Although adolescence is a new phenomenon in the history of our species, thanks to a stable and abundant food supply, we've already hit its limits—it's

not likely puberty onset will drop much below the age of 12.

If kids look like adults sooner than ever before, that doesn't mean they are. The brain begins to change when the body does, but it doesn't become a grown-up thinking organ as quickly as other systems of the body mature. The clash between physical maturity and mental immaturity not only throws parents a curve—they forget how to do their job, or even what it is—it catapults teens into some silly situations. They become intensely interested in romance, for example, only their idea of romance is absurdly simple, culminating in notes passed across the classroom: "Do you like me? Check yes or no."

Puberty isn't the only marker of adolescence. There's a slowly increasing capacity for abstract reasoning and relative thinking. Their new capacity for abstraction allows teens to think about big things—Death, Destruction, Nuclear War—subjects that depress them, especially since they lack the capacity to ameliorate them.

The idea that everything is relative suddenly makes every rule subject to debate. As time passes, teens attain the ability to make finer abstract distinctions. Which is to say, they become better at choosing their fights.

Teens also move toward autonomy. They want to be alone, they say, because they have a lot on their minds. Yet much of the autonomy hinges on the growing importance of social relationships. Evaluating the ups and downs of social situations indeed requires time alone. Family ties, however, remain more important than you might expect as teens increase identification with their peers.

Whatever else turns teens into the moody creatures they are, hormones have been given far too much credit, contends Brooks-Gunn. In fact, she points out, the flow of hormones that eventually shapes their bodies actually starts around age seven or eight. "Certain emotional states and problems increase between ages 11 and 14, at the time puberty takes place. These changes are probably due to the increased social

and school demands, the multiple new events that youth confront, their own responses to puberty, and to a much lesser extent hormonal changes themselves."

The nutritional abundance that underlies a long adolescence also prompted the extension of education, which has created a problem entirely novel in the animal kingdom—physically mature creatures living with their parents, and for more years than sexually mature offspring ever have in the past. College-bound kids typically depend on their parents until at least age 21, a decade or more after hitting puberty.

Historically, children never lived at home during the teen years, points out Temple University's Laurence Steinberg. Either they were shipped out to apprenticeships or off to other relatives.

Among lower primates, physically mature beasts simply are not welcome in the family den; sexual competition makes cohabiting untenable. But for animals, physical maturity coincides with mental acuity, so their departure is not a rejection.

The formal study of adolescence began in the 1940s, just before James Dean changed our perception of it forever. There is a long-standing tradition of professional observers looking at adolescence as a pathology—and this one really did start with Freud. It continues still.

A 1988 study reported that although the under-18 population actually declined from 1980 to 1984, adolescent admissions to private psychiatric hospitals increased—450 percent! The study suggests a staggering cultural taste for applying mental health care to any problem life presents. It also hints at the negative feelings Americans have toward adolescence—we consider it a disease.

The study of adolescence has come with a context—a culture of, by, and for youth, arising in the postwar boom of the 1950s and epitomized by James Dean. Once the original badass depressive teenager from hell, Dean seems quaintly tame by today's standards. But the fear and loathing he set in motion among adults is a powerful legacy today's teens are still struggling to live down.—V.R.

Many times teenagers are thought of as a problem that no one really wants to deal with. People are sometimes intimidated and become hostile because teenagers are willing to challenge their authority. It is looked at as being disrespectful. Teenagers are, many times, not treated like an asset and as innovative thinkers who will be the leaders of tomorrow. Adults have the power to teach the younger generation about the world and allow them to feel they have a voice in it.—**Zula, 16, Brooklyn, NY**

SILENCED SEX

Who can talk about teens without talking about sex? The topic of teenage sexuality, however, heightens parents' sense of powerlessness. Adults hesitate to acknowledge their own sexual experience in addressing the issue. They resolve the matter by pretending sex doesn't exist.

Sexuality was conspicuous by its absence in all the family interviews Steinberg, Montemayor, or Larson observed. Calling sex a hidden issue in adolescence verges on an oxymoron. Sprouting pubic hair and expanding busts aren't particularly subtle phenomena. But adolescent sexuality is only heightened by the silence.

I think Al Gore is a super environmentalist. With no ozone layer, the world is just going to melt. It's hard not to worry. The environment is really messed up and with no environment there will be no economy, no education, nothing. I hate it when people throw six-pack rings in the lake. We need to think about the environment because we need to get on with the rest of our lives. I don't think adults generally look to kids for opinions.—**Sam, 13, New York City**

So it's up to parents to seek more contact with their kids—despite the conflict they'll encounter. "The role of parents is to socialize children, to help them become responsible adults, to teach them to do the right thing. Conflict is an inevitable part of it" says Montemayor. He notes that one of the biggest sources of conflict between parents and teens is time management. Teens have trouble committing to plans in advance. They want to keep their options wide open all the time. The only surefire way to reduce conflict is to withdraw from teenagers—an equally surefire way to harm them.

"In other countries parents don't shy away from conflict. In the United States we have this idea that things are going to be hunky-dory and that we are going to go bowling and have fun together. Most people in the world would find that a pretty fanciful idea. There is an inevitable tension between parents and adolescents, and there's nothing wrong with that."

Doing the right thing and being good at what you're doing is important to me.

As teenagers we have a lot of things on our back, a lot of people are looking for us to do many great things. We also take in a lot of things and we know a lot of things. I care about the environment because it's a place that we all have to live in, not just us but our families and children. Even though I'm 15, I still have to keep those things in mind because it's serious. As for my own future, I've had a good upbringing and I see all open doors.—**Semu, 15, New York City**

culture, worship teen sexuality, mistakenly believing adolescence is the peak of human sexuality. Boys have more hard-ons than their dads, while the girls have less cellulite than their moms.

These kids may have the biological equipment, says Schnarch, but they don't yet know how to make love. Sex isn't just about orgasms, it is about intimacy. "All of our sex education is designed to raise kids to be healthy, normal adults. But we are confused about what we believe is sexually normal. Textbooks say that boys reach their sexual peak in late adolescence; girls, five to 10 years later. The adolescent believes it, parents believe it, schools believe it. In the hierarchy dictated by this narrow biological model of sexuality, the person with the best sex is the adolescent. On the one hand we are telling kids, 'we would like you to delay sexual involvement.' But when we teach a biological model of sexuality, we imply

I think there is going to be a lot of destruction and violence. There are all these peace treaties, but I don't think they are going to work out.

—Julia, 12, Albuquerque, NM

A postpubescent child introduces a third sexually mature person into the household, where once sex was a strictly private domain restricted to the older generation. It's difficult for everyone to get used to.

No matter how you slice it, sex can be an awkward topic. For parents, there's not only the feeling of powerlessness, there's discomfort. Most parents of adolescents aren't experiencing much sexual activity—neither the mechanics of sex nor its poetry—in this stage of the marriage (though this eventually improves).

The fact that fathers' marital satisfaction decreases when their kids start to date suggests the power of kids' sexuality, no matter how silenced, to distort parental behavior. Sex and marital therapist David Schnarch, Ph.D., points out that families, and the mythology of the

The future sounds alright. It is probably going to be more modern and really scientific. Things will be run by computers and computers will do more for people.
—Emily, 13, New York City

to the kids 'we know you can't delay. We think these are the best years of your life.' "

Parents can help their children by letting them know that they understand sex and have valuable experience about decisions related to sex; that they know it isn't just a mechanical act; that they recognize that teens are going to figure things out on their own with or without guidance from their parents; and that they are willing to talk about it. But often, the experience or meaning of sex gets lost.

I asked a woman whose parents had handed her birth control pills at age 15 how she felt about it now, at age 30. "I wish sex had been a little more taboo than it was. I got into a lot more sexual acting out before I was 20, and that didn't go very well for me. Even though my parents talked about the health consequences of sex, they did not mention other consequences. Like what it does to your self-esteem when you get involved in a series of one-night stands. So I guess I wish they had been more holistic in

> I don't feel any pressure about sex. It's a frequent topic of conversation, but we talk about other things, too—when I'm going to get my history paper done, movies, music. I listen to classical music a lot. I think about my maturity a lot, because I have recently had losses in my immediate family and it feels like I am maturing so fast. But then sometimes I feel so young compared to everything out there. I think adults have always felt that teens were more reckless.—Amanda, 16, New York City

their approach to sex. Not just to tell me about the pill when I was 15, but to understand the different issues I was struggling with. In every other aspect of my life, they were my best resource. But it turns out sex is a lot more complicated

> Teenagers, like adults, are all different. One has a job that is hard, another has more money and more education, and one just gets by. It is unfair to look at all teens the same way. You have maturity in you, but you just don't want to show it because it's no fun. We've got problems, but not really big ones like my uncle who came over from China when he was 16, or going to war when you're 18. If teenagers make it through this era, adults will just bash the next generation of teenagers.—Mike, 14, Brooklyn, New York

than I thought it was when I was 15. At 30, sex is a lot better than it was when I was a teenager."

The distortions parents create about teen sexuality lead directly to events like the "Spur Posse," the gang of teenage football stars in Southern California who systematically harassed and raped girls, terrorizing the community in the late 80s. The boys' fathers actually appeared on talk shows—to brag about their sons'

> *Jackie Joyner-Kersee, the Olympic track star, is my hero because she has accomplished so much and she is one of the main female athletes.*
> *—Kristy, 12, Woodbridge, New Jersey*

conquests. "The fathers were reinforcing the boys' behavior. It was as if it were a reflection on their own sexuality," observes Schnarch.

By closing their eyes to teen sexual behavior, parents don't just disengage from their kids. They leave them high and dry about understanding anything

> *My hero is Queen Latifah. She is herself and doesn't try to be somebody else. My mother is also my hero because she raises me as well as she can and she is a single parent.*
> *—Maria, 15, Bronx, New York*

more than the cold mechanics of sex. Kids raised this way report feeling very alone when it gets down to making intimate decisions for the first time. They feel like they haven't been given any help in what turns out to be the bigger part of sex—the relationship part of it.

Returning to the authoritarian, insular family of Ward, June, Wally, and the Beaver is not the solution for teenagers any more than it is for their parents. But teenagers do need parents and other responsible adults actively involved in their lives, just as younger children do. Only when it comes to teenagers, the grown-ups have to tolerate a lot more ambiguity—about authority, safety, responsibility, and closeness—to sustain the connection. If they can learn to do that, a lot of young people will be able to avoid a whole lot of trouble.

How Teens Strain the Family

What's most likely to set off a parent's midlife crisis? The presence of a child entering adolescence, says a psychologist who studied the stresses in 204 families.

Murray Dubin

Inquirer Staff Writer

When Dad makes a mistake around the house, 10-year-old Benjamin Steinberg of Ardmore either laughs hysterically "or he'll rub my face in it," says his father, Laurence Steinberg.

Steinberg, 42, the director of the developmental psychology department at Temple University, understands what's happening psychologically with his pre-adolescent son.

He knows that in the next few years, Benjamin will alter his view of his parents and take them off the pedestal. He knows that it's necessary for his son to separate himself and establish his own identity. Intellectually he understands, but it's still annoying when the kid pokes fun at the old man. And it will likely become more annoying as Benjamin gets older.

The reaction of adults to their adolescents' behavior is the subject of Steinberg's new book, *Crossing Paths—How Your Child's Adolescence Triggers Your Own Crisis* (Simon & Schuster), coauthored with his wife, Wendy, public relations coordinator at the Institute of Contemporary Art.

The book focuses on 204 families with adolescents that Steinberg and his project team studied in Wisconsin. It was there he discovered that the trigger for a parent's midlife crisis is likely to be a child becoming an adolescent.

Adolescence, Steinberg learned, has a far greater impact than previously imagined on the emotional well-being of parents. And it doesn't matter whether the parents are divorced, stepfamilied or in an intact family, living in a city or a suburb, working in a factory or a law firm, skin color of black, white or brown.

What does matter is the age of the children. If it's between 11 to 14 or so, there's a good chance that the kids are making mom or dad a little crazy.

Most of the psychological literature about families with teens looks at the impact that parents have on children. Just twice in the family life cycle has the literary spotlight illuminated children's impact on parents—at birth and when the kids leave home. For the most part, says Steinberg, the in-between time has been ignored by those who study and write about families.

And he did not set out to study it, either.

Steinberg's expertise is adolescent behavior and development. He set out in Wisconsin to find out more about how families "negotiated the change" as children grew into adolescence. A series of detailed questionnaires to family members was the initial research tool. Interviews came later.

"We had a good sense beforehand that this was a time of transformation of relationships in the family and we knew it was more likely to happen in early adolescence—11 to 14—than in late," he says in his Temple office.

"But we didn't know for sure it was affecting people's well-being. There's a difference between parents complaining about their adolescents and really being affected psychologically by what's going on. The surprise was the extent that they were affected.

"We looked at midlife literature and almost none of it talks about kids. They talk about work. They talk about physical changes."

He found that about 40 percent of the parents studied in a three-year period had a decline in their "psychological well-being" during their children's adolescence.

Steinberg is quick to point out that most adolescents get through adolescence fine and most adults get through their midlife just fine, thank you. But the 44-year-old parent with a 13-year-old is more likely to have difficulty than the 44-year-old parent with an 8-year-old.

One reason is de-idealization, a long word to describe the process in which a growing child learns that mom and dad make mistakes, too.

"The kids filled out the questionnaire, too, and the more they de-idealized their parents, the lower the parents' mental health.

"The kids are pointing out things and criticizing, and it all has an element of truth to parents. Some parents are more susceptible than others. Just because something is normative, that doesn't mean it won't bother you."

Reprinted with permission from *The Philadelphia Inquirer*, November 16, 1994, pp. H1, H3.

Laurence Steinberg and his wife, Wendy, of Ardmore know what to expect in the years ahead with their son, Benjamin, 10.

"Some of the criticism goes on in front of the spouse. It can be, 'You're no good at math. I'll ask Dad.' We don't talk much in this society about the ambivalent feelings that parents have about their children and we don't talk much about criticism of parents by kids."

Besides causing a decline in mental health, adolescence also may cause a decline in marital happiness.

Steinberg points out that most marriages that fail collapse early, but that marital happiness does dip into a trough at about 15 years. Couples that do not have children experience the same dip, but the decline is more precipitous for parents with teens.

"Bickering and squabbling between parents and kids and de-idealization makes a contribution to worsening marriages," he says. "When parents feel worse about themselves, it hurts the marriage."

Steinberg studied three types of families with teens or pre-teens: single parents, stepfamilies, and intact two-parent families.

SINGLE PARENTS

All of the single parents in the study were divorced women.

"Even good parents become less good following a divorce. They become less consistent, less vigilant, less organized."

Other studies show that single mothers and their sons—more so than their daughters—have a difficult time in the two-to-three-year period following a divorce.

"In the face of adversity, boys seem to do worse. We saw a lot of power struggles between single mothers and sons. In all families, the period of adolescence is when moms and sons go at it. In an intact family, the mom may say, 'Wait until your father gets home.' That works. Kids *are* more afraid of

their fathers. In single-parent families, there's no back-up defense to bring in."

In fact, a single mother is more likely to simply let her adolescent son go his own way than a mother in an intact family or in a stepfamily. "I was really surprised by this, but single mothers would say, 'He's so big, I can't control him anymore.' Must be something symbolic that he's now bigger and stronger."

While sons may be a problem, single mothers draw closer to their teenage daughters.

"There's an increase in closeness following the divorce and an increase in the quality of the closeness. Many single mothers had better relationships with their daughters than married mothers."

But, Steinberg says, when that daughter begins to separate and seek her own friends and her own space, "the single mom has more to lose if the adolescent becomes more emotionally distant."

Faced with the fact that adolescents are more likely to get into serious trouble than younger children, single parents react in one of two ways:

"One pattern is that the mother throws up her hands and sort of checks out. It is a to-hell-with-them attitude and it underlies the powerlessness and helplessness they feel. The second way is to start a crackdown, but they are unable to do that consistently and it doesn't work."

Steinberg says that it's difficult to be stricter as a child ages because the teenager is seeking fewer strictures.

He adds that single mothers are more permissive than mothers in intact families or in stepfamilies. The only more permissive parent is a single father.

STEPFAMILIES

New stepfamilies with teenagers have a more difficult time than if the children are small.

"The most common situation is mom remarries. Now there's a divided loyalties problem. She's torn between her children and her husband, and that's much more of a problem in adolescence because kids speak up at that age, they challenge."

The relationship between spouses is not on the firmest ground because the relationship is a new one. "Stepfamilies are sometimes like newlyweds, and when you are a newlywed you're more interested in pleasing your spouse."

Another problem is the break in continuity. "In two-parent families, parents may disagree, but not after doing things one way for five years. Stepfamilies have abrupt changes in family routines," Steinberg says.

"Lack of a biological and historical connection between father and child makes the authority of the parent less legitimate in the child's eye."

Unlike sons with divorced mothers, it is daughters who have the most difficulty with stepparents.

"If a remarriage occurs, it pulls the mother away from the daughter. They perceive their mother's remarriage as a loss of their mother. We didn't anticipate that. The reaction is more variable for boys."

He adds that other research shows that the story of the evil stepparent is a myth. "Most often it is really the evil stepchild."

INTACT FAMILIES

The dip in mental and emotional health strikes parents in intact families as well.

One parent may react well to the transformation of a child into an adult while the other may see it as a loss of control or, perhaps, an unwanted change in the parent-child relationship. Dad may be jealous of a son's success or mom may be depressed that a daughter is repeating youthful mistakes that she once made.

"If at the end of the day where you have been bickering and squabbling with your teenager, how ready are you to have fun with your spouse?"

Steinberg acknowledges that there is a flip side. "When the marriage is very happy, then marriage provides a buffer. Happily married men and women are less affected."

Work is also a buffer, no matter what the family configuration is. "We measured work satisfaction, and parents with satisfying careers are less likely to be negatively affected by their children's adolescence."

Many parents with adolescents are coping very well. The ones that seem to do the best have pleasures and pursuits other than parenting.

"A lot of parents out there, in a valiant way, have invested every part of themselves in being a parent," Steinberg says. "They are terrific parents, but . . . if all your eggs are in the parenting basket, that parent is the most vulnerable and will be hit hardest by their children becoming adolescents."

Enjoying summer
YOUR CHILD'S TEENAGE YEARS
*Some old-fashioned new advice about turning
the painful teen years into a fulfilling time to be a parent.*

Yep. Your adoring cherub has metamorphosed into a confused, insecure, sometimes volatile teenager. But that doesn't mean that you as a parent should become confused, insecure and volatile too.

"Where did you go?"

"Out."

"What did you do?"

"Nothing."

This little exchange is your cue that your child has embarked upon a new stage of his/her development — the struggle for independence. Teenagers want and need to take charge of their own lives. Not telling you everything (or anything) is merely part of the process.

The relationship between parent and child must change as adolescents become less an extension of the family and more an individual in their own right. Their families used to be the center of their emotional life; now peers and other adults are just as important to feelings of self-worth and self-esteem — and sometimes more so.

Parents often interpret this growth toward independence as rejection. Rather suddenly, your adolescent begins questioning your values, challenging your opinions, debating your rules, and telling you in countless small ways to go away. Actually, adolescents need to partially dissociate from the family. Yet the early development of independence is almost always played out in the home because the adolescent knows (at

"Where did you go?"

"Out."

"What did you do?"

"Nothing."

Laurence Steinberg Ph.D., and Ann Levine

least on an unconscious level) that home is a place where mistakes will not be too costly. And it is usually at home that adolescents express their need for independence through criticism and quarreling, silence and secrecy.

Accordingly, there may be a period of disequilibrium as family members adjust to the new person in their midst. But while disagreements are normal and common, constant fighting and out-and-out rebellion (running away, using drugs, truancy, delinquency) are not and may require professional help.

Adolescent insecurity has predictable consequences which parents can deal with if they expect some or all of the following:

Moodiness — Adolescents may be ecstatic one moment, despondent the next. The intensity of their emotions seems totally out of proportion to the events that inspire them.

Sulking — Adolescents do not have much experience talking about feelings. They may feel down but not know why, not be able to verbalize their feelings, or not want to do so.

Short Tempers — With little or no provocation, adolescents may blow up at their parents and siblings. This is a familiar defense mechanism we all use on occasion. When we are frustrated or anxious, we displace these feelings, and parents are frequent targets of displacement because, consciously or unconsciously, the teen believes that they will love him no matter how awful he is.

Standoffishness—Be prepared for your adolescent to reject your efforts to be helpful, reassuring, or affectionate. Your son may fly off the handle when you offer to help him fix his tape recorder—not because he doesn't need help, but because he doesn't want to be reminded that he still does. Requested to fuss over Aunt Suzy whom she hasn't seen in a year, your 13-year-old daughter disappears into her room. Some teenagers see routine gestures of affection not only as childish (and therefore inappropriate for them), but also as phony.

And teenagers don't want to be seen with their parents; they want to appear older and more independent. Ways to handle this situation are to invite the adolescent to bring a friend along; allow him to sit separately (in a movie theater); choose restaurants and movie theaters that are not school hangouts; and permit him to stay home alone sometimes without a hassle.

In addition, adolescents have a need for emotional as well as physical privacy. Small children like to tell their parents about what happened in school; adolescents jealously guard their personal lives. When you ask your adolescent daughter how her day went, you get a one-word answer (if that). One way adolescents establish their emotional independence is by keeping their thoughts and feelings to themselves. Being on stage all the time is tiring; closing the door to one's room allows a teenager to relax.

Criticism — Adolescents will look for (and find) their parents' personal weaknesses. Small children idealize their parents; adolescents can be hypercritical. Giving up a childish image of parents as all-knowing and all-powerful for a more realistic (and critical) appraisal of them is a necessary part of growing up.

Choosing friends before family — You used to spend Saturdays with your child. Now she'd rather be with her friends. This isn't a rejection of you, but an expression of her widening horizons.

Belief in a personal fable — The feeling that one is the center of attention can lead to feelings of exaggerated self-importance. Adolescents see themselves as unique; social and natural laws that apply to other people do not apply to them. On an abstract level, adolescents understand that playing with drugs can lead to addiction or an overdose; sex without contraception to pregnancy; driving above the speed limit to a ticket or an accident. But they don't have the life experience to understand that these facts apply to them, too. And feelings of uniqueness are another source of egocentrism: she honestly believes that no one has ever loved as deeply, hurt as badly, or understood things as clearly as she.

Hypocritical behavior — They expound lofty principles one minute, violate those same principles the next, and become indignant if an adult points out the discrepancy. Your daughter may spend hours talking about how she can't stand so-and-so because she's such a gossip. A crowd of teenagers may hold a rally for the environment and leave the site littered with soda cans. This apparent hypocrisy is the result of immaturity, not moral weakness.

WHAT NOT TO DO

Don't take the adolescent's steps toward independence personally. Try to remember that your adolescent is reacting to your role as a parent —to what you represent. She is going to want privacy no matter how understanding you have been; seek the advice of friends no matter how "with it" you are; and challenge you on day-to-day decisions no matter how democratic you have been.

Don't be afraid to say no. However much they may fuss and fume, adolescents appreciate limits. Setting limits shows you care. Decide where to draw the line. "No, you can't walk home by yourself at 10 p.m." "No, you are not allowed to go to a party unless there is adult supervision." "No, you're too young to drink." A good rule with adolescents is to say "yes"

when you can, "no" when you have to. But don't cut off discussion. Debating controversial issues like sex and drugs with parents helps adolescents to develop and espouse their own (not their peers') values and beliefs.

Don't overreact. Parents often feel helpless in the face of their teenager's misery; exasperated by unsuccessful attempts to make him or her "snap out of it." One of the hardest lessons for parents to learn is that they are not responsible for bringing their child out of his/her unhappiness. What adolescents and the rest of us want most when we are down is someone to listen, not a lecture. If your daughter is upset because her boyfriend left her, declaring cheerfully "There are other fish in the sea" won't help.

Don't pry. Respect your adolescent's desire to work things out for himself. Let him know that you see he is feeling blue and that you're available if he wants to talk. But don't persist in asking what's wrong. What he needs to know is that you are on his side and that it is safe to be himself at home, bad moods and all.

Don't give up. All parents want to raise good children — individuals who have a strong set of values and the courage to stand up for what they believe is right. The peer group may promote norms and values that undermine what parents are attempting to teach their children. TV soaps and serials treat violence, law-breaking, and casual sex as normal everyday events. The motto of the 1960s — "Do your own thing" — acquired new, materialistic, yuppie overtones in the 1980s that made the old ethics of self-discipline, self-denial, sacrifice, and service to others seem just that — old.

WHAT TO DO

Allow minor victories. Adolescents learn to make choices by having choices. Your job is not to solve their problems for them, but to protect them from making mistakes that will cause irreparable harm. Think about issues which you can defer to your child's judgment. Some good choices are how your adolescent dresses, how he decorates his room, what music he listens to, and (within reason) how he spends his allowance and what he does on weekends. A leather jacket, fatigue pants, and combat boots may not be your idea of chic, but they won't harm his health or hurt his future.

At the same time, be clear about the standards you expect your child to live up to. You won't tell him what to wear, but you expect his clothes to be clean. You won't tell him how to spend his Saturdays, but you expect him to tell you where he is going, with whom, and what they plan to do.

Expect some mistakes. In part, because of their immaturity and inexperience, all adolescents make foolish decisions. Your son may take a bus to the beach, spend half the afternoon playing Pac Man, only to realize later that he doesn't have the fare to get home. Your daughter may have spent her birthday money on an outfit that looks horrible. Ridicule ("How could you be so stupid?"), only undermines their confidence in their ability to make decisions.

Help the adolescent save face ("Everybody makes mistakes") and also learn to avoid such mistakes in the future. Did he think about buying a round-trip ticket? Did she ask about the store's return policy? These safety measures may seem obvious to you, but they won't be to new decision-makers who are going places by themselves and buying things for themselves for the first time.

Praise effort and achievement. However independent they may seem, adolescents still need your love and encouragement. Tell them you love them (even if they act as if they didn't hear you). Praise their efforts "You've really been helpful today." Try not to use shaming ("You should know better than that"), intimidation ("At the rate you're going, I doubt you'll make it to ninth grade"), or denigrating comparisons ("Your sister always got A's"). Such parental statements may be designed to prod an adolescent into behaving better, but the underlying message is a negative one: "You don't measure up."

Support friendships. Adolescents who have supportive friends, or even just one good friend, are less likely to be swayed by the crowd.

But draw the line. There is no reason to tolerate rudeness and disrespect. Feeling confused is not an excuse for throwing out everything you have taught her about manners and civility. If your adolescent snaps at you for asking how her day was, for example, say, "If you had a bad day and don't feel like talking about it, just say so. I have days like that myself."

HOW TO MINIMIZE CONFLICT

When your teenager acquires the use of logic, you will have met your match. And the adolescent's new intellectual independence can be disorienting. Your adolescent may point out — correctly — that you are irritable, short-tempered, irrational, and dictatorial. A few simple guidelines can make life easier.

Debating is not arguing. Quite simply, the teenager has become a better arguer. Like adults, teenagers look for the rationale behind a request. If they are being asked to do or not do something, they want to know why. And, like adults, when adolescents feel that a request is unreasonable, they respond with defiance.

Too often parents only see the negative side of this development. Would you want your son to go along with friends who decide to spray-paint racial slurs on a wall? Your daughter to give in when her boyfriend says she would go "all the way" if she really loved him? Do you want your adolescent to sit quietly in class, memorizing what the teacher says, never disagreeing, never asking a question?

If adolescents learn at home to stand their ground, and how to lose an argument without losing face, they will be better prepared to deal with peer pressure and illegitimate demands by other adults.

THE GOOD NEWS

The bad news about adolescence has been around for a long time. The good news is new. In the 1970s and 1980s a new wave of research swept through the field. Psychologists began to study how adolescents think, why they behave as they do, and how they respond to different types of parents. They looked not only at troubled young people, but also at ordinary, everyday kids. As a result of this research, common assumptions about adolescence have been exposed as myths.

It was established, for example, that psychological problems, problem behavior, and family conflict are no more common in adolescence than at any other stage of the life cycle. To be sure, some adolescents are troubled and some get into trouble. But the great majority (almost nine out of ten) do not. The problems we have come to see as a "normal" part of adolescent development — drugs, delinquency, irresponsible sex, opposition to any and all authority — are not normal at all. The bottom line is that good kids don't suddenly go bad in adolescence.

Studies also indicate that the evils of peer pressure have been overrated. To be sure, adolescents are concerned about what their friends think; they do want to fit in; and they are susceptible to peer pressure. But peer pressure is not a monolithic force.

What's more, the decline of the family has been overstated. In today's world, the story goes, the decline of neighborhoods, high divorce rates, women working, the youth culture, and the media all combine to undermine parental authority. This is nonsense. Parents remain the major influence on their child's attitudes and behavior through adolescence and into young adulthood. Adolescents care what you think and listen to what you say, even if they don't always admit it or agree. The majority of teenagers like their parents, respect them, agree with them on the big issues (though they might disagree over matters of taste and style), and want to please them. Good parent-child relationships do not deteriorate because of adolescence or household arrangements.

And cultural stereotypes die hard. A mother's apron declares, "Mother Nature, in all her wisdom, gave me 13 years to love my son before he became a teenager;" a father's coffee mug asserts, "Insanity is hereditary; you get it from your children." When parents of adolescents get together, they often play "Can you top this?" The parents who have survived the worst battles with their teenager get the most medals. Parents who haven't run into serious problems, who actually enjoy their teenagers, end up being apologetic: "I guess we are just lucky."

Yes, luck helps, but how you as a parent react to your adolescent is more important in laying the groundwork for good or bad times in your family.

When your young adult takes responsibility for his or her own life, you will become more like friends. The adolescent still needs you, but in a different way. The parent-adolescent relationship is like a partnership in which the senior partner has more expertise in many areas but looks forward to the day when the junior partner will take over the business of running his or her own life. Parents who resist the adolescent's desire for self-determination are missing the boat. Like it or not, your child is going to try to grow up. If you don't make room for her friends, grant her privacy, and let her make her own decisions about clothes and music, she will find other less benign ways to assert her independence.

But when parents welcome signs that their child is growing up and adjust gracefully to the new person in their midst, they often find adolescence the most rewarding time in their parental career. It's interesting to have a child with whom you can have an adult conversation (the kind of open-ended, all-nighters you haven't had since you were their age); exciting to be in touch with the latest fashions in clothes and music; fun to be able to share activities with a teenager (if you don't mind the fact that your daughter can beat you in tennis or knows more about computers than you do); and liberating to know that your child is on her way to becoming a self-reliant adult.

Laurence Steinberg is a professor of psychology at Temple University. Ann Levine is a New York-based writer specializing in human development.

"Don't talk back!"

Does your preteen have to argue about everything? Yes, but you can keep it all in perspective.

RICHARD M. LERNER, PH.D., AND CHERYL K. OLSON

Richard M. Lerner, Ph.D., is the director of the Institute for Children, Youth, and Families at Michigan State University, in East Lansing. Cheryl K. Olson is a specialist in youth and health communications.

Mark Twain once wryly noted, "When I was a boy of 14, my father was so ignorant that I could hardly stand to have the old man around. But when I got to be 21, I was astonished at how much he had learned in seven years."

If you're the parent of a preteen, you know all too well what it's like to be on the receiving end of that attitude. The youngster who once saw you as the source of all wisdom now cuts you off in midconversation with utterances such as "You can't tell me what to do" and "Why do I bother explaining things to you? You can't possibly understand." In addition, he suddenly seems to question every statement that comes out of your mouth. He

may even use the occasional obscenity.

It's easy for a parent to lose patience when a child starts mouthing off this way; none of us enjoys being treated disrespectfully or having to justify everything we say. Back talk is also disturbing because it signifies your loss of control over your child's behavior.

But as inappropriate and disrespectful as a preteen's language might be, it's actually a step toward mature behavior. Learning to assert individual opinions is a developmental milestone every bit as significant, and universal, as cutting teeth or walking. As annoying as this stage in your child's life can be at times, there is no way you can absolutely abolish back talk. There are, however, a number of ways for you to recognize and provide outlets for your child's opinions, emotions, and growing skills at debate.

Begin by understanding why your child needs to talk back. Her "smart mouth" is, in some ways, exactly that—a sign that she's smarter. Her logic is growing more sophisticated, although it's not

quite up to adult level yet. She now sees her parents' opinions, once regarded as the absolute truth, as one possible truth—and a version of it that she sometimes finds hard to swallow.

Chalk that up to another aspect of preadolescence: **your child's need to establish herself as a person separate from you. Just as it is your job to watch over and protect your child, it is your child's job to stake out her own emotional turf, to discover who she is and what she stands for.**

An increase in back talk often coincides with a developmental transition, such as starting middle or junior high school. Hanging out with a new group of kids may lead your child to think that a certain level of repartee is expected of her. You may need to tell your adolescent, "I know you talk this way with your friends, but I find it unpleasant to hear that kind of language at home."

Don't belittle your child. In the heat of the moment, this rule can be tough to follow, but it's crucial. No matter

how adult your preteen wants to be, he is still a child, with easily hurt feelings and little experience in the art of persuasion.

For example, if you take your child to task for doing his homework in front of the television, he may answer you dismissively with, "This isn't homework. It's just answering questions." You could easily answer him with something like, "That's ridiculous! Do you think I don't know what homework is?"

Although understandable, this response will only serve to embroil you further in an unproductive argument. What you might do instead is say something such as, "Whatever you call it, I want you to try your best at your schoolwork, and I don't think you can do that if you're working in front of the television."

Similarly, if your child is using unpleasant language toward a sibling and you tell him to stop it, he might say, **"I'm not being mean; I'm just defending myself!" Your impulse might well be to say, "That's baloney! I heard the way you talked**

If your child is hanging out with a new group of kids, he may start talking like them.

to her." But it's probably more helpful if you respond by saying something like," Standing up for yourself is a good thing, but you have to try to do it without using words that hurt others' feelings."

Fight fair, even when your child doesn't. Resist the temptation to fight fire with fire, especially if your preteen gets so angry during an argument that she curses at you, shoves you, or even spits on you. If something like this happens, as calmly as you can, say, "I want you to let me know how you feel about things, but I can't tolerate this behavior. The conversation is over." Follow up with appropriate discipline.

Stick to your values. Debates with your child will be more fruitful for both of you if you know what is negotiable and what is not. If you have a habit of arguing and then giving in, you'll get more of an argument from your child because he knows that it pays off. Put forward your deeply held values, and don't retreat from them—but be prepared to justify your position to your child.

Set limits on profanity. Preadolescents often use foul language to signal their grown-up status. It's hard to deny that cursing is an activity associated with adults. It is as reasonable to set limits on profanity, however, as it is on other adult behaviors, such as staying up late. What those limits are depends on how much foul language upsets you.

If your child says, "How come you get to say any words you want, and I don't?" tell her that using profanity is a habit of yours that you don't especially like and are trying to control, but that it sometimes happens when you're very angry or upset. You can also say to her, "By using those words, you're going to offend someone or create an **impression you'll regret later on.**"

Make sure you give your child credit for what he does right. Because one of your child's primary motives for talking back is to show that he is capable of holding his own in a grown-up conversation, acknowledge him when he succeeds, You won't lose ground by saying, "That's a good point you've made."

Suppose your 12-year-old son wants to sleep over at a friend's house and you say, "No, I don't want you to spend the night there. Blair's parents are lax about supervision."

Your child might respond with, "How do you know? *You've* never spent the night there."

Instead of treating this response as insolence, you might reply, "That's absolutely true. I've heard from other parents, however, that Blair's mom and dad sometimes go out and leave the kids alone. Maybe that isn't so, but the possibility worries me because I'm concerned about your safety."

After some discussion, your child might suggest a solution: "I'll call and make sure his parents will be there all night." After you agree to this—with the understanding that you can telephone the parents to confirm the arrangement—praise your child for respecting your concerns and solving the problem creatively.

Don't expect conflicts—or back talk—to be solved overnight. Arguments often do not have clear-cut resolutions. If you've both had your say and the conversation has become unproductive, you may have to tell your child, "We've been over this too many times. Let's wrap it up. Maybe if we think about it and talk tomorrow, it'll be easier for us to agree on something."

And remember that arguing with a child you love can be a highly emotional and exasperating experience. Don't expect perfection from yourself. Stay as calm and evenhanded as you can, and keep reminding yourself how smart you're going to be in just a few years.

Gay Families Come Out

SAME-SEX PARENTS are trying to move out of the shadows and into the mainstream. Will they—and their kids—be accepted?

BY BARBARA KANTROWITZ

THERE WERE MOMENTS IN Claire's childhood that seemed to call for a little . . . ingenuity. Like when friends came over. How could she explain the presence of Dorothy, the woman who moved into her Chicago home after Claire's dad left? Sometimes Claire said Dorothy was the housekeeper; other times she was an "aunt." In the living room, Claire would cover up the titles of books like "Lesbian Love Stories." More than a decade later, Claire's mother, Lee, recalls silently watching her daughter at the bookcase. It was, she says, "extremely painful to me." Even today, Lee and Claire—now 24 and recently married—want to be identified only by their middle names because they're worried about what their co-workers might think.

Hundreds of miles away, a 5-year-old girl named Lily lives in a toy-filled house with her mommies—Abby Rubenfeld, 43, a Nashville lawyer, and Debra Alberts, 38, a drug- and alcohol-abuse counselor who quit working to stay home. Rubenfeld and Alberts don't feel they should have to hide their relationship. It is, after all, the '90s, when companies like IBM offer gay partners the same benefits as husbands and wives, and celebrity couples like Melissa Etheridge and Julie Cypher proudly announce their expectant motherhood (interview).

Lily was conceived in a very '90s way; her father, Jim Hough, is a gay lawyer in New York who once worked as Rubenfeld's assistant and had always wanted to have kids. He flew to Nashville and the trio discussed his general health, his HIV status (negative) and logistics. They decided Rubenfeld would bear the child because Alberts is diabetic and pregnancy could be dangerous. They all signed a contract specifying that Hough has no financial or legal obligation. Then Rubenfeld figured out when she would be ovulating, and Hough flew down to donate his sperm so Alberts could artificially inseminate her at home. Nine months later, Lily was born.

Two daughters, two very different families. One haunted by secrecy, the other determined to be open. In the last few years, families headed by gay parents have stepped out of the shadows and moved toward the mainstream. Researchers believe the number of gay families is steadily increasing, although no one knows exactly how many there are. Estimates range from 6 million to 14 million children with at least one gay parent. Adoption agencies report more and more inquiries from prospective parents—especially men—who identify themselves as gay, and sperm banks say they're in the midst of what some call a "gayby boom" propelled by lesbians.

But being open does not always mean being accepted. Many Americans are still very uncomfortable with the idea of gay parents—either because of religious objections, genuine concern for the welfare of the children or bias against homosexuals in general. In a recent NEWSWEEK survey, almost half of those polled felt gays should not be allowed to adopt, although 57 percent thought gays could be just as good at parenting as straight people. Despite the tolerance of big companies like IBM, most gay partners do not receive spousal health benefits. Congress recently passed—and President Clinton signed—a bill allowing states to ban same-sex marriages. Only 13 states specifically permit single lesbians or gay men to adopt, according to the Lambda Legal Defense and Education Fund, a gay-rights advocacy group. Even then, usually only one partner is the parent of record—leaving the other in legal limbo. Courts have allowed adoptions by a second parent (either gay or straight) in some of those states, although the law is still in flux. In California, for example, Gov. Pete Wilson has been lobbying hard against his state's fairly open procedure for second-parent adoptions.

Dealing with other people's prejudices continues to be a rite of passage for children in gay families. Merle, 14, lives north of Boston with her mother, Molly, and her mother's partner, Laura. Over the years she has learned to ignore the name-calling—gay, queer, faggot—from kids who know her mother is a lesbian and assume she must be one, too (as far as she knows, she isn't). And there are other painful memories, like the time in fifth grade when a friend suddenly "changed her mind" about sleeping over. Merle later learned that the girl's parents had found out about Molly and Laura and wouldn't let their daughter associate with Merle. One day in sixth-grade health class, the teacher asked for examples of different kinds of families. When Merle raised her hand and said, "lesbian," the teacher responded: "This is such a nice town. There wouldn't be any lesbians living here."

Gays say they hope that being honest with the outside world will ultimately increase tolerance, just as parenthood makes them feel more connected to their communities. "It sort of gets you into the Mom and Dad clubs of America," says Jenifer Firestone, a lesbian mother and gay-family educator in Boston. Having a child can also repair strained family relations; mothers and fathers who may have once turned their backs on gay sons and daughters often find it emotionally impossible to ignore their grandchildren.

Still, the outlook for children in this new generation of gay families is unclear. Only a few have even reached school age, so there are

FOR THIS NEWSWEEK POLL, PRINCETON SURVEY RESEARCH ASSOCIATES TELEPHONED 929 ADULTS NATIONWIDE OCT. 17-18. THE MARGIN OF ERROR IS +/- 4 PERCENTAGE POINTS. THE NEWSWEEK POLL ©1996 BY NEWSWEEK, INC.

In the most recent Newsweek Poll, 57% of the adults surveyed said they think gay people can be as good at parenting as straight people; only 31% said they didn't think so

no long-term studies available of what the effects of growing up in such a family might be. Researchers do have some data on kids who grew up about the same time that Claire was living with Lee and Dorothy in Chicago. Most were born to a married mother and father who later split up. If the children were young, they generally wound up living with their mother, as did the majority of children of divorce. Pressures were often intense. The children worried about losing friends, while the mothers worried about losing custody if anyone found out about their sexual orientation. Yet despite these problems, the families were usually emotionally cohesive. In a comprehensive 1992 summary of studies of gay parenting, psychologist Charlotte Patterson of the University of Virginia concluded that the children are just as well adjusted (i.e., they do not have any more psychological problems and do just as well in school) as the offspring of heterosexual parents. The studies also show that as adults, they are no more likely to be gay than are children of straight parents.

The new generation of gay parents is far more diverse and will be harder to analyze. Often they are already in stable partnerships when they decide to start a family. They include lesbian couples who give birth through artificial insemination (the donors can be friends or anonymous contributors to a sperm bank); gay dads who adopt, hire surrogate mothers or pair up with lesbian friends to co-parent, and the more traditional—in this context, at least—parents who started out in heterosexual unions.

Usually they try to settle in a relatively liberal community within a large urban area like Boston, Chicago or Los Angeles, where their children will be able to mix with all kinds of families. They often join one of the many support groups that have been springing up around the country, like Gay and Lesbian Parents Coalition International or COLAGE, an acronym for Children of Lesbians and Gays Everywhere. The support groups form a kind of extended family, a shelter against the often hostile outside world.

A decade ago, when gay parents routinely hid their sexual orientation, the issues of differences rarely came up in school. But now gay parents say they try to be straightforward from the first day of class. Marilyn Morales, 34, and her partner, Angela Diaz, 37, live on Chicago's Northwest Side with their son, Christopher, 6, and their 4-month-old daughter, Alejandra, both conceived through artificial insemination. Registering Christopher for school proved to be an education for everyone. Because Morales appeared to be a single mother, a school official asked whether the family was receiving welfare. When Morales explained the situation, the woman was clearly embarrassed. "People don't know how to react," says Diaz. At Christopher's first soccer game, Diaz had to fill out a form that asked for "father's name." She scratched out "father's name" and wrote "Marilyn Morales." Both Morales and Diaz feel Christopher is more accepted now. "At birthday parties people say, 'Here comes Christopher's moms'," says Morales. Dazelle Steele's son Kyle is a friend of Christopher's, and the two boys often sleep over at each other's home. "They're such great parents," Steele says of Diaz and Morales. "Their actions spoke louder to me than rhetoric about their political decisions."

To the parents, each new encounter can feel like coming out all over again. Brian and Bernie are a Boston-area couple who don't want their last names used because they are in the process of finalizing the adoptions of two boys, ages 12 and 6. A few years ago, Brian dreaded meeting the older boy's Cub Scout leader because the man had actively tried to block a sex-education curriculum in the schools. But his son Ryan wanted badly to join the Scouts, and Bri-

an felt he needed to tell the man that the boy's parents were gay. As it turned out, the session went better than Brian had expected. "People challenge themselves, and people grow," Brian says. But, he adds, "as out as I am, I still feel the blood pressure go up, I sweat profusely, I'm red in the face as I tell him I'm gay, that I have a partner and that Ryan has two dads. I always think how it looks to Ryan. I'm always hoping he doesn't see me sweat."

Even in the relatively more tolerant '90s, gay parents "always feel threatened," says April Martin, a New York family therapist who is also a lesbian mother and the author of "The Lesbian and Gay Parenting Handbook." "How can you feel secure when it's still legal for someone to tear apart your family?" The parents are haunted by such well-publicized legal cases as the 1995 Virginia Supreme Court ruling that Sharon Bottoms was an unfit parent because she is a lesbian; she had to surrender custody of her 5-year-old son, Tyler, to her mother. In Florida this summer, the state appeals court ruled that John Ward, who was convicted of murdering his first wife in 1974, was a more fit parent than his ex-wife Mary, a lesbian.

Catherine Harris, 41, a university administrator in Boston, knows only too well the pain of these legal battles. Ten years ago, she was married and the mother of a toddler daughter, Tayler. Then she fell in love with Paula Vincent, now 38, a nurse-midwife. During the divorce Harris's husband fought for custody of Tayler, and Harris's parents, who disapproved of her new identity as a lesbian, testified against her. Her ex-husband won.

Harris is still on rocky terms with her parents and her ex-husband, but she and Vincent have started a new family of their own that now includes Sora, 7, and her twin siblings, Kaelyn and Marilla, 22 months. In contrast to Tayler, Sora knows her biological father only as "the donor." She has seen the vial his sperm came in and knows that her biological mother, Vincent, and Harris chose him because—according to the questionnaire he filled out at the sperm bank—he was well educated, spiritual and optimistic. "I don't really want a dad," says Sora. "I like having two moms."

Looking for Comfort Zones

The acceptance of gay men and lesbians as parents varies from state to state. This overview is based on information provided by the Lambda Legal Defense and Education Fund, a gay civil-rights group that looked at adoption law and custody decisions.

Highly tolerant ☐ Tolerant Varying tolerance Intolerant Highly intolerant

36% of those surveyed think gay couples should have the right to adopt, as compared with 29% in 1994; 47% oppose gay adoption rights, down from 65% in 1994

But problems can arise even in the most innocent situations. Wayne Steinman and Sal Iacullo didn't truly understand their fragile footing until Labor Day weekend a few years ago, when they drove to Disney World from their home in New York City. As they passed through Virginia, Steinman was at the steering wheel; Iacullo was in the back seat with their adopted daughter, Hope, now 9. They noticed a pickup truck sticking close to them, and when they pulled off the highway to get lunch the truck followed. Just as they were getting ready to pay the bill, two highway patrolmen walked in and started questioning them. The driver of the pickup had called the cops because he suspected the fathers of kidnapping. Fortunately, Steinman and Iacullo were able to convince the patrolmen that they were, in fact, Hope's parents. "From that point on, we carried the adoption papers in our pockets," says Iacullo.

Legalities aside, gay parents—and those who disapprove of gay families—are also concerned about issues of the children's emotional development. Most same-sex parents say they make a special effort to ensure that their kids learn to relate to adults of the opposite sex. Their situation is not that different from that of heterosexual single parents, and the solution is often the same: persuading aunts, uncles or grandparents to be part of their children's lives. Hope Steinman-Iacullo, for example, often visits with her grandmother, her aunts and her teenage cousins. "There are a lot of female role models," says Iacullo.

Psychologists say the best time to tell kids how their families are different is either in childhood or in late adolescence. Young adolescents—from about ages 11 to 15—are particularly vulnerable because they are struggling with their own issues of sexual identity. George Kuhlman and his ex-wife shared joint custody of their daughter, Annie, who was 13 when their marriage fell apart in the early 1980s. But although Annie talked to her father nearly every day of her life, he never told her he was gay. "Several of my friends and even family members had been of the opinion that there might be some real psychological damage and some anger if I didn't make the disclosure," says Kuhlman, now 49 and the ethics counsel for the American Bar Association in Chicago. "That was the bear breathing down my neck." But the timing never seemed right.

Then, one day when Annie was a college freshman, he called to say goodbye as he was about to head off for a Caribbean vacation with a male friend. "She just said, 'Dad, I know. I've known for a long time . . . I just thought you and Tom would have a much nicer time and a happier vacation if you know that I knew and I love you.' I pretty much fell to pieces." Annie, now 24, says she is happy she learned about her father when she was an adult. His sexuality isn't an issue now, she says. "When you have a dedicated parent, it matters less."

And, ultimately, it is the quality of the parenting—not the parents' lifestyle—that matters most to kids. Sexual orientation alone doesn't make a person a good or bad parent. In Maplewood, N.J., Charlie and Marc are raising 17-month-old Olivia, whom they adopted. Last Christmas she had a lead role in their church's holiday pageant. "So you had a little Chinese girl of two gay parents who was the baby Jesus," says Charlie. Adds Marc: "It gives a whole new meaning to the word 'Mary'." As she gets older, Charlie and Marc say, they'll explain to Olivia why her family is unusual. "I think Olivia is so lucky to have the opportunity to be different," says Marc. "And that's what I intend to teach her."

With KAREN SPRINGEN *in Chicago,* CLAUDIA KALB
in Boston, MARC PEYSER *in New York,*
MARK MILLER *in Los Angeles*
and DANIEL GLICK *in Denver*

BRINGING UP FATHER

**The message dads get is that they are not up to the job.
And a record number don't stick around—even as fathers
are needed more than ever.**

NANCY R. GIBBS

"I don't have a dad," says Megan, 8, a tiny blond child with a pixie nose who gazes up at a visitor and talks of her hunger. "Well, I do have a dad, but I don't know his name. I only know his first name, Bill."

Just what is it that fathers do?

"Love you. They kiss you and hug you when you need them. I had my mom's boyfriend for a while, but they broke up." Now Megan lives with just her mother and older brother in Culver City, California.

What would you like to do with your dad?

"I'd want him to talk to me." She's hurting now. "I wish I had somebody to talk to. It's not fair. If two people made you, then you should still be with those two people." And she's sad. "I'm not so special," she says, looking down at the floor. "I don't have two people."

She imagines what it would be like for him to come home from work at night.

"It would be just like that commercial where the kids say, 'Daddy, are you all right?'" She smiles, dreaming. "The kids show the daddy that they care for him. They put a thermometer in his mouth. They think he's sick because he came home early. They are sitting on the couch watching TV, and it's like, wow, we can play with Dad!"

Megan thinks her father is in the Navy now. "One day when I get older, I'm gonna go back to Alabama and try to find him."

More children will go to sleep tonight in a fatherless home than ever in the nation's history. Talk to the experts in crime, drug abuse, depression, school failure, and they can point to some study somewhere blaming those problems on the disappearance of fathers from the American family. But talk to the fathers who do stay with their families, and the story grows more complicated. What they are hearing, from their bosses, from institutions, from the culture around them, even from their own wives, very often comes down to a devastating message: We don't really trust men to be parents, and we don't really need them to be. And so every day, everywhere, their children are growing up without them.

Corporate America, for a start, may praise family life but does virtually nothing to ease it. Managers still take male workers aside and warn them not to take a paternity leave if they want to be taken seriously. On TV and in movies and magazine ads, the image of fathers over the past generation evolved from the stern, sturdy father who knew best to a helpless Homer Simpson, or some ham-handed galoot confounded by the prospect of changing a diaper. Teachers call parent conferences but only talk to the mothers. When father arrives at the doctor's office with little Betsy, the pediatrician offers instructions to pass along to his wife, the caregiver presumptive. The Census Bureau can document the 70 million mothers age 15 or older in the U.S. but has scant idea how many fathers there are. "There's no interest in fathers at all," says sociologist Vaughn Call, who directs the National Survey of Families and Households at the University of Wisconsin. "It's a nonexistent category. It's the ignored half of the family."

Mothers themselves can be unwitting accomplices. Even women whose own progress in public life depends on sharing the workload in private life act as "gatekeepers" in the home, to use Harvard pediatrician T. Berry Brazelton's description. Dig deeply into household dynamics, and the tensions emerge. Women say they need and want their husbands to be more active parents but fear that they aren't always reliable. Men say they might like to be more involved, but their wives will not make room for them, and jealously guard their domestic power.

Most troubling of all to some social scientists is the message men get that being a good father means learning how to mother. Among child-rearing experts, the debate rages over whether men and women parent differently, whether there is some unique contribution that each makes to the emotional health of their children. "Society sends men two messages," says psychologist Jerrold Lee Shapiro, father of two and the author of *A Measure of the Man*, his third book on fatherhood. "The first is, We want you to be involved, but you'll be an inadequate mother. The second is, You're invited into the birthing room and into the nurturing process—but we don't want all of you. We only want your support. We're not really ready as a culture to accept men's fears, their anger or their sadness. This is the stuff that makes men crazy. We want men to be the protectors and providers, but we are scared they won't be if they become soft."

So now America finds its stereotypes crushed in the collision between private needs and public pressures. While some commend the nurturing nature of the idealized New Father, others cringe at the idea

 From *Time*, June 28, 1993, pp. 52-56, 58, 61. © 1993 by Time Inc. Magazine Company. Reprinted by permission.

of genderless parenting and defend the importance of men being more than pale imitations of mothers. "If you become Mr. Mom," says Shapiro, "the family has a mother and an assistant mother. That isn't what good fathers are doing today." And fathers themselves wrestle with memories of their own fathers, vowing to do it differently, and struggling to figure out how.

THE DISAPPEARING DAD

Well into the 18th century, child-rearing manuals in America were generally addressed to fathers, not mothers. But as industrialization began to separate home and work, fathers could not be in both places at once. Family life of the 19th century was defined by what historians call the feminization of the domestic sphere and the marginalization of the father as a parent. By the 1830s, child-rearing manuals, increasingly addressed to mothers, deplored the father's absence from the home. In 1900 one worried observer could describe "the suburban husband and father" as "almost entirely a Sunday institution."

What alarms modern social scientists is that in the latter part of this century the father has been sidelined in a new, more disturbing way. Today he's often just plain absent. Rising divorce rates and out-of-wedlock births mean that more than 40% of all children born between 1970 and 1984 are likely to spend much of their childhood living in single-parent homes. In 1990, 25% were living with only their mothers, compared with 5% in 1960. Says David Blankenhorn, the founder of the Institute for American Values in New York City: "This trend of fatherlessness is the most socially consequential family trend of our generation."

Credit Dan Quayle for enduring the ridicule that opened the mainstream debate over whether fathers matter in families. In the year since his famous Murphy Brown speech, social scientists have produced mounting evidence that, at the very least, he had a point. Apart from the personal politics of parenting, there are larger social costs to reckon in a society that dismisses fathers as luxuries.

Studies of young criminals have found that more than 70% of all juveniles in state reform institutions come from fatherless homes. Children from broken families are nearly twice as likely as those in two-parent families to drop out of high school. After assessing the studies, economist Sylvia Hewlett suggested that "school failure may well have as much to do with disintegration of families as with the quality of schools."

Then there is the emotional price that children pay. In her 15 years tracking the lives of children of divorced families, Judith Wallerstein found that five years af-

ter the split, more than a third experienced moderate or severe depression. After 10 years a significant number of the young men and women appeared to be troubled, drifting and underachieving. At 15 years many of the thirtyish adults were struggling to create strong love relationships of their own. Daughters of divorce, she found, "often experience great difficulty establishing a realistic view of men in general, developing realistic expectations and exercising good judgment in their choice of partners."

For boys, the crucial issue is role modeling. There are psychologists who suggest that boys without fathers risk growing up with low self-esteem, becoming overly dependent on women and emotionally rigid. "Kids without fathers are forced to find their own ways of doing things," observes Melissa Manning, a social worker at the Boys and Girls Club of Venice, Cali-

It Takes Two

WOMEN'S VOICES ARE MORE SOOTHING. THEY CAN READ THE SIGNALS A CHILD SENDS BEFORE HE OR SHE CAN TALK. BUT AS TIME PASSES, THE STRENGTHS THAT FATHERS MAY BRING TO CHILD REARING BECOME MORE IMPORTANT.

fornia. "So they come up with their own ideas, from friends and from the gangs. Nobody is showing them what to do except to be drunk, deal drugs or go to jail." Then there are the subtler lessons that dads impart. Attorney Charles Firestone, for instance, recently decided it was time to teach his 11-year-old son how to play poker. "Maybe it will help if he knows when to hold 'em, when to fold 'em," he says.

THE ANTI-FATHER MESSAGE

Given the evidence that men are so vital to a healthy home, the anti-father messages that creep into the culture and its institutions are all the more troubling. Some scholars suggest that fatherhood is by its very biological nature more fragile than motherhood, and needs to be encouraged by the society around it. And yet for all the focus on the New Father (the kind who skips the corporate awards dinner to attend the school play), the messages men receive about how

they should act as parents are at best mixed and often explicitly hostile.

Employers that have been slow to accommodate the needs of mothers in their midst are often even more unforgiving of fathers. It is a powerful taboo that prevents men from acknowledging their commitment to their children at work. A 1989 survey of medium and large private employers found that only 1% of employees had access to paid paternity leave and just 18% could take unpaid leave. Even in companies like Eastman Kodak, only 7% of men, vs. 93% of women, have taken advantage of the six-year-old family-leave plan.

Those who do soon discover the cost. "My boss made me pay a price for it emotionally," says a prominent Washington executive who took leaves for both his children. "He was very generous with the time, but he never let me forget it. Every six seconds he reminded me what a great guy he was and that I owed him really, really big. You don't get a lot of points at the office for wanting to have a healthy family life." Men, like women, are increasingly troubled by the struggle to balance home and work; in 1989, asked if they experienced stress while doing so, 72% of men answered yes, compared with 12% a decade earlier, according to James Levine of the Fatherhood Project at the Families and Work Institute of New York City.

Many men will freely admit that they sometimes lie to employers about their commitments. "I announced that I was going to a meeting," shrugged a Washington journalist as he left the office in midafternoon one day recently. "I just neglected to mention that the 'meeting' was to watch my daughter play tennis." Now it is the fathers who are beginning to ask themselves whether their careers will stall and their incomes stagnate, whether the glass ceiling will press down on them once they make public their commitment as parents, whether today's productivity pressures will force them to work even harder with that much less time to be with their kids. In the higher reaches of management, there are not only few women, there are also few men in dual-income families who take an active part in raising their children. "Those who get to the top today," says Charles Rodgers, owner of a 10-year-old family-research organization in Brookline, Massachusetts, called Work/Family Directions, "are almost always men from what used to be the traditional family, men with wives who don't work outside the home."

Many men insist that they long to veer off onto a "daddy track." In a 1990 poll by the Los Angeles *Times,* 39% of the fathers said they would quit their jobs to have more time with their kids, while another survey found that 74% of men said they would rather have a daddy-track job than a fast-track job. But in real life, when they are not talking to pollsters, some fathers recognize the power of their atavistic impulses to earn bread and compete, both of which often leave them ambivalent about their obligations as fathers.

George Ingram, 48, lives on Capitol Hill with his sons Mason, 15, and Andrew, 10. He is the first to admit that single fatherhood has not helped his career as a political economist. "We're torn between working hard to become Secretary of State and nurturing our kids," he says. "You make the choice to nurture your kids, and people think it's great. But does it put a crimp on your career? Yes, very definitely. When I finish this process, I will have spent 15 years on a professional plateau." Ingram finds that his colleagues accept his dual commitments, his leaving every night before 6, or by 5 if he has a soccer practice to coach. In fact they are more accepting of his choices than those of his female colleagues. "I get more psychic support than women do," he says. "And I feel great about spending more time with my kids than my father did."

MATERNAL GATEKEEPERS

The more surprising obstacle men say, arises in their own homes. Every household may be different, every division of labor unique, but sociologists do find certain patterns emerging when they interview groups of men and women about how they view one another's parenting roles. Men talk about their wife's unrealistic expectations, her perfectionism, the insistence on dressing, feeding, soothing the children in a certain way. "Fathers, except in rare circumstances, have not yet become equal partners in parenthood," says Frank Furstenberg, professor of sociology at the University of Pennsylvania. "The restructuring of the father role requires support and encouragement from wives. Presumably, it is not abnormal for wives to be reluctant to give up maternal prerogatives."

Many men describe in frustration their wife's attitude that her way of doing things is the only way. "Dad is putting the baby to bed," says Levine. "He's holding his seven-month-old on his shoulders and walking around in circles. Mom comes in and says, 'She likes it better when you just lay her down on her stomach and rub her back.' Dad gets mad that Mom is undermining his way of doing things, which he thinks works perfectly well."

In most cases, it is still the mother who carries her child's life around in her head, keeping the mental daybook on who needs a lift to piano practice and who needs to get the poetry folder in on time. After examining much of the research on men's housework and child care, Sylvia Hewlett con-

cluded that married men's average time in household tasks had increased only 6% in 20 years, even as women have flooded the workplace. Psychologists Rosalind Barnett and Grace Baruch found that fathers were often willing to perform the jobs they were assigned but were not responsible for remembering, planning or scheduling them.

Women often respond that until men prove themselves dependable as parents, they can't expect to be trusted. A haphazard approach to family responsibilities does nothing to relieve the burdens women carry. "Men haven't been socialized to think about family appointments and how the household runs for kids," notes Marie Wilson of the Ms. Foundation for Women, who constantly hears of the hunger women feel for their husbands to participate more fully at home. "They don't really get in there and pay attention. Mothers often aren't sure they can trust them—not just to do it as they do it, but to do it at a level that you can get away with without feeling guilty."

Some women admit that their own feelings are mixed when it comes to relinquishing power within the family. "I can probably be overbearing at times as far as wanting to have it my way," says the 35-year-old wife of a St. Louis, Missouri, physician. "But I would be willing to relax my standards if he would be more involved. It would be a good trade-off." Here again the attitude is changing with each generation. Women under 35, researchers find, seem more willing than older women, whose own fathers were probably less engaged, to trust men as parents. Also, as younger women become more successful professionally, they are less fearful of relinquishing power at home because their identity and satisfaction come from many sources.

THE NEW FATHER

The redefinition of fatherhood has been going on in virtually every arena of American life for well over 20 years. As women worked to broaden their choices at home and work, the implicit invitation was for men to do likewise. As Levine has observed, Dr. Spock had carefully revised his advice on fathers by 1974. The earlier version suggested that fathers change the occasional diaper and cautioned mothers about "trying to force the participation of fathers who get gooseflesh at the very idea of helping to take care of a baby." The new version of *Baby and Child Care*, by contrast, offered a prescription for the New Fatherhood: "The father—any father—should be sharing with the mother the day-to-day care of their child from birth onward . . . This is the natural way for the father to start the relationship, just as it is for the mother."

By the '80s, bookstores were growing fat with titles aimed at men: *How to Father,*

Expectant Father, Pregnant Fathers, The Birth of a Father, Fathers Almanac and *Father Power.* There were books about child-and-father relations, like *How to Father a Successful Daughter,* and then specific texts for part-time fathers, single fathers, stepfathers and homosexual fathers. Bill Cosby's *Fatherhood* was one of the bestselling books in publishing history, and *Good Morning, Merry Sunshine,* by Chicago *Tribune* columnist Bob Greene, a journal about his first year of fatherhood, was on the New York *Times* best-seller list for almost a year. Parents can now pick up *Parents' Sports,* a new magazine dedicated to reaching the dad market with stories on the joys of soccer practice.

Institutions were changing too. In his book *Fatherhood in America,* published this month, Robert L. Griswold has traced the history of a fast-changing role that today not only allows men in the birthing room (90% of fathers are in attendance at their child's birth) but also offers them

Mixed Emotions

"WE'RE NOT READY TO ACCEPT MEN'S FEARS . . . OR THEIR SADNESS. WE WANT MEN TO BE THE PROTECTORS . . . BUT WE ARE SCARED THEY WON'T BE IF THEY BECOME SOFT."

postpartum courses in which new fathers learn how to change, feed, hold and generally take care of their infant. Some fathers may even get in on the pregnancy part by wearing the "empathy belly," a bulge the size and weight of a third-trimester fetus. Suddenly available to men hoping to solidify the father-child bond are "Saturday with Daddy Outings," special songfests, field trips and potlucks with dads. Even men behind bars could get help: one program allows an inmate father to read children's stories onto cassette tapes that are then sent, along with the book and a Polaroid picture of Dad, to his child.

"It's become cool to be a dad," says Wyatt Andrews, a correspondent for CBS News who has three children: Rachel, 8, Averil, 7, and Conrad, 5. "Even at dinner parties, disciplinary techniques are discussed. Fathers with teenagers give advice about strategies to fathers with younger kids. My father was career Navy. I don't think he ever spent two seconds thinking about strategies of child rearing. If he said anything, it was 'They listen to me.' "

BRING BACK DAD

These perceptual and behavioral shifts have achieved enough momentum to trigger a backlash of their own. Critics of the New Fatherhood are concerned that something precious is being lost in the revolution in parenting—some uniquely male contribution that is essential for raising healthy kids. In a clinical argument that sends off political steam, these researchers argue that fathers should be more than substitute mothers, that men parent differently than women and in ways that matter enormously. They say a mother's love is unconditional, a father's love is more qualified, more tied to performance; mothers are worried about the infant's survival, fathers about future success. "In other words, a father produces not just children but socially viable children," says Blankenhorn. "Fathers, more than mothers, are haunted by the fear that their children will turn out to be bums, largely because a father understands that his child's character is, in some sense, a measure of his character as well."

When it comes to discipline, according to this school of thought, it is the combination of mother and father that yields justice tempered by mercy. "Mothers discipline children on a moment-by-moment basis," says Shapiro. "They have this emotional umbilical cord that lets them read the child. Fathers discipline by rules. Kids learn from their moms how to be aware of their emotional side. From dad, they learn how to live in society."

As parents, some psychologists argue, men and women are suited for different roles at different times. The image of the New Fatherhood is Jack Nicholson surrounded by babies on the cover of *Vanity Fair*, the businessman changing a diaper on the newly installed changing tables in an airport men's room. But to focus only on infant care misses the larger point. "Parenting of young infants is not a natural activity for males," says David Popenoe, an associate dean of social studies at Rutgers University who specializes in the family. He and others argue that women's voices are more soothing; they are better able to read the signals a child sends before he or she can talk. But as time passes, the strengths that fathers may bring to child rearing become more important.

"At a time when fatherhood is collapsing in our society," warns Blankenhorn, "when more children than ever in history are being voluntarily abandoned by their fathers, the only thing we can think of talking about is infant care? It's an anemic, adult-centered way of looking at the problem." Why not let mothers, he says, do more of the heavy lifting in the early years and let fathers do more of the heavy lifting after infancy when their special skills have more relevance? As children get older, notes William Maddox, director of research and policy at the Washington-based Family Research Council, fathers become crucial in their physical and psychological development. "Go to a park and watch father and mother next to a child on a jungle gym," he said. "The father encourages the kid to challenge himself by climbing to the top; the mother tells him to be careful. What's most important is to have the balance of encouragement along with a warning."

This notion that men and women are genetically, or even culturally, predisposed to different parenting roles strikes other researchers as misguided. They are quick to reject the idea that there is some link between X or Y chromosomes and, say, conditional or unconditional love. "To take something that is only a statistical tendency," says historian E. Anthony Rotundo, "and turn it into a cultural imperative—fathers must do it this way and mothers must do it that way—only creates problems for the vast number of people who don't fit those tendencies, without benefiting the children at all." While researchers have found that children whose fathers are involved in their early rearing tend to have higher IQs, perform better in school and even have a better sense of humor, psychologists are quick to say this is not necessarily a gender issue. "It has to do with the fact that there are two people passionately in love with a child," says Harvard's Brazelton.

The very fact that psychologists are arguing about the nature of fatherhood, that filmmakers are making movies based entirely on fatherlove, that bookstores see a growth market in father guides speaks not only to children's well-being but to men's as well. As much as families need fathers, men need their children in ways they are finally allowed to acknowledge, to learn from them all the secrets that children, with their untidy minds and unflagging hearts, have mastered and that grownups, having grown up, long to retrieve.

—Reported by Ann Blackman/Washington, Priscilla Painton/New York and James Willwerth/Los Angeles

Longitudinal Studies of Effects of Divorce on Children in Great Britain and the United States

ANDREW J. CHERLIN, FRANK F. FURSTENBERG, JR., P. LINDSAY CHASE-LANSDALE,
KATHLEEN E. KIERNAN, PHILIP K. ROBINS, DONNA RUANE MORRISON,
JULIEN O. TEITLER

National, longitudinal surveys from Great Britain and the United States were used to investigate the effects of divorce on children. In both studies, a subsample of children who were in two-parent families during the initial interview (at age 7 in the British data and at ages 7 to 11 in the U.S. data) were followed through the next interview (at age 11 and ages 11 to 16, respectively). At both time points in the British data, parents and teachers independently rated the children's behavior problems, and the children were given reading and mathematics achievement tests. At both time points in the U.S. data, parents rated the children's behavior problems. Children whose parents divorced or separated between the two time points were compared to children whose families remained intact. For boys, the apparent effect of separation or divorce on behavior problems and achievement at the later time point was sharply reduced by considering behavior problems, achievement levels, and family difficulties that were present at the earlier time point, before any of the families had broken up. For girls, the reduction in the apparent effect of divorce occurred to a lesser but still noticeable extent once preexisting conditions were considered.

AT CURRENT RATES, ABOUT 40% OF U.S. CHILDREN WILL witness the breakup of their parents' marriages before they reach 18 (1). The research literature leaves no doubt that, on average, children of divorced parents experience more emotional and behavioral problems and do less well in school than children who live with both biological parents (2). But much less is known about why children whose parents divorce do less well. Most observers assume that their troubles stem mainly from the difficult adjustment children must make after their parents separate. Studies emphasize how difficult it can be for a recently separated mother or father to function effectively as a parent. "Put simply," wrote Wallerstein and Kelly, "the central hazard which divorce poses to the psychological health and development of children and adolescents is in the diminished or disrupted parenting which so often follows in the wake of the rupture and which can become consolidated within the post-divorce family" (3). Largely because of the widespread perception that marital disruption makes children more vulnerable to problems, a series of social policies and legal reforms were enacted in the 1970s and 1980s to increase and enforce child support payments and to encourage new custody practices that promote contact and cooperation between divorced parents (4).

We agree that events occurring after the separation can be critical for children's adjustment and that adequate child support payments and workable custody arrangements are indispensable. However, we present evidence that, at least for boys, tempers the conclusion that the aftermath of divorce is the major factor in children's adjustment. Our evidence, which comes from statistical analyses of national, longitudinal studies of children in both Great Britain and the United States, indicates that a substantial portion of what is usually considered the effect of divorce on children is visible before the parents separate. For boys, the apparent effect of divorce on behavior problems and school achievement falls by about half to levels that are not significantly different from zero, once preexisting behavior problems, achievement test scores, and family difficulties evident before the separation are taken into account. For girls, the same preexisting conditions reduce the effects of divorce to a lesser but still noticeable degree.

The observed differences between children from families in which the parents have separated or divorced and children from two-parent families may be traced to three distinct sources. The first source is the effect of growing up in a dysfunctional family—a home where serious problems of the parents or the children make normal development difficult. Parents with psychological impairments are reportedly more prone to divorce and their children are more likely to experience developmental difficulties (5). A second source, often accompanying the first, is severe and protracted marital conflict, which is known to harm children's development and often leads to divorce (6). The third source is the difficult transition that occurs only after couples separate—the emotional upset, fall in income, diminished parenting, continued conflict, and so forth. Although some researchers acknowledge the potentially adverse contribution of each source (7), nearly all empirical studies have focused exclusively on the third—the period after the separation—and have collected information only after the separation occurred (8).

Moreover, the current understanding of the effects of divorce on children is largely based on intensive, observational studies of a

A. J. Cherlin and D. R. Morrison are in the Department of Sociology, Johns Hopkins University, Baltimore, MD 21218. F. F. Furstenberg, Jr., and J. O. Teitler are in the Department of Sociology, 3718 Locust Walk, University of Pennsylvania, Philadelphia, PA 19104. P. L. Chase-Lansdale is at the Chapin Hall Center for Children, University of Chicago, 1155 East 60 Street, Chicago, IL 60637. K. E. Kiernan is at the Family Policy Studies Centre, 231 Baker Street, London NW1 6XE, United Kingdom. P. K. Robins is in the Department of Economics, University of Miami, Coral Gables, FL 33124.

relatively small number of families (9). These studies are invaluable because of the detailed observations of family interaction and child development they provide, but they typically are based on nonrandom samples of the population. In some influential clinical studies, there has not been a comparison group of intact families (3).

The British National Child Development Study

We describe two prospective studies that began with large samples of intact families. The British data come from the National Child Development Study (NCDS). Originally a study of perinatal mortality, the NCDS began as a survey of the mothers of all children born in England, Scotland, and Wales during the week of 3 to 9 March 1958 (10). Interviews were completed with 17,414 mothers, representing 98% of all women giving birth (11). In 1965, when the children were 7, the parents (usually the mothers) of 14,746 children were successfully reinterviewed. Local authority health visitors (trained nurses who normally saw every family before and after the birth of a child and frequently conducted follow-up visits, especially to families with difficulties) asked the mothers the majority of questions from the Rutter Home Behaviour Scale, which measured the children's behavior problems (12), and reported on the family's difficulties and use of social welfare services.

Our factor analyses of the Rutter items identified the two clusters of behavior problems typical of assessments such as these: "externalizing disorders" (aggression, disobedience) and "internalizing disorders" (depression, anxiety). However, the reliability of the internalizing subscale was considerably lower than that of the externalizing subscale. Consequently, we constructed a single, 18-item summated scale (α reliability = 0.72). The items were: temper tantrums, reluctance to go to school, bad dreams, difficulty sleeping, food fads, poor appetite, difficulty concentrating, bullied by other children, destructive, miserable or tearful, squirmy or fidgety, continually worried, irritable, upset by new situations, twitches or other mannerisms, fights with other children, disobedient at home, and sleepwalking.

In addition, the children's teachers filled out a detailed behavioral assessment at age 7, the Bristol Social Adjustment Guide (BSAG) (13). Again, our factor analyses showed the externalizing versus internalizing distinction, but the internalizing subscale was weaker. So again we constructed a single scale (α = 0.68). The children also were given reading and mathematics tests (14) and physical examinations at age 7. Then in 1969, when the children were 11, another round of interviews and testing was undertaken. Parents again were asked questions on children's behavior problems, and teachers once again filled out the BSAG (15). The reading and mathematics tests that had been given earlier were not appropriate for 11-year-olds; instead, the study used reading and mathematics achievement tests constructed specifically for this round of the NCDS, and standardized against normal populations, by the National Foundation for Educational Research in England and Wales (16).

Divorce and Children's Adjustment

We use parent-rated and teacher-rated behavior problems and reading and mathematics achievement, all measured at age 11, as the four outcome measures of children's adjustment in our analyses. In order to evaluate the relative contributions of pre- and post-separation sources of children's adjustment at age 11, we restricted our analyses to children whose parents were in an intact, first marriage in 1965, when the children were 7—the first time we have

detailed information about the children's behavior and achievement. Then we followed these children as they split into two groups by age 11: those whose parents had divorced or separated and those who parents had remained together (17). (Henceforth by "divorce" we mean divorce or marital separation; we do not distinguish between them.)

The number of children living with both parents at age 7 and for whom outcome variables were observed at age 11 ranged from 11,658 to 11,837 for the four outcome variables. Among these, there were 239 instances of a divorce occurring between ages 7 and 11. A remarriage before age 11 occurred in only 47 of these instances, so we have not analyzed separately data on non-remarried and remarried cases but rather have combined them. One limitation of the NCDS is that it did not obtain the exact date at which a marital disruption occurred. We can determine whether or not a divorce occurred between the age 7 and age 11 interviews, but we cannot determine the exact timing of the divorce. We conducted all analyses separately by the child's gender because of evidence in the literature that the effect of divorce is different for boys than for girls (2).

As expected, we found that boys and girls whose parents had divorced between the age 7 and age 11 interviews showed more behavior problems at age 11, as rated by parents and by teachers, and scored lower than other children on reading and mathematics achievement tests at age 11, even after controlling for predictors such as social class and race (18) (model 1 in Fig. 1). On average, the magnitude of the differences was modest, although significantly different from zero. For example, boys whose parents divorced showed 19% [standard error (SE) = 8%] more behavior problems at age 11, according to ratings by their parents, than did boys whose

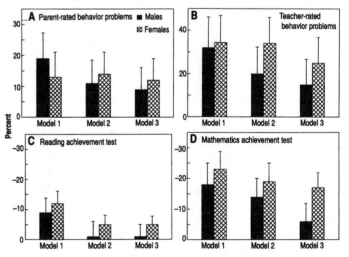

Fig. 1. Effects of a parental divorce or separation between ages 7 and 11 on four outcome measures for children age 11 in 1969 from the National Child Development Study, Great Britain (estimates restricted to children living with two married parents in 1965). (**A**) Behavior problems scale score as reported by parents. (**B**) Behavior problems scale score as reported by teachers. (**C**) Reading achievement test score. (**D**) Mathematics achievement test score. The height of the boxes shows the percentage by which the score of children whose parents divorced or separated between ages 7 and 11 was greater or less than the score of children whose parents remained married. In each of the four diagrams, three estimates of the effects of divorce are shown. Model 1 controls only for the social class and race of the child; model 2 controls additionally for the child's score on the same outcome measure at age 7, before anyone's parents were divorced; and model 3 adds further controls for characteristics of the child and family when he or she was 7. These included scales of family problems and difficulties from the Health Visitor's report and physician's reporting of physical handicap, mental retardation, or emotional maladjustment. Error bars represent one standard error.

parents were together, controlling for social class and race (Fig. 1A).

Unlike nearly all previous studies, we were able to introduce information on the children and parents before any of the families broke up. The measures we introduce may be proxies for family dysfunction and marital conflict. We first added the comparable 7-year-old behavior problems scale or achievement test score of the child (model 2 in Fig. 1). This step essentially adjusted the estimated effect of divorce for preexisting differences in behavior or achievement between children whose families would later divorce and children whose families would remain intact. For boys, the apparent effects of divorce dropped for all four outcome measures; for girls there was a drop in reading and mathematics achievement test scores. Finally, we controlled for other age 7 characteristics of the child and his or her family, such as the physician's rating of the child's mental and physical health and the Health Visitor's rating of the family's difficulties and use of social services (19) (model 3 in Fig. 1). After all the preseparation characteristics were taken into account, the apparent effect of divorce for boys fell by about half to levels that no longer were significantly different from zero for all four outcomes. For example, boys whose parents divorced now showed just 9% (SE = 7%) more behavior problems, according to parent ratings. For girls, the decline was smaller, and the remaining effect was significantly different from zero for two of the four outcomes (20).

The U.S. National Survey of Children

In order to determine whether these findings were generalizable beyond Great Britain in the 1960s, we estimated a similar set of models from U.S. data from the National Survey of Children (NSC), which began in 1976 with a random-sample survey of 2279 children aged 7 to 11 from 1747 families (21). In 1981, when the children were ages 11 through 16, additional interviews were conducted with parents and children in all families in which there already had been a separation or a divorce by 1976 or in which there was substantial marital conflict in 1976, and in a randomly selected subsample of intact, low-conflict families in 1976.

In both waves of the survey, a parent, usually the mother, was asked a series of questions about behavior problems similar in content to the Rutter Home Behaviour Scale in the NCDS (12) and to items in the Achenbach Child Behavior Checklist (22). In parallel with the procedure for the NCDS, we constructed single-factor scales from nine items in the 1976 data ($\alpha = 0.69$) and 24 items in the 1981 data ($\alpha = 0.90$). The items in the 1976 scale are fights too much, cannot concentrate, often tells lies, easily confused, breaks things, acts too young, very timid, has strong temper, and steals things. The items in the 1981 scale are changes in mood, feels no one loves him or her, high strung, tells lies, too fearful, argues too much, difficulty concentrating, easily confused, cruel to others, disobedient at home, disobedient at school, impulsive, feels inferior, not liked by other children, has obsessions, restless, stubborn or irritable, has strong temper, sad or depressed, withdrawn, feels others are out to get him or her, hangs around with kids who get into trouble, secretive, and worries too much.

Married parents in 1976 also were asked questions about conflict with their spouses covering nine areas, as follows: "Most married couples have some arguments. Do you ever have arguments about (i) chores and responsibilities, (ii) your children, (iii) money, (iv) sex, (v) religion, (vi) leisure time, (vii) drinking, (viii) other women or men, or (ix) in-laws?" We constructed a scale of marital conflict, which was the number of affirmative responses; scores ranged from 0 to 8 with a mean of 2.26 ($\alpha = 0.63$).

As with the British data, we restricted our analyses to children who were living with both of their parents at the first interview in 1976. As in the British study, these children were followed as their families split into divorced and nondivorced groups by 1981. Parent-rated behavior problems was the only outcome that could be compared adequately with the British findings (Fig. 2). The results for U.S. boys are similar to the results for British boys. Controlling for social class, race, and whether the mother was employed outside the home in 1976, boys whose parents had divorced between 1976 and 1981 showed 12% (SE = 4%) more behavior problems, on average (model 1). But when a control was added for behavior problems in 1976, before any of the parents divorced, the effect of divorce fell (model 2). And after a second control was introduced for the amount of marital conflict that was present in the home in 1976, the effect of divorce had fallen by approximately half, as in the British data, to 6% (SE = 4%), and it was no longer significantly different from zero.

For girls, however, the results are different from the British study. Controlling for class and race (model 1), there is little difference between girls from divorced families and girls from intact families. But with controls for 1976 behavior problems (model 2) and 1976 marital conflict (model 3), girls whose parents had divorced were showing somewhat fewer behavior problems than girls from intact families. In view of the inconsistency with the British data, we think it is prudent to be skeptical of this finding until it can be confirmed.

Conclusion

Overall, the evidence suggests that much of the effect of divorce on children can be predicted by conditions that existed well before the separation occurred. These predivorce effects were stronger for boys than for girls. Just when children begin to experience the process that precedes a divorce we cannot say. Our survey-based studies do not allow us to differentiate between a generally dysfunctional family and a family that has functioned adequately until the time that marital conflict becomes acute and the divorce process begins. It is also possible that the effects of divorce may differ for children older or younger than the ones in our studies or that divorce may have long-term effects on adult behavior. Nevertheless, the British and U.S. longitudinal studies suggest that those concerned with the effects of divorce on children should consider reorienting their thinking. At least as much attention needs to be paid to the processes that occur in troubled, intact families as to the trauma that children suffer after their parents separate.

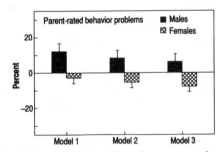

Fig. 2. Effects of a parental divorce between 1976 and 1981 on the behavior problems of children in 1981, when the children were ages 11 to 16, based on a behavior problems scale score as reported by parents from the U.S. National Survey of Children (estimates are restricted to children living with two married parents in 1976). The height of the boxes shows the percentage by which the score of children whose parents divorced between 1976 and 1981 was greater (or less) than the score of children whose parents remained married. Three estimates of the effects of divorce are shown: model 1 controls only for social class, race, and whether the mother was employed outside the home in 1976; model 2 controls additionally for the child's score on the behavior problems scale in 1976, as reported by parents, before anyone's parents were divorced; and model 3 adds further controls for the parents' score on a nine-item marital conflict scale in 1976. Error bars represent one standard error.

REFERENCES AND NOTES

1. L. L. Bumpass, *Demography* **21**, 71 (1984).
2. R. E. Emery, *Marriage, Divorce, and Children's Adjustment* (Sage, Beverly Hills, CA, 1988); P. L. Chase-Lansdale and E. M. Hetherington, in *Life-Span Development and Behavior*, P. B. Baltes, D. L. Featherman, R. M. Lerner, Eds. (Erlbaum, Hillsdale, NJ, 1990), vol. 10, pp. 105–150; S. S. McLanahan, *Am. J. Sociol.* **94**, 130 (1988).
3. J. S. Wallerstein and J. B. Kelly, *Surviving the Breakup: How Children and Parents Cope with Divorce* (Basic Books, New York, 1980), p. 316.
4. See, for example, L. J. Weitzman, *The Divorce Revolution: The Unexpected Consequences for Women and Children* (Free Press, New York, 1985); M. A. Glendon, *Abortion and Divorce in Western Law* (Harvard Univ. Press, Cambridge, MA, 1987); I. Garfinkel and S. S. McLanahan, *Single Mothers and Their Children: A New American Dilemma* (The Urban Institute Press, Washington, DC, 1986).
5. K. E. Kiernan, *Popul. Stud.* **40**, 1 (1986).
6. R. E. Emery, *Psychol. Bull.* **92**, 310 (1982).
7. E. M. Hetherington, M. Cox, R. Cox, in *Mother-Child, Father-Child Relations*, J. H. Stevens and M. Mathews, Eds. (National Association for the Education of Young Children Press, Washington, DC, 1978); E. M. Hetherington and K. Camara, in *Review of Child Development Research*, R. D. Parke, Ed. (Univ. of Chicago Press, Chicago, 1984), vol. 7.
8. But see J. H. Block, J. Block, P. F. Gjerde, *Child Dev.* **57**, 827 (1986); N. Baydar, *J. Marriage Family* **50**, 967 (1988).
9. The leading set of studies of this type have been conducted by E. M. Hetherington, M. Cox, and R. Cox [in *Nontraditional Families, Parenting, and Child Development*, M. E. Lamb, Ed. (Erlbaum, Hillsdale, NJ, 1982); *J. Am. Acad. Child Psychiatr.* **24**, 518 (1985)] and E. M. Hetherington [in *Remarriage and Stepparenting Today*, K. Pasley and M. Ihinger-Tallman, Eds. (Guilford Press, New York, 1987)].
10. The NCDS is described in a paper by P. M. Shepherd, "The National Child Development Study: An introduction to the background to the study and the methods of data collection" (Social Statistics Research Unit, City University, London, October 1985).
11. Information in medical records at birth also was recorded. Between 1958 and 1965, a supplementary sample was added consisting of 1142 children from recent immigrant families who had 3 to 9 March 1958 birth dates. We include this sample in our analyses.
12. M. Rutter, J. Tizard, K. Whitmore, Eds., *Educaton, Health, and Behaviour* (Longman, London, 1970).
13. D. H. Stott, *The Social Adjustment of Children* (Univ. of London Press, London, 1969).
14. V. Southgate, *Southgate Group Reading Tests: Manual of Instructions* (Univ. of London Press, London, 1962); M. L. K. Pringle, in *The Sixth Mental Measurements Yearbook*, O. K. Buros, Ed. (Gryphon Press, Highland Park, NJ, 1965). The mathematics test was developed for the NCDS by M. L. K. Pringle, N. Butler, and R. Davie [*11,000 Seven Year Olds* (Longman, London, 1966)].
15. Ten of the 11 items in the parent-rated scale ($\alpha = 0.68$) were identical to the items in the age 7 parent-rated scale *(12)*. For the BSAG scale at age 11, $\alpha = 0.71$.
16. K. Fogelman, *Br. J. Educ. Psychol.* **48**, 148 (1978).
17. There are two sources of nonrandomness that could have arisen with respect to the sample of families analyzed in 1969, when the children were 11: (i) the restriction that when the child was 7 the family was intact, was successfully found and reinterviewed, and had valid data on behavior and achievement; and (ii) the restriction that when the child was 11 the family was successfully reinterviewed and had valid data on behavior and achievement. To determine whether these sources of nonrandomness could possibly have biased our results, we specified and estimated several selection models. [G. S. Maddala, *Limited Dependent and Qualitative Variables in Econometrics* (Cambridge Univ. Press, Cambridge, 1983).] The coefficients for the effect of divorce were nearly identical in the selection models and the ordinary least squares (OLS) models we present here.
18. Among boys, the coefficient for the effect of divorce on three of the four outcomes was positive and at least twice its standard error in model 1 of Fig. 1 (for the reading test, the coefficient was 1.8 times its standard error). Among girls, all the coefficients for the effect of divorce, except on parent-rated behavior problems, were more than twice their standard errors in model 1. As in any nonexperimental study, it is possible that the variables we "control" for are actually markers for other, unmeasured variables. However, we have relied on a large literature in sociology and developmental psychology to guide our choice of variables. In the OLS regressions *(17)* for the NCDS, which form the basis for Fig. 1, we used the natural logarithms of the outcomes as dependent variables because the logarithmic transformation resulted in a more normally shaped distribution of the scale scores. The key independent variable was a dummy variable that indicated whether or not a divorce occurred during the time between the age 7 and age 11 interviews . Let β be the coefficient for the divorce dummy variable. Then, for the logarithmically transformed outcomes, the percentage change in the scale score produced by the occurrence of a divorce is $(e^{\beta} - 1) \cdot 100$. In model 1, the only additional independent variables in the equation (all measured at age 7) were father's social class (six-category classification), housing tenure (whether renting from a public agency, renting in the private market, or owning one's home), number of persons per room, and race (white, Asian, black, mixed). In our regression models, mean values were imputed for missing information on independent variables.
19. From the health visitor's report at age 7 we constructed five scales: use of children's services (five items, $\alpha = 0.56$), family conflict (two items, $\alpha = 0.44$), family problems (two items, $\alpha = 0.64$), and use of mental health services (three items, $\alpha = 0.60$). For models in which behavior problems at age 11 were the dependent variables, the age 7 reading test score was entered at this stage; and for models in which age 11 achievement tests were the dependent variables, age 7 teacher-rated behavior problems were added at this stage.
20. For boys, none of the model 3 estimates in Fig. 1 was twice its standard error; for girls, two of four were twice their standard errors. The death of a parent between the ages of 7 and 11 had no significant effects for girls on any of the four outcome measures and no significant effect on behavior problems for boys, even before controls for age 7 characteristics. The death of a parent did have a negative effect on reading and mathematics achievement at 11 for boys; this effect was reduced by age 7 controls but remained statistically significant.
21. See F. F. Furstenberg, Jr., C. W. Nord, J. L. Peterson, N. Zill, *Am. Sociol. Rev.* **48**, 656 (1983). We restricted the sample to include only families that were intact in 1976, in which the biological mother of the child or children was the parent respondent at both times and was living with the target child or children, and in which the father was not reported to have died between 1976 and 1981. Among this subsample of 822 children, there were 65 cases of a divorce or separation occurring between the 1976 and 1981 interviews.
22. T. M. Achenbach and C. S. Edelbrock, *Monogr. Soc. Res. Child Dev.* **33** (no. 166) (1981).
23. Supported primarily by NICHHD grant HD25936, with additional support from NSF grant SES-8908503. We thank M. Trieb for computer programming assistance. Complete sets of the estimated coefficients and other detailed documentation are available from A.J.C.

Peers and Youth Culture

My son won't spend time with the family anymore! All my daughter cares about is what her friends think! Parents bemoan the loss of influence over their children's behavior and the increasing insinuation of peers into their children's lives. The image of the powerless parent vs. the persuasive peer is inconsistent with current research and theory about relationships during adolescence. Parents who believe this stereotype run the risk of missing danger signals in their children's behavior and of abdicating too much responsibility when their children still need parental guidance and structure.

Adolescents are without a doubt more peer-oriented than any other age group. But it is simplistic to assume that peer influence is always negative and that it outweighs parental influence. The nature of the parent-child relationship is consistently the best predictor of adolescent psychological health and well-being. Adolescents who have poor relationships with their parents are precisely the adolescents who are most susceptible to negative peer influences. Poor parent-adolescent relationships are not the norm during the pubertal years, but they more likely represent a continuation of poor family relationships from childhood.

Research indicates that most adolescents feel close to and respect their parents. Most adolescents share their parents' values, especially when it comes to moral, religious, political, and educational values. Peers often reinforce parental values as the adolescent's peer group is influenced by parental choices: What school does the adolescent attend? What kind of neighborhood do the parents live in? Do parents attend religious services? What do the parents do for a living? Parental choices such as these impact on the network of potential friends for their children.

Several factors have contributed to this misconception that adolescents reject their parents in favor of peers. First, peers do play a greater role in the adolescent's life and influence day-to-day activities, style of dress, and musical tastes. Second, parents often confuse the adolescent's struggle for autonomy with rebellion. G. Stanley Hall's views of adolescence as a biologically necessary time of "storm and stress" contributed to this confusion. Anna Freud, arguing from her father's psychoanalytic tradition and her experience with troubled adolescents, also maintained that the adolescent-parent relationship should be highly conflictual and that adolescents need to turn to peers. Such conflict would ensure a successful resolution of the Oedipal/Electra complex. This model of intense parent-adolescent conflict has not been empirically supported and can be detrimental if parents fail to seek help because they believe that intense conflict is "normal" during adolescence.

Another myth about peer influence during adolescence is that it is primarily negative. As Thomas Berndt discusses in this unit, peer influence is mutual and has both positive and negative effects. Peer pressure is rarely coercive, as is popularly envisaged. It is a more subtle process where adolescents influence their friends as well as being influenced by them. Like adults, adolescents choose friends who already have similar interests, attitudes, and beliefs. Until recently, researchers paid little attention to the positive effects of peers on adolescent development. Among other things, friends help adolescents develop role-taking and social skills, conquer the imaginary audience, and act as social supports in stressful situations. Although they decry peer pressure as an influence on their children, no thinking parents would want their son or daughter to be a social outcast with few friends.

Another misconception about peer relations is that teen culture is a unified culture with a single way of thinking and acting. A visit to any secondary school today will reveal the variety of teen cultures that exist. The formation of peer groups and adolescent crowds is partly a function of school structure and school activities. As in past decades, one can find jocks, populars, brains, delinquents, and nerds. Today, one might also run into members of the grunge and body-piercing crowds. Media attention is often drawn toward bizarre or antisocial groups, further contributing to the myth that peer influence is primarily negative.

Music is very much a part of youth culture, although there is no universal type of music liked by all adolescents. One way that adolescents have always tried to differentiate themselves from adults has been through music. Adults today are concerned that music lyrics, movies, and television programs have gone too far in the quest for ever more shocking and explicit sexual and violent content. Media influences have also been blamed for recent increases in teenage smoking and drug use. Product ratings, similar to movie ratings, are more commonly used to help parents and adolescents make informed choices about what they are listening to and watching. One reading focuses on the V-chip, a recent invention that can help parents monitor their children's access to television programming. Other articles examine reasons for the recent increase in smoking and marijuana use.

UNIT 6

In addition to school and leisure activities, adolescents today spend considerable time in the part-time workforce. Work has usually been seen as a positive influence on adolescent development. Society points to positive outcomes such as developing responsibility and punctuality, knowledge of the working world, and appreciating the value of money. Research does corroborate some positive effects of working, but adolescents have been spending increasing hours in the workforce. Recent studies, such as those described in the unit's readings, find that adolescents who work over 20 hours per week are more involved in drug use and delinquent activity, have more psychological and physical complaints, and perform more poorly in school. Although there may be a tendency for adolescents who are predisposed toward such behaviors to be disengaged from school and, therefore, work more in the first place, longitudinal data suggest that working exacerbates these tendencies.

Looking Ahead: Challenge Questions

What makes an adolescent more socially acceptable or popular? How does an adolescent gain prestige with peers? Have the norms for this changed? What differences are there for boys vs. girls?

How has recent research and theory changed our ideas about peer pressure? What are some myths about peer influence? Is peer influence mostly negative? Do most adolescents engage in regular drug and alcohol use because of peer pressure?

Does part-time work take too much time away from studies? Do adolescents have too much discretionary income? How does working affect the adolescent? How does working affect the parent-adolescent relationship?

Why does alcohol play such a rite of passage role in youth culture? How does U.S. culture compare to other cultures in this respect? Should the drinking age be lowered? What drugs are popular with adolescents today? How does marijuana use today differ from in the 1960s and 1970s?

Do you believe that violence on television and in music contributes to aggressive behavior in children and adolescents? Why or why not? Will blocking television programs and putting warning labels on music make a difference in curbing violence? Defend your answer.

Football, Fast Cars, and Cheerleading: Adolescent Gender Norms, 1978–1989

J. Jill Suitor and Rebel Reavis

ABSTRACT

This paper examines changes in adolescent gender norms in the 1980s, using data collected from 496 college students who graduated from high school in 1979–82 (*N* = 271), and 1988–89 (*N* = 225). Each student was asked to list five ways in which male and female students could gain prestige in the high school from which they had recently graduated. The findings indicate relatively little change in gender norms across the decade. While there are some indications of less traditionalism—most importantly, an increase in girls' acquisition of prestige through sports, and a decrease in girls' acquisition of prestige through cheerleading—the overall pattern shows that boys and girls continue to acquire prestige through largely different means. Boys continue to acquire prestige primarily through participation in sports and school achievement, while girls continue to acquire prestige primarily through a combination of physical appearance, sociability, and school achievement.

During the past decade, there has been substantial interest in examining and explaining changes in gender-role attitudes and behaviors in the United States. This line of research has shown that gender-role attitudes have become markedly less traditional over the past two decades (cf. Mason & Lu, 1988; McBroom, 1987; Thornton, Alwin, & Camburn, 1983). This work has also revealed a decrease in traditionalism regarding the division of household labor across the 1970s and early 1980s (cf. Robinson, 1988; Shelton & Coverman, 1988), although the changes on these behavioral dimensions of gender roles are far less dramatic than are the changes in stated attitudes.

While this literature has shed a great deal of light on changes in *adults'* gender-role attitudes and behaviors, much less attention has been directed toward changes in gender roles among adolescents. This segment of the population should be

of particular interest to scholars since adolescents are the harbingers of American gender roles in the coming decades.

Data from several sources suggest that adolescents entered the 1980s with surprisingly traditional gender-role attitudes. For example, Thornton and her colleagues' 1980 findings (1983) revealed that although adolescents held more liberal gender-role attitudes than did their mothers, a substantial proportion maintained relatively traditional attitudes. In fact, almost half of the adolescents agreed with the statement that "It is much better for everyone if the man earns the living and the woman takes care of the home and family." Similarly, Corder and Stephan (1984) found that while 70% of the school-age girls they surveyed in 1978 wanted to combine parenting, marriage, and employment, only 40% of the boys wanted their future wives to combine these roles. Consistent with this pattern, Hansen and Darling (1985) found that the majority of the adolescents they studies in 1981 held relatively traditional attitudes toward the division of household labor.

Studies of adolescents' views toward girls' participation in sports in the late 1970s and early 1980s also demonstrated the persistence of traditional gender-role attitudes, and the characteristics of the people they would most like to date or be friends with. Feltz (1978) reported that participation in sports accrued less status for girls than did other behaviors and attributes, while Williams and White (1983) found that the lowest ratings were assigned to girls who participated in sports. Kane (1988), using data collected in 1982, found that girls were least likely to choose athletics as the way they would like to be remembered in high school. She also found that the "gender-appropriateness" of the sport in which the girls participated greatly affected both girls' and boys' choices of friends and dating partners. Girls who were associated with sports that were seen as gender-appropriate (e.g., tennis) were substantially more likely to be viewed as desirable friends and partners that were girls who were associated with less gender-appropriate sports (e.g., basketball).

Studies of other dimensions of adolescents' behaviors also suggest the persistence of traditional gender roles a decade ago. For example, Canaan's (1990) findings revealed that boys used different mechanisms from girls to create and maintain their position in the social hierarchy in their high schools in the late 1970s and early 1980s. While boys used joke-telling

This paper was presented at the August 1992 Meetings of the American Sociological Association, Pittsburgh, Pennsylvania.

The authors wish to thank Scott Feld, Karl Pillemer, and Patricia Ulbrich for their comments on earlier drafts of this paper, and to acknowledge Karl Pillemer, Sheryl Zebrowsky, and Bruce Hare for their assistance in collecting the data.

Reprint requests to J. Jill Suitor, Associate Professor, Dept. of Sociology, Louisiana State University, Baton Rouge, LA 70803.

Table 1

College Students' Reports of Mechanisms by Which Girls and Boys Acquired Prestige in Their High Schools in 1978–82 and 1988–89 (per cent of students mentioning each mechanism)

Mechanism for Gaining Prestige	1978–82 (n = 271)			1988–89 (n = 225)			Cohort Difference (sig. of diff.) between cohorts	
	Reports on			Reports on				
	Girls		Boys	Girls		Boys	Girls	Boys
Participation in Sports	33.6	**1	90.0	43.6	**	84.0	*	*
Grades/Intelligence	56.1		55.0	60.1		56.0	ns	ns
Physical Attractiveness	59.0	**	39.1	58.2	**	41.8	ns	ns
Popularity with Opposite Sex	43.2		40.6	41.8	*	35.1	ns	ns
General Sociability	56.8	**	42.1	54.7	**	44.4	ns	ns
Clothes	40.6	**	15.9	36.9	**	22.2	ns	ns
Ownership/Use of Car	5.9	**	45.0	5.3	**	25.3	ns	**
Participation in School Clubs/Government	35.4	*	29.9	29.3	*	23.1	ns	ns
Cheerleading	32.9	**	0.0	23.6	**	0.0	*	ns
Drugs/Drinking	2.6	**	11.4	2.7	**	6.7	ns	ns
"Class Clown"	3.0	**	11.1	1.8	**	9.8	ns	ns
"Toughness"/Physical Aggressiveness	1.9	**	17.7	3.6	**	13.8	ns	ns
Sexual Activity	1.9	*	4.8	8.4		7.6	**	ns

[1] Level of significance shown is difference between girls and boys within each cohort.
*p < .05
**p < .01

to demonstrate their masculinity by defining their superiority to other males and females, girls used note-passing to develop friendships and to subordinate other females. Further, Eckert (1989) found that physical appearance and dress were of greater importance to girls' than boys' social status among adolescents in the early 1980s. Last, while cheerleading was an important means by which girls could accrue prestige (Eckert, 1989; Eicher, Baizerman, & Michelman, 1991; Foley, 1990), this activity was never mentioned as an avenue by which boys could do so.

Taken together, these findings suggest that American adolescents entered the 1980s with relatively traditional gender roles, as exemplified by both their stated attitudes and differences in the ways in which boys and girls accrued prestige. However, if changes in adolescents' attitudes and behaviors paralleled those of adults during the 1980s, we would expect to find substantially less gender-role traditionalism among teenagers who were graduating from high school at the end of the 1980s. On this basis, it was anticipated that there would be fewer differences in the ways boys and girls acquired prestige in high schools by the end of the decade.

The data used in the present paper were collected between 1978 and 1982, and between 1989 and 1990 from students enrolled in a large public university in the northeastern United States. A total of 565 students completed questionnaires; 69

students were omitted from the analysis because their date of graduation from high school was either before 1978, or between 1983 and 1988. The final sample included 271 students who graduated between 1978 and 1982, and 225 students who graduated between 1988 and 1989. Fifty-nine per cent of the students were women; 41% were men.

All of the students were enrolled in introductory-level sociology courses: 85% of the students were enrolled in Introduction to Sociology; 15% were enrolled in a lower division course in family sociology. There were no statistically significant differences between the responses of students enrolled in the two courses; therefore, the data were combined for the analysis.

The data were collected during the first few weeks of the semester, prior to any discussion of issues involving gender roles. Data were collected from students enrolled in a total of nine classes taught by four professors; the findings did not differ significantly by instructor or class (within cohort).

Measurement

The students were asked to respond to the following requests: (1) "List five ways in which males could gain prestige in the high school you attended"; and (2) "List five ways in which females could gain prestige in the high school you attended." The logic behind this approach is that individuals generally acquire prestige by adhering to group norms. Therefore, the means of acquiring prestige should provide an indicator of the norms that exist in a particular group.

The respondents mentioned a total of 61 ways in which students in their high schools acquired prestige. Since several categories were similar, they were combined for the analysis. For example, "being friendly," "being outgoing," and "having a good personality" were combined into the category labeled "sociability"; "pretty," "handsome," and "having a good body" were combined into the category labeled "physical attractiveness." The 13 categories that were listed most frequently are included individually in the analysis; the remainder were combined in an "other" category which was taken into consideration in the analysis, but is not shown in Table 1.

The students were also asked to specify their gender, the year in which they graduated from high school, and the city/town in which they attended high school.[1]

RESULTS

Table I shows the distribution of students' reports of ways in which boys and girls acquired prestige in the high schools from which they had recently graduated. For example, 33.6% of the students who graduated between 1978 and 1982 reported that participation in sports was one of the ways in which girls gained prestige, while 90% of the students reported participation in sports as a way boys gained prestige.

The findings presented in the left-hand columns of Table I show substantial differences in most of the avenues by which boys and girls acquired prestige in high school in the early 1980s. Boys gained prestige primarily through (1) sports, (2) grades and intelligence, (3) access to cars, (4) sociability, (5) popularity with the opposite sex, (6) physical appearance, and (7) participation in school activities (e.g., school government, clubs). In contrast, girls gained prestige primarily through (1) physical attractiveness, (2) sociability, (3) grades and intelligence, (4) popularity with the opposite sex, (5) clothes, (6) participation in school activities, and (7) cheerleading.

The reports of students who graduated in the late 1980s are shown in the middle column of Table I. Boys in the late 1980s continued to acquire prestige primarily through sports and grades and intelligence, while girls continued to accrue prestige primarily through grades and intelligence, and physical attractiveness. Thus, while grades and intelligence were important for both boys and girls throughout the 1980s, sports continued to play a much larger role in the prestige structure for boys than girls, while physical attractiveness continued to play a much larger role for girls than boys.

Some other behaviors and attributes by which students gained prestige also remained highly segregated by gender throughout the 1980s. For example, while a notable minority of students in both cohorts stated that boys in their high school had gained prestige through "toughness" or rowdiness, or by being a "class clown," almost no students in either cohort re-

ported that these were avenues by which girls gained prestige. Conversely, although cheerleading was mentioned with some frequency by members of both cohorts as a way in which girls gained prestige, not one student in either cohort mentioned cheerleading as a way in which boys gained prestige.

The most important change between the earlier and later cohorts was in the area of prestige acquired through participation in sports—particularly for girls; 34% of the students who graduated in 1978–82 mentioned sports participation as a way in which girls gained prestige, compared to 44% of those who graduated in 1988–89. In contrast, sports became a slightly less important avenue for boys; 90% of the 1978–82 graduates mentioned sports for boys, compared to 84% of the 1988–89 graduates. While these changes suggest a move toward parity in the role of sports for boys' and girls' prestige, it is important to recognize that among the 1988–89 graduates, sports participation is still almost two times more likely to be named as a source of prestige for boys than girls.

Another difference worth noting is the decrease in the role of cheerleading. While almost 33% of the students who graduated in 1978–82 reported that cheerleading was a means of gaining prestige for girls, only 24% mentioned it in 1988–89. However, the fact that almost one-quarter of the members of the later cohort listed cheerleading for girls, while none listed it for boys, suggests that this activity remains gender segregated, and continues to be an important means of acquiring prestige for girls.

It is interesting to note that boys' acquisition of prestige through access to cars declined substantially across the decade, going from third to sixth place. The reasons for this remain unclear, and cannot be accounted for by any of the variables included in the study. For example, although a slightly larger proportion of students from the 1988–89 cohort attended high school in a city, this factor does not account for the finding; the importance of access to cars declined to the same degree among the subsample of students who attended high school in the suburbs.

Separate analyses by gender of the respondent revealed that men and women had generally similar perceptions of the ways in which boys and girls had acquired prestige in high school (tables not shown). The few differences of interest involved girls' participation in sports and girls' sexual activity.

When the responses are divided by gender, it becomes clear that the overall change in the prestige girls acquired through participation in sports was due to changes in the boys' perceptions. Between 1978–82 and 1988–89, the percentage of women who mentioned sports as a way in which girls gained prestige increased only slightly (from 39% to 44%); however, the percentage of men who listed girls' sports as a means of gaining prestige almost doubled (from 26% to 46%).

The other interesting difference between women's and men's reports involved sexual activity as a means through which girls gained prestige. As shown in Table I, sexual activity for girls was mentioned substantially more frequently among 1988–89 than among 1978–82 graduates. However, this change was due almost entirely to reports by men. In the early 1980s, women and men were approximately equally likely to report that girls gained prestige through being sexually active. In contrast, among members of the later cohort, 16% of the men reported that girls in their high school gained prestige through sexual activity, compared to only 4% of the women.

SUMMARY
AND CONCLUSIONS

The findings presented here suggest there was relatively little change in gender norms among high school students between the early and late 1980s. A comparison between the reports of students who graduated in 1978–82 and those who graduate in 1988–89 shows that boys continued to acquire prestige in high school primarily through sports, grades, and intelligence, while girls continued to acquire prestige primarily through a combination of physical appearance, sociability, grades, and intelligence. The only noteworthy differences between the reports in the early and late 1980s were an increase in girls' acquisition of prestige through participation in sports and sexual activity, a decrease in the role of cheerleading, and a reduction in the importance of car ownership as a means by which boys accrued prestige.

The findings also indicated that most of the change that occurred in the ways girls accrued prestige could be accounted for by changes in *boys'*, rather than girls' perceptions. Further, the particular mechanisms that boys viewed as increasingly important were those that have traditionally been avenues by which men, rather than women, have gained prestige—participation in sports and engaging in sexual activities. Thus, much of the change that occurred involved a greater acceptance of girls in traditionally "male" activities rather than the reverse, a pattern consistent with changes that have occurred in the occupational structure across the same period (U.S. Bureau of the Census, 1992).

One limitation of the present study is that the data were collected from only one university. It is possible that this university differs from many others in ways that could affect the findings. However, data collected at another university, but not presented in the present paper, suggest that the findings presented here may be replicated elsewhere. Between 1985 and 1989 one of the authors collected data from students enrolled in a medium-sized state university in New England. Analysis of those data revealed the same pattern of findings presented here, although the student bodies of the two universities differ substantially on demographic dimensions that might have affected gender norms (percentage of minorities; socioeconomic status; religion; percentage who attended high school in urban areas). The similarity between the reports of students in the two universities provides further support for the contention that there has been relatively little change in high school gender roles across the 1980s.

Thus, it appears that gender-role traditionalism continues to play an important role in the prestige structure of American adolescents.

REFERENCES

Canaan, J. E. (1990). Passing notes and telling jokes: Gendered strategies among American middle school teenagers. In F. Ginsburg, & A. L. Tsing (Eds.), *Uncertain terms: Negotiating in American culture.* Boston: Beacon Press.

Corder, J., & Stephan, C. W. (1984). Females' combination of work and family roles: Adolescents' aspirations, *Journal of Marriage and the Family, 46,* 391–402.

Eckert, P. (1989). *Jocks and burnouts: Social categories and identity in the high school.* New York: Teachers College.

Eicher, J. B., Baizerman, S., & Michelman, J. (1991). Adolescent dress, Part II: A qualitative study of suburban high school students. *Adolescence, 26,* 679–686.

Feltz, D. (1978). Athletics in the social status system of female adolescents. *Review of Sport and Leisure, 3,* 98–108.

Foley, D. E. (1990). The great American football ritual: Reproducing race, class, and gender inequality. *Sociology of Sport Journal, 7,* 111–135.

Hansen, S. L., & Darling, C.A. (1985). Attitudes of adolescents toward division of labor in the home. *Adolescence, 20,* 60–72.

Kane, M. J. (1988). The female athletic role as a status determinant within the social systems of high school adolescence. *Adolescence, 23,* 253–264.

Mason, K. O., & Lu, Y. H. (1988). Attitudes toward women's familial roles: Changes in the United States, 1977–1985. *Gender and Society, 2,* 39–57.

McBroom, W. H. (1987). Longitudinal change in sex-role orientations: Differences between men and women. *Sex Roles, 16,* 439–452.

Robinson, J. P. (1988). Who's doing the housework? *American Demographics, 10,* 24–29.

Shelton, B. A., & Coverman S. (1988). *Are men's roles converging with women's?: Estimating change in husbands' domestic labor time,* 1975–1981. Paper presented at the Annual Meetings of the American Sociological Association, Atlanta, Georgia.

Thornton, A., Alwin, D. F., & Camburn, D. (1983). Causes and consequences of sex-role attitudes and attitude change. *American Sociological Review, 48,* 211–227.

Williams, J. M., & White, K. A. (1983). Adolescent status systems for males and females at three age levels. *Adolescence, 70,* 381–389.

U.S. Bureau of the Census. (1992). *Statistical Abstract of the United States, 1992.* Washington, DC.

NOTES

1. Students in the 1978–81 cohorts were not asked where they had attended high school.

Friendship and Friends' Influence in Adolescence

Thomas J. Berndt

Thomas J. Berndt is Professor of Psychological Sciences at Purdue University. He is coeditor of *Peer Relationships in Child Development* (Wiley, 1989) and author of *Child Development* (Harcourt Brace Jovanovich, 1992). Address correspondence to Thomas J. Berndt, Department of Psychological Sciences, Purdue University, West Lafayette, IN 47907; e-mail: BERNDT@PURCCVM.BITNET.

Friendships have an important influence on adolescents' attitudes, behavior, and development. Theorists do not agree, however, on whether this influence is generally positive or generally negative. One theoretical perspective emphasizes the positive effects of close friendships on the psychological adjustment and social development of adolescents. Theorists who adopt this perspective argue that interactions with friends improve adolescents' social skills and ability to cope with stressful events.[1] A second theoretical perspective emphasizes the negative influence of friends on adolescents' behavior. Theorists who adopt this perspective argue that friends' influence often leads to antisocial or delinquent behavior.[2]

The two perspectives differ not only in their assumptions about the effects of friends' influence, but also in their assumptions about processes or pathways of influence. In the first perspective, the influence of friendships depends on the features of these relationships. For example, friendships that are highly intimate are assumed to enhance adolescents' self-esteem and understanding of other people. In the second perspective, friends' influence depends on the attitudes and behaviors of friends. For example, adolescents whose friends drink beer at parties are assumed to be likely to start drinking beer themselves. Thus, the first pathway of influence focuses on features of friendship and the second focuses on friends' characteristics.

Each perspective contains a kernel of truth, but each provides a one-sided view of the effects of friendships. Theorists who emphasize the positive features of friendship seldom acknowledge that friendships can have negative features, too. Adolescents often have conflicts with friends, and these conflicts can negatively affect adolescents' behavior toward other people. Theorists who emphasize the negative influence of friends' characteristics seldom ac-

knowledge that many adolescents have friends with positive characteristics. These friends are likely to influence behavior positively.

In sum, friends can have positive or negative effects on adolescents via either of the two pathways of influence. In this review, I present evidence for these assertions and argue for more comprehensive and balanced theories of friendship in adolescence.

FRIENDSHIP FEATURES

"How can you tell that someone is your best friend?" Open-ended questions like this one were used by several researchers to assess the age changes in conceptions of friendships. The responses of children and adolescents confirmed that they regard several features of friendship as important. They said that friendships involve mutual liking, prosocial behavior (e.g., "we trade tapes with each other"), companionship (e.g., "we go places together"), and a relative lack of conflicts (e.g., "we don't fight with each other"). Many adolescents, but few elementary school children, also referred to intimacy in friendships. Adolescents

From *Current Directions in Psychological Science*, October 1992, pp. 156-159. © 1992 by the American Psychological Society. Reprinted by permission of Cambridge University Press.

Adolescents correlate the degree of their friendship's intimacy with loyalty, generosity, and helpfulness. Intimate adolescent friendships are comparable to the supportive social relationships that help adults cope with stressful life events. (Credit UN Photos/ Margot Granitsas)

said, for example, that they "talk about their problems with best friends" and that "a best friend really understands you." These findings are consistent with hypotheses that intimate friendships emerge in adolescence.[1]

Gradually, researchers shifted from studies of conceptions of friendship to studies of the actual features of friendships. Researchers also devised structured rating scales for assessing the features identified in earlier studies. The new measures made it possible to examine several questions about the nature and effects of friendships.[3]

Recent research has confirmed that intimacy becomes a central feature of friendship in early adolescence. Adolescents usually rate their own friendships as more intimate than do elementary school children.

The increase in intimacy may be due partly to adolescents' growing understanding of the thoughts, feelings, and traits of self and others. It may also be due to the fact that adolescents spend more time with their friends than younger children do. Friendships are more significant relationships in adolescence than earlier.

Girls describe their friendships as more intimate than do boys. Some writers have suggested that the sex difference is merely a matter of style: Girls express their intimacy with friends by talking about personal matters, and boys express their intimacy in nonverbal ways. However, scattered evidence suggests that boys' friendships are less intimate because boys trust their friends less than girls do.[4] More boys than girls say that friends might tease them if

they talk about something clumsy or foolish that they did. More girls than boys say that they share intimate information with friends because their friends listen and understand them.

This sex difference does not simply reflect a developmental delay for boys. In adulthood, women also tend to have more intimate friendships than men.[5] Still, the difference should not be exaggerated, because significant differences have not been found on all measures in all studies. Yet when differences are found, females' friendships usually appear more intimate than males' friendships.

Intimacy is closely related to other features of friendship. Adolescents' ratings of the intimacy of their friendships are correlated with their ratings of the friends' loyalty, generosity, and helpfulness. In short, friendships that are highly intimate tend to have many other positive features. Such friendships are comparable to the supportive social relationships that help adults cope with stressful life events.[6]

We might ask, then, if intimate and supportive friendships have equally positive effects on adolescents' adjustment and coping. In several studies, adolescents with more supportive friendships had higher self-esteem, less often suffered from depression or other emotional disorders, and were better adjusted to school than subjects with less supportive friendships.[7] These data are consistent with theories about the benefits of friendship, but come from correlational studies and so are open to alternative interpretations. Most important is the possibility that self-esteem and other indicators of adjustment contribute to the formation of supportive friendships rather than vice versa.

Longitudinal studies help to answer questions about causal direction, but longitudinal studies of adolescents' friendships are rare. The available data suggest that supportive friendships have significant but modest effects on some aspects of behavior and adjustment. Supportive friendships are not a panacea: They do not appear to have as powerful or as general an influence on adolescents as some theorists have suggested. Additional research is needed to identify the specific aspects of behavior and development that are most strongly affected by variations in positive features of friendship.

Equally important for future research is greater attention to the negative features of friendship. Adolescents interviewed about their conceptions of friendship commented on conflicts with friends, but many researchers ignored these comments. Many measures of friendship focus exclusively on positive or supportive features. This is a serious omission, because recent studies suggest that conflicts with friends can contribute to negative in-

teractions with other peers and with adults.[8] With friends, adolescents may develop an aggressive interaction style that they then display with other interaction partners. Theories that emphasize the positive effects of supportive friendships need to be expanded to account for the negative effects of troubled friendships. Researchers need to measure both the positive and the negative features of friendships. New research with both types of measures should provide a more complete picture of friendship effects via the first pathway of influence.

FRIENDS' CHARACTERISTICS

You and your friends found a sheet of paper that your teacher must have lost. On the paper are the questions and answers for a test that you are going to have tomorrow. Your friends all plan to study from it, and they want you to go along with them. You don't think you should, but they tell you to do it anyway. What would you really do: study from the paper or not study from it?

Many researchers have used hypothetical dilemmas like this one to measure friends' influence on adolescents. In this dilemma, friends supposedly put pressure on an adolescent to engage in antisocial behavior, cheating on a test. Adolescents' responses to similar dilemmas are assumed to show the degree of adolescents' antisocial conformity to friends. Research with these dilemmas has provided the most direct support for theories of friends' negative influence.[2]

However, research with other methods has shown that the hypothetical dilemmas are based on faulty assumptions about the processes and outcomes of friends' influence in adolescence.[7] Some researchers observed friends' interactions in schools, summer camps, and other settings. Other researchers recorded friends' discussions, in experimental settings, as they tried to

reach a consensus on various decisions. Both types of research suggest that the studies of conformity dilemmas—and popular writings about peer pressure—seriously distort reality.

In natural settings, influence among friends is a mutual process. Adolescents influence their friends as well as being influenced by them. Mutual influence is most obvious during interactions between a pair of friends. When two friends talk together, each has chances to influence the other. Even when friends interact in a group, decisions are usually made by consensus after group discussion. Groups rarely divide into a majority that favors one decision and one person who favors another. Therefore, models of group decision making describe friends' influence better than do models of individuals conforming to a majority.

In natural settings, influence seldom results from coercive pressure by friends. Friends' influence often depends on positive reinforcement. For example, friends express their approval of certain opinions and not others. Adolescents who are engaged in a discussion also listen to the reasons that friends give for their opinions. The influence of reasoning, or informational influence, may be as important in adolescents' groups as it is in adults' groups.[9] In addition, friends' influence does not always result from explicit attempts to influence. Adolescents admire and respect their friends, so they may agree with friends simply because they trust the friends' judgment.

Of course, friends sometimes do try to put pressure on adolescents. Adolescents also know that they risk disapproval or ridicule if they advocate opinions different from the opinions of most of their friends. In extremely cohesive groups, like some urban gangs, adolescents may even be threatened with physical harm if they do not go along with important group decisions, such as to attack another gang. But such situations and such groups are uncommon. Few friendship groups are as highly organized as an urban gang. Most adolescents simply choose new friends if they constantly disagree with the decisions of their old friends. The freedom of adolescents to end friendships limits their friends' use of coercive pressure as an influence technique.

Research on adolescents' responses to antisocial dilemmas is also misleading because it implies that friends usually pressure adolescents to engage in antisocial behavior. Experimental studies of friends' discussions suggest a different conclusion. So do longitudinal studies in which friends' influence is judged from changes over time in the attitudes or behavior of adolescents and their friends.[7] These studies show that the direction of friends' influence depends on the friends' characteristics. For example, if an adolescent's friends do not care about doing well in school, the adolescent's motivation to achieve in school may decrease over time. By contrast, if an adolescent's friends have good grades in school, the adolescent's grades may improve.

Viewed from a different perspective, the usual outcome of the mutual influence among friends is an increase over time in the friends' similarity. Often, the increased similarity reflects a true compromise: Friends who differ in their attitudes or behaviors adopt a position intermediate between their initial positions. Some adolescents, however, are more influential than their friends. Other adolescents are more susceptible to influence than their friends. The sources of these individual differences need further exploration.

Finally, longitudinal studies suggest that the power of friends' influence is often overestimated.[10] In one study, friends' influence on adolescents' educational aspirations was nonsignificant. In another study, friends' influence on adolescents' alcohol use was nonsignificant. These findings are unusual, but even the statistically significant effects that are found are often small.

The conclusion that friends have only a small influence on adolescents is so contrary to the conventional wisdom that its validity might be questioned. Many studies seem to support the assertion of popular writers that friends have a strong influence on adolescents, but these studies often have serious flaws.[7] Researchers have frequently used adolescents' reports on their friends' behavior as measures of the friends' actual behavior. Then the researchers have estimated the friends' influence from correlations for the similarity between adolescents' self-reports and their reports on friends. Yet recent studies have shown that adolescents' reports on their friends involve considerable projection: Adolescents assume their friends' behavior is more like their own than it actually is.

Another flaw in many studies is the estimation of friends' influence from correlations for friends' similarity at a single time. However, influence is not the only contributor to friends' similarity. Adolescents also select friends who are already similar to themselves. On some characteristics (e.g., ethnicity), friends' similarity is due entirely to selection rather than to influence. To distinguish between selection and influence as sources of friends' similarity, longitudinal studies are needed. Recent longitudinal studies suggest that friends' influence on adolescents is relatively weak.

However, weak effects should not be interpreted as null effects. Underestimating the influence of friends would be as serious a mistake as overestimating it. At all ages, human beings are influenced by individuals with whom they have formed close relationships. Adolescents have close relationships with friends and, therefore, are influenced by friends. Friends influence adolescents' attitudes toward school and the broader social world. Friends influence adolescents' behavior in school and out of school.

This influence is not a social problem unique to adolescence, but one instance of a universal phenomenon. To understand friends' influence better, theorists need to abandon the simplistic hypothesis of peer pressure toward antisocial behavior and consider the multiple processes of friends' influence and the varied effects of these processes.

CONCLUSION

Current thinking about adolescents' friendships is dominated by two theoretical perspectives that are incomplete and one-sided. One perspective emphasizes the benefits of friendships with certain positive features, such as intimacy. Intimacy is a more central feature of friendships in adolescence than in childhood. Intimate friendships have positive effects on adolescents, but these friendships seem to affect only some aspects of psychological adjustment. Moreover, some adolescents have friendships with many negative features, such as a high rate of conflicts. These conflicts often spill over and negatively affect other relationships. Adults concerned about adolescents' friendships should not only try to enhance the positive features of close friendships, but also try to reduce their negative features.

The second theoretical perspective emphasizes the negative influence of friends whose attitudes and behaviors are undesirable. Adolescents are influenced by their friends' attitudes and behaviors, but adolescents also influence their friends. Over time, this mutual influence increases the similarity between adolescents and their friends. Friends' influence does not generally lead to shifts either toward more desirable or toward less desirable attitudes and behaviors. These findings imply that adults concerned about negative influences of friends should try not to reduce friends' influence but to channel that influence in a positive direction.

Acknowledgments—The author's research was supported by grants from the Spencer Foundation, the National Science Foundation, and the National Institute of Mental Health.

Notes

1. T.J. Berndt, Obtaining support from friends in childhood and adolescence, in *Children's Social Networks and Social Supports,* D. Belle, Ed. (Wiley, New York, 1989); R.L. Selman and L.H. Schultz, *Making a Friend in Youth: Developmental Theory and Pair Therapy* (University of Chicago Press, Chicago, 1990); J. Youniss and J. Smollar, *Adolescent Relations With Mothers, Fathers, and Friends* (University of Chicago Press, Chicago, 1985).

2. U. Bronfenbrenner, *Two Worlds of Childhood* (Russell Sage Foundation, New York, 1970); L. Steinberg and S.B. Silverberg, The vicissitudes of autonomy in early adolescence, *Child Development, 57,* 841–851 (1986).

3. T.J. Berndt, Children's comments about their friendships, in *Minnesota Symposium on Child Psychology: Vol. 18. Cognitive Perspectives on Children's Social Behavioral Development,* M. Perlmutter, Ed. (Erlbaum, Hillsdale, NJ, 1986); R.C. Savin-Williams and T.J. Berndt, Friendships and peer relations during adolescence, in *At the Threshold: The Developing Adolescent,* S.S. Feldman and G. Elliott, Eds. (Harvard University Press, Cambridge, MA, 1990).

4. T.J. Berndt, Intimacy and competition in the friendships of adolescent boys and girls, in *Gender Roles Through the Life Span,* M.R. Stevenson, Ed. (University of Wisconsin Press, Madison, in press).

5. W.K. Rawlins, *Friendship Matters: Communication, Dialectics, and the Life Course* (Aldine de Gruyter, Hawthorne, NY, 1992); M.S. Clark and H.T. Reis, Interpersonal processes in close relationships, *Annual Review of Psychology, 39,* 609–672 (1988).

6. S. Cohen and T.A. Wills, Stress, social support, and the buffering hypothesis, *Psychological Bulletin, 98,* 310–357 (1985); H.O.F. Veiel and U. Baumann, *The Meaning and Measurement of Social Support* (Hemisphere, New York, 1992).

7. T.J. Berndt and R.C. Savin-Williams, Variations in friendships and peer-group relationships in adolescence, in *Handbook of Clinical Research and Practice With Adolescents,* P. Tolan and B. Cohler, Eds. (Wiley, New York, in press).

8. T.J. Berndt and K. Keefe, *How friends influence adolescents' adjustment to school,* paper presented at the biennial meeting of the Society for Research in Child Development, Seattle (April 1991); see also W.W. Hartup, Conflict and friendship relations, in *Conflict in Child and Adolescent Development,* C.U. Shantz and W.W. Hartup, Eds. (Cambridge University Press, Cambridge, England, in press).

9. T.J. Berndt, A.E. Laychak, and K. Park, Friends' influence on adolescents' academic achievement motivation: An experimental study, *Journal of Educational Psychology, 82,* 664–670 (1990).

10. J.M. Cohen, Sources of peer group homogeneity, *Sociology of Education, 50,* 227–241 (1977); D.B. Kandel and K. Andrews, Processes of adolescent socialization by parents and peers, *International Journal of the Addictions, 22,* 319–342 (1987).

Too Old, Too Fast?

Millions of American teenagers work, but many may be squandering their futures

STEVEN WALDMAN
AND KAREN SPRINGEN
With Marcus Mabry in Washington

Anyone who thinks teenagers spend their afternoons playing hoops, hanging out at the mall—or, for that matter, studying—should meet 18-year-old Dave Fortune of Manchester, N.H. He wakes up at dawn, slurps some strawberry jam for a sugar rush, goes to the high school until 2:30 p.m., hurries home to make sure his little sister arrives safely, changes and goes off to his job at a clothing store. He gets home at around 10:30, does maybe an hour of homework—"if I have any"—and goes to sleep around midnight. The routine begins anew five hours later. Fortune knows he's sacrificed some of his school life for his job. He misses playing soccer and baseball as he did in junior high, and he had to give up a challenging law class because he had so little time for studying. "I have to work," Dave says. "I *have* to work."

Grade-Point Averages

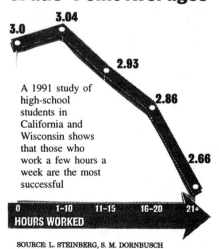

3.0
3.04
2.93
2.86
2.66

A 1991 study of high-school students in California and Wisconsin shows that those who work a few hours a week are the most successful

HOURS WORKED
0   1-10   11-15   16-20   21+

SOURCE: L. STEINBERG, S. M. DORNBUSCH

A peek in Fortune's closet suggests otherwise. His back-to-school wardrobe: two leather jackets, six sweaters, 12 pairs of jeans, four pairs of shoes, two pairs of sneakers, two belts, "loads of shirts," and a half-dozen silk pants and shirts that would make a jockey proud. Price tag for the spree (with his store discount): $550.

After-school jobs have become a major force in teen life. More than 5 million kids between 12 and 17 now work, according to Simmons Market Research Bureau. Teens are twice as likely to work as they were in 1950. The change has been fueled by the growth of the service sector after World War II, the rise of the fast-food industry in the 1960s and '70s and an increase in the number of girls entering the work force. About two thirds of seniors today work more than five hours a week during the academic year. While Wally Cleaver's afternoons were occupied by varsity track, basketball and hanging around with Eddie Haskell, Brandon Walsh on "Beverly Hills, 90210" waits on tables at the Peach Pit because his wealthy parents think it will teach him responsibility—and so that he could buy a Mustang convertible.

As political attention focuses on improving the quality of high schools—and producing a highly trained work force better fit for global competition—states have begun restricting the hours teens can work during the school year. In their senior year, about 47 percent of male student workers and 36 percent of females put in more than 20 hours per week at their jobs. Psychologists and teachers see the strain on students. They have little time for homework, and teachers who regularly watch exhausted students struggling to keep their heads up all too often respond by lowering standards. "Everybody worries why Japanese and German and Swed-

ish students are doing better than us," says Laurence Steinberg, a psychology professor at Temple University. "One reason is they're not spending their afternoons wrapping tacos."

The significance of after-school work goes beyond sagging test scores and eyelids. In interviews with 64 high-school students in New Hampshire, Iowa, Virginia, Illinois and Maryland, an unsettling picture emerges. The prevalence of youth employment has transformed what it means to be a teenager. Kids who take jobs by choice, not necessity, have worked themselves into what one scholar called "premature affluence"—the ability to finance consumer binges even as their parents are cutting back.

They buy clothing with all the well-heeled restraint of Imelda Marcos. Many have cars, which they use to go on lavish dates. Despite the recession, only 10 percent of high-school seniors surveyed last year said they were saving most of their earnings for college, and just 6 percent said they used most of it to help pay family living expenses. Finally, jobs even play a role in changing the relationships between teens and their parents. Pulled in many directions, parents grant their working children striking amounts of autonomy. Working at the local McDonald's, in short, has enabled many teens to buy out of adolescence.

There are those, of course, who must work. The recession has forced some kids into the labor force to help their parents survive. Teachers, students and social scientists also agree that work can teach discipline, self-respect and efficiency. Fortune's father, for example, insisted his son work to learn some responsibility—and the son says he has. Some studies show that kids who work moderately actually do better in school than those who don't take jobs at all. Students on the verge of dropping out—or into criminality—can be kept on track by a good job. It can even teach tolerance by forcing them to meet kids of different social cliques.

Nonetheless, educators worry that while the benefits of work have been known for years, a range of problems has been left unexplored. Some are apparent at Pembroke Academy, a public high school near Concord, N.H.:

■ Vanessa Thompson saw her grades plummet from B's to D's when she increased her schedule last year from 25 to 30 hours a week at a movie theater and Lady Foot Locker. "You either do homework at study hall or it just doesn't get done," she says. Her boss at the shoe store questioned whether she was keeping up with school. "Of course I lied to her because I needed the hours," Thompson says. "School's important but so's money. Homework doesn't pay. Teachers say education is your payment, and that just makes me want to puke."

■ Andrew Cutting points to a small red scar above his right eye, a reminder of what might be called a job-related injury. Last month Cutting was in study hall writing a composition when, midsentence, he fell asleep, slamming his head down on the tip of his pen cap. "It hurt wicked bad," he says. "I felt like an idiot." He was tired from pumping gas at a nearby Mobil station the night before. He says he's managing his sleep better now and will keep the job so he can buy a car and pay for his own clothes instead of the "queer shirts with butterflies on the collar" his parents get. His head probably hurts less, too.

■ Artie Bresby stocks shelves at Shaw's Supermarket. To sustain his job pace, he takes six Vivarin pills (equivalent to about 15 cups of coffee), plus two liters of turbo-charged Mountain Dew. That, however, did not stop him from dozing off during a group interview with NEWSWEEK.

Are these three the exception or the norm? Their schedules, at least, are typical. A 1989 study by the state of New Hampshire found that 77 percent of seniors were employed and more than half of them worked more than 20 hours. Does working too much really hinder academic performance? Some scholars cite Japan, where students do better in school—and work at jobs less. According to a forthcoming study by University of Michigan professor Harold Stevenson, 74 percent of juniors surveyed in Minneapolis worked—compared with 21 percent in Sendai, Japan. Indeed, almost half the public schools in Tokyo prohibit students from working.

Other U.S. studies have shown a more direct link between hours worked and academic achievement. A study by the Educational Testing Service concluded that kids who work longer hours are less likely to take biology and chemistry courses, and earn lower achievement scores in math, science, history, literature and reading. Another study of more than 68,000 students nationally linked working more than 20 hours to increased cigarette and alcohol use, less sleep and more truancy. While the author of the ETS study points out that these kids might not do well in school even if they weren't working, other researchers say that a heavy workload exacerbates poor performance.

Slipping standards: The job frenzy may even harm students who don't work. Some teachers demand less. Knowing that students were unlikely to read books outside class in part because of their job schedules, Ken Sharp, an English teacher at Pembroke, has his pupils spend a week reading a play aloud in class. A study of 1,577 Wisconsin teenagers in the early 1980s revealed that teachers shortened reading assignments, simplified lectures and reduced out-of-class assignments—all to accommodate teen work schedules. It "was a factor in demoralizing teachers and giving the students, in turn, a message that little of significance would happen at school," wrote Linda M. McNeil, the Rice University professor who conducted the study.

In some schools, standards are so low that it's become easy to get decent grades even while holding down a time-consuming job; there just isn't that much schoolwork to do. Parents, too, may lower expectations. Michael Szpisjak, a senior at Glenbrook South High School in Glenview, Ill., more than doubled his hours at a publishing company, though he knew it would hurt his grades. His father encouraged him to work. "Usually people at the bottom of the class are the most successful if you measure it in terms of how much money they make," says Stephen Szpisjak.

Teen work is also threatening extracurricular activities—which can be the best part of high school. Musical aptitude of students has declined since the days when "work was limited to summers and maybe a paper route," because students no longer have time to practice, says Terry Grossberg, the band teacher at Waukegan High in Illinois. William Turner played wide receiver his freshman year at Largo High in suburban Maryland, but quit last year to bag groceries so he'd have money for "clothes and girls." It turned out that was the year the team went to the state semifinals. His grades dropped as well, from 3.67 down to 2.50, so he cut back on his job this year.

Every individual reacts differently to work, but two groups seem immune to a job's detriments: weak and gifted students. "Some kids are not real good students, but at work, they're Queen of the May," says guidance counselor Gloria Mueller of Glenbrook South. The other group is that small slice at the top: the Roboteens who manage to do, and excel at, everything. John Fiorelli of Glenbrook wakes up at 5:30, runs three miles, earns grades in the top 10 percent, runs seven or eight miles after school for the cross-country team, serves as senior-class president and still works 15 to 20 hours washing dishes at a nearby hospital. "I like the pressure," he says.

Kids willingly make the sacrifice in part because high school's frenzy of consumerism has grown only more intense. Teens have always coveted thy friends' belongings, but could do little about it when their pockets were empty. But teen earning power increased from $65 billion in 1986 to $95 billion last year, far outpacing inflation and parental income, according to Teenage Research Unlimited, a marketing firm. Teens spent $82 billion in 1991, and have maintained the pace despite the recession. The more money Johnny has, the more he buys.

Some run-of-the-mill purchases by middle-class teens capture the 90210-ish expectations of teen life: Chris Lamarre, who works at a Manchester carpet store, bought his girlfriend a $100 Gucci watch and himself a $600 car stereo. Mary Kane of Olney, Md., spent $1,000 of her earnings from Lady Foot Locker to go to Cancún for eight days with her friends. More and more students at Glenbrook South are spending hundreds of dollars to get beepers—not to consummate drug deals, but to retrieve messages from friends. Blame it on peer pressure: when you go out with friends, "you don't want to say, 'I can't do that, I don't have the money'," explains Kirsten Fournier, a senior at Manchester West High.

The growth of the youth spending culture raises an ironic question: wasn't work supposed to teach kids the "value of the dollar"? Well, in a way, it does. "You see a two-for-one deal at a store and you're like, 'Whoaaa!'" says Chris Weir of Pembroke. Jerald Bachman, program director of the University of Michigan's Institute for Social Research, argues that students who develop premature affluence become accustomed to spending large percentages of their take-home pay. Why can Rasheda Stevenson, a Largo High senior, who worked 20 hours a week last year as a cashier, be so profligate? "If I see some dress shoes and they're, like, $80," she says, "my mother's going to wait until they go on sale. But if I want them I can get them right then and there. I don't have bills to pay. I don't have any children. It's just me." Stevenson has 20 pairs of dress shoes—and "a purse to go with every pair"—plus 10 pairs of tennis shoes.

The most important thing students can "buy" with their jobs is an altered relationship with their parents. Time after time, students say employment gave them more freedom. Parents who would contemptuously refuse to buy their children a shelf of color-coordinated Nikes can take the posture "It's your money; you can spend it on what you want." The net effect is that teens can feel, and are treated, more like adults. "It was like I just lived there, like a tenant," says Marvin Silver of Largo High. Last year he had dinner with his parents just on weekends while he was working at Morton's department store roughly 25 hours a week. "I'm losing my kid," says Betty Miller, whose daughter, Kris, a Wakefield High senior, fixes pastries and cappuccino at Bistro Bistro four and a half hours, four nights a week.

Parents often agree to the new arrangement because maintaining authority has become so difficult. Vetoing a son's purchase of Calvins or a used Mustang would mean forcing him to swim against a tidal wave of materialism at school. Patricia Turner, mother of the Largo student who missed the football championship, says parents now confront the extra fear that if they don't allow their kids to earn the trappings of adolescence legally, they will be lured by the easy money of drug dealing.

Cash relief: A kid's self-sufficiency can also relieve a parent of financial burden, even if the teen isn't directly pitching in for rent. But saying that a daughter can't sacrifice the glee club to buy a car means that parents might have to pick her up at school; with both working, that might be impossible. By accepting this assistance, parents in effect sell some of their authority for cash relief. They're selling too low, says Dr. Lawrence Hartmann, past president of the American Psychiatric Association. "Parents should be parents, and children should be children."

For those empathetic children who try to take care of their families as well as do "youthful" activities, the pressure can be enormous. Mary Clark's mother encourages her to participate in Wakefield High activities because "you're only young once." But Mary was proud she was able to pay for redecorating her room so she wouldn't have to ask her mom, who is single and holds down two jobs, as a waitress and a secretary. But taking on so much can be overwhelming. Last March, she was baby-sitting three nights a week, helping take care of her nephew, trying to learn her lines for her role in "Julius Caesar" and worrying about an academic project soon due. She sat in class realizing that in addition to all that, she wasn't understanding the algebra lesson. In the middle of class, she broke down and quietly sobbed.

Only in recent years have states, parents and business owners tried to preserve the numerous benefits of work while eliminat-

Teens in Two Societies

In different cities, here's where teenagers get their money and how they spend their time.

	Sendai, Japan	Minneapolis, U.S.
Percent working	21%	74%
Mean number of hours worked weekly	9.8 hrs.	15.6 hrs.
Percent feeling stress at least once a week	43.4%	71.2%
Portion of spending money from parents	94.7%	47.5%
Weekly amount received from jobs and parents	$86	$205
Percent dating	36.8%	84.5%
Weekly TV watching	16.7 hrs.	12 hrs.

SOURCE: UNIVERSITY OF MICHIGAN

ing the excesses. Washington state last month imposed a 20-hour limit for 16- and 17-year-olds while school is in session—half the previous level. Wisconsin, Indiana, New York, North Carolina and Maine have restricted work hours this year, and, since 1990, eight other states have changed their rules. But some business groups have mobilized to block restrictions. In Washington state, fast-food companies bused in burger flippers to protest against the proposed reduction to 20 hours a week.

Such restrictions mean nothing, of course, if they're not enforced. A child-labor crackdown by former labor secretary Elizabeth Dole has all but disappeared under the administration of Lynn Martin. The number of federal investigators has dropped from 970 to 841 in three years, and the department has asked for only 825 next year. States have cut back, too. Illinois now has only 13 child-labor inspectors for the entire state, down from 18 five years ago. And while lax enforcement can lead to sleepy students, it also allows for far worse: more than 71,000 teenagers were injured at work in 1990, according to a recent study by the National Safe Workplace Institute.

Burger bonus: Attitudes of individual bosses range from cruel to paternal. One student said he was forced to miss graduation ceremonies to keep his job. "I would have employers write me the nastiest letters be-

cause I wouldn't drop a chemistry class because they wanted a kid to work at 1 [p.m.]" says Manchester West principal Robert Baines. "I finally wrote back and said, 'Please leave them alone until 2:33'." Yet other students reported that their supervisors helped them with homework or crafted schedules around exams and athletics. The owners of 25 McDonald's in Baton Rouge, La., last year started offering bonuses to kids with good grades. A 3.0 average earns an extra 15 cents per hour. Schools are increasingly taking the posture that if students are going to work, it should at least be at a meaningful job. High-school students in rural Rothsay, Minn., actually run the local hardware and grocery stores so students can gain supervised experience tied to a curriculum. A program in Chicago helps teens run New Expression, a paper with a circulation of 70,000.

Ultimately, though, it is neither legislators nor employers who will have to solve the conundrum of teen work. Most parents are proud of their children earning a paycheck, but find themselves unaware of the problems their children's jobs can create. All parents want the best future for their kids. Once upon a time, after-school work seemed a perfect way to teach sons and daughters a little something about the real world and reward them with some cash at the same time. Now, for too many teenagers, too much of a wise thing may be squandering that very future.

WHY WORKING TEENS GET INTO TROUBLE

Teenagers who work have more money, but they also have more problems.

Adults often say that a good way to keep kids out of trouble is to keep them busy. Maybe they're wrong, but teenagers who work for pay are sometimes more likely to abuse drugs and develop behavioral problems.

Nearly three-fourths of students worked for pay during their last year of high school, according to the experiences of more than 70,000 high school seniors surveyed in the late 1980s. Forty-two percent of this group worked more than 20 hours a week. The likelihood that a senior will smoke cigarettes, drink al-

> **Seniors who work 30 or more hours a week display higher levels of aggression.**

cohol, and use illegal drugs increases with hours worked, according to researchers Jerald G. Bachman and John Schulenberg of the University of Michigan's Institute for Social Research in Ann Arbor.

Even when factors such as educational success and family background are taken into account, students who work a lot have more problems. Seniors who work 30 or more hours a week display higher levels of aggression and they are also

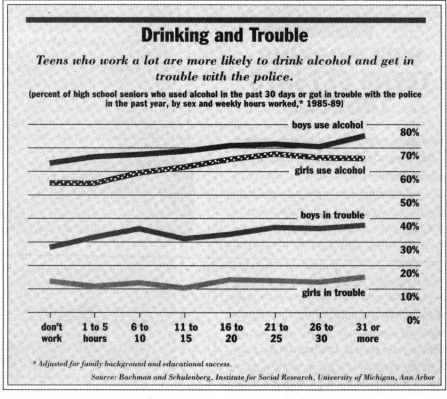

Drinking and Trouble

Teens who work a lot are more likely to drink alcohol and get in trouble with the police.

(percent of high school seniors who used alcohol in the past 30 days or got in trouble with the police in the past year, by sex and weekly hours worked,* 1985-89)

* Adjusted for family background and educational success.

Source: Bachman and Schulenberg, Institute for Social Research, University of Michigan, Ann Arbor

more likely to be victims of violence. This is apparently unrelated to their exposure to danger at workplaces, because most of the aggression takes place at or near school. Students who work are also slightly more likely to get in trouble with the police. Bachman and Schulenberg say that "these findings do little to support the notion that having students actively involved in part-time jobs will keep them 'out of trouble.'"

Work schedules affect teens' health, which may in turn affect their behavior. The more students work, the less likely they are to get a good night's sleep or eat

> **Work schedules affect teens' health, which may in turn affect their behavior.**

breakfast on a regular basis. Seniors who put in at least 30 hours a week are less likely than others to be satisfied with their leisure time, and the girls are less likely to be satisfied with their lives in general. On the other hand, the propensity to date rises somewhat with work hours.

In many respects, students with light work schedules seem to be the best-balanced group. Those who work one to five hours a week are more likely than those who don't work at all to eat breakfast and exercise vigorously. Boys in this category are also more likely to get a good night's sleep. Light-working teens also have the highest self-esteem, although this factor varies little for all seniors by hours worked.

Further research reveals that the types of jobs teens have can make a difference. Among more than 20,000 seniors surveyed between 1982 and 1991, those who perceived their jobs as relevant to their educational and career goals were less likely than other working teens to experience the problems associated with heavy work hours.

For more about seniors and their jobs, see the article by Bachman and Schulenberg in *Developmental Psychology* (Vol. 29, No. 2). To learn more about the Monitoring the Future project, which has been conducting annual and nationally representative surveys of high school seniors since 1975, contact the Institute for Social Research's Survey Research Center, University of Michigan, P.O. Box 1248, Ann Arbor, MI 48106-1248; telephone (313) 764-8365.   —*Diane Crispell*

Perils of Prohibition

Why we should lower the drinking age to 18

Elizabeth M. Whelan

My colleagues at the Harvard School of Public Health, where I studied preventive medicine, deserve high praise for their recent study on teenage drinking. What they found in their survey of college students was that they drink "early and . . . often," frequently to the point of getting ill.

As a public-health scientist with a daughter, Christine, heading to college this fall, I have professional and personal concerns about teen binge drinking. It is imperative that we explore *why* so many young people abuse alcohol. From my own study of the effects of alcohol restrictions and my observations of Christine and her friends' predicament about drinking, I believe that today's laws are unrealistic. Prohibiting the sale of liquor to responsible young adults creates an atmosphere where binge drinking and alcohol abuse have become a problem. American teens, unlike their European peers, don't learn how to drink gradually, safely and in moderation.

American teens don't learn how to drink safely and in moderation.

Alcohol is widely accepted and enjoyed in our culture. Studies show that moderate drinking can be good for you. But we legally proscribe alcohol until the age of 21 (why not 30 or 45?). Christine and her classmates can drive cars, fly planes, marry, vote, pay taxes, take out loans and risk their lives as members of the U.S. armed forces. But laws in all 50 states say that no alcoholic beverages may be sold to anyone until that magic 21st birthday. We didn't always have a national "21" rule. When I was in college, in the mid-'60s, the drinking age varied from state to state. This posed its own risks, with underage students crossing state lines to get a legal drink.

In parts of the Western world, moderate drinking by teenagers and even children under their parents' supervision is a given. Though the per capita consumption of alcohol in France, Spain and Portugal is higher than in the United States, the rate of alcoholism and alcohol abuse is lower. A glass of wine at dinner is normal practice. Kids learn to regard moderate drinking as an enjoyable family activity rather than as something they have to sneak away to do. Banning drinking by young people makes it a badge of adulthood—a tantalizing forbidden fruit.

Christine and her teenage friends like to go out with a group to a club, comedy show or sports bar to watch the game. But teens today have to go on the sly with fake IDs and the fear of getting caught. Otherwise, they're denied admittance to most places and left to hang out on the street. That's hardly a safer alternative. Christine and her classmates now find themselves in a legal no man's land. At 18, they're considered adults. Yet when they want to enjoy a drink like other adults, they are, as they put it, "disenfranchised."

Comparing my daughter's dilemma with my own as an "underage" college student, I see a difference—and one that I think has exacerbated the current dilemma. Today's teens are far more sophisticated than we were. They're treated less like children and have more responsibilities than we did. This makes the 21 restriction seem anachronistic.

For the past few years, my husband and I have been preparing Christine for college life and the inevitable partying—read keg of beer—that goes with it. Last year, a young friend with no drinking experience was violently ill for days after he was introduced to "clear liquids in small glasses" during freshman orientation. We want our daughter to learn how to drink sensibly and avoid this pitfall. Starting at the age of 14, we invited her to join us for a glass of champagne with dinner. She'd tried it once before, thought it was "yucky" and declined. A year later, she enjoyed sampling wine at family meals.

When, at 16, she asked for a Mudslide (a bottled chocolate-milk-and-rum concoction), we used the opportunity to discuss it with her. We explained the alcohol content, told her the alcohol level is lower when the drink is blended with ice and compared it with a glass of wine. Since the drink of choice on campus is beer, we contrasted its potency with wine and hard liquor and stressed the importance of not drinking on an empty stomach.

Our purpose was to encourage her to know the alcohol content of what she is served. We want her to experience the effects of liquor in her own home, not on the highway and not for the first time during a college orientation week with free-flowing suds. Although Christine doesn't drive yet, we regularly reinforce the concept of choosing a designated driver. Happily, that already seems a widely accepted practice among our daughter's friends who drink.

We recently visited the Ivy League school Christine will attend in the fall. While we were there, we read a story in the college paper about a student who was nearly electrocuted when, in a drunken state, he climbed on top of a moving train at a railroad station near the campus. The student survived, but three of his limbs were later amputated. This incident reminded me of a tragic death on another campus. An intoxicated student maneuvered himself into a chimney. He was found three days later

when frat brothers tried to light a fire in the fireplace. By then he was dead.

These tragedies are just two examples of our failure to teach young people how to use alcohol prudently. If 18-year-olds don't have legal access to even a beer at a public place, they have no experience handling liquor on their own. They feel "liberated" when they arrive on campus. With no parents to stop them, they have a "let's make up for lost time" attitude. The result: binge drinking.

We should make access to alcohol legal at 18. At the same time, we should come down much harder on alcohol abusers and drunk drivers of all ages. We should intensify our efforts at alcohol education for adolescents. We want them to understand that it is perfectly OK not to drink. But if they do, alcohol should be consumed in moderation.

After all, we choose to teach our children about safe sex, including the benefits of teen abstinence. Why, then, can't we—schools and parents alike—teach them about safe drinking?

Whelan is president of the American Council on Science and Health.

Surge in Teen-Age Smoking Left an Industry Vulnerable

By BARNABY J. FEDER

David Bernt, a 17-year-old high school junior in the affluent Chicago suburb of Oak Park, remembers being one of the few who smoked in junior high school. "But now if you go by there it seems to be everywhere," he said.

Not everywhere, perhaps, but researchers calculate that teen-age smoking rates, after declining in the 1970's and leveling off in the 1980's, have climbed sharply over the last five years. Although everything from why the trend began to what might stop it is disputed, it adds up to a huge health problem for the country and a public relations disaster for the tobacco industry. Indeed, the trend has played a crucial role in driving the once intractable industry into negotiations for a global settlement with regulators and its legal adversaries. The negotiations are expected to resume today.

Teen-age smoking rates are still lower than in the 1970's. But last year, the percentage of 12th graders who smoked daily was up 20 percent from 1991, to 22 percent, according to the most recent edition of the University of Michigan's Monitoring the Future Survey, an annual study widely followed by tobacco researchers. The rate among 10th graders jumped 45 percent, to 18.3 percent, and the rate for 8th graders was up 44 percent, to 10.4 percent.

Five million people now younger than 18 will eventually die of tobacco-related illnesses, at current smoking rates, according to the most recent projections from the Centers for Disease Control and Prevention in Atlanta. If youth smoking rates had not climbed but instead continued downward to the lowest levels achieved by any segment of the teenage population in recent years—those for black teen-agers in the early 1990's—fewer than one million of today's youth would be likely to die prematurely of tobacco-related illness, said Terry Pechacek, an epidemiologist in the Office on Smoking and Health at the disease-control agency.

Rising youth smoking rates have been cited by the Food and Drug Administration and President Clinton as evidence that the industry is marketing its products to youths and should be restricted by the F.D.A. The rates are also fueling demands in many states and nationally for higher taxes on tobacco, based on research showing that price increases typically discourage teen-age smokers more than adults. And lawyers in private class actions on behalf of adult smokers and in many of the 23 state lawsuits seeking compensation for Medicaid spending on tobacco-related illnesses have demanded restrictions aimed at reducing youth smoking in addition to financial compensation.

Teen-Age Smoking Makes a Comeback

The number of 12th graders who try cigarettes has declined over the last two decades, but the number who smoke occasionally and who develop heavier habits has increased sharply in recent years.

Of 12th graders surveyed:

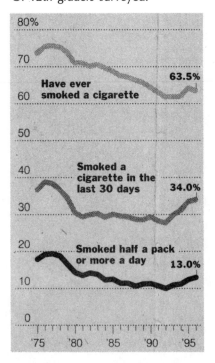

Source: University of Michigan

The New York Times

"A lot of this wouldn't be happening if youth smoking rates had been declining," said William Novelli, director of the National Center for Tobacco-Free Kids in Washington.

The National Center itself is a sign of the times, having emerged in the last year as the command station in Washington for much of the activity in the anti-tobacco movement, even though some tobacco critics say there is a danger in concentrating so much on children. Matthew Myers, the center's general counsel, has been the one representative of health groups involved in the settlement talks, which began early this month. In the talks, the nation's two largest tobacco companies, RJR Nabisco and Philip Morris, have demanded near-total immunity from lawsuits in return for concessions including new advertising curbs, more government regulation and payments to compensate states and individuals for tobacco's health costs.

Steve Berman, a plaintiffs' lawyer from Seattle who represents attorneys general from four states involved in the talks, said one proposal was to make the size of the cigarette producers' financial liabilities dependent on their contributions to lowering youth smoking rates through reducing advertising and marketing efforts and through other means.

Richard Blumenthal, the Connecticut Attorney General, said that the talks had involved what is being referred to as a "look back" provision that would kick in five to seven years after any settlement was approved, depending on smoking rates. Such a look-back might call for expanded Federal regulation of the industry if youth smoking rates were not cut. And states that failed to enforce Federal regulations governing marketing and advertising of cigarettes to young smokers might be denied some payments from the compensation fund. "We are looking at reducing the numbers of all smokers but particularly teen-age smokers," Mr. Blumenthal said.

Just what has caused the teen-age smoking rate to rise so sharply is hotly debated. The tobacco industry says the increase is due to a broad range of social forces. Industry officials note that other kinds of risk-taking among teen-agers, especially the use of marijuana and other drugs, have risen more sharply than tobacco use. The industry also cites teen-agers' naturally rebellious reaction to the increasing efforts to stop them from smoking.

Critics of the tobacco industry agree that rebelliousness and other forces are at work. But they say the industry itself is the most important factor. The industry's spending on domestic advertising and promotions soared to $4.83 billion in 1994, or 250 percent after adjusting for inflation, from $361 million in 1970, according to the latest data published by the Federal Trade Commission.

Just how that huge pie has been divided is a secret closely guarded not only from critics but even among companies in the industry. Much of the money goes into promotions to encourage retailers to run sales or to display particular brands and signs more prominently. Tobacco companies say they have adopted practices to focus their messages on adults, like requiring that all models be—and look—older than 25.

But critics like John Pierce, head of the Cancer Prevention Center at the University of California at San Diego, say it is most telling that spending rose most rapidly in the 1980's, when the decline in youth smoking was halted. They also point to research showing that children have been strongly attracted to some of the biggest marketing campaigns, notably R. J. Reynolds Tobacco's use of the ever-hip Joe Camel and Philip Morris's use of the rugged Marlboro man and the Marlboro Adventure Team, a merchandise promotion.

The surge in teen-age smoking in the 1990's coincided with a sharp expansion by both Reynolds and Philip Morris in giveaways of items like T-shirts in return for coupons accumulated by buying their ciga-

Half a Pack At an Early Age

Percentage in each grade who told surveyors that they smoke at least half a pack of cigarettes a day.

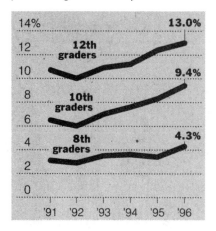

Source: University of Michigan

The New York Times

rettes. Research showed that the companies had limited success in preventing distribution of the merchandise to children—30 percent of teen-age smokers have it—and that the items are just as appealing to teen-agers as to adults.

Tobacco companies say critics grossly exaggerate the effects of their marketing. They point out that teen-age smoking is also rising in countries where most forms of advertising have been banned.

The latest indicator of the distance between the two sides is Philip Morris's creation of a record company—Woman Thing Music—to promote its Virginia Slims brand. The company will be selling bargain-priced compact disks by its female artists along with its cigarettes. Its first artist, Martha Byrne, a nonsmoking actress from the soap opera "As the World Turns," is on a concert tour, appearing, the tobacco company said, in venues where only those older than 21 are allowed.

Nevertheless, anti-tobacco groups have been organizing demonstrations, saying in part that the music is directed at making the Virginia

Slims brand more popular with female teen-agers.

Making matters worse, some critics say, is that Hollywood's long love affair with smoking seems to be heating up. Cigars are being widely used to symbolize success in movies like "The Associate," with Whoopi Goldberg. And even though today's stars are not as inseparable from their cigarettes as former cultural icons like Humphrey Bogart, Bette Davis and James Dean, actors who show up puffing on cigarettes include John Travolta and Uma Thurman, as anti-heroes in "Pulp Fiction," and Winona Ryder, as a Generation X drifter in "Reality Bites." Leonardo DiCaprio went so far as to light up as Romeo in last year's updated "Romeo and Juliet."

Whether smoking in films contributes to the teen-age trend or simply picks up on it is one of many questions. Teen-agers say that movie and music stars do shape their sense of what is "cool" and that a desire to be cool is often a reason the youngest smokers first try cigarettes. But many researchers doubt that an effect can be reliably measured.

Moreover, high school students who smoke regularly say it is so common that no one thinks of it as cool. Some concede that they enjoy doing something forbidden, but more often they cite a desire to relieve stress or to stay thin, the taste, or simply the need to fill time as reasons they kept smoking to the point of becoming addicted. Many, like David Bernt of Oak Park, agree with the industry's contention that its marketing had nothing to do with the decision to smoke but influences brand choice.

"If I buy anything but Camel, it feels like I wasted money because I collect Camel cash," he said, referring to the coupons that can be redeemed for Camel merchandise.

Ultimately, the debate about what is driving up teen-age smoking rates is also a debate about what should be done to try to halt it. Mr. Novelli has in mind higher taxes on tobacco products, strict enforcement of laws against selling tobacco to minors, more public education about the risks of tobacco, more anti-tobacco advertising and broader restrictions on where smokers can light up to reduce nonsmokers' exposure to secondhand smoke. He also wants full enforcement of the F.D.A.'s new marketing curbs, which the industry is challenging in a Federal court in North Carolina.

Cigarette makers say rebelliousness has caused more youths to light up.

The increased smoking rates since 1991 are expected to translate into tens of thousands of additional early deaths because one out of three teenage smokers is expected to develop fatal tobacco-related illnesses. About 46,000 more eighth graders are smoking at least half a pack a day than would have been smoking had the rate remained at its 1991 level, and 250,000 more have smoked within the last 30 days than would have at the 1991 rate, judging from the application of census data to results from the Monitoring the Future surveys. And because of the rising smoking rate since 1991, an extra 110,000 10th graders are half-a-pack-a-day smokers, and nearly 366,000 more of them have smoked in the last 30 days.

The new pot culture

Marijuana is back, more available and accepted than before. Blame blasé parents and the '60s revival.

Monika Guttman

Monika Guttman last wrote for the magazine about the increased use of Ritalin for children.

IT'S THE KIND OF STORY that in the free-wheeling '60s would have been dismissed as "reefer madness"—an outlandish tale of the dangers of smoking marijuana, designed (like the movie of the same name) to scare kids away from the evil weed. But for Kevin West this story is all too real.

"I felt I could stand out if I did crazy things," says West, of Little Rock. That's why he agreed when a friend suggested a game of Russian roulette. West removed all the bullets except one from his mother's .38. Then 17, he'd spent the earlier part of the evening moving from friend's house to friend's house, smoking joints, "getting high on top of high." He put the gun to his head. Had he been in his right mind, he says, he simply would have taken his finger off the trigger. "But on weed you can't think straight." Next thing he knew, he was on the ground in a puddle of blood, a hole in his head the size of a golf ball.

After three operations and months of therapy, West, now 19 remains paralyzed on his left side and takes a daily regimen of anti-seizure and other medications. "I only smoked for a few months. Now I'm on drugs for the rest of my life. I thought marijuana was no big deal."

West's attitude, that pot is "no big deal," reflects what experts say is at the root of a stunning resurgence of pot use among younger and younger kids. "Reefer madness" hysteria has been replaced in some quarters by a culture of complacency about pot, especially among adults who grew up around it and may still consider marijuana "no big deal."

INDEED, MANY TEENS SEE MARIJUANA as a harmless, even healthful, alternative to cigarettes and alcohol. They call it dank, bo, chronic and hemp, and survey after recent survey shows that after more than a decade of decline, growing numbers of teenagers are inhaling (*see chart,*

Out in the open

Today, marijuana is openly promoted at concerts, on CDs, even on clothes—sending teens a message of social acceptance that alarms many experts.

■ **Open market.** Young people look at pipes and other pot paraphernalia. Purpose of the event: to "educate the public on historical, industrial and medicinal uses of the hemp plant [and] rally in support of decriminalization of marijuana."

■ **Blunt message.** A man sells "Phillies blunts"—cigars hollowed out and refilled with marijuana—last year in New York City. The nicotine helps increase the high.

■ **Paraphernalia.** • Capricorn Records' *Hempilation* CD has songs by artists like Cypress Hill, the Black Crowes and Blues Traveler extolling pot. • A pot-themed T-shirt design. • Hats with pot emblems are big sellers among teens. • Last month, outgoing U.S. drug czar Lee Brown scolded Adidas for its new shoe, the Hemp. ("Hemp" is a term for "marijuana"; the shoe is partly made from the plant.) Adidas' president responded: "I don't believe you will encounter anyone smoking our shoes."

■ **Warning.** Duane Garcia, 18, of Queens, N.Y., started smoking marijuana at age 12. "I wanted to be accepted, and it was cool." Later he began stealing to buy pot. Now Garcia appears in a public service TV campaign telling how the drug messed up his life.

From *USA Weekend*, February 16–18, 1996, pp. 4-7. © 1996 by Monika Guttman. Reprinted by permission.

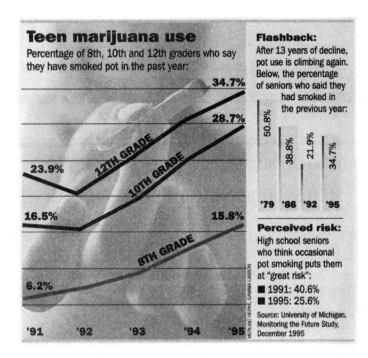

Teen marijuana use

Percentage of 8th, 10th and 12th graders who say they have smoked pot in the past year:

12TH GRADE — 23.9% → 34.7%
10TH GRADE — 28.7%
— 16.5%
8TH GRADE — 6.2% → 15.8%

'91 '92 '93 '94 '95

Flashback: After 13 years of decline, pot use is climbing again. Below, the percentage of seniors who said they had smoked in the previous year:

'79	'86	'92	'95
50.8%	38.8%	21.9%	34.7%

Perceived risk: High school seniors who think occasional pot smoking puts them at "great risk":
■ 1991: 40.6%
■ 1995: 25.6%

Source: University of Michigan, Monitoring the Future Study, December 1995

MERLING HERVE, GAMMA LIAISON

"Teen marijuana use"). The government's National Household Survey on Drug Abuse last September found that the number of teens who smoked pot nearly doubled between 1992 and 1994. In fact, so many studies show teen pot use climbing rapidly that Steve Dnistrian of the Partnership for a Drug-Free America contends "we face a possible epidemic."

Any drug use at this age, notes John Schowalter, clinical director of the Yale Child Study Center, can have lifelong consequences. In the teen years, he says, "social, educational and physical development is taking place at the fastest rate ever except for a child's first year. [Pot] will completely mess up their reality testing." Besides, regular pot use makes kids less interested in school, sports and other activities, adds Schowalter. Even NORML (the National Organization for the Reform of Marijuana Laws), in its policy statement, says it is "strongly committed to the concept that growing up should be drug-free."

Why, then, after more than a decade of decreasing interest, are more teens toking? The most-cited explanation points to a generation of adults for whom pot was almost a rite of passage. Many parents "had an experience with marijuana and don't consider it as serious as other drugs," says U.S. Health and Human Services Secretary Donna Shalala. Susie Williams Manning, director of an adolescent alcohol and drug program in Lexington,

S.C., says she often sees that dynamic at work with client families: "I've had parents tell me they'd rather see their child smoke dope at home than go out and use alcohol."

"One of the things we learned in the '80s [when marijuana use declined] is when all sectors of society speak in unison, it's heard," says Lloyd Johnston, author of the University of Michigan's respected annual teen drug study. "Now we've seen an erosion of that single voice, and [teens get] either no voice in some quarters or conflicting voices in others."

As a result, many teens think pot is more or less endorsed by a majority of adults—and point to success stories like Vice President Al Gore and House Speaker Newt Gingrich, who have admitted trying it.

WHAT MANY ADULTS MAY NOT REALIZE is that marijuana and its use have changed in four significant ways:

■ **Age is down.** Users are starting younger. In the 1992 Adolescent Drug Survey, the average age of first-time users dropped to between 13 and 15, from 14–17 the year before. Treatment centers report 12- and 13-year olds enrolling, formerly a rare event.

■ **The effects now are clear.** Unlike the drug experimentation days of the 1960s and '70s, the effects of pot use now have been studied extensively. Among the conclusions: Marijuana reduces coordination; slows reflexes; interferes with the ability to measure distance, speed and time; and disrupts concentration and short-term memory. According to Donald Tashkin at the UCLA Medical School, there are also cancer risks: A marijuana smoker is exposed to six times as many carcinogens as a tobacco smoker.

■ **Quantity is up.** Kids today smoke larger amounts than their elders did, thanks to innovations such as "blunts": short cigars hollowed out and restuffed with pot or a pot-and-tobacco mix. Marijuana is now often laced with other drugs, as in "primos" (with cocaine) and "illies" (with formaldehyde, making the smoker ill). Result: In 1994, 50 percent more 12- to 17-year olds ended up in emergency rooms for smoking pot as in 1993.

■ **Potency is up.** The pot teens smoke today is not their parents' cannabis. The U.S. Drug Enforcement Administration says the THC, or primary psychoactive chemical, of pot on the street has double in the past decade, thanks to sophisticated cloning and genetic manipulation. (Some experts, however, say pot is no stronger now.) Sample review in *High Times* magazine: three hits and you're "absolutely, totally and righteously screwed up for hours."

"When we smoked marijuana, no one said to us it was harmful to our health, " says HHS' Shalala. "Now we know it's clearly dangerous to [users'] health, that young marijuana users get hooked and smoke it for a very long time." And it's now understood that pot serves as a "gateway" drug. A 1994 study by the Center on Addiction and Substance Abuse found 43 percent of teens who use pot by age 18 move on to cocaine.

A PANOPLY OF CULTURAL FACTORS draws kids to pot. Top of the list: the current glamorization of the '60s and '70s, from the Beatles revival to fashion trends and hairstyles. Media watchers also cite references on TV, such as Roseanne and Dan smoking pot in the bathroom on *Roseanne*; in music, such as Yo-Yo's *I.B.W.* ("Intelligent Black Women") video showing the hip-hop star making a blunt, or the recent *Hempilation* CD to raise funds for pot decriminalization; and in movies such as *How to Make an American Quilt, Home for the Holidays and Dazed and Confused*. Merchandise and clothing with marijuana symbols are popular items nationwide in stores frequented by teens. "Some people are influenced by images," agrees Marcus Harcus, 17, a senior at Minneapolis' Patrick Henry High School who says he has tried pot but didn't like it. "You see it on TV all the time."

Like so many other baby boomers who once experimented with pot, President Clinton has cautioned his own child against drugs. His style, says former drug czar Lee Brown: using daughter Chelsea's interest in science to help make his case.

Pot use also fits a movement that the Rhinebeck, N.Y.-based *Trends Journal* defines as one of the top 10 trends of 1996, "a new anti-Establishment activism simmering among teenagers and preteens." This activism aims at greed, materialism and the get-ahead-at-any-cost attitude that some teens think their parents' generation personifies. One example: Teens on Internet chat boards overwhelmingly support legalization.

Drug abuse also has taken the political and media back burner recently. A decline in news coverage may have given the public a sense that the drug problem is over, says Rick Evans of the National Family Partnership, which provides substance abuse information to families. Indeed, a White House survey found that drug coverage dropped from 518 stories on network newscasts in 1989 to 66 in 1993.

In an election year, teen drug use could turn into a political football. Republicans such as Sen. Orrin Hatch of Utah and Rep. William H. Zeliff Jr. of New Hampshire criticize what they call President Clinton's lack of leadership on the issue. Others agree. Until recently, Clinton "hasn't used the bully pulpit to keep attention on this issue," says Diane Barry, communications director of Join Together, a national resource clearinghouse for more than 3,000 substance abuse organizations. But former drug czar Lee Brown charges that the same congressional leadership proposed a 60 percent cut in funding for anti-drug programs. (Clinton has named Army Gen. Barry McCaffrey to replace Brown; the White House recently held a conference to focus attention on the drug problem.)

One surprising factor in increased pot use by teens: Because of decreased use throughout the '80s, they have seen few examples of pothead burnout, which can be persuasive. "It shows how pot makes you lazy," says Harcus, the 17-year-old in Minneapolis. A neighbor "smokes all the time, and this is his third year as a senior."

FINALLY, MORE KIDS may be smoking simply because pot is cheap and easy to find. According to the DEA, prices are down—loose joints sell for $3–$5; ounces that sold for $200 in 1990 now sell for $125—and supply is up—marijuana currently is the USA's largest cash crop. New technology, particularly hydroponics (growing plants in super-nutrient-rich solutions), means pot can be grown indoors in any neighborhood. More than 20 teens from around the nation interviewed for this article said the average time it would take them to find and buy pot was 3 minutes. "That's 3 minutes here in the inner city. I hear it takes only a minute out in the suburbs," says 15-year-old Amy Lawler of

How to talk about pot

Norman and Janet Dill of Charlottesville, Va., don't want their five kids—four in their teens—to use pot. Problem is, the Dills are among the many baby boomers who experimented with the drug in the 1960s and '70s. Here's what the Dills and several experts recommend.

■ **Don't avoid the topic:** Make it clear you don't want your kids to use pot, and listen to what they have to say, advises the new book *Keeping Youth Drug-Free*, from the Center for Substance Abuse Prevention. (For a free copy, call 1-800-729-6686.) It includes a section for parents who are past drug users, says the center's George Marcelle. Those parents "felt hypocritical talking to their kids about pot, although they felt very strongly that they didn't want their kids using it."

■ **Reveal the past:** "If you did use marijuana when you were young, it's useful to admit that," says Victor Strasburger, author of *Getting Your Kids to Say No in the '90s When You Said Yes in the '60s*. "But you have to say, 'If I had it to do over again, I'd do it differently.' Parents can admit that they did things foolishly."

■ **Don't demonize pot:** "That makes it more alluring" says norman Dill. "I put [pot] in the same category as watching horror films. It's a waste of time and doesn't do you any good."

■ **Appeal to their interests:** This is President Clinton's approach. "Chelsea is interested in science, so he has long talks with her using this interest to explain the dangers of drugs," says former drug czar Lee Brown.

■ **Don't glamorize the past:** "The mistake I see people making is saying, 'Wow! It was so cool when we got really stoned and went to the Frank Zappa concert. But don't *you* do it,' " says Dill. "It's like a lot of things [I did] when I was young, and it was probably a little dumb."

By Richard Vega

Minneapolis, who doesn't smoke pot. "It's easier to get than alcohol."

"Parents aren't paying attention," says Bill Van Ost, a pediatrician and co-director, with his wife, Elaine, of a family drug treatment center in affluent Englewood, N.J. The Van Osts recently gave a free lecture about dealing with drugs at a private school for girls where a drug problem was developing. "Nine parents showed up," says Bill Van Ost. "It's the 'not my kid' syndrome in spades."

Kevin West's mother, Elise, said she had no idea he was smoking pot before he shot himself. "I didn't smell anything out of the ordinary. He'd wait until I'd gone to sleep, then he'd go out."

Because so many factors have contributed to the upswing in teen marijuana use, the search for solutions is scattered. Suggestions range from putting prevention back on the national agenda to focused community action.

The most persuasive messages, for now, seem to come from teens themselves. A program in San Antonio called Fighting Back claims a 16 percent drop in teen pot use since 1993 with youth-initiated anti-drug projects emphasizing respect. The message teens tell one another: "If anything lowers your inhibitions so you take risks you wouldn't normally take, then you're disrespecting your community," says executive director Beverly Watts Davis. The Partnership for a Drug free America, which produced such notable campaigns as the "This is your brain on drugs" ads, now has teenagers telling first-person stories about pot messing up their lives.

What if the message doesn't get through? "The alternative to educating our kids," says the University of Michigan's Lloyd Johnston," is to let them have their own drug epidemic and learn the hard way. And that's not particularly desirable."

CHIPS AHOY

As a new study warns that violence saturates the airwaves, a technological quick fix promises to help. But will the V chip really protect our children?

Richard Zoglin

On NBC's *Law & Order* last week, a white racist set off a bomb that killed 20 people on a New York City subway train. Tori Spelling, in the CBS movie *Co-Ed Call Girl,* grabbed a gun and shot a sleazy pimp. Batman (the cartoon character) was almost thrown into a vat of flames by the Penguin. Lemuel Gulliver (the Ted Danson character) battled gigantic bees in the land of Brobdingnag. And Nick Nolte and Eddie Murphy slapped around bad guys in the umpteenth cable showing of *48 HRS.*

It was, in other words, a pretty typical week of TV in the mid-'90s America. Another week, in the view of troubled parents and concerned politicians, in which TV continued to assault youngsters with violent images, encouraging aggressive behavior in a culture where handguns and street violence are rampant. But it was also a landmark week that brought new hope to many parents worried that scenes like the above are doing untold damage to their kids.

As President Clinton signed into law the sweeping telecommunications bill passed by Congress, he officially launched the era of the V chip. A little device that will be required equipment in most new TV sets within two years, the V chip allows parents to automatically block out programs that have been labeled (by whom remains to be seen) as high in violence, sex or other objectionable material. Last week also saw the release of a weighty academic study that said, in effect, it's about time. Financed by the cable industry and conducted by four universities, the study concluded that violence on TV is more prevalent and more pernicious than most people had imagined. Of nearly 2,700 shows analyzed in a 20-week survey of 23 channels, more than half—57%—were said to contain at least some violence. And much of it was the kind that, according to the study, can desensitize kids and encourage imitation: violence divorced from the bad consequences it has in real life.

The study drew an outcry from network executives, who argued, with some justification, that they have reduced the amount of violence they air and have added warning labels for the little that remains. Indeed, a UCLA study (financed by the networks) last year found "promising signs" that levels of network violence are declining. And upon closer scrutiny, the new study's methodology does seem to overstate the case a bit. Nevertheless, it pins some hard numbers on a problem that is popping up increasingly in the public forum: What effect is TV violence having on kids? And what should we do about it?

Politicians of all stripes have jumped in. Democratic Senator Paul Simon has held well-publicized hearings on TV violence and first proposed that networks sponsor independent audits like last week's report. Bob Dole last year called for action against violence on TV as well as in movies and rock music. Democratic Senator Joseph Lieberman of Connecticut last week joined the conservative Media Research Center in urging the networks to clean up the so-called family hour, the first hour of prime time each evening. President Clinton and Vice President Gore have both embraced the V Chip and called for a summit meeting on TV violence with top network and cable executives at the end of February. The antinetwork rhetoric from many reformers sounds strikingly like that directed against another industry charged with making a harmful product. "The TV industry has to be socially responsible," says Harvard child psychiatrist Dr. Robert Coles. "We're now going after the tobacco companies and saying, 'Don't poison people.' It seems to me, the minds of children are being poisoned all the time by the networks. I don't think it's a false analogy."

The analogy depends, of course, on accepting the proposition that TV has a harmful effect on young viewers. Researchers have been sparring over that question for years, but the debate seems to have swung in favor of the antiviolence forces. The study released last week did no original research on the effect TV violence has on children's behavior. But it summarized a growing body of research and concluded that the link between TV violence and aggressive behavior is no longer in doubt.

Even if true, the exact nature and extent of that link is unclear. Is the effect of watching TV violence brief or lasting? Is TV as important a factor in fostering societal violence as economic poverty, bad schools and broken homes? And in any event, is it really possible—or desirable—to manage kids' exposure to a cultural environment that can never be entirely beneficial or benign? From gangster movies in the '30s to horror comics and rock 'n' roll in the '50s, pop culture has always been strewn with pitfalls for youngsters. Sheltering kids from such things is largely futile; most seem to survive in spite of it.

The current wave of concern about TV violence seems oddly timed. The violent action shows that flourished on TV a decade or so ago—*The A-Team; Magnum, P.I.; Miami Vice*—have largely disappeared. The few crime shows left are cerebral dramas like *Law & Order* and *NYPD Blue,* which, though grittier than the older shows, have little overt violence. The sniggering sex talk on network sitcoms is a far more alarming trend. But even if there are some shows that young kids should be shielded from, the question is whether all TV should be held to the standard of safe-for-children. If TV were to be scrubbed clean for kids, it would be a pretty barren place for adults.

The V chip offers what appears to be an easy solution to this problem. Rather than removing or trying to tone down objectionable shows, it enables parents simply to keep them out of kids' reach. The current V-chip technology, developed by a Canadian engineer named Tim Collings, is essentially a computer chip that, when installed in TV sets (added cost: as little as $1), can receive encoded information about each show. Parents can then program the TV set to block out shows that have been coded to indicate, say, high levels of violence. If, after the kids have gone to bed, parents want to watch Tori Spelling on a shooting spree, they can reverse the blocking by pushing one or more buttons.

The V chip will be welcomed by many parents who despair of monitoring the multitude of TV programs available to their kids. The device has already been a godsend for politicians—a way of seeming to take action on TV violence while avoiding sticky issues of censorship or government control. Most children's activists welcome the device, yet recognize it is not a panacea. "The V chip doesn't do anything to decrease violence," says Arnold Fege of the National Parent-Teacher Association. "There are parents who are not going to use it at all. But it does give parents some control."

Widespread use of the V chip is probably years off. New TV sets are not required to have them for at least two years (legal challenges from the networks are expected to extend that further), and there are still all those chipless RCAs and Sonys currently in people's living rooms. Every set in the house would have to have the V chip, or else kids could just go into the bedroom to watch forbidden shows. Some critics warn, moreover, that it's only a matter of time before kids learn how to break the code and counteract the blocking mechanism.

The trickiest problem of all is, Who will rate the shows, and how they will be rated? The telecommunications bill encourages the networks to devise their own rating system; if they haven't done so in a year, the FCC is empowered to set up a panel for creating one. One possible system is currently being tested in Canada. Programs are given a rating of from 0 to 5 in each of three categories: violence, sex and profanity. By setting their V-chip dial to numbers of their choice, parents can block out all shows with higher than that level of offensive material.

Some V-chip critics see the centralized rating concept as too rigid. They support instead one of several devices currently in development that enable parents to make their own choices of which shows to block out. FCC chairman Reed Hundt, a V-chip booster, contends that it will be only "the first of a slew of products. I predict remote-control devices with selection programs. There will be a variety of ways to receive TV."

Broadcasters, for their part, object that a ratings system mandated by the government threatens their free-speech rights. "A centralized rating system that is subject to review and approval by the government is totally inconsistent with the traditions of this country," says NBC general counsel Richard Cotton. "This legislation turns the FCC into Big Brother." Former CBS Broadcast Group president Howard Stringer argues, "The V chip is the thin end of a wedge. If you start putting chips in the television set to exclude things, it becomes an all-purpose hidden censor."

The rhetoric may invoke the First Amendment, but the networks' more pressing concern is the bottom line. The V chip will, inevitably, reduce the potential audience for shows marked with the scarlet letter. That means advertising revenue will go down. What's more, a violence label may scare off many advertisers and thus cause programmers to steer clear of provocative shows. "The thing nobody is taking into account," says *Law & Order* creator Dick Wolf, "is that there's going to be a V-chip warning on *Homicide, NYPD Blue, Law & Order, ER, Chicago Hope*— any of the adult dramas that deal with real-life substantive issues. Once that happens, you are going to have a television landscape that's far, far different from what you have today."

There is another possible scenario. If the networks and advertisers learn to live with a V rating, producers might find themselves liberated—able to produce even more adult fare, secure in the knowl-

So What's On in Tokyo?

IS THE REST OF THE WORLD AS CONCERNED about sex and violence on TV as America? Channel surf elsewhere and U.S. television begins to seem as though it were run by so many Roman Catholic schoolgirls. In Japan—where TV programming is virtually unregulated and concerns about media amorality are scant—prime-time TV is a mixed menu of soft-core porn, bloodletting drama and violent animation. Log some viewing time in Brazil, and you will find erotic soaps and specials featuring naked women dancing the samba in heels and sparkling body paint. This kind of spectacle could just as easily turn up on European TV, where nudity, sex and tastelessness are also unavoidable. Consider *The Word*, a lewd late-night variety show that aired on Britain's Channel 4 for five years and once depicted a viewer eating other peoples' scabs. (Don't tell Ricki Lake.)

So where do foreign broadcasters draw the line? In Britain, where programming is regulated by the TV industry and the government, shows considered unfriendly to families are prohibited from airing before 10 p.m. Similar rules apply throughout Europe. Definitions of unsuitable fare are so vague, however, that networks often run what turns out to be objectionable programming and pay the penalties later. The Independent Television Commission, one of various monitoring groups in Britain, recently fined MTV Europe $90,000, in part for running explicit sex-themed talk shows in the morning and early evening. In France a government-operated FCC equivalent known as the CSA fined two French networks a total of $2 million in 1989 for airing violent movies during prime-time hours.

Efforts to curtail indecency have been far more efficient in Germany. Starting in 1993 the country's leading TV manufacturer voluntarily included V chips in new sets. The chip can automatically block out movies that the German film-industry board has deemed unacceptable for young audiences. The chip also filters out all TV shows—including soft-core porn—that individual stations decide are potentially inappropriate. The FSF, a TV industry watchdog group, frequently guides networks in scheduling. In December 1994 it convinced the RTL network to run the *Mighty Morphin Power Rangers* on a weekly rather than daily basis, following public outcries that the show preached combativeness.

In Canada, where concerns about violence on TV have been mounting as clamorously as they have in the U.S., broadcasters air expurgated versions of the *Power Rangers*. Canada is also experimenting with V-chip technology in several cities. This week a third round of tests will begin in about 400 homes where encoded programming will allow parents to selectively block out material rated on a scale of 0 to 5 for offensiveness. So far the V chip has sparked few objections in Canada. By mid-March the government is expected to decide whether or not to enact it as law. —*By Ginia Bellafante, with bureau reports*

edge that children will be shielded from it. Which could, of course, lead either to more sophisticated adult fare or sleazier entertainment. Says Wolf: "If all these shows have warnings on them, you could have a situation where producers are saying to standards people at the networks, 'I've got a warning. I can say whatever I want. I can kill as many people as I want.'"

THEY'RE ALREADY KILLING A LOT, if the National Television Violence Study is to be believed. Billed as the "most thorough scientific survey of violence on television ever undertaken," the study not only found a surprisingly high percentage of violent shows; it also made some damning observations about the way violence is presented. According to the survey, 47% of the violent acts shown resulted in no observable harm to the victim; only 16% of violent shows contained a message about the long-term negative repercussions of violence; and in a whopping 73% of all violent scenes, the perpetrator went unpunished. These figures, however, were based on some overly strict guidelines: perpetrators of violence, for example, must be punished in *the same scene* as the violent act. By that measure, most of Shakespeare's tragedies would be frowned on; Macbeth, after all, doesn't get his comeuppance until the end of the play.

The study found significant variations in the amount of violence across the dial. On network stations, 44% of the shows contained at least some violence, vs. 59% on basic cable and 85% on premium channels like HBO and Showtime. Yet it was the broadcast networks that squawked the loudest. "Someone would have to have a lobotomy to believe that 44% of the programs on network television are violent," exclaims Don Ohlmeyer, NBC West Coast president. (Actually, the study referred to network stations, meaning that syndicated shows like *Hard Copy* were also included.) "Since I've been here, I can't think of a program we've had that's glorified violence, that hasn't shown the pain of violence and attempted to show there are other ways to resolve conflicts."

The researchers' definition of violence did, at least, avoid some of the absurdities of previous studies, in which every comic pratfall was counted. Violent acts were defined as those physical acts intended to cause harm to another; also included were verbal threats of physical harm as well as scenes showing the aftermath of violence. Thus, finding a body in a pool of blood on *NYPD Blue* counts as a violent act; Kramer bumping into a door on *Seinfeld* does not. A cartoon character whacking another with a mallet counts; but the accidental buffoonery of *America's Funniest Home Videos* doesn't.

Yet just one of these acts was enough to classify a program as violent. In addition, the survey covered a number of cable channels—among them USA, AMC, TNT, HBO and Showtime—whose schedules are filled with network reruns (including many action shows like *Starsky and Hutch* and *Kung Fu)* or theatrical films. This served to boost the overall totals of violent shows while masking the fact that violence in the most watched time periods—network prime time—has declined.

"We didn't want to get into a show-by-show debate," says Ed Donnerstein, communications and psychology professor at the University of California at Santa Barbara, where most of the monitoring was done. "We didn't want to point fingers." George Gerbner, former dean of the University of Pennsylvania's Annenberg School for Communication and a longtime chronicler of TV violence, agrees with the study's big-picture approach. "Anytime you give a name of a program, it lends itself to endless quibbling," he says. "The question is not what any one program does or doesn't do. The question is, What is it that large communities absorb over long periods of time?"

Whatever its defects, the study could have a major impact as development of the V chip begins. "This is the foundation of any rating system that will be developed," says Representative Edward Markey of Massachusetts, the V chip's original champion in Congress. The irony is that some of the most objectionable shows, in the survey's view, are cartoons and other children's shows: they are the ones that portray violence "unrealistically," without consequences or punishment. "When you show a young kid somebody being run over and they pop back up without harm, that's a problem," says Donnerstein. Maybe so, but a kid who grows up without Batman or Bugs Bunny misses something else: a chance to engage in playful fantasy. And the V chip can't make up for that.

—Reported by Hannah Bloch/Washington, Georgia Harbison and William Tynan/New York and Jeffrey Ressner/Los Angeles

Teenage Sexuality

Sexual Attitudes and Behavior (Articles 41–47)
Sex Education (Articles 48–51)

Based on the music they listen to, the television shows they watch, or the movies they attend, it is clear that sex is frequently on the minds of adolescents. In fact, one statistic indicates that teenage boys think of sex on the average of once every five minutes! Unfortunately for adolescents today, the sexual issues that concern them run the gamut from "When should I start dating?" to "Will I get AIDS?" How has society, whether in the form of the government, the schools, or the family, dealt with these concerns? The answer seems to be, not very consistently and, frequently, not very well.

The articles in this unit have been organized into two subsections. The first, *Sexual Attitudes and Behavior*, addresses the concerns adolescents have about a variety of areas related to sexuality, and how adolescents behave in these areas. Although prepubescent children are interested in sex and may engage in some sexual exploration of their own or other people's bodies, interest in dating and in interacting in a sexual manner with others seems to increase rapidly with the onset of puberty. The vast majority of adolescents indicate that they have a boyfriend or girlfriend. By age 13 about 20 percent of boys indicate that they have touched a girl's breasts; a similar proportion of girls concur. Between ages 16 and 17, half of American girls are no longer virgins. By the end of the teen years, the majority of adolescents have engaged in coitus. Ten percent of teenagers in the United States become pregnant each year—twice the rate of other industrialized nations. Twenty-five percent of new cases of HIV are in adolescents under age 18.

Adolescents are clearly engaging in sexual behaviors. This is not only normal, but it is an important part of development. Understanding oneself as a sexual being is a significant component of identity formation. It seems, therefore, that society would want to understand how adolescents view their sexuality. The reality is that research on what adolescents want more information about, and how much adolescents already know, is surprisingly limited. Part of the reason for this lack of information is the taboos our society has concerning talking about sex. For example, when was the last time a study asking adolescents how often they masturbated was described in a magazine? Probably not recently. This is a sensitive topic, and parents are reluctant to allow their adolescents to talk about it even though the majority of people have masturbated. How much less is known, then, about the concerns of adolescents who are homosexual—a far more controversial area? How much

is really known regarding how girls feel about sexual harassment as opposed to flirting?

Research on sexuality is limited not only by taboos but also by society's clinging to myths involving romantic relationships. Ours is a society that worries about adolescent sexuality, yet it does not train adolescents in social skills for dating or flirting. Adolescents are presented with the myth that they should find love with no problems, yet in reality romance and relationships must be worked on. Adolescents are expected to date, but they are not taught how to act on a date, how to communicate with a partner, or how to avoid or remove themselves from uncomfortable situations while on a date. When adults discuss sex with adolescents they generally focus on the dangers surrounding sexual behavior. They do little to prepare adolescents for the emotional aspects of dating relationships. Knowledge about many significant areas of adolescent sexuality is severely limited. The articles selected for this first section demonstrate the wide variety of issues faced by adolescents, including dating, homosexuality, emotional involvement, virginity, sexual harassment, and some of the ways in which adolescents respond to these concerns.

The second subsection, *Sex Education,* includes articles discussing how parents, teachers, and society inform adolescents about sex and how their approaches to sex education may be improved. Research on where adolescents learn about sex has been performed for about 60 years. The results of this research are quite consistent—adolescents' primary sources of information on sex are other adolescents. Schools and mothers also seem to contribute some information. Adolescents are most likely to learn about sexually transmitted diseases, including HIV, from teachers. Many, though by no means all, girls learn about menstruation and conception from their mothers. Fathers are less frequently cited by adolescents as a source of information on sex.

Why aren't parents and schools assuming more responsibility for educating children about sex? Researchers have speculated that parents do not know what to discuss with their children or how to effectively present information. Parents may also be inhibited by their own embarrassment with the topic. This does not mean parents wish their children to be completely ignorant about sex. Some surveys indicate that 85 percent of American families want schools to include sex education. Part of the reason for this is because parents wish their children to be knowledgeable about transmission of HIV. However, when sex education is left up to the schools, other problems are incurred. For example, what topics should be covered in school? In how much detail should various topics be covered? It may be acceptable to teach adolescents about conception or pregnancy, but if the adolescents have children, should the school teach child care? How much information on transmission of HIV and prevention of transmission should be included? The first article in this subsection approaches the topic of sex education in general. In the second article the effect school-based programs can have on teen parenting is presented. The last two articles focus on AIDS.

Looking Ahead: Challenge Questions

What kinds of factors should parents consider when deciding whether their children should be allowed to date?

How may acknowledgement of one's sexuality differ for homosexual as compared to heterosexual adolescents? What kinds of problems may homosexual adolescents face that may not even occur to heterosexuals?

How may adults prepare adolescents for the emotional aspects of intimate relationships?

What combination of social and educational factors seems to encourage sexual abstinence in adolescents?

What are possible emotional consequences of premature sexual involvement?

What is the difference between sexual harassment and flirting? What are problems with overidentifying sexual harassment?

When may teen pregnancy actually benefit the mother and child?

How can schools effectively educate adolescents about sex?

What are the benefits of having programs for teen mothers in schools? What are the characteristics of the programs?

How can schools and society effectively increase the safer sex behaviors of adolescents?

Too Young *To* Date?

Definitely—and you can help your preteen resist peer pressure.

**Debra
Morgenstern
Katz**

Ben began dating last year, when he was 11. According to his mother, Annie, it started when he and his friends suddenly announced that they were "going out" with girls. Ben's first relationship, Annie recalls, lasted all of one day. The second one was a couple of months long, and the third hung on until the end of the school year. These relationships consisted primarily of phone conversations; dating, Annie says, was strictly in name only.

However, now that he's 12, Ben goes on group outings with his current girlfriend and other couples. Although Annie says she doesn't allow the two of them to spend time together alone, she adds, "I constantly think this is happening too soon, but I'm not sure how to put the brakes on."

Putting the brakes on preteen dating is something virtually every expert endorses. "For kids this age, dating is developmentally inappropriate," says Karen Zager, Ph.D., a psychologist in private practice in New York City who specializes in adolescents. "Ten-, 11-, and 12-year-olds are, by and large, not ready. It's like trying to drive an 18-wheel truck before you even know how to drive a car. There's too

much information—and too many complicated feelings—for kids that age to integrate."

Furthermore, the same-sex friendships that dominate preteens' lives allow them to develop skills such as sharing emotions and learning give-and-take—skills that come into play in later romantic relationships—without social or sexual pressure. According to David Elkind, Ph.D., professor of child study at Tufts University, in Medford, Massachusetts, and the author of The Hurried Child (Addison-Wesley), "If children this age spend too much time in opposite-sex relationships, they don't get to hone these skills."

There's no denying that preteens feel pushed to begin their romantic lives at an ever earlier age. It used to be that 13-year-olds were the ones who were forced to straddle the boundary between childhood and adolescence. Zager says, "Now it's an issue with clients I'm seeing who are 10, 11, and 12."

Why? "Kids this age are exposed to much more 'mature' material on TV and in the movies than kids were a generation ago," explains Zager. Another reason is the classic one, peer influence. However, preteens often

find that there's another subtle source of pressure: parents themselves. In many neighborhoods all over the country, parents organize dances for elementary-school-age children—even when the children view these events with nervousness and discomfort. In my own neighborhood, several mothers have described their preteens' dating rituals as "cute."

Most parents, thankfully, don't look at preteen romance that way. They are genuinely perplexed about how they should handle this early rush into the dating game. As Annie says, "What do you say when all your son's friends are going out with girls? 'No, you can't go'?" If you're concerned, try these suggestions.

Listen to your child—and yourself. Children this age are still more inclined to listen to their parents' advice than to their friends'. When your child comes to you with questions about her personal life, it means that she wants and values your honest answer. You'll help a lot if you place a higher priority on hearing your child out than on judging her.

If your daughter came home from sleep-away camp and told you that she didn't know what to do when a boy she met there gave her a

French kiss, some parents' instinct would be to say, "French kissing? There's no way you're going to see that boy again!" However, that response is practically guaranteed to close the lines of communication, notes Leah Blumberg Lapidus, Ph.D., professor of psychology at Columbia University and clinical psychologist in private practice. "It shuts down trust. In effect, the parent is saying that the child can't be in charge of her own social life," she explains.

A better response, Lapidus says, is something like, "It sounds like this made you kind of nervous." If your child indicates that it did, you might suggest that the next time she's in a romantic situation that makes her uncomfortable, she might say, "I don't want to do this. Let's go get something to eat." By talking to your daughter in this way, you let her know that she can trust her own feelings, that she doesn't have to go along with peers if their activities make her uncomfortable—and that you are an ally in whom she can confide freely.

Define "dating" clearly. If your preteen tells you he wants to date, your response should depend on

 From *Parents*, October 1995, pp. 92-93. © 1995 by Debra Morgenstern Katz. Reprinted by permission.

whether or not you feel comfortable with what that means in his social group. For some, it is a serious commitment — spending Friday nights, weekend afternoons, and some days after school together. Also part of the definition is the way in which "dating" children spend their time. Do they go to movies, indoor arcades, or ice cream parlors with other couples? Are they alone at each other's houses?

Sometimes their outings resemble traditional dates, with boys paying for girls, and a goodnight kiss when they part. However, in other instances, dating is far more innocent and informal. Kids who call each other boyfriend and girlfriend may not spend much time together, even on the phone.

If your child wants to take dating further than you'd like, don't be afraid to set limits in a firm but loving way. According to Elkind, if your son says he wants to be alone with his girlfriend, "You can say, 'You're not ready for this yet. Some day you will be, but not yet. You're not supposed to drive. You're not supposed to drink alcohol. There are a lot of things you can't do until you're older.'"

If he makes the request with his girlfriend present, calmly say you'd like to speak with him alone for a minute; preteens can easily feel humiliated by parents when peers are around.

Don't hesitate to offer compromises and alternatives. If you have no problem with your child occasionally having phone conversations with a boyfriend, but object to their going to a movie together, suggest another activity that's acceptable. Preteens often enjoy supervised outings such as trips to sports events or amusement parks, where they can be active. Just make sure the activity is suited to their age; even something as supposedly corny as taking a group of preteens bowling is more appropriate than getting them into an R-rated movie—and more fun for the kids, who generally feel less pressure to act grown-up when they're among adults than they do in a group of their peers.

If your child is among a mixed-gender group going to a movie, it's not a bad idea to have a parent or two in the theater during the movie; they can sit away from the kids, who will feel independent, but still have the reassuring presence of a grown-up nearby.

Debra Morgenstern Katz is a freelance writer based in North Woodmere, New York.

A CLACK
OF TINY SPARKS

Remembrances of a gay boyhood

Bernard Cooper

Bernard Cooper is the author of Maps to Anywhere, *a collection of essays published by the University of Georgia Press. His essay "Nick's Barber Shop" appeared in the June 1990 issue of* Harper's Magazine. *He lives in Los Angeles.*

Theresa Sanchez sat behind me in ninth-grade algebra. When Mr. Hubbley faced the blackboard, I'd turn around to see what she was reading; each week a new book was wedged inside her copy of *Today's Equations*. The deception worked; from Mr. Hubbley's point of view, Theresa was engrossed in the value of X, but I knew otherwise. One week she perused *The Wisdom of the Orient*, and I could tell from Theresa's contemplative expression that the book contained exotic thoughts, guidelines handed down from high. Another week it was a paperback novel whose title, *Let Me Live My Life*, appeared in bold print atop every page, and whose cover, a gauzy photograph of a woman biting a strand of pearls, head thrown back in an attitude of ecstasy, confirmed my suspicion that Theresa Sanchez was mature beyond her years. She was the tallest girl in school. Her bouffant hairdo, streaked with blond, was higher than the flaccid bouffants of other girls. Her smooth skin, plucked eyebrows, and painted fingernails suggested hours of pampering, a worldly and sensual vanity that placed her within the domain of adults. Smiling dimly, steeped in daydreams, Theresa moved through the crowded halls with a languid, self-satisfied indifference to those around her. "You are merely children," her posture seemed to say. "I can't be bothered." The week Theresa hid *101 Ways to Cook Hamburger* behind her algebra book, I could stand it no longer and, after the bell rang, ventured a question.

"Because I'm having a dinner party," said Theresa. "Just a couple of intimate friends."

No fourteen-year-old I knew had ever given a dinner party, let alone used the word "intimate" in conversation. "Don't you have a mother?" I asked.

Theresa sighed a weary sigh, suffered my strange inquiry. "Don't be so naive," she said. "Everyone has a mother." She waved her hand to indicate the brick school buildings outside the window. "A higher education should have taught you that." Theresa draped an angora sweater over her shoulders, scooped her books from the graffiti-covered desk, and just as she was about to walk away, she turned and asked me, "Are you a fag?"

There wasn't the slightest hint of rancor or condescension in her voice. The tone was direct, casual. Still I was stunned, giving a sidelong glance to make sure no one had heard. "No," I said. Blurted really, with too much defensiveness, too much transparent fear in my response. Octaves lower than usual, I tried a "Why?"

Theresa shrugged. "Oh, I don't know. I have lots of friends who are fags. You remind me of them." Seeing me bristle, Theresa added, "It was just a guess." I watched her erect, angora back as she sauntered out the classroom door.

She had made an incisive and timely guess. Only days before, I'd invited Grady Rogers to my house after school to go swimming. The instant Grady shot from the pool, shaking water from his orange hair, freckled shoulders shining, my attraction to members of my own sex became a matter I could no longer suppress or rationalize. Sturdy and boisterous and gap-toothed, Grady was an inveterate backslapper, a formidable arm wrestler, a wizard at basketball. Grady was a boy at home in his body.

My body was a marvel I hadn't gotten used to; my arms and legs would sometimes act of their own accord, knocking over a glass at dinner or flinching at an oncoming pitch. I was never singled out as a sissy, but I could have been just as easily as Bobby Keagan, a gentle, intelligent, and introverted boy reviled by my classmates. And although I had always been aware of a tacit rapport with Bobby, a suspicion that I might find with him a rich friendship, I stayed away. Instead, I emulated Grady in the belief that being seen with him, being like him, would somehow vanquish my self-doubt, would make me normal by association.

Apart from his athletic prowess, Grady had been gifted with all the trappings of what I imagined to be a charmed life: a fastidious, aproned mother who radiated calm, maternal concern; a ruddy, stoic father with a knack for home repairs. Even the Rogerses' small suburban house in Hollywood, with its spindly Colonial furniture and chintz curtains, was a testament to normalcy.

Grady and his family bore little resemblance to my clan of Eastern European Jews, a dark and vociferous people who ate with abandon—matzo and halvah and gefilte fish; foods the goyim couldn't pronounce—who cajoled one another during endless games of canasta, making the simplest remark about the weather into a lengthy philosophical discourse on the sun and the seasons and the passage of time. My mother was a chain-smoker, a dervish in a frowsy housedress. She showed her love in the most peculiar and obsessive ways, like spending hours extracting every seed from a watermelon before she served it in perfectly bite-sized, geometric pieces. Preoccupied and perpetually frantic, my mother succumbed to bouts of absentmindedness so profound she'd forget what she was saying mid-sentence, smile and blush and walk away. A divorce attorney, my father wore roomy, iridescent suits, and the intricacies, the deceits inherent in his profession, had the effect of making him forever tense and vigilant. He was "all wound up," as my mother put it. But when he relaxed, his laughter was explosive, his disposition prankish: "Walk this way," a waitress would say, leading us to our table, and my father would mimic the way she walked, arms akimbo, hips liquid, while my mother and I were wracked with laughter. Buoyant or brooding, my parents' moods were unpredictable, and in a household fraught with extravagant emotion it was odd and awful to keep my longing secret.

One day I made the mistake of asking my mother what a "fag" was. I knew exactly what Theresa had meant but hoped against hope it was not what I thought; maybe "fag" was some French word, a harmless term like "naive." My mother turned from the stove, flew at me, and grabbed me by the shoulders. "Did someone call you that?" she cried.

"Not me," I said. "Bobby Keagan."

"Oh," she said, loosening her grip. She was visibly relieved. And didn't answer. The answer was unthinkable.

For weeks after, I shook with the reverberations from that afternoon in the kitchen with my mother, pained by the memory of her shocked expression and, most of all, her silence. My longing was wrong in the eyes of my mother, whose hazel eyes were the eyes of the world, and if that longing continued unchecked, the unwieldy shape of my fate would be cast, and I'd be subjected to a lifetime of scorn.

During the remainder of the semester, I became the scientist of my own desire, plotting ways to change my yearning for boys into a yearning for girls. I had enough evidence to believe that any habit, regardless of how compulsive, how deeply ingrained, could be broken once and for all: The plastic cigarette my mother purchased at the Thrifty pharmacy—one end was red to approximate an ember, the other tan like a filtered tip—was designed to wean her from the real thing. To change a behavior required self-analysis, cold resolve, and the substitution of one thing for another: plastic, say, for tobacco. Could I also find a substitute for Grady? What I needed to do, I figured, was kiss a girl and learn to like it.

This conclusion was affirmed one Sunday morning when my father, seeing me wrinkle my nose at the pink slabs of lox he layered on a bagel, tried to convince me of its salty appeal. "You should try some," he said. "You don't know what you're missing."

"It's loaded with protein," added my mother, slapping a platter of sliced onions onto the dinette table. She hovered above us, cinching her housedress, eyes wet from onion fumes, the mock cigarette dangling from her lips.

My father sat there chomping with gusto, emitting a couple of hearty grunts to dramatize his satisfaction. And still I was not convinced. After a loud and labored swallow, he told me I may not be fond of lox today, but sooner or later I'd learn to like it. One's tastes, he assured me, are destined to change.

"Live," shouted my mother over the rumble of the Mixmaster. "Expand your horizons. Try new things."

And the room grew fragrant with the batter of a spice cake.

The opportunity to put their advice into practice, and try out my plan to adapt to girls, came the following week when Debbie Coburn, a member of Mr. Hubbley's algebra class, invited me to a party. She cornered me in the hall, furtive as a spy, telling me her parents would be gone for the evening and slipping into my palm a wrinkled sheet of notebook paper. On it were her address and telephone number, the lavender ink in a tidy cursive. "Wear cologne," she advised, wary eyes darting back and forth. "It's a make-out party. Anything can happen."

The Santa Ana wind blew relentlessly the night of Debbie's party, careening down the slopes of the Hollywood hills, shaking the road signs and stoplights in its path. As I walked down Beachwood Avenue, trees thrashed, surrendered their leaves, and carob pods bombarded the pavement. The sky was a deep but luminous blue, the air hot, abrasive, electric. I had to squint in order to check the number of the Coburns' apartment, a three-story building with glitter embedded in its stucco walls. Above the honeycombed balconies was a sign that read BEACHWOOD TERRACE in lavender script resembling Debbie's.

From down the hall, I could hear the plaintive strains of Little Anthony's "I Think I'm Going Out of My Head." Debbie answered the door bedecked in an Empire dress, the bodice blue and orange polka dots, the rest a sheath of black and white stripes. "Op art," proclaimed Debbie. She turned in a circle, then proudly announced that she'd rolled her hair in orange juice cans. She patted the huge unmoving curls and dragged me inside. Reflections from the swimming pool in the courtyard, its surface ruffled by wind, shuddered over the ceiling and walls. A dozen of my classmates were seated on the sofa or huddled together in corners, their whispers full of excited imminence, their bodies barely discernible in the dim light. Drapes flanking the sliding glass doors bowed out with every gust of wind, and it seemed that the room might lurch from its foundations and sail with its cargo of silhouettes into the hot October night.

Grady was the last to arrive. He tossed a six-pack of beer into Debbie's arms, barreled toward me, and slapped my back. His hair was slicked back with Vitalis, lacquered furrows left by the comb. The wind hadn't shifted a single hair. "Ya ready?" he asked, flashing the gap between his front teeth and leering into the darkened room. "You bet," I lied.

Once the beers had been passed around, Debbie provoked everyone's attention by flicking on the overhead light. "Okay," she called. "Find a partner." This was the blunt command of a hostess determined to have her guests aroused in an orderly fashion. Everyone blinked, shuffled about, and grabbed a member of the opposite sex. Sheila Garabedian landed beside me—entirely at random, though I wanted to believe she was driven by passion—her timid smile giving way to plain fear as the light went out. Nothing for a moment but the heave of the wind and the distant banter of dogs. I caught a whiff of Sheila's perfume, tangy and sweet as Hawaiian Punch. I probed her face with my own, grazing the small scallop of an ear, a velvety temple, and though Sheila's trembling made me want to stop, I persisted with my mission until I found her lips, tightly sealed as a private letter. I held my mouth over hers and gathered her shoulders closer, resigned to the possibility that, no matter how long we stood there, Sheila would be too scared to kiss me back. Still, she exhaled through her nose, and I listened to the squeak of every breath as though it were a sigh of inordinate pleasure. Diving within myself, I monitored my heartbeat and respiration, trying to will stimulation into being, and all the while an image intruded, an image of Grady erupting from our pool, rivulets of water sliding down his chest. "Change," shouted Debbie, switching on the light. Sheila thanked me, pulled away, and continued her routine of gracious terror with every boy throughout the evening. It didn't matter whom I held—Margaret Sims, Betty Vernon, Elizabeth Lee—my experiment was a failure; I continued to picture Grady's wet chest, and Debbie would bellow "change" with such fervor, it could have been my own voice, my own incessant reprimand.

Our hostess commandeered the light switch for nearly half an hour. Whenever the light came on, I watched Grady pivot his head toward the newest prospect, his eyebrows arched in expectation, his neck blooming with hickeys, his hair, at last, in disarray. All that shuffling across the carpet charged everyone's arms and lips with static, and eventually, between low moans and soft osculations, I could hear the clack of tiny sparks and see them flare here and there in the dark like meager, short-lived stars.

I saw Theresa, sultry and aloof as ever, read three more books—*North American Reptiles, Bonjour Tristesse,* and *MGM: A Pictorial History*—before she vanished early in December. Rumors of her fate abounded. Debbie Coburn swore that Theresa had been "knocked up" by an older man, a traffic cop, she thought, or a grocer. Nearly quivering with relish, Debbie told me and Grady about the home for unwed mothers in the San Fernando Valley, a compound teeming with pregnant girls who had nothing to do but touch their stomachs and contemplate their mistake. Even Bobby Keagan, who took Theresa's place behind me in algebra, had a theory regarding her disappearance colored by his own wish for escape; he imagined that Theresa, disillusioned with society, booked passage to a tropical island, there to live out the rest of her days without restrictions or ridicule. "No wonder she flunked out of school," I overheard Mr. Hubbley tell a fellow teacher one afternoon. "Her head was always in a book."

Along with Theresa went my secret, or at least the dread that she might divulge it, and I felt, for a while, exempt from suspicion. I was, however, to run across Theresa one last time. It happened during a period of torrential rain that, according to reports on the six o'clock news, washed houses from the hillsides and flooded the downtown streets. The halls of Joseph Le Conte Junior High were festooned with Christmas decorations: crepe-paper garlands, wreaths studded with plastic berries, and one requisite Star of David twirling above the attendance desk. In Arts and Crafts, our teacher, Gerald (he was the only teacher who allowed us—*re-quired* us—to call him by his first name), handed out blocks of balsa wood and instructed us to carve them into bugs. We would paint eyes and antennae with tempera and hang them on a Christmas tree he'd made the previous night. "Voilà," he crooned, unveiling his creation from a burlap sack. Before us sat a tortured scrub, a wardrobe-worth of wire hangers that were bent like branches and soldered together. Gerald credited his inspiration to a Charles Addams cartoon he'd seen in which Morticia, grimly preparing for the holidays, hangs vampire bats on a withered pine. "All that red and green," said Gerald. "So predictable. So *boring.*"

As I chiseled a beetle and listened to rain pummel the earth, Gerald handed me an envelope and asked me to take it to Mr. Kendrick, the drama teacher. I would have thought nothing of his request if I hadn't seen Theresa on my way down the hall. She was cleaning out her locker, blithely dropping the sum of its contents—pens and textbooks and mimeographs—into a trash can. "Have a nice life," she sang as I passed. I mustered the courage to ask her what had happened. We stood alone in the silent hall, the reflections of wreaths and garlands submerged in brown linoleum.

"I transferred to another school. They don't have grades or bells, and you get to study whatever you want." Theresa was quick to sense my incredulity. "Honest," she said. "The school is progressive." She gazed into a glass cabinet that held the trophies of track meets and intramural spelling bees. "God," she sighed, "this place is so . . . barbaric." I was still trying to decide whether or not to believe her story when she asked me where I was headed. "Dear," she said, her exclamation pooling in the silence, "that's no ordinary note, if you catch my drift." The envelope was blank and white; I looked up at Theresa, baffled. "Don't be so naive," she muttered, tossing an empty bottle of nail polish into the trash can. It struck bottom with a resolute thud. "Well," she said, closing her locker and breathing deeply, "bon voyage." Theresa swept through the double doors and in seconds her figure was obscured by rain.

As I walked toward Mr. Kendrick's room, I could feel Theresa's insinuation burrow in. I stood for a moment and watched Mr. Kendrick through the pane in the door. He paced intently in front of the class, handsome in his shirt and tie, reading from a thick book. Chalked on the blackboard behind him was THE ODYSSEY BY HOMER. I have no recollection of how Mr. Kendrick reacted to the note, whether he accepted it with pleasure or embarrassment, slipped it into his desk drawer or the pocket of his shirt. I have scavenged that day in retrospect, trying to see Mr. Kendrick's expression, wondering if he acknowledged me in any way as his liaison. All I recall is the sight of his mime through a pane of glass, a lone man mouthing an epic, his gestures ardent in empty air.

Had I delivered a declaration of love? I was haunted by the need to know. In fantasy, a kettle shot steam, the glue released its grip, and I read the letter with impunity. But how would such a letter begin? Did the common endearments apply? This was a message between two men, a message for which I had no precedent, and when I tried to envision the contents, apart from a hasty, impassioned scrawl, my imagination faltered.

Once or twice I witnessed Gerald and Mr. Kendrick walk together into the faculty lounge or say hello at the water fountain, but there was nothing especially clandestine or flirtatious in their manner. Besides, no matter how acute my scrutiny, I wasn't sure, short of a kiss, exactly what to look for—what semaphore of gesture, what encoded word. I suspected there were signs, covert signs that would give them away, just as I'd unwittingly given myself away to Theresa.

In the school library, a *Webster's* unabridged dictionary lay on a wooden podium, and I padded toward it with apprehension; along with clues to the bond between my teachers, I risked discovering information that might incriminate me as well. I had decided to consult the dictionary during lunch period, when most of the students would be on the playground. I clutched my notebook, moving in such a way as to appear both studious and nonchalant, actually believing that, unless I took precautions, someone would see me and guess what I was up to. The closer I came to the podium, the more obvious, I thought, was my endeavor; I felt like the model of The Visible Man in our science class, my heart's undulations, my overwrought nerves legible through transparent skin. A couple of kids riffled through the card catalogue. The librarian, a skinny woman whose perpetual whisper and rubber-soled shoes caused her to drift through the room like a phantom, didn't seem to register my presence. Though I'd looked up dozens of words before, the pages felt strange beneath my fingers. *Homer* was the first word I saw. *Hominid. Homogenize.* I feigned interest and skirted other words before I found the word I was after. Under the heading HO·MO·SEX·U·AL was the terse definition: *adj. Pertaining to, characteristic of, or exhibiting homosexuality. –n. A homosexual person.* I read the definition again and again, hoping the words would yield more than they could. I shut the dictionary, swallowed hard, and, none the wiser, hurried away.

As for Gerald and Mr. Kendrick, I never discovered evidence to prove or dispute Theresa's claim. By the following summer, however, I had overheard from my peers a confounding amount about homosexuals: They wore green on Thursday, couldn't whistle, hypnotized boys with a piercing glance. To this lore, Grady added a surefire test to ferret them out.

"A test?" I said.

"You ask a guy to look at his fingernails, and if he looks at them like this"—Grady closed his fingers into a fist and examined his nails with manly detachment—"then he's okay. But if he does this"—he held out his hands at arm's length, splayed his fingers, and coyly cocked his head—"you'd better watch out." Once he'd completed his demonstration, Grady peeled off his shirt and plunged into our pool. I dove in after. It was early June, the sky immense, glassy, placid. My father was cooking spareribs on the barbecue, an artist with a basting brush. His apron bore the caricature of a frazzled French chef. Mother curled on a chaise longue, plumes of smoke wafting from her nostrils. In a stupor of contentment she took another drag, closed her eyes, and arched her face toward the sun.

Grady dog-paddled through the deep end, spouting a fountain of chlorinated water. Despite shame and confusion, my longing for him hadn't diminished; it continued to thrive without air and light, like a luminous fish in the dregs of the sea. In the name of play, I swam up behind him, encircled his shoulders, astonished by his taut flesh. The two of us flailed, pretended to drown. Beneath the heavy press of water, Grady's orange hair wavered, a flame that couldn't be doused.

I've lived with a man for seven years. Some nights, when I'm half-asleep and the room is suffused with blue light, I reach out to touch the expanse of his back, and it seems as if my fingers sink into his skin, and I feel the pleasure a diver feels the instant he enters a body of water.

I have few regrets. But one is that I hadn't said to Theresa, "Of course I'm a fag." Maybe I'd have met her friends. Or become friends with her. Imagine the meals we might have concocted: hamburger Stroganoff, Swedish meatballs in a sweet translucent sauce, steaming slabs of Salisbury steak.

Teen Sex Wars

Learning to Love

JESSE HELMS SAYS TEENS MUST CHOOSE BETWEEN "SEXUAL DECADENCE" AND "RESTRAINT." BUT, JUST LIKE ADULTS, OUR KIDS NEED A HUMAN CONNECTION.

Nell Bernstein

Nell Bernstein is the editor of YO! (Youth Outlook), a Bay Area newspaper produced by Pacific News Service. She writes frequently on youth issues.

WHEN THE UNIVERSITY OF CHICAGO RELEASED A COMPREHENSIVE sex survey last fall detailing what Americans are doing in private, one bedroom door remained firmly shut—the one at the end of the hall with the Pearl Jam poster and the "Keep Out" sign.

It's public knowledge that federal funding for the sex survey (which looked at Americans age 18 to 59) had been scratched in 1991 by the Bush administration, and that private foundations ended up footing the bill. What's gone unreported, however, is that a comprehensive study of adolescent sexual behavior was also in the works, and it was not revived after the federal funding cut.

The adolescent survey was even more politically unpalatable than its adult counterpart. Dr. Richard Udry, a social scientist at the University of North Carolina, is one of the researchers who planned the five-year, 24,000-teen survey. He recalls that Louis Sullivan, then secretary of Health and Human Services, "said the study might give the wrong message to adolescents, when the official policy of the administration was to encourage abstinence." The researchers talked to a few foundations but concluded that they would not be able to raise enough money to do the study properly.

The final nail in the American Teenage Study's coffin came when the Senate approved a Jesse Helms-sponsored bill and subsequent amendment: the first transferred the original funding for both the adult and adolescent surveys to the abstinence-only Adolescent Family Life program, and the second prohibited the government from ever funding either study in the future. Helms argued that the Senate faced "a clear choice—between support for sexual restraint among our young people, or, on the other hand, support for homosexuality and sexual decadence."

"I don't trust anybody. No one. I was just a carefree kind of guy who loved everybody, but in high school that doesn't go. I found that there's a lot more bigotry against gays among blacks. And it angers me, because black people, of all people, should know what it feels like to be oppressed. I don't see any hope for society. The most important things, like accepting ourselves as individuals, and not judging or being judged, I don't see."

RAPHAEL, 19

"I didn't feel any pressure to have sex. I always said to myself that when I was ready, I'd have sex. I didn't set an age on it. It just so happened that when I was 16, I felt ready. It could've been when I was 27."

MICHELLE, 18

The death of the American Teenage Study is right in line with the country's unofficial policy on teen sex, which might be described as "Don't Ask, Tell." As panic over teen pregnancy and AIDS escalates, adults have defined their role as dispensing warnings and imperatives, rather than examining the complexities of young people's lives.

Teen sex, like teen violence, has come to be seen as a national crisis, both symptom and symbol of a "generation out of control." But even as it reaches a near-hysterical pitch, the national dialogue on adolescent sexuality remains painfully abstract. Sex is to the '90s what drugs were to the '80s: the locus of adult anxiety over what the kids are doing when we're not around (which is more and more of the time); something we want desperately to stop but not necessarily to understand.

Efforts to manage the "crisis" of adolescent sexual activity consistently focus on consequences rather than motivations, and are driven in great part by political enmities. The left accuses the right of imposing its own repressive mores on defenseless teens, of driving young girls to back-alley abortions and lives of shame. The right charges the left with fostering legions of junior Murphy Browns, who drain the public coffers with their babies and diseases. This ideological battle is reflected back to teenagers in lectures about "values" and "choices"—sex education buzzwords that are also, not coincidentally, the rallying cries of political movements.

As the chasm widens between the rhetoric of their elders and the word on the street, young people are left alone with their deepest questions about relationships, pleasure, and risk.

> *"Most of the guys I know put up a front to get girls. They try to make their voices sound deeper on the phone. Being tough—that's what's in. If you get girls, you got 'game.' Game is just what helps you get a girl. Whatever works for you, works for you. I got my game. I don't lie with a girl. I'll tell her straight up about myself. The truth is I'm just myself, I'm the funny man. That's my way, and it's worked for me so far. That seems to attract the right girls for me, so I'm gonna stick with it."*
>
> **GERMAINE, 16**

In North Carolina, educators are training junior high school girls to counsel friends whose boyfriends assault them, having found that most battered girls do not discuss it with an adult. A recent study showed that half of all 15-year-old girls have never discussed birth control or STDs with a parent, and one-third have never discussed how pregnancy occurs.

Another study indicates that growing numbers of teenagers are having sex at home in the afternoon, while their parents are out of the house—a far cry from the era of backseats and drive-ins, of sneaking out from under the watchful parental eye. And what are we offering those kids left all by themselves in the downstairs bedroom? A "True Love Waits" button, or a condom and a map of their genitals—neither of which addresses the underlying loneliness of a generation raised in empty houses.

Most of the research on adolescent sexual behavior focuses on declining virginity rates and growing social costs. We know, for example, that more than half of American women and three-quarters of American men have had intercourse by their 18th birthday, compared to a quarter of women in the mid-1950s (they didn't count men then). We know that 3 million teens acquire a sexually transmitted disease each year, and that 1 million become pregnant, a third of whom have abortions. And although the number of reported AIDS cases among teenagers is still very small, we know that 20 percent of AIDS cases are among people in their 20s, many of whom probably contracted HIV as teenagers.

What we don't know is why young people do what they do, and how it makes them feel. "There's a tremendous amount of information about a truly small number of questions," says Mindy Thompson Fullilove, associate professor of clinical psychology and public health at Columbia University. "Anything that is not about contraception is missing. We tend to be very obsessed with counting things. We don't value asking, 'What do you mean?'"

While teen sexual activity is increasing, condom use among teenagers is also on the rise: among urban adolescent males, it nearly doubled between 1979 and 1988. Teenage girls are no more likely than older unmarried women to have multiple partners, and are actually less likely to have an unwanted pregnancy. But if advocates across the political spectrum agree on one thing, it's that teen sex is fraught with danger—and they tailor their messages accordingly. "It's always 'Don't get AIDS,'" points out Dr. Lynn Ponton, a professor of psychiatry at the University of California at San Francisco, "never 'Have a good time.'"

A study of state guidelines for sexuality education done last year by the Sexuality Information and Education Council of the United States found that HIV and other STDs were among the most widely covered topics; "shared sexual behavior" and "human sexual response," among the least. In other words, young people are learning in school that sex can hurt or kill them without learning that it can also bring them pleasure or give them a connection to another person.

"Fear messages never persuade anybody to do anything except for a very short period of time," says John Gagnon, a sociologist at the State University of New York at Stony Brook and co-author of the Chicago sex study. He notes that adults lose credibility when they feed young people oversimplified warnings instead of trusting them to understand ambiguous realities. "It's absolutely irresponsible not to give kids sex ed, including information on condoms, and the possibility of not having sex. But it's also irresponsible not to mention that many people find sex a great source of pleasure."

Also lost in the "Just Say No" frenzy are ways for young people to say yes—not just to sex, but to love, family, each other. All around them, adults are rewriting the social script: bearing children out of wedlock; introducing kids to stepfathers, ex-wives, casual girlfriends, and other "options"; publicly venting fury at each other in vicious divorce and custody battles. As we struggle to sort things out for ourselves, we are offering fewer and fewer coherent models for conducting and sustaining intimate relationships. Lifelong marriage, whether or not the desirable norm for sexual relationships, at least had the advantage of being imitable.

With our relentless focus on disease and pregnancy, we leave our children without much explicit guidance when it comes to high-risk activities of the heart. We talk to young people as if their genitals were a matter of public concern, while their souls were none of our business. "People say 'Use a condom,'" says Stephanie Brown, who manages the teen clinic at a Planned Parenthood in Northern California, "but not 'Why are you having sex with this person?'"

Those who do ask that question say they often hear surprisingly sentimental answers. "The degree to which adolescents believe in being in love is absolutely extraordinary," says Gagnon. Surveys show that the vast majority of young people want to marry and raise children with a spouse. Unlike the children of the '60s—for whom the fear of ending up like their parents manifested itself as a terror of being old, married, and bored—today's teens fear ending up old and alone.

One of the better-kept secrets about teen pregnancy is that many of the babies born to adolescents are anything but "unwanted." Ask a 15-year-old why she got pregnant and she's more likely to tell you that she wanted company than that she didn't know how to use a condom. One pregnant 18-year-old I know—a girl who spent last Christmas alone in her apartment, while her mother and stepfather went on vacation together—told me she'd always planned to have a baby right after high school, to make a person all her own, who would love her and not leave. Like most of her friends, she had no illusions that the young man she made the baby with—or any man—would fill that role. "Do you think I'm selfish?" she wanted to know.

With responsible adults focusing mainly on the pitfalls of sexual activity, the task of showing young people what sex and love have to offer is left to that trusted family friend, the television. And television—along with movies, music, and advertising—offers up a sexual universe that has little room for either "values" or "choices." In this universe, sex is everything—and the beautiful people, the glamorous people, the people who *matter*, are having it all the time.

"Abstinence makes the heart grow fonder," promise the advocates. Meanwhile the media map out a very different route to love and fulfillment, hammering home the message that—as Woody Allen put it when called upon to explain his own sexual involvement with a teenager—"the heart wants what it wants."

Perhaps most dangerously for teenagers, points out Sexuality Information and Education Council of the United States director Debra Haffner, the media reinforce the idea that good sex means being swept away: "It just happens. There's almost no sexual negotiation, no portrayal of sexual communication, no limit setting, very little condom and contraceptive use. What we see on TV is that people kiss and then they have intercourse."

The Chicago study painted a picture of sex in America that was much more moderate and restrained. But when Baltimore-based sex educator Deborah Roffman asked her students what they *thought* the study would find, she says, "They predicted the image of sexual behavior that is presented in the media—that there was a lot of intercourse, that married people were less happy with their sex lives than single people, that Americans are sex bunnies." The effect of the dissonance between the official teachings on sex and what the media dish up, says Roffman, is clear: "Any teacher knows that when students get mixed messages from adults, they test."

Gagnon is even more explicit about the role of adults in convincing young people that they are "ready" for sex. "The

'raging hormones' argument is nonsense," he says. "Society *elicits* sexual behavior in kids." But—as with so many problems that plague our children—we rarely acknowledge our own complicity. We prefer to define adolescent sexuality as a crisis of self-control that we, the responsible (but not culpable) adults, must find ways to manage.

Bombarded with messages telling them both that sex is the ticket to love, glamour, and adulthood—and that it is bad and will kill them, adolescents in America are ultimately left with few models and little guidance in the area where they need it most: human relationships. Busy with their battles over propaganda and prophylactics, adults aren't addressing young people's yearning for intimacy, for contact, for connections that prove they matter. "Adults are so evasive, so unwilling to confront the reality of young people's lives," says Gagnon. "It's a maelstrom. And we've abandoned kids to it."

For Further Reading

Everything you ever wanted your children to know about sex but were afraid to say out loud: Let Robie Harris say it all before it's too late. Her hip intro to puberty and sexuality for preteens, *It's Perfectly Normal* (Massachusetts: Candlewick Press, 1994), is rounded out by Michael Emberley's funky illustrations, celebrating the diversity of life and love.

Don't let *Sassy* magazine's cheeky attitude and neon graphics fool you: This teen glossy is a lot smarter and more progressive than its puffy counterparts. (When a reader inquires about the "average age for a girl to start shaving," a *Sassy* advice columnist shoots back: "By answering this question, I'm not advocating shaving, OK?") The magazine's frank and realistic approach to sexuality has, sadly, distanced advertisers; its profit margin is skinnier than its models.

Whether you want to read it yourself or pass it to your teenager, Judy Blume's back-of-the-school bus classic, *Forever . . .* (New York: Simon & Schuster, 1975) still keeps, with one crucial caveat: In a preface added to newer editions of the novel, Blume urges her teenage readers to use condoms (unlike her '70s-era protagonist, who leaves a Planned Parenthood clinic with only a prescription for the pill).

Go back to school with Paul Goodman's *Growing Up Absurd* (New York: Random House, 1956), a somewhat dated and stuffy sociological look at adolescence that, to its credit, was one of the first to seriously consider the ways in which teenagers fit into our screwed-up world.

Most films aimed at capturing angst are either sappy, mindless, or just plain lame. But Chicago Sun-Times film critic Roger Ebert recommends *The Man in the Moon* (directed by Robert Mulligan, 1991), a Southern weeper about a 14-year-old girl's unrequited love for a boy who is, alas, captivated by her sister.

For insight into teenagers' music, listen to your *Offspring*. Spawning top-40 singles like "Self-Esteem" and the anti-gun "Come Out and Play," the group's second LP, "Smash" (released by Epitaph, 1994) reflects all of the frustration (or is it naïveté?) of their suburban upbringing.

Virgin Cool

A lot of kids are putting off sex, and not because they can't get a date. They've decided to wait, and they're proud of their chastity, not embarrassed by it. Suddenly, virgin geek is giving way to virgin chic.

Michele Ingrassia

Fredda Chalfin's students drag their chairs into a circle, joking and jostling until, finally, 31 pairs of baggy-jeaned legs are sitting knee to knee. Their style is haute teen: flannel shirts, fist-size earrings, baseball caps and bandannas tied Aunt Jemima style. Standard, too, is the pose of adolescent ennui. But it dissolves the moment Chalfin closes the door. Here, in a basement classroom at DeWitt Clinton High School in the Bronx, Chalfin leads a daily encounter group, and the box of Kleenex on the floor is just the most visible sign that, for the next 45 minutes, there will be no routine academics. Chalfin, casual in jeans and ankle boots, grew up in the age of peace and love, and her rules are gentle but firm: no lateness, no gum, no breaking confidences. No one needs a reminder. Three weeks into the term, her 14- to 18-year olds are already each other's protectors, offering enough security to reveal an early-childhood sexual abuse, to applaud a schoolyard refusal to smoke some weed—and to support a choice to forgo sex in a teenager's sex-crazy world.

With a note of innocence—or maybe it's shyness—they recite the affirmation scrawled on the board: I LOVE MY SEXUALITY • I AM AT PEACE • I AM FREE TO MAKE MY OWN DECISIONS REGARDING SEX •. Chalfin jumps in, challenging the students to defend their resolve. "Look at that statement. *Do* you call the shots regarding sex? Or do you feel pressure? Do you feel you're going to lose that person if you don't have sex? How free are you really?"

Even here, in a corner of the Bronx that runs the economic and social gamut, it's obvious that abstinence is looking good to a lot more kids. "If you don't want to give it up, you don't have to," says Myra. "If that's what he wants, tell him to *forget* about it."

"What's a guy supposed to do when he wants to do it and she doesn't?" Phil chides.

"What happens when he gets hot and horny and you're a virgin?" Chalfin asks. "How are you gonna work it out? It's like you're a vegetarian and he loves steak—where are you going to eat?"

"If your relationship is based on sex, you don't *have* a relationship," says Sweeney. "You can't do it 24-7."

"I want to be different from other girls," says Betsy. "I want a guy to look at me in another way. I want to have respect for myself. I see girls getting into trouble, and I don't want to get hurt. I *want* to be a virgin."

Just a year ago, teenagers and abstinence would have seemed as unlikely a pair as Lisa Marie Presley and Michael Jackson. But after a decades-long explosion in births among unmarried teens and a growing number of AIDS cases among young adults, forgoing sex—or at least delaying it—is finding new respect. Some of the impetus comes from parents, many of them baby boomers who charged, buck naked, into the sexual revolution. Teachers who've offered up the abstinence message with a wink and a yawn are also starting to treat it as seriously as they do safe sex. Even the most liberal president in 30 years is talking the talk: Bill Clinton has made abstinence a cornerstone of his proposed $400 million campaign against teen pregnancy, turning virginity into a matter of public health, not just private morality.

Pop Images: But when you're a teenager, even the president is just another droning voice. What counts is what flits by on the tube and pulses through the headphones of your Discman. And out there, in the supersexed world of pop culture, the image of abstinence is shifting from the pimply dweeb who can't get a date; virgin geek is giving way to virgin chic. Winsome rocker Juliana Hatfield, 26, announced her virginity a few years back, in Interview magazine, no less. MTV veejay Kennedy declared her virginity with a whatcha'-gonna-make-of-it-air. NBA star A. C. Green has his own athletes-for-abstinence campaign. And up and down the TV channels, writers who once rushed characters into bed are hot to keep them out. Witness virgin goddess Tori Spelling, whose "Beverly Hills 90210" character clings to her virtue even when she feels like the last virgin on Rodeo Drive. And though the fictional Sarah Owens gave up her chastity on "Models, Inc.," Cassidy Rae, the 18-year-old actress who plays her, has become virginity's most visible standard-bearer. "I want to stay as pure as I can for my [future] husband," Cassidy says.

TRUST ME I'M A VIRGIN

It's tough to deal with peer pressure—and hormone pressure

Jacques M. Chenet—Newsweek

Of course, this isn't a return to the '50's, when the moral code was as rigid as the cone-shaped bras. Today three quarters of boys and half of girls have had sex by the time they graduate high school. A century ago girls reached puberty at about 15 and married at 22; today, the age of puberty has dropped to 12.5, the marrying age has jumped to 24.3—and no one expects teens to ignore the call of their hormones for a dozen years. "Once you're 12, the pressure starts," Sweeney, 15, says after class as she and some friends sprawl on the linoleum floor in a guidance office. "To hold on three years until you're 15, you may not think it's a long time, but it is."

Still, teachers, counselors and social scientists say more kids are waiting, though these changes in attitudes and behavior won't show up in statistics for years. The question is, why now? Eugene Genovese, scholar-in-residence at the University Center in Georgia and an observer of campus life for 25 years, calls abstinence "a broad-based counterattack against the counterculture that developed since the 1960s." In Thousand Oaks, Calif., a diverse bedroom community where the streets are wide, the air unpolluted and many of the families intact, Wayne Tanaka, 47, takes a more personal view. He explains what 12 used to be like. "We were riding bicycles and going to the corner drugstore and getting a soda and reading a comic book." Sounds very Stone Age, he concedes. "Now, by the time a child has reached 16 or 18, they've seen so much that they're missing out on childhood," says Tanaka, who has a 12-year-old daughter and a 20-year-old son. "A 12-year-old should be enjoying 12-year-old things."

Teens Who Abstain

The median age for first intercourse is 16.6 years for boys and 17.4 for girls, according to the latest available data. But nearly 20 percent (of both sexes) remain virgins throughout their teenage years.

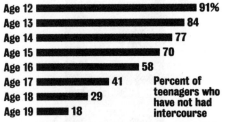

Age 12	91%
Age 13	84
Age 14	77
Age 15	70
Age 16	58
Age 17	41
Age 18	29
Age 19	18

Percent of teenagers who have not had intercourse

SOURCE: 'SEX AND AMERICA'S TEENAGERS,' ALAN GUTTMACHER INSTITUTE 1994

But 12-year-old things aren't the same. Teen bibles like Seventeen, Sassy and YM serve up all sorts of sexual frankness. Sexual positions, sexual satisfaction are all part of a startling adolescent discourse—so are whirlpooling, the Spur Posse, sexual harassment, domestic violence and regular reports of high-school boys sexually assaulting junior-high-school girls. Not surprising, in less than a generation, some kids have

come to view sex as a sadistic sideshow. Instead of an act meant to bring two people together, it can drive them apart. This is *fun*?

In hindsight, the sexual revolution seems terribly quaint. Back when do-I-love-him was their biggest worry, girls actually said things like "If I sleep with him tonight, will I be able to look at myself in the mirror tomorrow?" That was before AIDS. Now kids sound like Damien Ritter, a 15-year-old from Missoula, Mont., who wears his virginity as defiantly as the ponytail that sticks straight up from his head. "A person can have sex once and be *dead* six months later," Damien says with a dose of adolescent theatrics. AIDS among teens is still relatively rare—partly because it can take a decade for the virus to develop into full-blown AIDS. But that doesn't make AIDS less frightening.

"My uncle died of AIDS this year. He was 32," a 14-year-old named Ruth says quietly, sitting in the DeWitt Clinton guidance office. She's staring down at her snub-nosed sneakers, her wavy black hair covering her creamy olive cheeks. As her friends nod in recognition, Ruth explains that, when she hit high school last year, she was sure she was the last virgin alive. She decided that she didn't care. "My uncle made me think about it so much," says Ruth, whose mother is an AIDS educator and whose father is a minister. "Try to imagine his emotional thing. Seeing him go through so much pain, I realized I don't ever want to look at my little sister—she's my whole world—or my cousin and have to say 'Please, help me'."

Even if they're not scared of AIDS, kids are worried about diseases that could leave them infertile or babies that could weigh them down with adult responsibilities. By the age of 21, according to the Centers for Disease Control, one in four young people is already infected with a sexually transmitted disease like chlamydia, syphilis or gonorrhea. And though teen-pregnancy rates are higher among the poor, it burdens all kids. Between 1960 and 1989, the percentage of teens who were unmarried when they had their first child rose from 33 percent to 81 percent, according to the Alan Guttmacher Institute, the research arm of Planner Parenthood. And a new Guttmacher study shows that nearly one third of girls who had a first baby by 16 had a second within two years. Jamal Richardson, a Brooklyn 15-year-old, needs only to look at his brother to know why he doesn't want to have sex yet. Just 17, Jamal's brother has a 1-year-old daughter, and most of what he earns in his after-school job goes to supporting the baby. "I don't know much about growing up, but I know he isn't having any fun

doing it," Jamal says. "He always tells me when I'm talking about the honeys to just keep my pants on."

Sex ed classes have to go beyond 'Just Say No'

Jacques M. Chenet—Newsweek

Abortion access: Every kid who's sat through even one sex ed class knows that condoms can make a difference, but teenagers are notoriously lax about using contraception, even when they can walk into a school health office and pick up a handful of Trojans. Abortion, never an easy alternative for anyone, is even more daunting when you're young. Back in the '70's—and even the '80's—any woman worth her Ms. subscription knew she could pass around the hat in her dorm and collect a few hundred bucks for an abortion. Access was rarely a problem: every big city and most college towns had a clinic or at least an abortion doctor, and if he wasn't Marcus Welby, well, at least he had an office. Now 25 states require parental consent or notification before a teenager can have an abortion, and 84 percent of all U.S. counties don't even have a provider. Before *Roe v. Wade*, women feared they could die if they had an abortion; now, doctors fear being killed if they perform one. The climate has chilled; even ardent pro-choicers don't treat "choice" so lightly.

Tapping into kids' fears, parents' natural protectiveness and the country's conservative moral sway, Richard Ross, a Baptist youth minister from Nashville, helped launch the virginity movement. Ross says he decided to act last year, when two 14-year-olds told him, "We're the only virgins left in our school." The result: an organization called True Love Waits. With unabashed boosterism, TLW offers a motto ("True love waits"), a theme song ("True Love Waits") and a pledge card for virgins to promise abstinence until marriage. Though critics dismiss it as the sexual equivalent of the "Just Say No" drug campaign, TLW struck a chord. This summer 22,000 "sexually pure" young people converged on Washington, D.C., in a show of strength that included the planting of 200,000 pledge cards on the Washington Mall. Not exactly Woodstock South, but the sea of rainbow-colored pledge cards and telegenic faces drove home the point.

Reasons to Wait

Eight in 10 abstinent teens cite fear of sexually transmitted diseases as one of the reasons they remain virgins. Less than half as many cite religion.

Want to wait until I'm in a committed relationship	87%
Worry about sexually transmitted diseases	85%
Worry about pregnancy	84%
Want to wait until I'm older	84%
Worry about AIDS	83%
Haven't met the right person yet	80%
Just not ready for sex yet	79%
Want to wait until I'm married	71%
Against my religion	40%

SOURCE: ROPER STARCH WORLDWIDE, 1994

Even Christian virgins will tell you it's not always easy being chaste. Walking hand in hand with her boyfriend during the Washington rally, Jill Clayton explained that abstinence would be nearly impossible if they didn't set strict limits. "We kiss, we French-kiss, we embrace," said Jill, 20, a junior at Carson Newman College in Jefferson City, Tenn., "and that's it." She cast a guilty look at her boyfriend of two years, Scott Dender. Well, once, after a romantic movie, they went further than they wanted to—though not all the way. Afterward, they talked about boundaries. "We just said we can't go that far again," said Scott, who proposed to Jill this summer.

Sex ed: The Christian right's real impact has been in bringing abstinence front-and-center in sex ed. Now most teachers embrace it. The reason: kids say they're looking for help—and support—in how not to have sex. "When you say a guy is coming up against you in the back of a car or in the hallway or in someone's house and what are you going to do about it, they need their sisters saying, 'Don't do it,' and understanding that, God, it's so scary," says consultant Lenore Roseman, who taught sex ed in New York City for 24 years and helped

rewrite the city's curriculum. But not all kids are hearing the same message. Conservatives, fueled by tens of millions of dollars in funding for "family centered" programs during the Reagan-Bush years, demanded a universal chastity theme and got it: 90 percent of sex ed courses now include abstinence (although some teachers still approach it with the enthusiasm of a cop reading a suspect his Miranda rights).

Nationwide, about 1 percent of sex ed courses preach abstinence—and nothing else. The best-known, and most controversial, is Sex Respect, an 11-year-old program that warns against all manner of sex, including necking. ("Petting [before] marriage can sometimes harm our sex life within marriage.") In fact, Sex Respect's student workbook is, in many ways, a throwback to sexual attitudes of the '50s. Every chapter offers catchy aphorisms ("Control your urgin', be a virgin." "Pet your dog, not your date"). And, for kids who've lapsed, there's the promise of "secondary" virginity ("Any person who wants it can have it by deciding to change.").

The problem is, abstinence-only programs rarely work. In a new review of sex ed courses, the CDC found that kids tune out one-note messages—abstinence-only as well as contraception-only. What does work? Courses that talk abstinence, teach safe sex and refuse to send kids out into a cold, cruel, sexually charged world on their own. "The only programs that have any impact teach kids how to say 'no' to someone you really like, someone you might want to say 'yes' to down the road," says Peter Scales of the Center for Early Adolescence at the University of North Carolina, Chapel Hill. "That's not an easy skill for a 14- or 15-year-old. Frankly, it's not an easy lesson for some 35-year-olds."

MY MOM THINKS I'M A VIRGIN

Maybe, says one parent, a little fear is a good thing

Jacques M. Chenet—Newsweek

Actually, it's easy to underestimate how much teenagers struggle with sex. Beth lost her virginity during the first week of May. "It was a Thursday, I think," says the feisty 13-year-old from working-class Manchester, N.H., who asked that her real name not be used. She was at a friend's house, and one thing led to another and before you knew it . . . "It was something I got pressured into," Beth says with a sigh. She recalls the afternoon with disjointed stream-of-consciousness. It was just like in the movies, Beth insists. "It felt good being with him." Physically, though, it hurt. A lot. It wasn't too safe, either—they didn't use birth control. But the worst part came when Beth and her boyfriend broke up—six weeks after they started going out, four days after they slept together.

Early Experience

Sexual experimenting soars in high school, especially between sophomore and junior years.

ASKED OF STUDENTS GRADES 9–12
What sexual activities have you engaged in?

Kissing	90%
Deep kissing	79%
Touching above the waist	72%
Touching below the waist	54%
Sexual intercourse	36%
Oral sex	26%
Mutual masturbation	15%

SOURCE: ROPER STARCH WORLDWIDE, 1994

Now, Beth's angry. Like many teenagers, she doesn't want to plumb the lofty issues of sex and social responsibility, or prosaic matters like pregnancy and AIDS. What she wants to talk about is more direct; the fear of getting hurt. After they'd had sex, Beth says, her boyfriend blabbed—to everyone. "Girls afterwards have all the pain, all the rumors. I couldn't take it," she says, chewing on a stick of Big Red.

No one has to explain Beth's fury to another girl. By the time she's bought her first bra, every female child knows that there's a double standard—and that she's doomed to be on the losing end. A steely edge cuts the air as some DeWitt Clinton girls explain how the boys view them:

"Guys have preconceived notions of what you are by what you look like" says Miesha, a 15-year-old woman-child who wears her long hair '70s-straight and studs her French manicure with tiny rhinestones.

"If you dress a little preppy, they think you're a virgin," adds Sweeney, shrouded, safely, in work shirt and jeans.

"And on the day you put on something nice, they call you a 'ho," says Miesha, wearing a tiny T shirt that does little to hide her curves "They say, 'She's oversexed—she's no virgin'."

Virginity isn't just about fear. Many teenagers say that they've actually weighed the demands of school with the demands of a sexual relationship and have decided, for now, to wait. The phone in the Basoukas house in suburban Manchester, N.H., rings a lot these days, and it's usually for 16-year-old Lindsay, who, according to her sister, has actually burned up several phones. Though the callers are often boys wanting to date the petite Molly Ringwald look-alike, Lindsay tells most of them, "Let's just stick to being friends." This summer Lindsay started seeing Matt, and though the subject of sex hasn't come up, she isn't worried. "I know what I want, and I know that's just not one of the things I want to do now," says Lindsay. "I'm having a great time being 16 and having tons of my friends around."

That's the kind of talk parents love to hear. David Leeman, the music director of a nondenominational church in Winnetka, Ill., has been open with his sons, Michael, 16, Philip, 17, and Jonathan, 21, about sex. To underscore how he feels about abstinence, Leeman will give each son a signet ring on his 18th birthday to remind him not to go all the way until he's married. Though the family beliefs are rooted in religion, Barbara Leeman says "you could do away with all the religious reasons" and they'd still feel the same. "They don't force stuff on us," says Michael, who plays soccer and basketball at New Trier High School. "It's not like, 'If you have sex and we find out, you're grounded for the rest of your life'."

Especially for baby boomers, teenage sexuality stirs wildly conflicting emotions. Theirs, after all, was the first generation to experience sexual freedom in an exuberant way. "The thrill of going to a party and thinking, Who do I want to sleep with? Who do I want to go home with? ... It was exciting," says Pam Rogers, 44, of Brookline, Mass. But those were college students marching into the sexual revolution, not high-schoolers or prepubescent kids. For any parent who same of age in the '60s, it's not easy knowing what to say without sounding like a hypocrite.

Maybe, suggests Judy Rosensweig, a little fear is good. Rosensweig, 45, grew up well-to-do in West Hartford, Conn., with parents who were politically liberal and generally permissive—except when it came to Judy and sex. So she did what any child of the '60s would do: she rebelled. At 14, she tried pot; at 16, she dropped acid, and at college at the University of New Mexico she was interviewed for a Playboy article on sex on campus. Last year, when Rosensweig's 12-year-old daughter, Brooke, confided that some of her friends were having sex, all the dangers—AIDS, pregnancy, STDs—raced through Rosensweig's mind. "Now, I don't regret anything I did, but I doubt I would do it again," says Rosensweig, a decorative house painter in Delray Beach, Fla. She tried to convey that to Brooke, using herself as an example. "When I was 14, I was going out with guys who were 20, 26," she says. "Now, I always say, 'Wait till you're older.' She asks, 'How old?' I say, '35'."

Middle ground: After 30 years of sexual exploration—and exploitation—it was inevitable that some sort of upheaval would happen. Don't think of it as another revolution: it's more like a midcourse correction, somewhere between free love and take-back-the-night marches. Virginity even offers its own post-post-feminist twist: the girls everyone is rushing to protect may actually turn out tougher and more self-reliant than their mothers. This, after all, is the first generation to really understand you-don't-have-to-be-touched-anywhere/you-don't-want-to-be-touched, and it already colors their lives.

Back when Mom was a fledgling feminist, it was hip to declare, "It's my body and I'll sleep with as many guys as I want to." Now, even high-schoolers insist, "It's my body and I don't have to sleep with *anyone* if I don't want to." Of course, it's always hard to lose a boyfriend—especially if it's because you didn't sleep with him—but life doesn't end. Sitting in her dorm room at tiny Rivier College in New Hampshire, Ebony Doran, a freshman and a virgin, admits that sex is a big part of life. "Yes, I think about it," says Ebony, 17. "But I know that I control my body and my mind." For many teenagers, that makes virginity even more liberating than sex.

With DEBRA ROSENBERG *in Manchester, N.H.,* KAREN SPRINGEN *in Chicago,* PATRICK ROGERS *in New York,* SUSAN MILLER *and* PAT WINGERT *in Washington, D.C., and bureau reports*

The Right Time

When asked the best age for first intercourse, teens say hold out until your 20s—or at least 18. Surprisingly, they have the same standards for girls as they do for boys.

ASKED OF STUDENTS GRADES 9–12
At what age is it reasonable to first have sexual intercourse?

	FOR MALES	FOR FEMALES
14 years or younger	2%	1%
15 years	5%	4%
16 years	15%	16%
17 years	14%	14%
18 years	20%	20%
19 years	5%	5%
20 years or older	22%	23%

SOURCE: ROLONDA/SEICUS SURVEY CONDUCTED BY ROPER STARCH WORLDWIDE, 1994; A NATIONAL SURVEY OF 252 MALES AND 251 FEMALES

THE NEGLECTED HEART

The Emotional Dangers of Premature Sexual Involvement

THOMAS LICKONA

You didn't get pregnant. You didn't get AIDS. So why do you feel so bad?
—Leslee Unruh, abstinence educator

There is no condom for the heart.
—Sign at a sex education conference

IN DISCUSSIONS of teen sex, much is said about the dangers of pregnancy and disease—but far less about the emotional hazards. And that's a problem, because the destructive psychological consequences of temporary sexual relationships are very real. Being aware of them can help a young person make and stick to the decision to avoid premature sexual involvement.

That's not to say we should downplay the physical dangers of uncommitted sex. Pregnancy is a life-changing event. Sexually transmitted disease (STD)—and there are now more than 20 STDs—can rob you of your health and even your life. Condoms don't remove these dangers. Condoms have an annual failure rate of 10 percent to 30 percent in preventing pregnancy because of human error in using them and because they sometimes leak, break, or slip off. Condoms reduce but by no means eliminate the risk of AIDS. In a 1993 analysis of 11 different medical studies, condoms were found to have a 31 percent average failure rate in preventing the sexual transmission of the AIDS virus.[1] Finally, condoms do little or nothing to protect against the two STDs infecting at least one-third of sexually active teenage girls: human papilloma virus (the leading cause of cervical cancer) and chlamydia (the leading cause of infertility), both of which can be transmitted by skin-to-skin contact in the entire genital area, only a small part of which is covered by the condom.[2]

Why is it so much harder to discuss sex and emotional hurt—to name and talk about the damaging psychological effects that can come from premature sexual involvement? For one thing, most of us have never heard this aspect of sex discussed. Our parents didn't talk to us about it. The media don't talk about it. And the heated debate about condoms in schools typically doesn't say much about the fact that condoms do nothing to make sex *emotionally* safe. When it comes to trying to explain to their children or students how early sexuality can do harm to one's personality and character as well as to one's health, many adults are simply at a loss for words, or reduced to vague generalities such as, "you're too young" or "you're not ready" or "you're not mature enough."

This relative silence about the emotional side of sex is ironic, because the emotional dimension of sex is what makes it distinctively human.

What in fact are the emotional or psychological consequences of premature, uncommitted sex? These consequences vary among individuals. Some emotional consequences are short-term but still serious. Some of them last a long time, sometimes even into marriage and parenting. Many of these psychological consequences are hard to imagine until they've been experienced. In all cases, the emotional consequences of sexual experiences are not to be taken lightly. A moment's reflection reminds us that emotional problems can have damaging, even crippling, effects on a person's ability to lead a happy and productive life.

Let's look at 10 negative psychological consequences of premature sexual involvement.

1. Worry About Pregnancy and AIDS

For many sexually active young people, the fear of becoming pregnant or getting AIDS is a major emotional stress.

Russell Henke, health education coordinator in the Montgomery County (Maryland) Public Schools, says, "I see kids going to the nurses in schools, crying a day after their first sexual experience, and wanting to be tested for AIDS. They have done it, and now they are terrified. For some of them, that's enough. They say, 'I don't want to have to go through that experience anymore.'"[3]

A high school girl told a nurse: "I see some of my friends buying home pregnancy tests, and they are so worried and so distracted every month, afraid that they might be pregnant. It's a relief to me to be a virgin."

2. Regret and Self-Recrimination

Girls, especially, need to know in advance the sharp regret that so many young women feel after becoming sexually involved.

Says one high school girl: "I get upset when I see my friends losing their virginity to some guy they've just met. Later, after the guy's dumped them, they come to me and say, 'I wish I hadn't done it.'"[4] A ninth-grade girl who slept with eight boys in junior high says, "I'm young, but I feel old."

Thomas Lickona is a developmental psychologist and professor of education at the State University of New York at Cortland. He is the father of two sons, ages 20 and 26, and author of the Christopher Award-winning book Educating for Character *(Bantam Books, 1992).*

From *American Educator*, Summer 1994, pp. 34-39. Adapted from *Sex, Love, and You: Making the Right Decision* by Thomas Lickona, Judith Lickona, and William J. Boudreau. © 1994 by Ave Maria Press, Notre Dame, IN 46556. Reprinted by permission.

Girls are more vulnerable than boys because girls are more likely to think of sex as a way to "show you care." They're more likely to see sex as a sign of commitment in the relationship.

If a girl expects a sexual interlude to be loving, she may very well feel cheated and used when the boy doesn't show a greater romantic interest after the event. As one 15-year-old girl describes her experience: "I didn't expect the guy to marry me, but I never expected him to avoid me in school."

Bob Bartlett, who teaches a freshman sexuality class in a Richfield, Minn., high school, shares the following story of regret on the part of one of his students (we'll call her Sandy):

Sandy, a bright and pretty girl, asked to see Mr. Bartlett during her lunch period. She explained that she had never had a boyfriend, so she was excited when a senior asked her out.

After they dated for several weeks, the boy asked her to have sex with him. She was reluctant; he was persistent. She was afraid of appearing immature and losing him, so she consented.

"Did it work?" Mr. Bartlett asked gently. "Did you keep him?"

Sandy replied: "For another week. We had sex again, and then he dropped me. He said I wasn't good enough. There was no spark.

"I know what you're going to say. I take your class. I know now that he didn't really love me. I feel so stupid, so cheap."[5]

Sandy hoped, naively, that sex would keep the guy. Here is another high school girl, writing to an advice column about a different kind of regret. She wishes she *could* lose the guy she's involved with, but she feels trapped by their sexual relationship.

I am 16, a junior in high school, and like nearly all the other girls here, I have already lost my virginity. Although most people consider this subject very personal, I feel the need to share this part of my life with girls who are trying to decide whether to have sex for the first time.

Sex does not live up to the glowing reports and hype you see in the movies. It's no big deal. In fact, it's pretty disappointing.

I truly regret that my first time was with a guy that I didn't care that much about. I am still going out with him, which is getting to be a problem. I'd like to end this relationship and date others, but after being so intimate, it's awfully tough.

Since that first night, he expects sex on every date, like we are married or something. When I don't feel like it, we end up in an argument. It's like I owe it to him. I don't think this guy is in love with me, at least he's never said so. I know deep down that I am not in love with him either, and this makes me feel sort of cheap.

I realize now that this is a very big step in a girl's life. After you've done it, things are never the same. It changes everything.

My advice is, don't be in such a rush. It's a headache and a worry. (Could I be pregnant?) Sex is not for entertainment. It should be a commitment. Be smart and save yourself for someone you wouldn't mind spending the rest of your life with.
—Sorry I Didn't And Wish I Could
Take It Back[6]

Regret over uncommitted sexual relationships can last for years. I recently received a letter from a 33-year-old woman, now a psychiatrist, who is very much concerned about the sexual pressures and temptations facing young people today. She wanted to share the lessons she had learned about sex the hard way. After high school, she says, she spent a year abroad as an exchange student:

I was a virgin when I left, but I felt I was protected. I had gotten an IUD so I could make my own decisions if and when I wanted. I had steeled myself against commitment. I was never going to marry or have children; I was going to have a career. During that year abroad, from 17½ to 18½, I was very promiscuous.

But the fact is, it cost me to be separated from myself. The longest-standing and deepest wound I gave myself was heartfelt. That sick, used feeling of having given a precious part of myself—my soul—to so many and for nothing, still aches. I never imagined I'd pay so dearly and for so long.

This woman is happily married now, she says, and has a good sexual relationship with her husband. But she still carries the emotional scar of those early sexual experiences. She wants young people to know that "sex without commitment is very risky for the heart."

3. Guilt

Guilt is a special form of regret—a strong sense of having done something morally wrong. Guilt is a normal and healthy moral response, a sign that one's conscience is working.

In his book for teenagers, *Love, Dating, and Sex*, George Eager tells the story of a well-known speaker who was addressing a high school assembly. The speaker was asked, "What do you most regret about your high school days?"

He answered, "The thing I most regret about high school is the time I singlehandedly destroyed a girl."

Eager offers this advice to young men: "When the breakup comes, it's usually a lot tougher on the girls than it is on the guys. It's not something you want on your conscience—that you caused a girl to have deep emotional problems."[7]

One 16-year-old boy says he stopped having sex with girls when he saw and felt guilty about the pain he was causing: "You see them crying and confused. They say they love you, but you don't love them."

Even in an age of sexual liberation, a lot of people who are having sex nevertheless have a guilty conscience about it. The guilt may come, as in the case of the young man just quoted, from seeing the hurt you've caused other people.

The guilt may come from knowing that your parents

168

would be upset if they knew you were having sex. Or it may stem from your religious convictions. Christianity, Judaism, and Islam, for example, all teach that sex is a gift from God reserved for marriage and that sexual relations outside marriage are morally wrong.

Sometimes guilt about their sexual past ends up crippling people when they become parents by keeping them from advising their own children not to become sexually involved. According to counselor Dr. Carson Daly: "Because these parents can't bear to be considered hypocrites, or to consider themselves hypocrites, they don't give their children the sexual guidance they very much need."[8]

4. Loss of Self-Respect and Self-Esteem

Many people suffer a loss of self-esteem when they find out they have a sexually transmitted disease. For example, according to the Austin, Texas-based Medical Institute for Sexual Health, more than 80 percent of people

Sometimes guilt about their sexual past ends up crippling people when they become parents by keeping them from advising their own children not to become sexually involved.

with herpes say they feel "less confident" and "less desirable sexually."[9]

But even if a person is fortunate enough to escape sexually transmitted disease, temporary sexual relationships can lower the self-respect of both the user and the used.

Sometimes casual sex lowers self-esteem, leading a person into further casual sex, which leads to further loss of self-esteem in an oppressive cycle from which it may be hard to break free. This pattern is described by a college senior, a young woman who works as a residence hall director:

> There are girls in our dorm who have had multiple pregnancies and multiple abortions. They tend to be filled with self-loathing. But because they have so little self-esteem, they will settle for any kind of attention from guys. So they keep going back to the same kind of destructive situations and relationships that got them into trouble in the first place.

On both sides of dehumanized sex, there is a loss of dignity and self-worth. One 20-year-old college male confides: "You feel pretty crummy when you get drunk at a party and have sex with some girl, and then the next morning you can't even remember who she was."

Another college student describes the loss of self-respect that followed his first sexual "conquest":

> I finally got a girl into bed—actually it was in a car—when I was 17. I thought it was the hottest thing there was, but then she started saying she loved me and getting clingy.
>
> I figured out that there had probably been a

dozen guys before me who thought they had "conquered" her, but who were really just objects of her need for security. That realization took all the wind out of my sails. I couldn't respect someone who gave in as easily as she did.

I was amazed to find that after four weeks of having sex as often as I wanted, I was tired of her. I didn't see any point in continuing the relationship. I finally dumped her, which made me feel even worse, because I could see that she was hurting. I felt pretty low.[10]

People aren't things. When we treat them as if they were, we not only hurt them; we lose respect for ourselves.

5. The Corruption of Character and the Debasement of Sex

When people treat others as sexual objects and exploit them for their own pleasure, they not only lose self-respect; they corrupt their characters and debase their sexuality in the process.

Good character consists of virtues such as respect, responsibility, honesty, fairness, caring, and self-control. With regard to sex, the character trait of self-control is particularly crucial. The breakdown of sexual self-control is a big factor in many of the sex-related problems that plague our society: rape, promiscuity, pornography, addiction to sex, sexual harassment, the sexual abuse of children, sexual infidelity in marriage, and the serious damage to families many of these problems cause. It was Freud who said—and it is now obvious how right he was—that sexual self-control is essential for civilization.

Sex frequently corrupts character by leading people to tell lies in order to get sex. The Medical Institute for Sexual Health reports: "Almost all studies show that many sexually active people will lie if they think it will help them have sex."[11] Common lies: "I love you" and "I've never had a sexually transmitted disease."

Because sex is powerful, once sexual restraint is set aside, it easily takes over individuals and relationships. Consider the highly sexualized atmosphere that now characterizes many high schools. A high school teacher in Indiana says, "The air is thick with sex talk. Kids in the halls will say—boy to girl, girl to boy—'I want to f— you.'"

In a 1993 study by the American Association of University Women, four of five high school students—85 percent of girls and 75 percent of boys—said they have experienced "unwelcome sexual behavior that interferes with my life" in school.[12] An example: A boy backs a 14-year-old girl up against her locker, day after day. Says Nan Stein, a Wellesley College researcher: "There's a Tailhook happening in every school. Egregious behavior is going on."

Another recently reported example of this corruption of character is the Spur Posse club at Lakewood High School in suburban Los Angeles. Members of this club competed to see how many girls they could sleep with; one claimed he had slept with 63. Sadly, elementary school-age children are beginning to mimic such behavior. In a suburb of Pittsburgh, an assistant superintendent reports that sixth-grade boys were found playing a sexual contact game; the object of the game was to earn points by touching girls in private parts, the most points being awarded for "going all the way."

In this sex-out-of-control environment, even rape is judged permissible by many young people. In a 1988 survey of students in grades six through nine, the Rhode Island Rape Crisis Center found that two of three boys and 49 percent of the girls said it was "acceptable for a man to force sex on a woman if they have been dating for six months or more."[13] In view of attitudes like these, it's easy to understand why date rape has become such a widespread problem.

In short, sex that isn't tied to love and commitment undermines character by subverting self-control, respect, and responsibility. Unchecked, sexual desires and impulses easily run amok and lead to habits of hedonism and using others for one's personal pleasure. In the process, sexual intercourse loses its meaning, beauty, and specialness; instead of being a loving, uniquely intimate expression of two people's commitment to each other, sex is trivialized and degraded.

6. Shaken Trust and Fear of Commitment

Young people who feel used or betrayed after the break-up of a sexual relationship may experience difficulty in future relationships.

Some sexually exploited people, as we've seen, develop such low self-esteem that they seek any kind of attention, even if it's another short-lived and demeaning sexual relationship. But other people, once burned, withdraw. They have trouble trusting; they don't want to get burned again.

Usually, this happens to the girl. She begins to see guys as interested in just one thing: Sex. Says one young woman: "Besides feeling cheap [after several sexual relationships], I began to wonder if there would ever be anyone who would love and accept me without demanding that I do something with my body to earn that love."[14]

However, boys can also experience loss of trust and fear of commitment as a result of a broken relationship that involved sex. Brian, a college senior, tells how this happened to him:

> I first had intercourse with my girlfriend when we were 15. I'd been going with her for almost a year, and I loved her very much. She was friendly, outgoing, charismatic. We'd done everything but have intercourse, and then one night she asked if we could go all the way.
>
> A few days later, we broke up. It was the most painful time of my life. I had opened myself up to her more than I had to anybody, even my parents.
>
> I was depressed, moody, nervous. My friends dropped me because I was so bummed out. I felt like a failure. I dropped out of sports. My grades weren't terrific.
>
> I didn't go out again until I got to college. I've had mostly one-night stands in the last couple of years. I'm afraid of falling in love.[15]

7. Rage Over Betrayal

Sometimes the emotional reaction to being "dumped" isn't just a lack of trust or fear of commitment. It's rage.

Every so often, the media carry a story about a person who had this rage reaction and then committed an act of violence against the former boyfriend or girlfriend. Read these accounts, and you'll find that sex was almost always a part of the broken relationship.

Of course, people often feel angry when somebody breaks up with them, even if sex has not been involved. But the sense of betrayal is usually much greater if sex has been part of the relationship. Sex can be emotional dynamite. It can lead a person to think that the relation-

Teenagers who are absorbed in an intense sexual relationship are turning inward on one thing at the very time in their lives when they should be reaching out.

ship is really serious, that both people really love each other. It can create a very strong emotional bond that hurts terribly when it's ruptured—especially if it seems that the other person never had the same commitment. And the resulting sense of betrayal can give rise to rage, even violence.

8. Depression and Suicide

In *Sex and the Teenager*, Kieran Sawyer writes: "The more the relationship seems like real love, the more the young person is likely to invest, and the deeper the pain and hurt if the relationship breaks up."[16] Sometimes the emotional turmoil caused by the rupture of a sexual relationship leads to deep depression. The depression, in turn, may lead some people to take their own lives.

In the past 25 years, teen suicide has tripled. In a 1988 survey by the U.S. Department of Health and Human Services, one in five adolescent girls said they have tried to kill themselves (the figure for boys was one in 10).

This is the same period during which the rate of teenage sexual activity has sharply increased, especially for girls. No doubt, the rise in youth suicide has multiple causes, but given what we know about the emotional aftermath of broken sexual relationships, it is reasonable to suspect that the pain from such break-ups is a factor in the suicide deaths of some young people.

9. Ruined Relationships

Sex can have another kind of emotional consequence: It can turn a good relationship bad. Other dimensions of the relationship stop developing. Pretty soon, negative emotions enter the picture. Eventually, they poison the relationship, and what had been a caring relationship comes to a bitter end.

One young woman shares her story, which illustrates the process:

> With each date, my boyfriend's requests for sex became more convincing. After all, we did love each other. Within two months, I gave in, because I had justified the whole thing. Over the next six months, sex became the center of our relationship....

At the same time, some new things entered our relationship—things like anger, impatience, jealousy, and selfishness. We just couldn't talk anymore. We grew very bored with each other. I desperately wanted a change.[17]

A young man who identified himself as a 22-year-old virgin echoes this warning about the damage premature sex can do to a relationship:

I've seen too many of my friends break up after their relationships turned physical. The emotional wreckage is horrendous because they have already shared something so powerful. When you use sex too early, it will block other means of communicating love and can stunt the balanced growth of a relationship.[18]

10. Stunting Personal Development

Premature sexual involvement not only can stunt the development of a relationship; it also can stunt one's development as a person.

Just as some young people handle anxieties by turning to drugs and alcohol, others handle them by turning to sex. Sex becomes an escape. They aren't learning how to cope with life's pressures.

Teenagers who are absorbed in an intense sexual relationship are turning inward on one thing at the very time in their lives when they should be reaching out—forming new friendships, joining clubs and teams, developing their interests and skills, taking on bigger social responsibilities.

All of these are important nutrients for a teenager's development as a person. And this period of life is special because young people have both the time and the opportunities to develop their talents and interests. The growing they do during these years will affect them all their lives. If young people don't put these years to good use, they may never develop their full potential.

The risk appears to be greater for girls who get sexually involved and in so doing close the door on other interests and relationships. Says New York psychiatrist Samuel Kaufman:

A girl who enters into a serious relationship with a boy very early in life may find out later that her individuality was thwarted. She became part of him and failed to develop her own interests, her sense of independent identity.[19]

REFLECTING ON her long experience in counseling college students and others about sexual matters, Dr. Carson Daly comments:

I don't think I ever met a student who was sorry he or she had postponed sexual activity, but I certainly met many who deeply regretted their sexual involvements. Time and time again, I have seen the long-term emotional and spiritual desolation that results from casual sex and promiscuity.

No one tells students that it sometimes takes years to recover from the effects of these sexual involvements—if one ever fully recovers.

Sex certainly can be a source of great pleasure and joy. But as should be amply clear—and youngsters need our help and guidance in understanding this—sex also can be the source of deep wounds and suffering. What makes the difference is the relationship within which it occurs. Sex is most joyful and fulfilling—most emotionally safe as well as physically safe—when it occurs within a loving, total, and binding commitment. Historically, we have called that marriage. Sexual union is then part of something bigger—the union of two persons' lives.

REFERENCES

1 Susan Weller, "A Meta-Analysis of Condom Effectiveness in Reducing Sexually Transmitted HIV," *Social Science and Medicine,* June 1993, p. 12.

2 See, for example, Kenneth Noller, *OB/GYN Clinical Alert-t,* September 1992; for a thorough discussion of the dangers of human papilloma virus, see "Condoms Ineffective Against Human Papilloma Virus," *Sexual Health Update* (April 1994), a publication of the Medical Institute for Sexual Health, P.O. Box 4919, Austin, Texas 78765.

3 "Some Teens Taking Vows of Virginity," *Washington Post* (November 21, 1993).

4 William Bennett, "Sex and the Education of Our Children," *America* (February 14, 1987), p. 124.

5 Bob Bartlett, "Going All the Way," *Momentum* (April/May, 1993), p. 36.

6 Abridged from Ann Landers, "A Not-So-Sweet Sexteen Story," *Daily News* (September 23, 1991), p. 20.

7 Eager's book is available from Mailbox Club Books, 404 Eager Rd., Valdosta, Ga. 31602.

8 Carson Daly, personal communication.

9 *Safe Sex: A Slide Program.* Medical Institute for Sexual Health, Austin, Texas: 1992.

10 Josh McDowell and Dick Day, *Why Wait: What You Need to Know About the Teen Sexuality Crisis* (Here's Life Publishers, San Bernardino, Calif.: 1987).

11 Medical Institute for Sexual Health, P.O. Box 4919, Austin Texas 78765.

12 *American Association of University Women Report on Sexual Harassment,* June 1993.

13 J. Kikuchi, "Rhode Island Develops Successful Intervention Program for Adolescents," *National Coalition Against Sexual Assault Newsletter* (Fall 1988).

14 McDowell and Day, op. cit.

15 Abridged from *Choosing the Best: A Values-Based Sex Education Curriculum,* 1993. (5500 Interstate North Parkway, Suite 515, Atlanta, Ga. 30328).

16 Kieran Sawyer, *Sex and the Teenager* (Ave Maria Press, Notre Dame, Ind.: 1990).

17 McDowell and Day, op. cit.

18 Ann Landers, "Despite Urgin', He's a Virgin." *Daily News* (January 15, 1994).

19 Quoted in Howard and Martha Lewis, *The Parent's Guide to Teenage Sex and Pregnancy* (St. Martin's Press, New York: 1980).

SEXUAL
Correctness

Has it gone too far?

SARAH CRICHTON

Watch what you say, watch what you do. Will the new rules of feminist politics set women free—or set them back?

THE WOMEN AT BROWN UNIversity play hardball. Three years ago, fed up with an administration that wasn't hopping into action, they scrawled the names of alleged rapists on the bathroom stalls. Brown woke up, revamped its disciplinary system and instituted mandatory sexual-assault education for freshmen. But that really hasn't calmed the siege mentality. This fall, Alan S., class of '94, returned to Brown after a one-year suspension for "non-consensual physical contact of a sexual nature," the first student to come back after such disciplinary action. And two weeks ago, all over Brown—on the doors of dorms, on bulletin boards, by the mailroom in Faunce House—posters cropped up. Under a mug shot cut from a class book, it read, "These are the facts: [Alan S.] was convicted of 'sexual misconduct' by the UDC, was sentenced to a one-year suspension; he has served his term and is back on campus." It was signed "rosemary and time." As these posters go, it was low-key. But that doesn't matter. Alan S. had been publicly branded as an "assaulter."

No big deal, said senior Jennifer Rothblatt, hanging out in the Blue Room, a campus snack bar. "As a protest against the system, it's valid and necessary," she said, brushing her long, golden-brown hair off her face. Besides, she added, the posters simply state the facts.

Well, wait. What are the facts? Who is the victimizer here and who is the victim? In the ever-morphing world of Thou Shalt Not Abuse Women it's getting mighty confusing. Crimes that hurt women are bad; we know that. But just as opportunities keep expanding for women, the list of what hurts them seems to grow, too. A Penn State professor claims Goya's luscious "The Naked Maja," a print of which hangs in her classroom, hurts her ability to teach; it sexually harasses her. A Northwestern University law professor is trying to make street remarks—your basic "hey baby" stuff—legally punishable as assaultive behavior that limits a woman's liberty. Verbal

coercion can now constitute rape. But what is verbal coercion—"Do me or die"? Or, "C'mon, Tiffany, if you won't, I'm gonna go off with Heather." If the woman didn't want it, it's sexual assault. And thanks to nature, he's got the deadly weapon.

Feminist politics have now homed in like missiles on the twin issues of date rape and sexual harassment, and the once broadbased women's movement is splintering over the new sexual correctness. "The Morning After: Sex, Fear and Feminism on Campus," a controversial new book by Katie Roiphe, argues that issues like date rape reduce women to helpless victims in need of protective codes of behavior. The much-publicized rules governing sexual intimacy at Antioch College seem to stultify relations between men and women on the cusp of adulthood. Like political correctness on campuses, there's pitifully little room for debate or diverse points of view. For expressing her ideas, Roiphe has received threats. A NEWSWEEK photographer at Antioch—a woman who had permission to photograph—was attacked by a mob of students and, yes, sexually harassed by several who exposed themselves.

The workplace, the campuses and the courts are the new testing grounds of sexual correctness. Complaints of harassment on the job have ballooned in the last three years as men and women try to sort out when they can and cannot flirt, flatter, offer a friendly pat. Too many rules? Maybe. The obsession with correct codes of behavior seems to portray women not as thriving on their hard-won independence but as victims who can't take care of themselves. Will the new rules set women free? Or will they set them back?

Young men and women used to be sent off to college with a clear sense of how it would be. Back in the dark ages, when guys still wielded mighty swords and girls still protected their virtue (which is to say, the mid-1960s), in a military school overlooking the Tennessee River, a colonel gathered his graduating cadets for the everything-you-need-to-know-about-sex lecture.

"Gentlemen," he drawled, "soon you'll go off and get married and before you do, you need to understand the differences between men and women."

He began to draw a chart on the blackboard. At the top of one column he wrote MEN, at the top of another, WOMEN. It looked like this:

MEN	WOMEN
love	LOVE
·SEX	sex

"That's what men and women believe in," he said, and then went on to describe a typical wedding night. When the bride finally climbs into bed and sees the groom, he warned, "chances are she'll scream and probably throw up. Don't worry: this is perfectly natural."

Bette Midler had a name for a night like that. Back in the early '70s, she sang of romantic disappointment in a little ditty called "Bad Sex." Everyone had bad sex back then and, to hear them tell, survived just fine. Now feminists on campus quote Andrea Dworkin: "The hurting of women is . . . basic to the sexual pleasure of men."

Rape and sexual harassment are real. But between crime and sexual bliss are some cloudy waters. To maneuver past the shoals, corporations and universities try a two-pronged approach: re-education and regulations. Some rules make sense: "It is unacceptable to have sex with a person if he/she is unconscious." Others seem silly. After attending mandatory sexual-harassment seminars at Geffen Records where she works, Bryn Bridenthal is rethinking every move she makes. "Everybody is looking for anything to be misinterpreted." Bridenthal used to quite innocently stroke the arm of a man who had a penchant for wearing luxuriously soft cashmere sweaters. "I never thought anything about it, but through the seminars I realized that I shouldn't do that," she says. "It's not worth doing anything that might be construed by anyone as sexual harassment."

If it's chilly in the workplace, it's downright freezing on campus. No school has

concocted guidelines quite as specific as Antioch College's. Deep among the cornfields and pig farms of central Ohio in the town of Yellow Springs. Antioch prides itself on being "A Laboratory for Democracy." The dress code is grunge and black; multiple nose rings are *de rigueur,* and green and blue hair are preferred (if you have hair). Seventy percent of the student body are womyn (for the uninitiated, that's women—without the dreaded m-e-n). And the purpose of the Sexual Offense Policy is to empower these students to become equal partners when it comes time to mate with males. The goal is 100 percent consensual sex, and it works like this: it isn't enough to ask someone if she'd like to have sex, as an Antioch women's center advocate told a group of incoming freshmen this fall. You must obtain consent every step of the way. "If you want to take her blouse off, you have to ask. If you want to touch her breast you have to ask. If you want to move your hand down to her genitals, you have to ask. If you want to put your finger inside her, you have to ask." Well, Molly Bloom would do fine.

How silly this all seems; how sad. It criminalizes the delicious unexpectedness of sex—a hand suddenly moves to here, a mouth to there. What is the purpose of sex if not to lose control? (To be unconscious, no.) The advocates of sexual correctness are trying to take the danger out of sex, but sex is inherently dangerous. It leaves one exposed to everything from euphoria to crashing disappointment. That's its great unpredictability. But of course, that's sort of what we said when we were all made to wear seat belts.

What is implicit in the new sex guidelines is that it's the male who does the initiating and the woman who at any moment may bolt. Some young women rankle at that. "I think it encourages wimpy behavior by women and [the idea] that women need to be handled with kid gloves," says Hope Segal, 22, a fourth-year Antioch student. Beware those boys with their swords, made deaf by testosterone and, usually, blinded by drink.

Drink—the abuse of it, the abuses that occur because of it—is key. In up to 70 percent of acquaintance rapes, alcohol plays a role, says Manhattan sex-crimes prosecutor Linda Fairstein, author of "Sexual Violence: Our War Against Rape." And because alcohol poses such a powerful problem, it is the rule at almost every school (and the law in most states) that "consent is not meaningful" if given while under the influence of alcohol, drugs or prescription medication. If she's drunk, she's not mentally there, and her consent counts for zip. If the man is just as drunk as the woman, that's no excuse. Mary P. Koss is a professor of psychology at the University of Arizona and the author of a highly regarded, if controversial, survey of rape

and college-age students. "The Scope of Rape" indicates that one in four college-age students has been the victim of a rape or an attempted rape. In those numbers Koss includes women who have been coerced into having sex while intoxicated. "The law punishes the drunk driver who kills a pedestrian," she argues. "And likewise, the law needs to be there to protect the drunk woman from the driver of the penis."

"Men and women just think differently," Antioch president Alan Guskin says, "and we've got to help the students understand the differences." It's a policy, he says, designed to create a "safe" campus environment. But for all the attempts to make them

---

A lot of young college women today just feel like sitting ducks

---

feel secure, a lot of young college women just feel like sitting ducks. "As a potential survivor . . ." a Barnard student said to a visiting reporter. As a *what?* Potential survivor equals an inevitable victim. Every Wednesday night at Dartmouth, a group of undergraduate women gather to warn one another about potential date rapists. At the University of Michigan, and several other schools as well, when sorority women attend frat parties, a designated "sober" monitor stands guard over her friends. "Whenever people start going upstairs, you go up to them right away," says Marcy Myers. "You ask, 'Do you know this guy? You're drunk, do you want to go home? You can call him tomorrow'." "My friends won't go to parties at Dartmouth without other women," says Abby Ross, and before they leave the dorm, they check each other's outfits, too. No one wears short skirts. "You should be able to wear whatever you want. But the reality is that you're not dealing with people who have the same set of values," says Ross.

This defensive mind-set is at the heart of the escalating battle over date rape. Critics charge feminists with hyping the statistics and so broadening the definition of rape that sex roles are becoming positively Victorian. Women are passive vessels with no responsibility for what happens; men are domineering brutes with just one thing on their minds. "People have asked me if I have ever been date-raped," writes Katie Roiphe in "The Morning After." "And thinking back on complicated nights, on too many glasses of wine, on strange and familiar beds, I would have to say yes. With such a sweeping definition of rape, I wonder how many people there are, male or female, who haven't been date-raped at one point or another . . . If verbal coercion constitutes rape, then the word 'rape' itself expands to include any kind of sex a woman experiences as negative."

Roiphe, 25, a Harvard graduate and now a doctoral candidate at Princeton, argues that a hysteria has gripped college campuses, fomented by "rape-crisis feminists." "The image that emerges from feminist preoccupations with rape and sexual harassment is that of women as victims, offended by a professor's dirty joke, verbally pressured into sex by peers. This image of a delicate woman bears a striking resemblance to that '50s ideal my mother and the other women of her generation fought so hard to get away from. They didn't like her passivity . . . her excessive need for protection . . . But here she is again, with her pure intentions and her wide eyes. Only this time it is the feminists themselves who are breathing new life into her."

ROIPHE IS GETTING WHOMPED FOR her provocative, though too-loosely documented, book. A "traitor," says Gail Dines, a professor of sociology and women's studies at Wheelock College, who lectures about rape and pornography. She calls Roiphe the "Clarence Thomas of women," just trying to suck up to the "white-male patriarchy." She thinks Roiphe will get her comeuppance. Warns Dines, in a most unsisterly fashion: "[When] she walks down the street, she's one more woman."

So how much of a threat is rape? What are women facing on dates with acquaintances or on the streets with strangers? Throughout her book, Roiphe wrestles with Koss's one-in-four statistic. "If I was really standing in the middle of an epidemic, a crisis," she asks, "if 25 percent of my female friends were really being raped, wouldn't I know about it?"

Heresy! Denial! Backlash! In an essay in The New Yorker, Katha Pollitt fired back: "As an experiment, I applied Roiphe's anecdotal method myself, and wrote down what I knew about my own circle of acquaintance: eight rapes by strangers (including one on a college campus), two sexual assaults (one Central Park, one Prospect Park), one abduction (woman walking down street forced into car full of men), one date rape involving a Mickey Finn, which resulted in pregnancy and abortion, and two stalkings (one ex-lover, one deranged fan); plus one brutal beating by a boyfriend, three incidents of childhood incest (none involving therapist-aided "recovered memories"), and one bizarre incident in which a friend went to a man's apartment after meeting him at a party and was forced by him to spend the night under the shower, naked, while he debated whether to kill her, rape her, or let her go."

Holy moly. Pollitt is one of the wisest essayists around; a fine poet, too. And far be it for us to question her list. So what does the list prove? Well, that even wise feminists fall precisely into the same trap as Roiphe: you can't extrapolate from your circle of acquaintance; friends don't constitute a statistical

average. What's more, Pollitt is almost 20 years older than Roiphe; her friends presumably have lived more years, too. Still, Pollitt's litany is shocking. It's punch-my-victim-card time: How full's yours.

"When one woman is raped on campus, all women are afraid to go to the library and finish their chemistry homework," Pat Reuss, a senior policy analyst with the NOW Legal Defense Fund, told a workshop at the NOW National Convention this summer. Today, college students are handed, as part of their orientation programs, pamphlets that spell out the threat and, over and over, the same dire figures appear: As Penn State's Sexual Assault Awareness pamphlet reads, in can't-miss-it type: "FBI statistics indicate that one in three women in our society will be raped during her lifetime."

Except there are no such FBI figures. The figures the FBI does have to offer are both out-of-date and so conservative that most people dismiss them. The FBI recognizes rape only as involving forcible penetration of the vagina with a penis. Oral sex, anal sex, penetration with an object—these do not officially constitute rape. It doesn't matter to the FBI if a woman was made incapacitated by alcohol or drugs, and the agency certainly isn't interested in verbal coercion. Rape is as narrowly defined by the FBI as could be imagined.

So, in the rape-crisis mentality, the numbers keep being bloated. Which is crazy, considering the fact that even the most conservative numbers are horrifying. College students are a high-risk group. The No. 1 group to be sexually assaulted in this country are 16- to 19-year-olds. The second largest group hit are the 20- to 24-year-old age bracket. Women are four times more likely to be assaulted during these years than at any other time in their lives. Forty-five percent of all rapists arrested are under 25. And as for the most conservative, yet trustworthy, numbers: according to the National Victim Center survey last year—a survey that did not include intoxication—13 percent of adult women are victims of forcible rape. That's one in seven.

THAT'S A LOT. BUT IT DOESN'T mean all women are victims—or survivors, as we are supposed to call them. And it sure doesn't mean all "suffering" warrants attention or retribution—or even much sympathy. When New York state Assemblyman Harvey Weisenberg misspoke during a speech and said "sex" instead of "six," he covered up his error by looking at Assemblywoman Earlene Hill (Democrat of Hempstead) and joked, "Whenever I think of Earlene, I think of sex." Another brutish colleague wouldn't move his legs so she could get to her seat and made her climb over him. Sexual harassment, she cried, saying: "If I don't

speak up, then they won't realize it's wrong and there will be a new victim." Oh, please. A student at the University of Virginia told The New York Times that she favored a ban on all student/faculty dating because "One of my professors asked me out and it made me really uncomfortable." So tell him to bug off. Artist Sue Williams plopped a six-feet-in-diameter piece of plastic vomit on the floor of the Whitney Museum as her protest against the male-dominated beauty-obsessed culture that makes women stick fingers down their throats. Tell them to get some therapy and cut it out. You want to talk victimization? Talk to the mothers all over America whose children have been slaughtered in urban cross-fire.

"I'm sick of women wallowing in the victim state," says Betty Friedan. "We have empowered ourselves. We are able to blow the whistle on rape. I am not as concerned with that as I am with violence in our whole society."

It does seem ironic that the very movement created to encourage women to stand up and fight their own battles has taken this strange detour, and instead is making them feel vulnerable and in need of protection. From the grade schools to the workplace, women are asking that everything be codified: How to act; what to say. Who to date; how to date; when to mate. They're huddling in packs, insisting on a plethora of rules on which to rely, and turning to authority figures to complain when anything goes wrong. We're not creating a society of Angry Young Women. These are Scared Little Girls.

If she's drunk, she's not mentally there, and her consent counts for zip

---

For all the major advances in the status of women in the last 25 years, the shifts in attitudes don't seem to have percolated down to our kids. Parents still raise girls to become wives, and sons to be sons. "I think to some extent we're dealing with a cultural lag," says Janet Hansche, a clinical psychologist and director of the Counseling and Testing Center at Tulane University. "Society still trains women to be pliant, to be nice, to try to avoid saying no, and my guess is that that's most everywhere."

And we're not doing any better raising boys. Obviously something's still screwy in this society. Boys are still being brought up to believe it's the height of cool to score—as if ejaculation were a notable achievement for an adolescent male. Young men still "get tremendous status from aggressiveness," says Debra Haffner, executive director of S[I]ECUS (the Sex Information and Education Council of the U.S.). "But no one teaches them how to live in the real world." It is a weird real world when "nice" boys in a "nice" community, good students, good athletes, good family, rape a mentally handicapped girl with a broomstick handle and a plastic baseball bat, and try to claim it was consensual. "Aren't they virile specimens?" Don Belman boasted to a New York Times reporter about his three Spur Posse sons, one of whom was awaiting trial for allegedly trying to run over several girls with a pickup truck while another had been arrested on sexual charges.

All right. Not all boys turn into Glen Ridge, Spur Posse, Tailhook-grabbing beings. But when it comes to human sexuality, the messages that are being sent to kids—male and female—remain cloaked in myth. In 1993, girls who want sex are still sluts, those who don't are still teases. And those who finally make it to college are completely befuddled.

Which is why it's time for everyone who doesn't have a serious problem to pipe down.

What is happening on the campuses is scary, because it is polarizing men and women. Rather than encouraging them to work together, to trust one another, to understand one another, it is intensifying suspicion. Brown sophomore David Danon complains, "Women have all the power here on sexual conduct . . . It's very dangerous for us." If women are so profoundly distrustful of men, how will they raise boys? And if men are so defensive about women, how will they raise little girls? The most pressing problem the majority of American women face isn't rape or sexual harassment. It's the fact that, in addition to holding down full-time work, they still are burdened with the lion's share of parenting and housework responsibility. Add it up, says sociologist Arlie Hochschild, and it comes to a full month's worth of 24-hour days. Line up the 100 most involved fathers you know and ask one question: what size shoes do your children wear?

Real life is messy, rife with misunderstandings and contradictions. There's no eight-page guide on how to handle it. There are no panels of mediators out there to turn to unless it gets truly bad. Those who are growing up in environments where they don't have to figure out what the rules should be, but need only follow what's been prescribed, are being robbed of the most important lesson there is to learn. And that's how to live.

With DEBRA ROSENBERG in Providence, STANLEY HOLMES in Yellow Springs, Ohio, MARTHA BRANT in New York, DONNA FOOTE in Los Angeles, NINA BIDDLE in New Orleans and bureau reports

IN DEFENSE OF TEENAGED MOTHERS

MIKE MALES

At the Crittenton Center for Young Women near downtown Los Angeles, seventeen-year-old LaSalla Jackson sets down her tiny infant and shows the scars on her calves where her drug-addicted mother beat her with an extension cord. Jackson left home when she had her baby to live at the Crittenton Center. After she graduates from the Center's high school, she plans to marry her child's twenty-three-year-old father, who visits twice a week. "I was watching five little brothers, sisters, cousins at home," she says. "Here it's one, and I'm not getting hit around."

Almonica, another Crittenton resident, saw her mother set on fire and murdered by her stepfather during a drunken fight. At age sixteen, she got pregnant by a twenty-one-year-old man. "It was a way out," she says.

To President Clinton, these unwed teenaged mothers represent an assault on family integrity and public coffers. "Can you believe that a child who has a child gets more money from the Government for leaving home than for staying home with a parent or grandparent? That's not just bad policy, it's wrong," the President declared in his State of the Union address. "We will say to teenagers: If you have a child out of wedlock, we'll no longer give you a check to set up a separate household." Clinton has won praise from liberals and conservatives alike for his "family values" campaign, which includes welfare sanctions to force unwed teen mothers back into their parents' homes. Some Congressional Republicans have proposed cutting off welfare to all teen mothers to achieve the same end. "We want families to stay together," Clinton says.

Mike Males, a graduate student in the University of California-Irvine's School of Social Ecology, reports on youth issues for In These Times.

But the supervising social worker at the Crittenton Center, Yale Gancherov, takes a different view. "The parents of these young women were violent, were drug abusers, were sexually abusive, were absent or neglectful. While privileged people may see a detriment in a teenager becoming a mother, these girls see it as a realistic improvement in their lives."

Current rhetoric about sex, values, and teenaged parenthood in the United States ignores several crucial realities. Contrary to welfare reformers' contention, many teenaged mothers cannot return home. Washington reasearchers Debra Boyer and David Fine's detailed 1992 study of pregnant teens and teenaged mothers showed that two-thirds had been raped or sexually abused, nearly always by parents, other guardians, or relatives.

Six in ten teen mothers' childhoods also included severe physical violence: being beaten with a stick, strap, or fist, thrown against walls, deprived of food, locked in closets, or burned with cigarettes or hot water.

Most teen mothers stay with their families even under difficult conditions. More than 60 per cent of the young mothers in Boyer and Fine's study lived with their parents, foster parents, or in institutions.

Nearly all the rest lived with adult relatives, husbands, or friends, often with combinations of the above. "Very few live apart from adults," says Fine. Those who did, Fine says, are often escaping intolerable situations at home. "Young mothers who live away from home are significantly more likely to have been physically or sexually abused at home than those who live with parents."

Despite all the talk of "children having children" the large majority of births—as well as sexually transmitted disease, including AIDS—among teenaged girls is caused by adults. The most recent National Center for Health Statistics data show that only one-third of births among teenaged mothers involved teenaged fathers. Most were caused by adult men over the age of twenty.

In order to mold teenaged pregnancy into a safe, expedient issue, some uncomfortable facts have been suppressed—even by groups that know better.

Child advocates such as the Children's Defense Fund might be expected to speak out against official distortions of "teen" parenthood. Not so. Despite its excellent research papers, which show the complexity of the problems teenaged mothers face, a popular poster campaign by the Children's Defense Fund promotes a two-dimensional—and misleading—picture of the issue. IT'S LIKE BEING GROUNDED FOR EIGHTEEN YEARS, says one poster, depicting teenaged mothers as naughty airheads. WAIT'LL YOU SEE HOW FAST HE CAN RUN WHEN YOU TELL HIM YOU'RE PREGNANT, says another, showing a stereotypical picture of a callous varsity jock.

"Teen-adult sex is not being dealt with," says Angie Karwan of Michigan's Planned

Parenthood. Part of the reason, Karwan theorizes, is that the Federal preoccupation with teenaged sex influences programs that receive grant funding. "That's how the money is awarded," she told a reporter from Michigan's *Oakland Press.*

The spin put on teen pregnancy, in turn, has some serious consequences for social policy. Present policy blames teenaged mothers for causing a multi-billion-dollar social problem. Says Health and Human Services Secretary Donna Shalala, "We will never successfully deal with welfare reform until we reduce the amount of teenaged pregnancy."

In fact, the opposite seems to hold: Poverty causes early childbearing. The rapid increase in child and youth poverty, from 14 per cent in 1973 to 21 per cent in 1991, was followed—after a ten-year lag—by today's rise in teenaged childbearing. Like Ronald Reagan's anecdotes about "welfare Cadillac" black mothers, the allegation by Clinton's welfare-reform task force and members of Congress that teens have babies to collect the "incentive" of $150 a month in AFDC benefits has been repeatedly disproven.

Recent studies show that, rather than "risking the future" (the title of a 1987 National Research Council report), most adolescent mothers may be exercising their best option in bleak circumstances when they latch onto older men who promise them a "way out" of homes characterized by poverty, violence, and rape.

"Troubled, abused girls who have babies become more centered emotionally," says social worker Gancherov.

"They often gain the attention of professionals and social services. Such girls are more likely to stay in school with a baby than without. Their behavioral health improves."

A 1990 study of 2,000 youths found that teenaged mothers show significantly lower rates of substance abuse, stress, depression, and suicide than their peers.

"Becoming a mother is not the ideal way to accomplish these goals," Gancherov emphasizes. But impoverished girls who get pregnant may not be the heedless, self-destructive figures politicians and the media portray.

To decrease the incidence of teen pregnancy, we must improve environments for teens, Gancherov argues. Girls who see a brighter future ahead have reason to delay childbearing. Dramatically lower rates of teenaged pregnancy in the suburbs, as opposed to the inner city, bear this out.

The Clinton Administration's budget and its rhetoric offer little to millions of youth subjected to poverty and physical, emotional, and sexual violence—conditions many girls form liaisons with older men to escape. Instead, the myth Clinton and those around him continue to foster is that of reckless teenaged mothers guilty of abusing adult moral values and welfare generosity. Female "survival strategies," in the words of sociologist Meda Chesney-Lind, are what the Government seeks to punish.

In an Administration led by the most knowledgeable child advocates ever, the concerted attack on adolescents has never been angrier, more illogical, or more potentially devastating to a generation of young mothers and their babies, who cannot fight back.

How Should We Teach Our Children About SEX?

Bombarded by mixed messages about values, students are more sexually active than ever, and more confused

Nancy Gibbs

SOME INGREDIENTS IN THE STEAMING HORMONAL STEW THAT IS American adolescence:

For Prom Night last week, senior class officers at Benicia High School in California assembled some party favors—a gift-wrapped condom, a Planned Parenthood pamphlet advocating abstinence and a piece of candy. "We know Prom Night is a big night for a lot of people, sexually," senior Lisa Puryear told the San Jose *Mercury News*. "We were trying to spread a little responsible behavior." But administrators confiscated the 375 condoms, arguing that the school-sponsored event is no place for sex education.

Fifty students in Nashville, Tennessee, stand in front of a gathering of Baptist ministers to make a pledge: "Believing that true love waits, I make a commitment to God, myself, my family, those I date, my future mate and my future children to be sexually pure until the day I enter a covenant marriage relationship."

Tonya, 17, began having sex when she was 12, but rarely uses a condom. "I know a lot of people who have died of AIDS," she says, "but I'm not that worried." Every six months she gets an AIDS test. "The only time I'm worried is right before I get the results back."

Last Wednesday the student leaders at Bremerton High in Seattle voted that no openly gay student could serve in their school government. The goal, they stated, was "to preserve the integrity and high moral standards that BHS is built upon."

Teenagers in York County, Pennsylvania, celebrate the Great Sex-Out, a sex-free day to reflect on abstinence. Among activities suggested as alternatives to sex are baking cookies and taking moonlit walks. Since the event was held on a Monday, it wasn't much of a problem. But Friday, said one student, "that would be harder."

Owen, 19, of Kill Devil Hills, North Carolina, carries a key chain bearing the inscription, A TISKET, A TASKET, A CONDOM OR A CASKET.

Just Do It. Just Say No. Just Wear a Condom. When it comes to sex, the message to America's kids is confused and confusing. The moral standards society once generally accepted, or at least paid lip service to, fell victim to a sexual revolution and a medical tragedy. A decade marked by fear of AIDS and furor over society's values made it hard to agree on the ethical issues and emotional context that used to be part of learning about sex. Those on the right reacted to condom giveaways and gay curriculums and throbbing MTV videos as signs of moral breakdown. Those on the left dismissed such concerns as the rantings of religious zealots and shunned almost any discussion of sexual restraint as being reactionary or, worse yet, unsophisticated. "Family values" became a polarizing phrase.

Now, however, the children of the sexual revolution are beginning to grapple with how to teach their own children about sex. Faced with evidence that their kids are suffering while they bicker, parents and educators are seeking some common ground about what works and what doesn't. It is becoming possible to discuss the need for responsibility and commitment without being cast as a religious fanatic and to accept the need for safe-sex instruction without being considered an amoral pragmatist.

In one sense, the arrival of AIDS in the American psyche a decade ago ended the debate over sex education. Health experts were clear about the crisis: By the time they are 20, three-quarters of young Americans have had sex; one-fourth of teens contract some venereal disease each year. About 20% of all AIDS patients are under 30, but because the incubation period is eight years or more, the CDC believes a large proportion were infected with HIV as teenagers.

In such a climate of fear, moral debate seemed like a luxury. Get them the information, give them protection, we can talk about morality later. There is a fishbowl full of condoms in the nurse's office, help yourself. While only three states mandated sex ed in 1980, today 47 states formally require or recommend it; all 50 support AIDS education.

But as parents and educators watch the fallout from nearly a decade of lessons geared to disaster prevention—here is a diagram of female anatomy, this is how you put on a condom—

there are signs that this bloodless approach to learning about sex doesn't work. Kids are continuing to try sex at an ever more tender age: more than a third of 15-year-old boys have had sexual intercourse, as have 27% of 15-year-old girls—up from 19% in 1982. Among sexually active teenage girls, 61% have had multiple partners, up from 38% in 1971. Among boys, incidents like the score-keeping Spur Posse gang in California and the sexual-assault convictions of the Glen Ridge, New Jersey, jock stars suggest that whatever is being taught, responsible sexuality isn't being learned.

Beyond what studies and headlines can convey, it is the kids who best express their confusion and distress. Audrey Lee, 15, has taken a sex-education class at San Leandro High School in California, but, she asserts, "there's no real discussion about emotional issues and people's opinions." The program consists mostly of films and slides with information on sex and birth control. It lacks any give-and-take on issues like date rape and how to say no to sexual pressure. "The school doesn't emphasize anything," she says. "If you have a question, you go to your friends, but they don't have all the answers." As for her family, "sex is not mentioned."

Adults have one foot in the Victorian era while kids are in the middle of a world-wide pandemic," complains pediatrician Karen Hein, of Albert Einstein College of Medicine in New York City, who has seen too many teens infected with HIV and other sexually transmitted diseases come through her hospital. She laments the fact that sex ed is only "about vaginas, ovaries and abstinence—not about intimacy and expressing feelings." Kids, she says, "don't know what they're supposed to be doing, and adults are really not helping them much."

America has long wrestled with the tension between its Puritan and pioneer heritages, and its attitude toward sex has often seemed muddled. Victorian parents, fearful of their children's sexuality, would try to delay the onset of puberty by underfeeding their children. By 1910 exploding rates of syphilis drove the crusade for sex education in much the way AIDS does today. In 1940 the U.S. Public Health Service argued the urgent need for schools to get involved, and within a few years the first standardized programs rolled into classrooms. But by the 1960s came the backlash from the John Birch Society, Mothers Organized for Moral Stability and other groups. By the early '70s they had persuaded at least 20 state legislatures to either restrict or abolish sex education.

"There's something wrong," sex educator Sol Gordon once said, "with a country that says, 'Sex is dirty, save it for someone you love.' " But families at least agreed on a social standard that preached, if not practiced, the virtues of restraint and of linking sex to emotional commitment and marriage. "It used to be easy to say it's just wrong to have sex before marriage. You could expect churches to say that, adults from many walks of life to somehow communicate that," notes Peter Benson, president of Minneapolis-based Search Institute, a research organization specializing in child and adolescent issues. "We went through a sexual revolution since the '60s that poked a major hole in that. And nothing has come along to replace it. What's responsible sexuality now? Does it mean no sex unless you're in love? No sex unless you're 21? No sex unless it's protected?

Nothing approaching a consensus has emerged to guide kids in their decisions. A TIME/CNN poll of 500 U.S. teenagers found that 71% had been told by their parents to wait until they were older before having sex: more than half had been told not to have sex until they were married. The teens were almost evenly split between those who say it is O.K. for kids ages 16 and under to have sex and those who say they should be 18 or older.

Some social scientists argue that there is nothing wrong with increased sexual expression among teens. "Feeling, thinking and being sexual is an endemic part of being a teenager," says UCLA psychologist Paul Abramson. "Let's say a couple has paired off, wants to be monogamous and uses condoms. I'd say that's a legitimate part of their sexual expression as a couple in the '90s."

There are many factors, besides increased permissiveness, that make the trend toward increased casual sex among kids seem almost inevitable. Since the turn of the century, better health and nutrition have lowered the average age of sexual maturity. The onset of menstruation in girls has dropped three months each decade, so the urges that once landed at 14 may now hit at 12. At the same time, the years of premarital sexual maturity are much greater than a generation ago. The typical age of a first marriage has jumped to 25, from 21 in the 1950s.

School cutbacks and working parents have left teens with a looser after-school life. Many use that time for afternoon jobs, but less to pay for college than for a car, for freedom and the chance to socialize more with peers, who may pressure each other into ever greater sexual exploration. Sandra, 17, in Des Moines, Iowa, pregnant and due in November, says she has slept with 33 boys. She keeps count and doesn't think her behavior is all that unusual. "A lot of girls do the same. They think if they don't have sex with a person, that person will not want to talk to them anymore."

In the inner cities the scarcity of jobs and hope for the future invites kids to seek pleasure with little thought for the fallout. "You'd think AIDS would be a deterrent, but it's not," says Marie Bronshvag, a health teacher at West Side High School in upper Manhattan. Their lives are empty, she observes, and their view of the future fatalistic. "I believe in God," says student Mark Schaefer, 19. "If he wants something bad to happen to me, it will happen. Anyway, by the time I get AIDS I think they'll have a cure."

Nor is fear of pregnancy any more compelling. "The kids feel," says Margaret Pruitt Clark, executive director of the Center for Population Options, "that the streets are so violent that they are either gonna be dead or in jail in their 20s, so why not have a kid." Most striking, she adds, is the calculation that young women in the inner cities are making. "They feel that if the number of men who will be available to them as the years go on will be less and less, the girls might as well have a child when they can, no matter how young they are."

Finally, there is the force that is easiest to blame and hardest to measure: the saturation of American popular culture with sexual messages, themes, images, exhortations. Teenagers typically watch five hours of television a day—which in a year means they have seen nearly 14,000 sexual encounters, according to the Center for Population Options. "Kids are seeing a

How often did you use birth control when you had sex?*

Every time	61%
Sometimes	26%
Never	13%

*Asked only of teens who said they have had sexual intercourse.

Where have you learned the most about sex?

	13-15	AGE 16-17
Parents	30%	22%
Friends	26%	37%
School	26%	15%
Entertainment	15%	18%

From a telephone poll of 500 American teenagers (age 13 to 17) taken for TIME/CNN on April 13-14 by Yankelovich Partners Inc. Sampling error is ± 4.5%.

Have you ever had sexual intercourse?

YES

Age 13-15	19%
Age 16-17	55%

How old were you when you first had sex?*

Under 14	23%
14	24%
16	20%
17	6%

How many different people have you had sex with?*

1	42%
2 to 3	29%
4	6%
5 or more	15%

*Asked only of those 151 teens who said they had had sexual intercourse. Sampling error ± 8%.

What are the reasons kids you know have sex?**

	GIRLS	BOYS
They were curious and wanted to experiment	80%	76%
They wanted to be more popular or impress their friends	58%	58%
They were in love	65%	50%
They were under pressure from those they were dating	65%	35%

**Asked only of those 373 teens who know another teen who has had sexual intercourse. Sampling error is ± 5%.

world in which everything is sensual and physical," says Dr. Richard Ratner, who this week takes office as president of the American Society for Adolescent Psychiatry. "Even in this era of feminism, rap songs preach, 'Take this bitch and ——— her.' Everything is more explicit. It's the difference between wearing a bathing suit and walking around nude."

The content of popular culture has been a favorite target among politicians caught up in the culture wars, but kids themselves have their own criticisms of what they see. Many recoil at the sexual pressures they feel from Calvin Klein ads, MTV, heavy-breathing movies, all the icy, staged or oddball sex they see in books by Madonna and rock videos. "If you turn on TV, there's a woman taking off her clothes," says Marcela Avila, a senior at Santa Monica High, who was among a group of students who sat down with TIME's Jim Willwerth to discuss the sexual landscape they face. "It makes you doubt yourself. Am I O.K.? You put yourself down—I'll never be able to satisfy a guy." Her classmate Elizabeth Young agrees. "The media doesn't make it seem like it's really about love," she says. "Nowadays sexuality is the way you look, the way you wear your hair. It's all physical, not what's inside you."

Many kids, who can be lethal critics of the sexual mores of their parents' generation, say they are offended that adults have so little faith in them. "Not all teenagers have sex. They're not all going to do it just because everyone else is," says Kristen Thomas, 17, of Plymouth, Minnesota. "They kind of have a lack of faith in us—parents and general society."

Traditionally, it's been the role of parents to convey the messages about love and intimacy that kids seem to be missing in their education about sex. Although today's parents are the veterans of the decade that came after free love and before safe sex, that doesn't automatically make them any more able to *talk* about sex with their children; if anything, the reverse may be true. Hypocrisy is a burden they carry. "Do as I say," they instruct their teenagers, "not as I did."

As for those who sat out the sexual revolution, they may be too embarrassed or intimidated to talk to teens—or afraid of giving the wrong information. Phyllis Shea, director of teen programs for the Worcester, Massachusetts, affiliate of Girls Inc. (formerly Girls Clubs of America), recently ran a sex-education workshop for 12 girls and their mothers. In many cases, she says, mothers lag far behind their daughters in knowledge. Five of the mothers had never seen a condom. A mother who had been completely unwilling to discuss sex with her daughter told the group that she had been molested as a child. On the way home, she and her daughter drove around for two hours, deep in conversation.

Of all the mixed messages that teenagers absorb, the most confused have to do with gender roles. The stereotypes of male and female behavior have crumbled so quickly over the past generation that parents are at a loss. According to the TIME/CNN poll, 60% of parents tell their daughters to remain chaste until marriage, but less than half tell their sons the same thing. Kids reflect the double standard: more than two-thirds agree that a boy who has sex sees his reputation enhanced, while a girl who has sex watches hers suffer.

That is not stopping girls from acting as sexual aggressors, however. Teenagers in TIME's survey say girls are just as interested in sex as boys are—an opinion confirmed by recent research. "My friends and I are a lot less inhibited about saying what we want to do," says Rebecca Tuynman of Santa Monica High. "A lot of the change is admitting that we like it." Tuynman says that while she was taught that boys don't like girls who come on too strong, her brother set her straight. "He said he'd like it if girls came after him. I'll always be grateful to him for saying that." Her classmate Tammy Weisberger notes that like so many boy jocks, girls on her soccer team brag about whom they've slept with—but with a difference. "The guys say how many girls they did it with. With the girls, it's *who* they did it with."

For all the aggressive girl talk, some experts are worried that what the sexual revolution has really done for teenage girls is push them into doing things they may not really want to do. "The irony is that the sexual revolution pressured girls into accepting sex on boys' terms," argues Myriam Miedzian, author of *Boys Will Be Boys: Breaking the Link Between Masculinity and Violence*. "If they don't engage in sex, they're not cool. At least under the old morality, girls had some protection. They could say their parents would kill them if they had sex."

As for boys, researchers are finding that among parents, the fear that their son will grow up to be aggressively promiscuous is nothing compared with the fear he will turn out to be gay. Manhattan social worker Joy Fallek has seen boys who fear that they might be gay if they haven't had sex with a girl by age 16. Parents have told Miedzian that they will not let their boys watch TV's Mr. Rogers because of his gentle demeanor. "This is a major barrier to parents' raising their sons to be caring and sensitive people," she contends. "Other parents have told me that they're afraid not to have their sons play with guns because they'll grow up gay. And yet there's not the slightest shred of evidence for this."

Schools are attempting to fill in where parents have failed. But it has been hard for educators over these past few years to know what to teach when society itself cannot agree on a direction. Absent any agreement over what is "proper" sexual conduct, teachers can be left reciting, word for word, the approved text on homosexuality or abortion or masturbation. The typical sex-ed curriculum is remarkably minimalist. Most secondary schools offer somewhere between 6 and 20 hours of sex education a year. The standard curriculum now consists of one or two days in fifth grade dealing with puberty; two weeks in an eighth-grade health class dealing with anatomy, reproduction and AIDS prevention, and perhaps a 12th-grade elective course on current issues in sexuality.

Joycelyn Elders, President Clinton's nominee for Surgeon General, is leading the fight for a more comprehensive approach from kindergarten through 12th grade. As head of the Arkansas health department, she was one of the country's most outspoken advocates of wide-ranging sex education. "We've spent all our time fighting each other about whose values we should be teaching our kids," she complains. "We've [been]

allowed the right to make decisions about our children for the last 100 years, and all it has bought us is the highest abortion rate, the highest nonmarital birth rate and the highest pregnancy rate in the industrialized world." But Elders is no advocate of values-free instruction. "Proper sex education would be teaching kids to develop relationships and about the consequences of their behavior. Kids can't say no if they don't first learn how to feel good about themselves."

But the issue of teaching kids about sex remains politically explosive. This week the results are expected to be announced in an unusually bitter election for New York City community school boards in which the religious right joined with the Catholic Church to try to elect more tradition-minded representatives. Earlier this year, the system's highly regarded Chancellor Joseph Fernandez was ousted largely because of his effort to expand condom distribution and teach children about gay lifestyles. The New York City Board of Education last week chose as its new president a conservative Queens mother who had cast the deciding vote against the chancellor.

If there is one point of agreement among all parties in the debate, it is that sex education has to be about more than sex. The anatomy lesson must come in a larger context of building relationships based on dignity and respect. The message these programs have in common: learn everything you want and need to know, and then carefully consider waiting.

Some of the most innovative and successful efforts have been launched by private religious and social-service organizations. Girls Inc., with 165 chapters nationwide, launched Preventing Adolescent Pregnancy (PAP) in 1985 to help low-income teens avoid cycles of early pregnancy, poverty and hopelessness. The first section, called Growing Together, invites girls ages 12 to 14 to talk over issues of sexuality with their mothers. The second section, Will Power/Won't Power, is designed to help girls develop strategies for postponing sexual activity and preventing pregnancy. "It's our experience that kids this age really know it's too early to be having sex," says Heather Johnston Nicholson, director of the National Resource Center for Girls Inc., in Indianapolis. "But when you're that age, you don't want to be considered a complete dweeb. We're establishing a peer group that says it's O.K. not to be sexually active."

In the third segment, Taking Care of Business, 15- to 17-year-olds are encouraged to focus on their goals. The final step, Health Bridge, helps older teens establish ties with a community clinic to ensure that they will have continued access to affordable reproductive health care. "It gives kids an opportunity to think through the reasons for not becoming sexually active," says Nicholson. But she cautions that "this is not a Just Say No program. When kids ask questions, they get straight answers. While we're focusing on postponement, we're not doing it in a context of fear and scare tactics."

That approach distinguishes PAP from the more hard-line abstinence programs that are gaining ground all across the country (*see box*). While both types of programs are designed to help teens make healthy decisions, there remains a fault line over whether to include detailed information on contraception or to focus on abstinence in a way that assumes that no lessons on applying condoms will be necessary.

Making the Case for Abstinence

By Philip Elmer-Dewitt

AMID ALL THE ANGUISH, CONFUSION AND MIXED SIGNALS surrounding teenage sexuality, the simplicity of one group's message is striking: sex outside marriage is just plain wrong. To instruct children in the mechanics of birth control or abortion, it argues, is to lead them down the path of self-destruction. That's the philosophy of the abstinence-only movement, a coalition of conservative parents, teachers and religious groups that, in the absence of any national sex-education consensus, has been remarkably successful in having its approach adopted as the official curriculum in schools across the U.S.

But is it the best approach? Its adherents claim the message is both morally correct and demonstrably effective. Opponents argue that in an age in which most teenagers are already sexually active, preaching the case for chastity without teaching the case for condoms is dangerously naive. "All the parents I know are absolutely in favor of abstinence," says Carole Chervin, senior staff attorney for the Planned Parenthood Federation. "It's the abstinence *only* approach that's bothersome. We believe sex education should be comprehensive."

The fight has moved into the courts. In what could become a landmark case, Planned Parenthood of Northeast Florida and 21 citizens in Duval County, Florida, have sued the local school board for rejecting a broad-based sex-education curriculum developed by the board's staff in favor of a controversial abstinence-only program from Teen-Aid, Inc. of Spokane, Washington. Planned Parenthood complains that the material in the text is biased, sensationalist and, at times, misleading. Some school-board members argue that the real issue is whether the local community has the right to choose the sex-education curriculum it wants, however flawed.

Late last week a similar case in Shreveport, Louisiana, went against the abstinence-only movement when a district judge ruled that a prochastity text called "Sex Respect" was biased and inaccurate and ordered it pulled from the Caddo-Parish junior high schools. The court is scheduled to rule this week on the fate of the abstinence-only text still being used in the high schools.

Abstinence is hardly a new idea, but the organized abstinence-only movement dates back to a Reagan-era program that set aside $2 million a year for the development of classroom materials to teach adolescents to say no to sex. Today there are more than a dozen competing curriculums on the market, each offering lesson plans, activities and workbook exercises designed to encourage abstinence among teenagers.

"Sex Respect," developed by Project Respect in Golf, Illinois, is one of the most widely used, having been adopted by a couple of thousand schools nationwide. Class activities include listing ways humans are different from animals, making bumper stickers that read CONTROL YOUR URGIN'/ BE A VIRGIN, and answering multiple-choice test questions about what kinds of situations put pressure on teens to have sex. The teacher's manual features a section on sexual messages in the media, a list of suggested alternatives to sex when on dates (bicycling, dinner parties, playing Monopoly) and a chapter on "secondary virginity"—the decision to stop having sex until marriage, even after one is sexually experienced.

Missing from the Sex Respect curriculum is the standard discussion of the comparative effectiveness of various birth-control methods found in most sex-education courses. Furthermore, it fails to offer any follow-up programs, outside counseling or guidance for teens who might become pregnant or contract a sexually transmitted disease. Kathleen Sullivan, director of Project Respect, defends her program: "We give the students a ton of information," she says. "We point out, for example, the tremendous failure rate of condoms."

One argument put forward for abstinence-only programs is that they work. Sullivan cites a study conducted by Project Respect showing that pregnancy rates among students who have taken the course are 45% lower than among those who have not. But critics say none of these studies have been reviewed by outside scientists and wonder whether any will bear close scrutiny. The San Diego *Union* looked into one of the most widely reported success stories—that the Teen-Aid program lowered the rate of pregnancy at a San Marcos, California, high school from 147 to only 20 in two years—and reported that while the 147 figure was well documented, the number 20 had apparently been made up.

The argument most often used against abstinence-only programs is that they are a thinly disguised effort to impose fundamentalist religious values on public-school students and thus violate the constitutional separation of church and state. Some of the texts started out as religious documents and were rewritten to replace references to God and Jesus with nonsectarian words like goodness and decency. Still, it makes little sense to criticize the programs simply because they originate from a religious perspective; what matters is not where the courses came from but what they say.

That's the real issue with the Teen-Aid text at the center of the Florida lawsuit. In making the case for chastity, Teen-Aid has asserted, among other things, that "the only way to avoid pregnancy is to abstain from genital contact" and that the "correct use of condoms does not prevent HIV infection but only delays it." Most teens don't need a school course to know that neither of those statements is correct. How are they going to believe in abstinence if those who preach don't have their facts straight?

—Reported by Lisa H. Towle/Raleigh

At least a dozen abstinence-based curriculums are on the market; one of the largest, Sex Respect, is used in about 2,000 schools around the country. What Sex Respect does not include is standard information about birth control, which prompts some critics to charge that purely abstinence-based programs are inadequate. Michael Carrera, who eight years ago founded a highly successful teen-pregnancy-prevention program in Harlem, deplores the "ungenerous, unforgiving" nature of some abstinence programs. "The way you make a safe, responsible abstinent decision is if you're informed, not if you're dumb." Carrera attributes the success of his program to this more comprehensive approach: in a part of Manhattan with a 50% dropout rate, 96% of Carrera's kids are still in school.

Trust Dr. Ruth Westheimer, the high priestess of pleasure, to provide parents and teens with a middle ground. She has just published *Dr. Ruth Talks to Kids,* in which she writes for ages 8 through 14. Her thesis: teach kids everything, and then encourage them to wait. "Make sure even the first kiss is a memorable experience, is what I tell kids," she says. "I don't think kids should be engaging in sex too early, not even necking and petting. I generally think age 14 and 15 is too early, in spite of the fact that by then girls are menstruating and boys may have nocturnal emissions."

Above all, she says, kids need to have their questions addressed. Learning and talking about sex do not have to mean giving permission, she insists. "On the contrary, I think that a child knowing about his or her body will be able to deal with the pressure to have sex. This child can say no, I'll wait." In fact, Westheimer is a big advocate of waiting. "I say to teenagers, What's the rush?"

—Reported by Wendy Cole, Margaret Emery and Janice M. Horowitz/New York, Lisa H. Towle/Raleigh and Marc Hequet/St. Paul

Key Skill for Teen Parents: Having Realistic Expectations

Today's parenting programs teach teen-age mothers how to care for their children and themselves.

Bridget Murray

Monitor staff

Becky Piatt is convinced she's become a better mother to her son, Christopher, ever since she took a parenting class at Kishwaukee College in rural Illinois near DeKalb.

Kishwaukee's parenting, or "family enrichment," program is geared for teen-age mothers like Piatt, who gave birth to Christopher when she was 17. She entered the program at age 19 when Christopher's bad behavior started to frustrate her.

"It taught me to turn something negative into something positive," said Piatt of the program. Instead of scolding Christopher and telling him to stop riding his bike on the street, she now uses a problem-solving approach and suggests that he ride it on the sidewalk.

Psychologist Karen Stoiber, PhD, a professor at the University of Wisconsin–Milwaukee who worked with teens at Kishwaukee, says such parenting programs strive to establish positive relations between mothers and

children and to promote financial independence for mothers.

In accordance with goal two of the National Education Goals 2000 legislation, which calls for more emphasis on high school completion, teen-parenting programs enable young mothers to finish school. The programs first caught on in the 1980s when pregnancy rates began to escalate, and psychologists have been heavily involved with them from the outset.

Teen-pregnancy rates rose 23 percent between 1972 and 1990, and as rates continue to climb and Congress threatens to reduce welfare support for single mothers, programs that move teen moms toward independence are becoming a necessity, experts say.

Counseling and school psychologists often coordinate and run the programs, while others act as consultants. Stoiber sees consulting with teen programs as a new frontier for school psychologists, in particular.

"There's room for school psychologists to become more aware of the is-

sues pregnant and parenting teens face—to help keep them in school and respond to their mental health needs," Stoiber said.

Improving Lives

A range of studies show that teen-parenting programs work. Psychologist Alice Honig, PhD, of Syracuse University found that a parenting program for inner-city teens in Syracuse lowers rates of child abuse and neglect from 40 percent to between 15 percent and 20 percent.

The program, funded by New York State and run by Syracuse's Consortium for Children's Services, sends child development specialists to the homes of first-time teen mothers on a weekly basis for 18 to 24 months. Home visitors often become surrogate mothers to the teens, who tend to live alone, draw welfare and relate poorly to their own families, said Honig.

Honig has also been studying outcomes of a teen-parenting program at

Photo by Lloyd Wolf

on mutual trust and appreciation, it starts off wrong and stays that way.

"We teach moms that they can have a happy relationship with their child and a good life for their child by understanding kids' needs and what to expect," said Sheridan.

In parenting groups Stoiber runs, she teaches that certain kinds of play, like shaking a rattle, and certain kinds of teaching, such as toilet training, are appropriate at specific developmental levels. At Kishwaukee, Stoiber tapped into young mothers' nurturing feelings by having them and their children wrap baby dolls in blankets and stick band-aids on them. To prevent parents from yelling and striking their children, she showed videos that demonstrate the difference between harsh and firm parenting.

Gearing Teens for Work

Teens need career strategies too. Hence, many programs are multifaceted, like the Lady Pitts school-age parenting program, a school for pregnant and parenting teens that Stoiber now works with in Milwaukee. Lady Pitts is geared towards predominantly African-American inner-city 12- to 18-year olds who are either pregnant or have children and are at risk of dropping out of school.

The program aims to keep teen mothers in school by providing them with high school courses and job counseling. Like Kishwaukee, it provides daycare for babies.

The programs teach teen mothers to put their job expectations in perspective, said Stoiber. Some mothers have spotty school attendance records and low grade point averages, but still think they can become physicians. Programs move them toward goals they can realistically achieve.

When financial independence became the primary goal for a young mother Stoiber worked with at Kishwaukee, she decided to pursue a two-year associate's degree and later a bachelor's degree in nursing.

"If I quit school now, I couldn't support my son and myself," the

Syracuse University that she and psychologist J. Ronald Lally, PhD, directed in the 1970s. Called the Family Development Research Program, the project served teen mothers who dropped out of school. Mothers received parenting and nutrition training from home visitors while other staff cared for their children. As the kids grew older, kindergarten teachers prepared them for kindergarten.

Honig's follow-up studies show that children of mothers who participated in the program had lower rates of delinquency than control children on such counts as burglary, robbery and assault. Girls had lower rates of school failure and, in early adolescence, girls performed better in school. Mothers reported higher rates of family unity and greater pride in their children.

At a time in their lives when teen mothers probably would rather have been flirting or dating than be tied

down with baby, the program taught them how to empathize with their infants and see them as people, said Honig.

"Teens need to understand that language and love are the two most powerful gifts a parent can give a child," said Honig. "Language develops only as we give it."

Stopping Child Abuse

Teen-parenting programs aim in part to prevent child abuse, says parenting expert Susan Sheridan, PhD, an associate professor in educational psychology at the University of Utah. To do that, they teach mothers to have more realistic expectations about parenting.

Teens learn that parenting is challenging work and a full-time commitment, Sheridan said. If the mother-child relationship is not based

mother told Stoiber. "I just figure if I plug away at it long enough, I'll get somewhere some day."

Including Fathers

The Really Awesome Parent groups in Minneapolis have made a point of including fathers and other partners of teen mothers in their teen-parenting program. University of Minnesota psychologist Patricia McCarthy, PhD, who ran the program last year and is awaiting funding to run it again, says dads are usually overlooked, but can make a positive difference in their children's lives.

The RAP program draws a large percentage of its participants from area alternative high schools and learning centers, which give students credit if they complete the program. The clientele are predominantly 15- to 20-year-old inner-city or suburban teen moms living below the poverty level.

Program leaders encourage participants to support and socialize with each other. In 15 sessions, the groups cover topics such as managing stress, disciplining children and building self-esteem.

Mothers tested after the program show a significant increase in parenting knowledge. The real challenge, says McCarthy, is getting them to attend sessions.

"They can't attend class because they get sick, their car breaks down, they get in fights with their boyfriends, or they're just being a teen-ager," McCarthy said. "If we could provide transportation for them as well, we'd have a lot more of them attend."

Research on the program also shows that parent education improves families' lives and benefits the communities they live in.

"Teen-parenting programs cut costs everywhere by lowering delinquency, abuse, neglect and joblessness," she said.

Will Schools Risk Teaching about the Risk of AIDS?

GERALD UNKS

U nlike many of the other risks that students face, the risks associated with AIDS are truly a life-or-death matter. Students who get AIDS are not simply *at risk* of losing their lives; they will certainly die. Since 1981, when it was first diagnosed in the United States, more than 243,000 Americans have died of AIDS. Of all persons who have been reported with AIDS in the United States, 61 percent are now dead. AIDS is the leading cause of death among men in the United States aged twenty-five to forty-four and the fourth leading cause of death among women in the same age group. Among persons of all ages in the United States, HIV infection/AIDS is the eighth leading cause of death. The number of AIDS cases increases approximately 3 percent each year (Centers for Disease Control and Prevention 1994b).

Although all humans are potentially at risk of becoming infected with the AIDS virus, teens, with their inexperience and lack of knowledge, are a particularly vulnerable group. Through June 1994, a total of 1,768 AIDS cases had been reported among adolescents. Although this number is relatively small, it is not the complete picture. HIV infection is increasing most rapidly among young people. One in four new infections in the United States occurs in people younger than twenty-two (Rosenberg, Bigger, and Goedert 1994). Considering that one in five reported AIDS cases is diagnosed in the twenty to twenty-nine age group, and that the incubation period between HIV infection and AIDS diagnosis is many years, it is clear that large numbers of

people who were diagnosed with AIDS in their twenties became infected with HIV as teenagers. Through June 1994, more than 15,000 persons aged twenty to twenty-four and more than 60,000 persons aged twenty-five to twenty-nine had been diagnosed with AIDS (Centers for Disease Control and Prevention 1994a).

Much has been written and broadcast about AIDS; thousands of pamphlets have been distributed, and AIDS hotlines have been established. It is not a disease about which little is known; nor is it a disease against which humans have no apparent defense. Most encouraging, it is a disease that is essentially preventable. Yet in the presence of this certain killer and in spite of mountains of information about AIDS prevention, the institution from which teens and other students should reasonably expect to receive complete, reliable information about the disease—the school—has been either silent or incredibly timid in its response.

Schools and Current AIDS Education

Although there are a few bright spots, the picture—considering the schools' potential for action—is generally bleak. Many schools continue to fear a negative reaction from the public more than they fear the potential for adolescents to become infected with HIV/AIDS. Currently, sixteen states still do not require HIV/AIDS education programs in their schools (Centers for Disease Control and Prevention 1994a), and many of the states that do mandate AIDS instruction have weak laws that allow school districts "local option" in choosing what to teach (including nothing) about AIDS. At least one-third of the nation's school districts do not require HIV education (Holtzman, Greene, Ingraham, Daily, Demchuk, and Kolbe 1992). Even among those states that indicate that they provide HIV/AIDS

Gerald Unks is a professor of education at the University of North Carolina at Chapel Hill.

From *Clearing House*, March/April 1996, pp. 205-210. © 1996 by the Helen Dwight Reid Educational Foundation. Reprinted by permission of Heldref Publications, 1319 Eighteenth Street, NW, Washington, DC 20036-1802.

instruction, their data are not necessarily a true or complete picture of what is actually going on in classrooms. In almost every instance, the data are self-reported, and states and school districts may not have wanted to show themselves in a negative light. Further, the figures provide information about what states and districts require, not what schools actually provide or what students actually receive in the way of HIV/AIDS education.

Part of the hesitant response from the schools can be explained by the history of AIDS in the United States, most importantly the fact that it was first diagnosed among homosexual males. It quickly became "the gay disease" in the minds of most Americans. In hindsight, we know that this idea was naive. AIDS had first been diagnosed in Africa; the majority of world AIDS cases were then, and still are, in Africans of both sexes. Today the trend in the spread of the disease in the United States is away from homosexuals "who now account for less than half" of the newly reported cases; nearly one-third of new cases are attributed to persons who inject drugs (Centers for Disease Control and Prevention 1994b). Among adolescents with AIDS in the United States, only 22 percent of cases are from the CDC category "men who have sex with men," and the proportion of girls among United States adolescents with AIDS has more than doubled, from 14 percent in 1987 to 32 percent by June 1994 (Centers for Disease Control and Prevention 1994a).

The image of AIDS as an exclusively homosexual disease remains in the minds of many Americans, and it persists in some schools. When suggestions are made to establish HIV/AIDS education programs in schools or to increase funding or the time allotted for HIV/AIDS education, some parents and teachers conclude that what is being advocated is a program of instruction about homosexuality. The discussion—particularly the media-attended discussion—then inevitably moves away from the merits of teaching about an always-fatal disease to the worthiness and morality of the homosexual lifestyle. Further, some schools continue to believe that they have no homosexual students—an absurd assumption (Unks 1995). But if schools reason that AIDS is a homosexual disease and that they have no homosexual students, then there is no need to teach about it. It is someone else's problem. Unfortunately this disposition—AIDS does not affect us—is also common among many nonhomosexual students, who also do not appreciate the importance of HIV/AIDS education (Shayne and Kaplan 1988). Unfortunately, as long as the homosexuality/AIDS linkage continues, schools will be very reluctant to say much of consequence about AIDS, and there will be little support for HIV/AIDS education.

However, most of the timidity on the part of many schools derives not so much from concerns about homosexuality as it does from another factor: The transmission of AIDS is almost always conjoined with sexual activity and drug use, and schools as a group are notorious in their desire to avoid controversy in any form—be it teaching

about evolution, communism, *The Catcher in the Rye*, or any of a host of other areas of discourse.

Avoiding teaching about issues of social consequence out of fear of stirring up a certain amount of public hostility is unfortunate school behavior, but perhaps it is forgivable when the issues are not life-or-death matters. AIDS, however, is without question such a matter, and by denying or limiting young people's access to knowledge about how AIDS can be prevented, schools increase the level of risk under which their students live.

This pattern of neglect does not have to continue. An age-appropriate, comprehensive AIDS awareness curriculum could save many lives by telling the facts about AIDS—the most important of which is that *students* are affected by the disease. It could also tell them the specific behaviors in which they *should not* engage if they want to avoid becoming infected. In the process, the schools could become one of the most effective institutions that adolescents have to reduce their risk of dying from AIDS.

Facts about AIDS

Although many students have some general ideas (sometimes mythological) about AIDS, most have had no systematic instruction about the disease. The "AIDS curriculum" in most school systems tends to be more of a patchwork quilt than a blanket. Nonetheless, the great majority of high school students know that AIDS is always fatal, and most know that it is usually caught through sexual and drug-injecting activity. They know that it is transmitted through blood and other bodily fluids. Most know that the best way for them to avoid getting AIDS is to avoid sexual activity and never inject drugs.

Unfortunately, although teenagers know the facts, they have not internalized them. For example, they do not *act* as if they knew that HIV is an "equal opportunity infector" and that *anyone* can become infected with HIV. When considering risk factors, they tend to think in terms of categories of people—particularly homosexuals, drug addicts, and prostitutes—rather than types of behaviors. They can articulate but they do not fully comprehend the fact that HIV infects persons of all ages, all sexual orientations, all sexes, and all levels of personal hygiene, as well as people living in all sorts of residences and regions of the country. Some students continue to believe that it is possible to tell if people are infected by the way they look or where or how they live. They do not fully appreciate the fact that people become infected with HIV because they make unwise decisions about how to behave.

Students appear to be even less knowledgeable about what *does not* cause AIDS—for example, that HIV is not spread through everyday school and social activities or that it is not spread through the air, casual contact, or water. Many do not know that a person cannot become infected from the bites of mosquitoes or other insects, from eating food that was prepared or is served by someone else, or from being around an infected person. Nor can infection result from using toilets or showers, drinking fountains, or

sport and gym equipment. Students are particularly ignorant about and suspicious of all bodily fluids and excre-
tions. They don't know that contact with feces, nasal fluid,
saliva, sweat, tears, urine, or vomit (unless these contain
visible blood) does not spread HIV infection. They also
don't know that HIV is extremely delicate and sensitive to
its environment; a weak solution of household bleach or hot
tap water will kill it.

One of the reasons that students are so ill informed about
AIDS is that some schools believe that the truth is too controversial to tell. However, the facts about AIDS and its pre-
prevention are not "far out," controversial material or ivory-
tower musings. They are demonstrated and incontrovert-
ible, supported by among the most impressive bodies of
research evidence ever assembled. All that is unusual about
this information is the fact that it is not systematically
taught in every school.

Teaching about Behavioral Change

The starting point in an AIDS awareness curriculum is
knowledge about what HIV/AIDS is and how it is (and is
not) transmitted, including information about how infection
can be avoided. But this information alone is insufficient.

> If information about the consequences of unhealthy or risky
> behaviors were sufficient to motivate people to adopt
> healthy behaviors, no one would smoke, everyone would
> wear a seat belt, all doctors' recommendations about diet
> and exercise would be followed, and there would be no
> drunk driving. Obviously, this is not the case, and most
> adults know how difficult the struggle can be to change
> entrenched, often pleasurable, behaviors. It is illogical, then,
> to expect young people to change their behavior based on
> information alone, even if that information included knowl-
> edge of their own HIV status. . . . Comprehensive HIV pre-
> vention should include information, exploration of values
> and attitudes, skills building, and access to services, includ-
> ing condom availability. (National Commission on AIDS
> 1994, 45–46)

Students must *internalize* the factual data, reject the
belief that "it can't happen to me," and change their personal behavior (Centers for Disease Control and Prevention
1994a). Effective behavioral change, however, will not
come from didactic preaching about how to behave. Rather,
the facts must be supported by an exploration of personal
values and attitudes as well as by skill-building opportunities in the areas of decision making, negotiation, and
refusal (Office of Technology Assessment 1991).

As the site where 91 percent of all persons between ages
five and nineteen in the United States are to be found, the
school is a logical and powerful place in which to locate
such activities and to advocate for changes in personal
behavior. Schools hesitate, however, to talk about personal
sexual behavior lest it alarm some members of the community. Yet, abstinence, the *primary* behavior advocated for
teens by public and private health agencies, is hardly controversial. Schools could teach their students not to have
sex, not to inject drugs, not to share needles or syringes,
and not to use alcohol or drugs without much, if any, pub-

lic censure. But the schools cannot simply stop at abstinence, and all too many have. Schools must also address
those students who do not choose to abstain—and here is
the rub.

The public and its schools often confuse statements of
values such as, "Students should not have sex or inject
drugs," with statements of fact such as, "Students do
engage in sex and they do inject drugs" (Centers for Disease Control and Prevention 1995a). In their desire to
affirm the former, they reject the latter as false. Most Americans value abstinence as a desired end for teen behavior,
but many also acknowledge the reality that a great many
adolescents are sexually active and do inject drugs. Studies
consistently show that by the twelfth grade, approximately
three-fourths of high school students have had sexual intercourse, and about one-fifth have had more than four sex
partners. One in sixty-two high school students reports having injected an illegal drug (Centers for Disease Control
and Prevention 1994a). The United States has more than
double the teenage pregnancy rate of any Western industrialized country; more than a million teenage girls become
pregnant each year (Centers for Disease Control and Prevention 1995c).

Public and private health agencies have acknowledged
the sizable number of adolescents who choose not to
abstain. While not approving of the reality of teenage sexual and drug behavior, these agencies have adopted a *secondary* line of defense by advocating changes in personal
behavior that, although not as effective as abstinence, are
nonetheless highly effective. The schools could do the
same. They could teach students that they should never
share needles or syringes, never use needles that have been
used by others, and never have sex without using a latex
condom.

Some adults contend that teaching both abstinence and
safer sexual and drug-use behaviors sends a mixed message
to teens that confuses them. In reality, although it is a complex message, it is not contradictory. It is much like the
message "don't drink, but if you do drink, don't drive." The
adult community has indicated the preferred behavioral
option, but it has then provided for other options if the preferred behavior is not chosen (National Commission on
AIDS 1994).

The Use of Condoms

Talking about the importance of using latex condoms as
well as making latex condoms available to students are two
areas of AIDS awareness education about which schools
are particularly nervous. Condom use is the behavioral skill
that is *least* likely to be addressed at any grade level in an
AIDS awareness curriculum (Holtzman et al. 1992).
Although more than three hundred schools make condoms
available on campus (Centers for Disease Control and Prevention 1995b), most schools assiduously avoid teaching
about the correct use of latex condoms or making them
available. Interestingly, they do not act this way with
respect to other diseases. If it were found, for example, that

a product was available that would prevent just 50 percent of all common colds, schools would advocate its use, perhaps even provide the product immediately. Using latex condoms during sex has been found to be 99 percent effective in preventing the spread of HIV. Yet schools balk at advocating the use of latex condoms, let alone making them available to their students.

The schools fear that there will be a negative response from the public, and in this instance the schools are probably correct; there *will* be a public response. But from *which* public, the informed or the uninformed, the majority or the minority? And what has the school done to educate that public? Have school officials stressed that no student is being *forced* to use a condom? Have they pointed out that the school is advocating not sex but rather the prevention of a fatal disease? When schools tell students to cover their noses and mouths when they sneeze or cough, they are not advocating sneezing or coughing. Instead, they are trying to prevent the potential spread of disease, and they know that students will, inevitably and unfortunately, sneeze and cough.

The school is a logical and powerful place in which to advocate for changes in personal behavior.

It is also possible that the schools have *overestimated* public hostility. Reichelt (1986) has found that there has been, over the last several decades, an upward trend in public approval of better contraceptive services and sex education for teenagers. He contends that public support for such measures runs counter to the popular wisdom that the public is increasingly opposed to these activities; consequently, schools could be far more proactive without encountering significant public opposition (Reichelt 1986). Media attention can also heighten the belief that there is more opposition than there actually is. Stories that are sensational or depict conflict are widely reported, while stories about successful projects may go unreported (National Commission on AIDS 1994).

Some members of the public will continue to believe that by advocating the use of latex condoms, the schools are encouraging sexual activity. On this point, the evidence is quite to the contrary. Five U.S. studies of specific sex education programs have demonstrated that HIV education and sex education that included condom information either had no effect upon the initiation of intercourse or resulted in delayed onset of intercourse (Centers for Disease Control and Prevention 1995a).

In spite of what media attention often implies, condom availability programs are increasing in number. The public

has apparently decided that making them available to those students who do not choose abstinence is a responsible decision in the presence of the threat of HIV infection/AIDS (Center for Population Options 1993).

An AIDS Awareness Curriculum

The AIDS awareness curriculum must extend across the disciplines and throughout a student's tenure in school. It should not be confined to a single subject area nor to the province of one school year. One disturbing pattern of HIV/AIDS education is its tendency to be reduced, both in amount of time spent and in number of students reached, just at the time when students are increasingly likely to engage in risk behaviors. A 1992 survey of HIV and health education policies and practices in the nation's schools found that requirements for both HIV and health education began to decline after grade seven. In the last two years of high school, fewer than 25 percent of school districts required HIV education, and even fewer required health education (Holtzman et al. 1992). At least one study conducted on the state level obtained similar results (Felts et al. 1992).

This decline is illustrative of an unfortunate, and often noted, characteristic of the United States curriculum: the older the student, the greater the irrelevance of the curriculum. "Practical" courses are moved aside to make room for "college prep" and/or "basic" courses. Ironically, the brighter the students, the more likely this pattern is to prevail. The college-bound seldom have room in their course of study for anything as "practical" or as much of a "frill" as HIV/AIDS instruction. Again, the school implicitly sends a message that AIDS is not something about which bright students should be concerned. Even below the high school level, there are school districts in which the so-called back-to-basics movement has sought to limit the time spent on HIV/AIDS instruction in order to increase the amount of time devoted to the "basic subjects." Considering the size of the AIDS epidemic and its obvious impact upon all students, it is difficult to imagine a subject that is more basic than HIV/AIDS instruction. Indeed, HIV/AIDS education may be exactly the sort of basic education that both students and the United States need.

> Conceptually, HIV prevention education fits well into educational reform. What is needed for America's future is a revamping of education to give students the critical thinking and analytic skills that allow them to apply knowledge, make decisions, and think independently. Those are the skills needed in both today's and tomorrow's technology and information-based workplaces. The best HIV prevention education provides young people with opportunities to learn and practice just such skills. (National Commission on AIDS 1994, 44)

HIV/AIDS education is the proper concern of science, particularly health education, biology, and chemistry, but it also has a social studies and a literature component. Students need to know the scientific basis of HIV infection and how AIDS develops, but they also need to be aware of the discrimination and prejudice that have accompanied the spread of the disease. All of the disciplines could be marshaled in an effective AIDS awareness curriculum, each contributing its unique perspective.

Schools and teachers are fortunate, for curricular materials and plans for lessons about AIDS are readily available from a wide variety of sources. Indeed, more curriculum development models have probably been written on promoting AIDS awareness than on almost any topic. Two excellent examples were developed by the United States Department of Health and Human Services (Centers for Disease Control 1988) and the Council of Chief State School Officers (1992).

The AIDS awareness curriculum should not be a one-shot effort. Students need different sorts of information at different times in their development. Simplistic explanations may satisfy a child; they will not cause adolescents to change their behavior. What may be appropriate for a teen would not be suitable (or understandable) for a child. The curriculum should, therefore, be age-appropriate. It should also recognize that, over time, even well-taught, appropriate material will be forgotten by the typical student. The AIDS awareness curriculum involves repetition—year after year and across the stages in human development (Shayne and Kaplan 1988). It is a lifelong process not ending in schools, but certainly beginning there—if the schools are willing.

HIV/AIDS Awareness and Sex Education

Earlier, in the context of discussing the use of latex condoms, it was noted that the schools' reaction to AIDS was different from their reaction to other diseases. The AIDS awareness curriculum is, of necessity, enmeshed with most of the problems inherent in sex education. If HIV infection and AIDS were not associated with sexual behavior, the schools might well be in the forefront, working for its prevention. It is a tragic irony: This always-fatal disease can be prevented by changing sexual behavior, but sexual behavior is an area generally closed to discussion in the schools.

There are a variety of reasons that some people reject the idea of sex education in schools, but none is more powerful than the belief that if students become aware of sexual function, they will become sexually active. This is an idea that continues to attract believers in spite of little more than folklore to support it and an impressive body of research, conducted throughout the world and over lengthy periods of time, that says it is false (Kirby, Short, and Collins 1994). "A World Health Organization (WHO) review cited 19 studies of sex education programs that found no evidence that sex education leads to earlier or increased sexual activity in young people" (Centers for Disease Control and Prevention 1995a). The burden of proof about whether sex education promotes sexual activity ought to rest firmly on those who say it does, not on those who say it does not.

Burdens of proof, however, hardly win the argument. Opponents of sex education—although a distinctly small minority of citizens—are well organized and financed; they can quickly bring enormous pressure to bear on a school

administration or a legislative body. It is always unfortunate when the side whose argument prevails is the one that can shout the loudest, not the one that has truth on its side; however, this condition is not unknown—particularly in issues involving the school curriculum. Considering the gravity of the AIDS crisis, this could be a deadly victory.

HIV/AIDS Awareness and Democratic Schooling

The schools generally have a good track record in preventing the spread of disease. Requiring inoculations and vaccinations prior to entering school and teaching about effective hygiene have dramatically reduced the spread of many communicable diseases that once threatened the nation's population. Schools in the 1930s and 1940s were the center for the detection of tuberculosis among young people, and when the polio vaccine was developed, the school was the site of choice for its administration to the youth population. Indeed, the school has often been *the leader* in fighting the spread of disease, and it has occupied that position because the citizens of the United States, more than most people, have an almost religious faith in education's presumed capacity to bring about universal good.

In the nation's history, schools have variously been seen as centers of political, social, and economic hope, but they have also been widely seen as places in which, at their best, a reliable sort of knowledge and morality could be found. If nothing else, the school as an American institution has said that it will tell the truth and assist its students in discovering it for themselves.

AIDS awareness education involves making choices, and choosing is not always pretty. When choice involves consequential social issues, it is not easy. Choosing the lesser of two evils or choosing to abandon cherished beliefs in the presence of new knowledge is difficult. In the choice process, however, the United States is fortunate in that it has a democratic model upon which it can rely. Democracy is based on the simple but elegant assumption that people, when possessed of sufficient knowledge, can be trusted to make intelligent and correct choices. Totalitarian regimes are distinguished by their habit of preventing citizens from making informed choices and by their withholding of information, and societies are undemocratic to the extent that they engage in these practices. The subverters of traditional American values are not those who want to give more knowledge to the population; they are those who advocate anything less. Difficult as the decision process may be in the field of AIDS awareness education, the schools must, in the final analysis, have faith in the power and ultimate correctness of democratic decision making.

REFERENCES

Center for Population Options. 1993. *Condom availability in schools: A guide for programs.* Washington, D.C.: Center for Population Options.
Centers for Disease Control. 1988. Guidelines for effective school health education to prevent the spread of AIDS. *Morbidity and Mortality Weekly Report* 37 No. S-2 (Jan.): 1–14.
Centers for Disease Control and Prevention. 1994a. *Adolescents and HIV/AIDS.* Rockville, Md.: CDC National AIDS Clearinghouse.

————. 1994b. *Recent trends in reported U.S. AIDS cases.* Rockville, Md.: CDC National AIDS Clearinghouse.

————. 1995a. *Condoms and their use in preventing HIV infection and other STD's.* Rockville, Md.: CDC National AIDS Clearinghouse.

————. 1995b. *Does sex education work?* Rockville, Md.: CDC National AIDS Clearinghouse.

————. 1995c. Youth risk behavior surveillance—United States—1993. *Morbidity and Morality Weekly Report* 44: 1–56.

Council of Chief State School Officers. 1992. *Lessons from the classroom.* Washington, D.C.: Council of Chief State School Officers.

Felts, M., R. Barnes, T. Chenier, and P. Dunn. 1992. *Prevalence and characteristics of HIV prevention education in North Carolina public schools, grades 7–12.* Greenville, N.C.: East Carolina University HIV Prevention Education Research Team.

Holtzman, D., B. Z. Greene, G. C. Ingraham, L. A. Daily, D. G. Demchuk, and L. J. Kolbe. 1992. HIV education and health education in the United States: A national survey of local school district policies and practices. *Journal of School Health* 62(9): 421–27.

Kirby, D., L. Short, and J. Collins. 1994. School-based programs to reduce sexual risk behaviors: A review of effectiveness. *Public Health Reports* 109(5): 339–60.

National Commission on AIDS. 1994. Preventing HIV/AIDS in adolescents. *Journal of School Health* 64(1): 39–51.

Office of Technology Assessment. U.S. Congress. 1991. *Adolescent Health. Volume 2: Background and the effectiveness of selected prevention and treatment services.* OTA- H-446. Washington, D.C.: U.S. Government Printing Office.

Reichelt, P. A. 1986. Public policy and public opinion toward sex education and birth control for teenagers. *Journal of Applied Social Psychology* 16(2): 95–106.

Rosenberg, P. S., R. J. Biggar, and J. J. Goedert. 1994. Declining age in HIV infection in the United States. *New England Journal of Medicine* 330(11): 789–90.

Shayne, V. T., and B. J. Kaplan. 1988. Aids education for adolescents. *Youth and Society* 20(4): 189–208.

Unks, G., ed. 1995. *The gay teen.* New York: Routledge.

Young adults and AIDS: 'It can't happen to me.'

Many young heterosexuals still shun condoms and have a false sense of security about their own risk for contracting HIV.

By Nathan Seppa
Monitor staff

Young Americans know all about safe sex. They've seen the statistics on AIDS risks, the MTV warnings and those "Russian roulette" public service announcements. And, as one might expect, young adults are practicing sex more safely than any previous generation.

But they still take chances. Studies of college students, for example, show a disturbing trend: New sweethearts often use condoms during their first month or two of sex, then discard the condoms in favor of another form of birth control, such as contraceptive pills, said Christopher Agnew, PhD, assistant professor of psychology science at Purdue University.

Ironically, it is trust in each other that places them at risk. They equate monogamy with security, regardless of their sexual histories. And many never get tested for the human immunodeficiency virus (HIV) that causes AIDS, said Paul Poppen, PhD, associate professor of psychology at George Washington University. Many young heterosexuals, whether in college or not, consider AIDS something that happens to "other people," he said. Studies show that at most, they use condoms only about half the time they have sex.

In the United States, young gay men and intravenous drug users face the greatest risk of contracting HIV. Historically they have been the main

John Michael Yanson

targets of education campaigns and other interventions.

But even as gains are made in the gay community and among drug users, the strides of *non-IV-drug-using* heterosexuals toward safer sex have stalled.

"The heterosexual population is where the greatest risk is to society, because of their huge numbers," said

Stevan Hobfoll, PhD, professor and director of the Applied Psychology Center at Kent State University. The data show that risk is rising: AIDS cases caused by heterosexual transmission in 1983 constituted 1 percent of the U.S. total; by 1993, the number rose to 9 percent. While a large portion of that rise stems from IV-drug users or their partners, the fact remains that

Condom sales are dropping

Condom sales in the United States fell between 1991 and 1994, based on scanner data from retail outlets.

Other research supports the notion that much unsafe sex is still being practiced in the young heterosexual community:

• Of sexually active college students, only 35 percent of females and 45 percent of males reported using a condom during their most recent sexual intercourse, the Centers for Disease Control and Prevention (CDC) reported in July.

• In 1995, 53 percent of high school students ages 14 to 18 had had sex at some point and 38 percent were still active sexually, numbers largely unchanged from five years earlier. But condom use during their most recent intercourse rose only slightly, from 46 percent in 1990 to 53 percent in 1995, the CDC found.

• A study of 109 black and adolescent girls in an East Coast city found that of the nearly three-fourths who had had intercourse in the past three months, only 29 percent had used a condom every time. Another 19 percent said they never used a condom in those three months.

—Nathan Seppa

getting other young heterosexuals to change their sexual practices has been a difficult task for psychologists and public health officials.

But sometimes events do it for them. For example, after pro basketball star Earvin "Magic" Johnson announced in 1991 that he had contracted HIV through unprotected heterosexual sex, condom use among blacks who had more than one sex partner in the past year rose significantly, research shows. Johnson stood as a real-life reminder that HIV can be spread by heterosexual sex—and that condoms, for the most part, prevent it.

Meanwhile, IV-drug use and unsafe sex form a dangerous combination. Most of the roughly 41,000 annual new HIV infections in the United States occur among IV drug users, their sexual partners or their offspring, said John Anderson, Phd, director of APA Office on AIDS.

For U.S. women, the second-highest cause of HIV infection—after IV drug use—is having sex with an HIV-positive man, according to a study in *Health Psychology,* 1992 Vol. 11. As a result, inner-city women are at risk because their partners have higher-than-average incidences of IV drug use, the study found.

The Centers for Disease Control and Prevention (CDC) reported in

1991 that nearly two-thirds of women who contracted HIV through heterosexual sex got it from an IV drug user.

And in 1994, African-American and Hispanic women showed the highest rates of new HIV/STD (sexually transmitted disease) infections, said psychologist Joseph Catania, PhD, associate professor in the department of medicine/Center for AIDS Prevention at the University of California–San Francisco.

But overall, these risks and incidents haven't ignited mass behavioral changes in the large population of young heterosexuals, most of whom have never met an IV-drug user or had sex with anyone in such a high-risk network. Thus, the move toward greater condom use in this broader group may be stalling in part because they simply don't know anyone who is HIV-positive and still see AIDS only in the abstract, psychologists say.

In any case, their risks could rise in the future as other strains of HIV arrive from abroad (see "New HIV strain likely to come West").

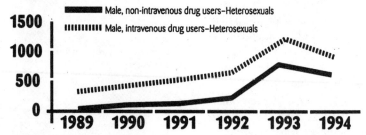

U.S. AIDS CASES CAUSED BY HETEROSEXUAL CONTACT

Number of AIDS Cases

━━━ Male, non-intravenous drug users–Heterosexuals
||||||||| Male, intravenous drug users–Heterosexuals

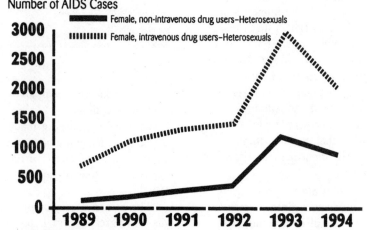

Number of AIDS Cases

━━━ Female, non-intravenous drug users–Heterosexuals
||||||||| Female, intravenous drug users–Heterosexuals

Sources: U.S. Department of Health and Human Services, Public Health Service, Centers for Disease Control and Prevention, National Center for Infectious Diseases.

The question is why

Why aren't young people using condoms? Hobfoll and his colleagues found that some fear that broaching the topic will wreck the mood during sexual encounters, cause embarrassment or ultimately limit sexual enjoyment. Adolescents often find sex to be awkward anyway, he said, and the embarrassment can run deep.

On study found that 12 percent of adolescent boys stole their first condom rather than ask a friend for one or face a check-out clerk. Other research found that adolescent girls asking for help in buying condoms in Washington, D.C., drug stores encountered resistance or condemnation from store clerks 40 percent of the time.

Moreover, young people find HIV transmission perplexing because it can be spread heterosexually after only a single sexual contact or not at all after 100, research shows.

And because HIV infection can take months to show up on a basic antibody test, getting tested with a new partner may not yield a valid picture of a person who has had multiple partners in recent months.

Gender role differences complicate heterosexual sex and can hinder condom use as well. Despite social changes of the past 30 years, men are still expected to ask women out on a date, propose marriage and initiate sex, psychologists note. But other research shows that men are several times more likely to give a woman HIV than to get it from a woman.

Communication is key. For example, while condom use has risen in colleges in the past 15 years, discussions about contraception *prior to sex* occurred no more often—about half the time—in 1989 as was the case in 1979, Poppen found.

Many young people also suffer from misconceptions about HIV. In a study of 289 single, pregnant inner-city women (average age 21), researchers in Ohio found that many didn't feel at risk for HIV because

New HIV strain likely to come West

While most HIV infections in Europe and North America are spread through intravenous drug use or by anal sex among gay men, HIV in Asia and Africa is largely a heterosexual disease. In Africa, for example, a much higher percentage of AIDS victims are women than in North America.

In the March 1996 issue of *Science,* a group of researchers from the Harvard AIDS Institute unveiled laboratory findings, which suggest that certain HIV subtypes (strains) seen in Asia and Africa are better able to infect an individual via the kinds of cells that appear along vaginal walls—through heterosexual sex.

Some scientists believe it's only a matter of time before heterosexuals in the West face these other strains of HIV.

If these strains are shown to behave in the population the same way they act in the laboratory, it could result in an incursion of HIV in the heterosexual community, said Joseph Catania, PhD, of the University of California–San Francisco. Unsafe sex, little knowledge of personal histories and multiple partners—combined with the arrival of new HIV strains—could spell trouble, he said.

"If you reach this set of conditions, where heterosexuals have all thrown their condoms away and said, '[HIV] isn't going to affect us,' you risk what happened to the gay community in '79 through '81," when many were unknowingly exposed to HIV, Catania said.

—Nathan Seppa

they had only one sex partner in the past year.

They failed to perceive the inherent risk they faced as a result of their partner's current or past behavior, Hobfoll and four colleagues wrote in *Health Psychology* (Vol. 12, 1993, pp. 481–488). White and black women were equally represented in the study.

Also, many college students feel safe from HIV because they are geographically isolated from big cities, where AIDS is more prevalent. They are, in some ways, correct, Poppen said. Only about one in 500 college students is HIV-positive, a 1990 study showed.

What to do?

Some encouraging data has surfaced. Between 1979 and 1989, college students' condom use rose from 35 percent to 49 percent for first-time-ever sex and 17 percent to 51 percent for first-time sex with the respondent's current sexual partner, Poppen said.

But young adults still account for nearly 70 percent of all STDs in the United States, according to data from the 1993 National AIDS Behavioral

Survey. The U.S. Public Health Service has found that 25 percent of sexually active women contract an STD by age 21. Hobfoll believes young adults need to learn better negotiation skills to satisfy their partner without reverting to unsafe sex.

Also, people need to become more forthcoming, to facilitate frank communication about sex between partners, he said.

Poppen promotes a multifaceted approach to changing sexual behavior among young people, including more condom use and better education. But most importantly, the norms of sexual behavior must change to include safe sex until a partner's sexual history is established, he said.

On the other hand, young people often "fall in love with the person they are having sex with," Poppen said; the idealized vision of their lover can fool them into thinking they can't catch the disease.

Young people need to remember that the AIDS epidemic is not like the flu, something that passes by, Catania said. Many young heterosexuals ignore the stealth nature of HIV and its ability to lie dormant in a person, he said.

Problem Behaviors and Interventions

That many adolescents engage in high-risk behavior is not subject to much debate. The statistics on causes of adolescent fatalities demonstrate their risk taking. The leading causes of death in adolescence are violent: accidents, suicide, and homicide. Alcohol use is frequently involved in these deaths, particularly in motor vehicle fatalities. About half of the fatal motor vehicle accidents involving an adolescent also include a drunk driver. In addition to violent causes of death, death from AIDS has tripled in about the last ten years in people under 30. Considering that people may be HIV positive for 10 years before showing symptoms of AIDS, many of these people probably contracted the virus in their teens. Almost all of these people contracted HIV through high-risk behaviors: injectable drug use or unprotected sexual activity.

Why adolescents engage in high-risk behaviors is debated. Some researchers believe the cause of adolescent risk taking is related to their cognitive development. They propose that adolescents have a sense of invulnerability. Adolescents believe that they are special and unique; things that could happen to others could not possibly happen to them. Other researchers believe this may apply at best to only young adolescents. By their mid-teens, most older adolescents are too sophisticated in their thinking to consider themselves invulnerable. Despite this, however, adolescents still take more risks than do adults.

If adolescents do not perceive themselves as invulnerable, then why do they take risks? There are several possible explanations. One proposal is adolescents may not perceive the risk. For example, adults may have a better sense of how fast they can safely drive given differing road conditions. Adolescents, simply because they are less experienced, may not recognize when road conditions are dangerous and so may not adjust their speed. Adolescents may engage in more high-risk behaviors than adults do simply because they have the time and energy to do so. Many adolescents have free time, money, and a car. Access to these may allow adolescents to put themselves in dangerous situations. Adults, in contrast, may work, do household chores, and take care of their children. These adults may not have the time to drink, or take drugs, or joy ride. Adolescents may also be less adept than are adults in extricating themselves from high-risk situations. For example, adults who attend a party where drugs are consumed may be more comfortable in declining offered drugs than are adolescents, or they may be able to leave the party without relying on transportation from others. Some researchers indicate that society must be somewhat to blame for adolescents' risk taking. If adolescents living in poverty have no chance of getting a meaningful job, have limited access to recreational activities, and have little encouragement in school, then participation in drug-related or violent activities may be the only options open to them. It is up to society to provide these adolescents with an increased number of safe choices.

Adolescents' risk taking activities may take many forms. The U.S. Public Health Service identifies several categories of behavior related to health risks for adolescents. Included are behaviors that may cause injuries such as suicide and violence; use of tobacco; use of drugs (including alcohol); and risky behaviors related to eating. All these can clearly threaten adolescents. Alcohol use seems to exacerbate many of the other risks, as indicated by the statistics on alcohol use and violent death. Drug use can be related to accidents, health problems, and violence. Violent behaviors are an increasing concern to society. Murder is the second leading cause of death in adolescence; it is the leading cause of death for African American male teenagers. Suicide rates in young people have tripled since the 1950s. Eating disorders are another threat to adolescents. Millions of adolescents, primarily girls, suffer from eating disorders in the United States. Young girls suffering from anorexia nervosa starve themselves in pursuit of thinness. Bulimic adolescents binge and purge, again in an attempt to be thin. Both anorexia and bulimia can be life threatening. Articles are included in this unit that address these areas of high-risk behavior. Articles describing risky behaviors and articles addressing interventions for these behaviors are presented.

The first unit article discusses prevention of risk taking. One provides advice for parents, the other describes programs that involve parents, schools, communities, and adolescents in an attempt to prevent drug abuse. The next two articles address violence. The first describes research on the genetic underpinnings of violent behavior and the controversies surrounding this. The next article discusses programs available for delinquent youth. Then, Cynthia Clark describes why adolescents may be attracted to cults and the different forms cults may take in her essay, "Clinical Assessment of Adolescents Involved in Satanism." The two articles that follow address adolescents' concerns with their bodies. In "The A's and B's of Eating Disorders: Eating to Extremes," anorexia and bulimia are described. "Biceps in a Bottle," by James Deacon, focuses on teenage boys' use of steroids and the risks associated with this. The final article in this unit is a discussion of adolescent suicide and prevention.

Looking Ahead: Challenge Questions

What are some of the factors underlying adolescents' risk taking? How can parents, schools, and communities work together to prevent adolescents from engaging in high-risk activities?

What is the evidence for a genetic basis for violent behaviors? What controversies result from a focus on genes rather than the environment?

What kinds of programs are available for adolescent ex-cons? What factors influence the effectiveness of these programs?

Why may adolescents join cults? What are the dangers of involvement in cults?

What are the causes and symptoms of eating disorders?

What are potential side effects of steroid use?

List at least five risk factors for adolescent suicide. What would you do if you suspected an acquaintance or friend was suicidal? Describe how postvention activities in schools can help peer survivors of an adolescent suicide.

Programs Go Beyond 'Just Saying No'

Innovative programs teach children the skills they need to resist substance abuse.

Bridget Murray

Monitor staff

Psychologists' new school-based approaches to drug-abuse prevention go a step beyond telling teen-agers to "just say no." They're teaching teens *how* to say no.

Instead of bombarding students with antidrug dogma that they often ignore, the programs build kids' drug-resistant skills and encourage them to get involved in their schools and communities, social scientists say.

"The programs show alienated kids that society offers better options than taking drugs and strengthen kids' ability to take advantage of those options," said Ronda C. Talley, PhD, APA's assistant executive director for education and head of the APA Center for Psychology in Schools and Education.

These new drug-abuse prevention programs are better than traditional drug-education programs at targeting risk factors for drug abuse, such as boredom, lack of parental support, feelings of failure and social pressures to drink or smoke, said Talley.

Moreover, using such programs to prevent drug abuse is ultimately less expensive and probably more effective than treating it, some psychologists contend.

(Photo by Lloyd Wolf)

But there is a hitch. The programs fail to reach adolescents who have already started smoking and drinking, said substance-abuse expert John Swisher, PhD, a psychology professor at Pennsylvania State University. Those adolescents do need more intensive treatment programs, he said.

The need for effective drug-abuse prevention programs has reached new heights, according to national survey data. An ongoing, annual study of 50,000 eighth-, 10th- and 12-graders led by social psychologist Lloyd Johnston, PhD, of the University of Michigan's Institute for Social Research, finds that adolescents are reporting greater use of illegal drugs, especially marijuana, than they did in the late 1980s.

School psychologists are working to curb these rates by developing students' social skills and fostering student support systems within and beyond the school, says Swisher.

A Social Fabric That Connects

One program that aims to substitute drug use with community responsibility is the Child Development Project, or CDP, run in elementary schools and based out of the Developmental Studies Center in Oakland, Calif. By building a social fabric that connects kids, parents and teachers with each other and the school, CDP seeks to build children's commitment to such community values as helpfulness and responsibility. Funded in part by the Center for Substance Abuse Prevention at the U.S. Department of Human Services, CDP helps kids become more responsible and academically motivated *before* they're exposed to drugs.

"We try to help schools provide children with a stronger sense of autonomy, belonging and competence—a new sense of the ABCs," said the program's founder, social psychologist Eric Schaps, PhD, director of the Development Studies Center.

CDP revamps school climate, discipline practice and parental involvement. For example, hall monitors report on peers' behavior, and in "buddies" programs, teachers assign each older student to a younger "buddy" to support during the school year. Families become more involved in school life through participation in events such as Family Read Aloud Nights, and in homework activities that relate family experience to what kids are learning in school.

The program also boosts the curriculum: Teachers receive intensive training in teaching methods and discipline practice over three years, and CDP staff provide them with on-site consultation and curriculum materials such as reading supplements. CDP significantly reduces alcohol and marijuana use relative to other schools. Students also work more collaboratively on classroom tasks, interact more with each other, and behave less

violently. Since 1992, schools have gradually phased in CDP in White Plains, N.Y.; Dade County, Fla.; Louisville, Ky.; and Salinas, Cupertino and San Francisco, Calif.

"THE PROGRAMS SHOW ALIENATED KIDS THAT SOCIETY OFFERS BETTER OPTIONS THAN TAKING DRUGS AND STRENGTHEN KIDS' ABILITY TO TAKE ADVANTAGE OF THOSE OPTIONS."

RONDA C. TALLEY, PHD

APA'S CENTER FOR PSYCHOLOGY IN SCHOOLS AND EDUCATION

A Community Approach

Project Star is another community-oriented program developed to steer kids away from alcohol and cigarettes. This program aims to stop youngsters from taking these "gateway drugs" and to prevent them from being tempted by "harder" illegal drugs.

The five-year program, partially funded by the National Institute on Drug Abuse and designed by school psychologist Mary Anne Pentz, PhD, has been adopted in the Indianapolis schools. Project Star is school-based but reaches out to parents and the community with prevention education.

The program, which usually starts in junior high school, involves five stages:

- **First year**—Students are taught drug awareness and resistance skills.
- **Second year**—Parents, children, teachers and principals communi-

cate about drug abuse, and parents create stronger rules about drug use.

- **Third year**—Experts train community leaders about prevention strategies and schools sponsor community-wide prevention activities like smoke-outs and alcohol-free sporting events.
- **Fourth year**—Program participants work on policy change such as creating a tax on beer and creating drug-free school zones.
- **Fifth year**—Participants target the mass media to deliver antidrug messages in advertisements and talk shows.

When community norms are addressed along with schools' prevention efforts, drug-abstinence levels are higher than when school-based programs are implemented alone, says Pentz.

In-school prevention programs typically report a 15 percent to 44 percent drop in drug-use, whereas Project Star reports a 20 percent to 60 percent decline.

The program has been shown to lower occasional use of gateway drugs throughout high school and to quell heavier use, such as daily drunkenness and chain-smoking, Pentz said.

Resistance Training

Still another preventive approach is Life Skills Training, which seeks to build adolescents' ability to deal with life stress rather than escaping it through drug use. LST is one of the first school-based projects to demonstrate durable prevention effects over time.

The project was developed by developmental and clinical psychologist Gilbert Botvin, PhD, director of the Institute for Prevention Research at Cornell University Medical College in New York City. LST is funded by NIDA and is being tested in New York State.

Botvin documented the program's success in 56 rural and suburban public schools in upper New York State and Long Island. In this study, nearly 6,000 seventh-graders were coached in LST in 1985. Botvin surveyed 3,600 of them six years later in 1991, and found that those exposed to LST were less likely to use alcohol, drugs and cigarettes than those not exposed to the program.

To implement the program, Botvin and his colleagues train teachers to conduct 15 LST classes, lasting from 45 to 50 minutes, to seventh-graders, each focused on a specific life skill objective. Instruction includes showing students such techniques as muscle-relaxation exercises to ease the anxiety and tension that can lead them to drugs and alcohol.

LST explains how to weigh options and think about long-term conse-quences of behavior. The program teaches students assertiveness skills, such as building up the nerve to return defective merchandise, and, most importantly, to resist offers and advertising pressure to drink, take drugs and smoke cigarettes.

LST also strives to polish students' conversation skills and improve their rapport with others. Kids learn how to introduce people, to sustain and gracefully end a conversation and to compliment people, said Botvin. The intention is to build supportive social networks that steer children toward academics and away from the isolation that sometimes leads them to drugs.

These classes are supported by out-of-class behavioral "homework," such as encouraging students to introduce themselves to five new people. These skills are reinforced and expanded through a series of 15 "booster" classes in the eighth and ninth grade.

Although programs designed by research psychologists typically rely on classroom teachers and health educators to deliver lessons, school psychologists can take an active role in setting up programs and training teachers, said Botvin. He hopes to see school health professionals, including psychologists, running LST in teams as they work to bring it into more schools and communities.

Seeking the Criminal Element

Scientists are homing in on social and biological risk factors that they believe predispose individuals to criminal behavior. The knowledge could be ripe with promise—or rife with danger

W. Wayt Gibbs, *staff writer*

Imagine you are the father of an eight-year-old boy," says psychologist Adrian Raine, explaining where he believes his 17 years of research on the biological basis of crime is leading. "The ethical dilemma is this: I could say to you, 'Well, we have taken a wide variety of measurements, and we can predict with 80 percent accuracy that your son is going to become seriously violent within 20 years. We can offer you a series of biological, social and cognitive intervention programs that will greatly reduce the chance of his becoming a violent offender.'

"What do you do? Do you place your boy in those programs and risk stigmatizing him as a violent criminal even though there is a real possibility that he is innocent? Or do you say no to the treatment and run an 80 percent chance that your child will grow up to (a) destroy his life, (b) destroy your life, (c) destroy the lives of his brothers and sisters and, most important, (d) destroy the lives of the innocent victims who suffer at his hands?"

For now, such a Hobson's choice is purely hypothetical. Scientists cannot yet predict which children will become dangerously aggressive with anything like 80 percent accuracy. But increasingly, those who study the causes of criminal and violent behavior are looking beyond broad demographic characteristics such as age, race and income

level to factors in individuals' personality, history, environment and physiology that seem to put them—and society—at risk. As sociologists reap the benefits of rigorous long-term studies and neuroscientists tug at the tangled web of relations between behavior and brain chemistry, many are optimistic that science will identify markers of maleficence. "This research might not pay off for 10 years, but in 10 years it might revolutionize our criminal justice system," asserts Roger D. Masters, a political scientist at Dartmouth College.

"With the expected advances, we're going to be able to diagnose many people who are biologically brain-prone to violence," claims Stuart C. Yudofsky, chair of the psychiatry department at Baylor College of Medicine and editor of the *Journal of Neuropsychiatry and Clinical Neurosciences*. "I'm not worried about the downside as much as I am encouraged by the opportunity to prevent tragedies—to screen people who might have high risk and to prevent them from harming someone else." Raine, Yudofsky and others argue that in order to control violence, Americans should trade their traditional concept of justice based on guilt and punishment for a "medical model" based on prevention, diagnosis and treatment.

But many scientists and observers do worry about a downside. They are con-

cerned that some researchers underplay the enormous complexity of individual behavior and overstate scientists' ability to understand and predict it. They also fear that a society desperate to reduce crime might find the temptation to make premature or inappropriate use of such knowledge irresistible.

Indeed, the history of science's assault on crime is blemished by instances in which incorrect conclusions were used to justify cruel and unusual punishments. In the early 1930s, when the homicide rate was even higher than it is today, eugenics was in fashion. "The eugenics movement was based on the idea that certain mental illness and criminal traits were all inherited," says Ronald L. Akers, director of the Center for Studies in Criminology and Law at the University of Florida. "It was based on bad science, but they thought it was good science at the time." By 1931, 27 states had passed laws allowing compulsory sterilization of "the feeble-minded," the insane and the habitually criminal.

Studies in the late 1960s—when crime was again high and rising—revealed that many violent criminals had an extra Y chromosome and thus an extra set of "male" genes. "It was a dark day for science in Boston when they started screening babies for it," recalls Xandra O. Breakefield, a geneticist at Massachusetts General Hospital. Subsequent studies revealed that although XYY men

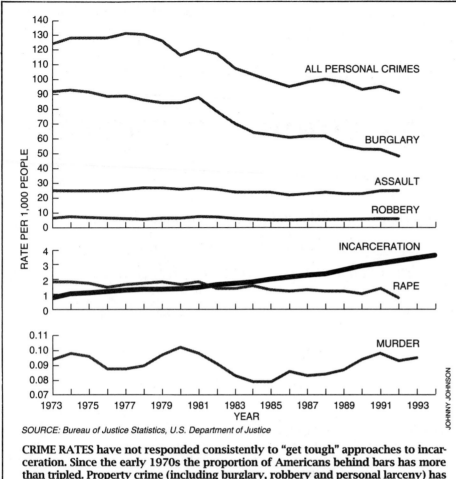

SOURCE: Bureau of Justice Statistics, U.S. Department of Justice

CRIME RATES have not responded consistently to "get tough" approaches to incarceration. Since the early 1970s the proportion of Americans behind bars has more than tripled. Property crime (including burglary, robbery and personal larceny) has dropped about 30 percent, but violent crime remains high.

pothesis on 319 boys from high-crime neighborhoods in Eugene. Last November at the American Society of Criminology meeting, she reported her findings: boys who had been arrested by age 14 were 17.9 times more likely to become chronic offenders than those who had not, and chronic offenders were 14.3 times more likely to commit violent offenses. "This is a good way of predicting," she says.

Good is a relative term. For if one were to predict that every boy in her study who was arrested early would go on to commit violent crimes, one would be wrong more than 65 percent of the time. To statisticians, those so misidentified are known as false positives. "All of these predictors have a lot of false positives—about 50 percent on average," says Akers, who recently completed a survey of delinquency prediction models. Their total accuracy is even lower, because the models also fail to identify some future criminals.

The risk factors that Akers says researchers have found to be most closely associated with delinquency are hardly surprising. Drug use tops the list, followed by family dysfunction, childhood behavior problems, deviant peers, poor school performance, inconsistent parental supervision and discipline, separation from parents, and poverty. Numerous other controlled studies have found that alcoholism, childhood abuse, low verbal IQ and witnessing violent acts are also significant risk factors. Compared with violent behavior, however, all these experiences are exceedingly common. The disparity makes it very difficult to determine which factors are causes and which merely correlates.

tend to score lower on IQ tests, they are not unusually aggressive.

False Positive ID

Social science studies on the causes of crime have been less controversial, in part because they have focused more on populations than on individuals. But as consensus builds among criminologists on a few key facts, researchers are assembling these into prediction models that try to identify the juveniles most likely to lapse into delinquency and then into violent crime.

Perhaps their most consistent finding is that a very small number of criminals are responsible for most of the violence. One study tracked 10,000 males born in Philadelphia in 1945 for 27 years; it found that just 6 percent of them committed 71 percent of the homicides, 73 percent of the rapes and 69 percent of the aggravated assaults attributed to the group.

Preventing just a small fraction of adolescent males from degenerating into chronic violent criminals could thus make a sizable impact on the violent crime rate, which has remained persistently high since 1973 despite a substantial decline in property crime. (Females accounted for only 12.5 percent of violent crime in 1992.) "For every 1 percent that we reduce violence, we save the country $1.2 billion," Raine asserts.

The problem, says Terrie E. Moffitt, a psychologist at the University of Wisconsin who is conducting long-term delinquency prediction studies, is that "a lot of adolescents participate in antisocial behavior"—87 percent, according to a survey of U.S. teens. "The vast majority desist by age 21," she says. The dangerous few "are buried within that population of males trying out delinquency. How do you pick them out? Our hypothesis is that those who start earliest are at highest risk."

Marion S. Forgatch of the Oregon Social Learning Center tested that hy-

Preventive Intervention

The difference is important, notes Mark W. Lipsey of Vanderbilt University, because "changing a risk factor if it is not causal may have no impact," and the ultimate goal of prediction is to stop violence by intervening before it begins. Unfortunately, improvements in predictive models do not necessarily translate into effective intervention strategies. Lipsey recently analyzed how well some 500 delinquency treatment programs reduced recidivism. "The conventional wisdom that nothing works is just wrong," he concludes. But he concedes that "the net effect is modest"—on average, 45 percent of program participants were rearrested, versus 50 percent of those left to their own devices. Half of that small apparent improvement, he adds, may be the result of in-

The Tangled Roots of Violence

The failure of expensive prison booms and welfare programs to beat back the historically high violent crime rates of the past 20 years has prepared fertile ground for new approaches to crime control. Encouraged by research that tentatively links a few instances of antisocial aggression with biological abnormalities, some politicians and activists are turning to science, perhaps too hastily, to identify and treat those who are likely to become dangerous.

Take the case of Everett L. "Red" Hodges, a California oilman who has spent more than $1 million to support research that implicates the trace metal manganese as a marker for violent criminal behavior. Hodges was struggling to tame a delinquent son in 1984 when he came across a *Science News* story on a study that had found high levels of lead, cadmium and copper in the head hair of violent felons.

Intrigued, Hodges offered funding to Louis A. Gottschalk, a psychiatrist at the University of California at Irvine, to conduct a controlled study to replicate the results. Analysis of hair clipped from convicted and accused felons at a prison and two county jails in southern California revealed no unusual levels of lead, cadmium or copper. But Gottschalk did find that average levels of manganese were about 3.6 times higher in the alleged felons than in men of similar age and race at local barbershops. "A new paradigm is opening in criminal justice," Hodges says, beaming. "It's a marker."

That judgment may be premature. Critics of Gottschalk's research, published in 1991 in a psychiatric (rather than a nutrition) journal, point out that average manganese levels varied from 2.2 parts per million in the prisoners to just 0.71 in one of the groups of jail inmates. Previous studies had found *lower* manganese levels in inmates than in control subjects. Skeptics also note that Gottschalk threw a wide net, measuring levels of 23 trace metals. "If you look at enough variables, you're bound to find a statistically significant association," comments Curtiss D. Hunt of the Grand Forks Human Nutrition Research Center in North Dakota. "But it may be meaningless." Hunt adds that the concentration of a metal in the hair does not tell one how much is in the blood or the brain. "We know so little about manganese's role in the body that we haven't even set an RDA [recommended daily allowance] for it."

Hodges remains convinced he is on the right track. "Violence can be detected and treated," he argues. In 1987 a mugger fractured the skull of another of Hodges's sons. That year Hodges founded the Violence Research Foundation (VRF) to lobby public officials to experiment with treatment programs that use what he calls "the power of nutrition" to pacify violent criminals.

The VRF found an ally in Senator Robert Presley of California, who pushed through a bill in 1989 authorizing a study of male prisoners by Stephen Schoenthaler of California State University at Stanislaus. In the first part of the study, 402 offenders were divided randomly into three groups and given vitamin-mineral supplements equivalent to the RDA, three times the RDA or a placebo. Preliminary results showed that rule violations among the first group dropped 38 percent during the study. Strangely, the behavior of inmates getting the higher dose did not improve significantly, and violations rose 20 percent among the placebo group.

Although encouraging, the equivocal results are so inconclusive that Schoenthaler has decided not to publish them until he completes further studies with more controls. Hodges, however, has publicized the results widely at conferences and on television talk shows, much to the scientist's annoyance. "We have asked that all reports on the study be embargoed until the final paper goes through the peer-review process," Schoenthaler says, "but he [Hodges] continues to make an example of it."

With two studies in hand, Hodges has redirected his crusade to Washington. "What we need is a leap of faith from the Justice Department," he says. So he has begun searching for converts. Hodges claims to have the support of former attorney general Edwin Meese, with whom he has met several times, and Senator Tom Harkin of Iowa. "I have an invitation from [Utah senator] Orrin G. Hatch to come up to Washington as soon as he becomes chairman of the Judiciary Committee," Hodges stated in December. A member of Hatch's staff says that Hodges's "material is under review, but no agreements have been made yet."

Trace element deficiencies are just one of many frequently cited but poorly demonstrated claims that nutritional problems can cause criminal and violent behavior. A 1992 report by the Federal Bureau of Prisons stated that correctional facilities in 46 states have incorporated a wide array of dietary intervention and testing programs, even though "such programs are perceived by many physicians, scientific researchers, registered dietitians, and other health care professionals as an incorporation of food faddism into public policy." —*Steven Vames and W. Wayt Gibbs*

consistency in the methods used to evaluate the programs.

Some strategies do work better than others, Lipsey discovered. Behavioral programs that concentrated on teaching job skills and rewarding prosocial attitudes cut rearrest rates to about 35 percent. "Scared straight" and boot camp programs, on the other hand, tended to increase recidivism slightly.

Patrick H. Tolan of the University of Illinois at Chicago has also recently published an empirical review of delinquency programs. To Lipsey's findings he adds that "family interventions have repeatedly shown efficacy for reducing antisocial behavior and appear to be among the most promising interventions to date." According to Forgatch, two experiments in Eugene, Ore., showed that teaching parents better monitoring and more consistent, less coercive discipline techniques reduces their kids' misbehavior. "We should make parenting skills classes compulsory for high school students," argues Raine of the University of Southern California.

Unfortunately, Tolan observes, family intervention is difficult and rarely attempted. The most common kinds of programs—counseling by social workers, peer mediation and neighborhood antiviolence initiatives—are hardly ever examined to see whether they produce lasting benefits. "It usually is hard to imagine that a good idea put into action by well-meaning and enlightened people cannot help," he noted in the paper. "It may seem that any effort is better than nothing. Yet our review and several of the more long-term and sophisticated analyses suggest that both of these assumptions can be dangerously wrong. Not only have programs that have been earnestly launched been ineffective, but some of our seemingly best ideas have led to worsening of the behavior of those subjected to the intervention."

Many researchers are thus frustrated that the Violent Crime Control and Law Enforcement Act of 1994 puts most of its $6.1 billion for crime prevention in untested and controversial programs, such as "midnight basketball" and other after-school activities. "Maybe these programs will help; maybe they won't," Tolan says. "No one has done a careful evaluation." The Crime Act does not insist that grant applicants demonstrate or even measure the effectiveness of their approach. For these and other reasons, Republicans vowed in their "Contract with America" to repeal all prevention programs in the Crime Act and to increase funding for prison construction. But that strategy also ignores research. "We do know," Tolan asserts, "that locking kids up will not reduce crime and may eventually make the problem worse."

All in Our Heads?

The failure of sociology to demonstrate conclusively effective means of controlling violent crime has made some impatient. "There is a growing recognition that we're not going to solve any problem in society using just one discipline," says Diana Fishbein, a professor of criminology at the University of Baltimore. "Sociological factors play a role. But they have not been able to

explain why one person becomes violent and another doesn't."

Some social scientists are looking to psychiatrists, neurologists and geneticists to provide answers to that question, ready or not. "Science must tell us what individuals will or will not become criminals, what individuals will or will not become victims, and what law enforcement strategies will or will not work," wrote C. Ray Jeffery, a criminologist at Florida State University, last year in the *Journal of Research in Crime and Delinquency*.

As medical researchers have teased out a few tantalizing links between brain chemistry, heredity, hormones, physiology and assaultive behavior, some have become emboldened. "Research in the past 10 years conclusively demonstrates that biological factors play some role in the etiology of violence. That is scientifically beyond doubt," Raine holds forth. The importance of that role is still very much in doubt, however.

As with social risk factors, no biological abnormality has been shown to *cause* violent aggression—nor is that likely except in cases of extreme psychiatric disorder. But researchers have spotted several unusual features, too subtle even to be considered medical problems, that tend to appear in the bodies and brains of physically aggressive men. On average, for example, they have higher levels of testosterone, a sex hormone important for building muscle mass and strength, among other functions. James M. Dabbs, Jr., of Georgia State University has found in his experiments with prison inmates that men with the highest testosterone concentrations are more likely to have committed violent crimes. But Dabbs emphasizes that the link is indirect and "mediated by numerous social factors," such as higher rates of divorce and substance abuse.

"Low resting heart rate probably represents the best replicated biological correlate of antisocial behavior," Raine observes, pointing to 14 studies that have found that problem children and petty criminals tend to have significantly lower pulses than do well-behaved counterparts. A slower heartbeat "probably reflects fearlessness and underarousal," Raine theorizes. "If we lack the fear of getting hurt, it may lead to a predisposition to engage in violence." But that hypothesis fails to explain why at least 15 studies have failed to find abnormal heart rates in psychopaths.

Jerome Kagan, a Harvard University psychologist, has suggested that an in-

hibited "temperament" may explain why the great majority of children from high-risk homes grow up to become law-abiding citizens. One study tested pulse, pupil dilation, vocal tension and blood levels of the neurotransmitter norepinephrine and the stress-regulating hormone cortisol to distinguish inhibited from uninhibited, underaroused two-year-olds. An expert panel on "Understanding and Preventing Violence" convened by the National Research Council suggested in its 1993 report that inhibited children may be protected by their fearfulness from becoming aggressive, whereas uninhibited children may be prone to later violence. The panel concluded that "although such factors in isolation may not be expected to be strong predictors of violence, in conjunction with other early family and cognitive measures, the degree of prediction may be considerable."

Perhaps the most frequently cited biological correlate of violent behavior is a low level of serotonin, a chemical that in the body inhibits the secretion of stomach acid and stimulates smooth muscle and in the brain functions as a neurotransmitter. A large body of animal evidence links low levels of serotonin to impulsive aggression. Its role in humans is often oversimplified, however. "Serotonin has a calming effect on behavior by reducing the level of violence," Jeffery wrote in 1993 in the *Journal of Criminal Justice Education*. "Thus, by increasing the level of serotonin in the brain, we can reduce the level of violence." A front-page article in the *Chicago Tribune* in December 1993 explained that "when serotonin declines… impulsive aggression is unleashed."

Such explanations do violence to the science. In human experiments, researchers do not generally have access to the serotonin inside their subject's braincase. Instead they tap cerebrospinal fluid from the spinal column and measure the concentration of 5-hydroxyindoleacetic acid (5-HIAA), which is produced when serotonin is used up and broken down by the enzyme monoamine oxidase (MAO). Serotonin does its job by binding to any of more than a dozen different neural receptors, each of which seems to perform a distinct function. The low levels of 5-HIAA repeatedly seen in violent offenders may indicate a shortage of serotonin in the brain or simply a dearth of MAO—in which case their serotonin levels may actually be high. Moreover, serotonin can rise or drop in different regions of the brain at different times, with markedly different effects.

Environment, too, plays a role: non-human primate studies show that serotonin often fluctuates with pecking order, dropping in animals when they are threatened and rising when they assume a dominant status. The numerous pathways through which serotonin can influence mood and behavior confound attempts to simply "reduce the level of violence" by administering serotonin boosters such as Prozac, a widely prescribed antidepressant.

Nevertheless, the link between 5-HIAA and impulsive aggression has led to a concerted hunt for the genes that control the production and activity of serotonin and several other neurotransmitters. "Right now we have in our hand many of the genes that affect brain function," says David Goldman, chief of neurogenetics at the National Institute on Alcohol Abuse and Alcoholism. Although none has yet been shown to presage violence, "I believe the markers are there," he says. But he warns that "we're going to have to understand a whole lot more about the genetic, environmental and developmental origins of personality and psychiatric disease" before making use of the knowledge.

Yudofsky is less circumspect. "We are now on the verge of a revolution in genetic medicine," he asserts. "The future will be to understand the genetics of aggressive disorders and to identify those who have greater tendencies to become violent."

A Compelling Option

Few researchers believe genetics alone will ever yield reliable predictors of behavior as complex and multifarious as harmful aggression. Still, the notion that biologists and sociologists might together be able to assemble a complicated model that can scientifically pick out those who pose the greatest threat of vicious attack seems to be gaining currency. Already some well-respected behavioral scientists are advocating a medical approach to crime control based on screening, diagnostic prediction and treatment. "A future generation *will* reconceptualize nontrivial recidivistic crime as a disorder," Raine predicted in his 1993 book, *The Psychopathology of Crime.*

But the medical model of crime may be fraught with peril. When the "disease" is intolerable behavior that threatens society, will "treatment" necessarily be compulsory and indefinite? If, to reexamine Raine's hypothetical example, prediction models are judged reliable but "biological, social and cognitive intervention programs" are not, might eight-year-old boys be judged incorrigible before they have broken any law?

Calls for screening are now heard more often. "There are areas where we can begin to incorporate biological approaches," Fishbein argues. "Delinquents need to be individually assessed." Mas-

ters claims that "we now know enough about the serotonergic system so that if we see a kid doing poorly in school, we ought to look at his serotonin levels."

In his 1993 article Jeffery emphasized that "attention must focus on the 5 percent of the delinquent population who commit 50 percent of the offenses.... This effort must identify high-risk persons at an early age and place them in treatment programs *before* they have committed the 10 to 20 major felonies characteristic of the career criminal."

Yudofsky suggests a concrete method to do this: "You could ask parents whether they consider their infant high-strung or hyperactive. Then screen more closely by challenging the infants with provocative situations." When kids respond too aggressively, he suggests "you could do careful neurologic testing and train the family how not to goad and fight them. Teach the children nonviolent ways to reduce frustration. And when these things don't work, consider medical interventions, such as beta blockers, anticonvulsants or lithium.

"We haven't done this research, but I have no doubt that it would make an enormous impact and would be immediately cost-effective," Yudofsky continues. While he bemoans a lack of drugs designed specifically to treat aggression, he sees a tremendous "opportunity for the pharmaceutical industry," which he maintains is "finally getting interested."

But some worry that voluntary screen-

For Biological Studies, Minorities Need Not Apply

Scientists pursuing the role of biology in violent behavior have been twice shy since 1992, when shrill public criticism forced the National Institutes of Health to withdraw financial support of a conference on the ethical implications of "Genetic Factors in Crime" and compelled former health secretary Louis Sullivan to abort his proposed "Violence Initiative." Led by firebrand psychiatrist Peter Breggin, critics charged that in a society where blacks account for 12.4 percent of the population but 44.8 percent of arrests for violent crimes, such research plays into the hands of racists.

The controversy did little to dissuade scientists from their studies, which continue to grow in number. The NIH has reinstated funding for the genetics conference and increased its budget for violence-related research to $58 million. Most Violence Initiative projects have found support in other programs. And last December the National Science Foundation began soliciting proposals for a $12-million, five-year violence research consortium.

But the political wrangling seems to have intimidated investigators from including minorities in any violence studies with a biological tinge—and from collecting medi-

cal data in multiracial studies. Designers of an 11,000-subject, eight-year study of the causes of crime in Chicago, for example, were forced last summer to ditch plans to collect blood and urine samples when Breggin organized rallies to block the project, says Felton Earls, a Harvard University professor and co-director of the study. As a result of such pressure, asserts Adrian Raine of the University of Southern California, "all the biological and genetic studies conducted to date have been done on whites. Scientifically, we can make no statements on the biological basis of violence and crime in blacks or Hispanics or Asians."

There is no reason to suspect that any genetic connection links race to antisocial behavior. But there is reason to be concerned that ostensibly objective biological studies, blindly ignoring social and cultural differences, could misguidedly reinforce racial stereotypes. Still, Earls, Raine and other researchers emphasize that biological factors, if they exist, are important only insofar as they protect individuals from—or make them vulnerable to—bad influences in their family, school and neighborhood. Research that excludes those who are most burdened by such pressures may be most expedient, but is it most useful?

ing for the good of the child might lead to mandatory screening for the protection of society. "It is one thing to convict someone of an offense and compel them to do something. It is another thing to go to someone who has not done anything wrong and say, 'You look like a high risk, so you have to do this,'" Akers observes. "There is a very clear ethical difference, but that is a very thin line that people, especially politicians, might cross over."

Even compelling convicted criminals to undergo treatment raises thorny ethical issues. Today the standards for proving that an offender is so mentally ill that he poses a danger to himself or others and thus can be incarcerated indefinitely are quite high. The medical model of violent crime threatens to lower those standards substantially. Indeed, Jeffery argues that "if we are to

follow the medical model, we must use neurological examinations in place of the insanity defense and the concept of guilt. Criminals must be placed in medical clinics, not prisons." Fishbein says she is "beginning to think that treatment should be mandatory. We don't ask offenders whether they want to be incarcerated or executed. They should remain in a secure facility until they can show without a doubt that they are self-controlled." And if no effective treatments are available? "They should be held indefinitely," she says.

Unraveling the mystery of human behavior, just like untangling the genetic code of human physiology, creates a moral imperative to use that knowledge. To ignore it—to imprison without treatment those whom we define as sick for the behavioral symptoms of their illness—is morally indefensible. But to

replace a fixed term of punishment set by the conscience of a society with forced therapy based on the judgment of scientific experts is to invite even greater injustice.

FURTHER READING

THE PSYCHOPATHOLOGY OF CRIME. Adrian Raine. Academic Press, 1993.
UNDERSTANDING AND PREVENTING VIOLENCE. Edited by A. J. Reiss, Jr., and J. A. Roth. National Academy Press, 1993.
WHAT WORKS IN REDUCING ADOLESCENT VIOLENCE. Patrick Tolan and Nancy Guerra. Available from the Center for the Study and Prevention of Violence, University of Colorado, 1994.
Crime statistics and violence prevention program information are available at gopher://justice2.usdoj.gov:70/1/ojp on the World Wide Web.

The Youngest Ex-Cons: Facing a Difficult Road Out of Crime

By PAM BELLUCK

They get out of jail, still young enough to go back to school.

And if they do return to school, juvenile justice experts find, they are much more likely to get a degree or job. But for a growing number of teen-agers across the country, getting into school after getting out of jail means crossing a precarious threshold, their home and street lives constantly threatening to unravel their progress or lure them back to a criminal world.

Herbert Carrasquillo, 17, said he has been selling drugs and stealing cars since he was 11. Released from Rikers Island last month, he wanted a high school diploma but instead worries about supporting his two daughters. He has yet to attend class.

Tim G., 17, got out of boot camp last year and went straight into school, an environment where counselors delved so deeply into his life that they moved him into foster care after learning that his father was selling cocaine from the living room. The school, which made Tim available on the condition his last name not be published, also helped him care for his crack-addicted mother, who has AIDS.

Lisa Lovejoy was 16 when she helped two other girls attack and stab a man nearly to death in a Queens subway station. She reentered school eight months ago, and has stayed there, trying to escape the drugs and violence around her and forget the memories of seeing her brother and boyfriend gunned down.

These young criminals fall into a subset of teen-agers far more common today than 10 years ago. The rate of serious felonies, especially violent ones, has increased among those 10 to 17 years old for most of the last 10 years, bucking the general decline in violence among adults. And experts predict a burgeoning number of young violent criminals in the next 10 years, if only because the number of teen-agers will grow.

In New York and elsewhere, turning around the lives of young criminals has been largely unsuccessful. To date, most rehabilitation efforts have occurred while teen-agers were still incarcerated, using boot camps, adult prisons or vocational programs intended to teach new skills.

But experts are beginning to realize that these approaches have little lasting influence outside of prison. About two-thirds of juvenile offenders are arrested again within 18 months of their release, and many become adult criminals. A survey of 100 youths released from Rikers last year found that after 6 months, only 25 had enrolled in school, and 4 of those had dropped out. Twenty-two had already returned to Rikers.

"The one thing we know now is that the real problem has been when these youngsters get out of these facilities," said David M. Altschuler, a principal researcher in juvenile crime at the Johns Hopkins Institute for Policy Studies. "It doesn't matter how well they do in an institution. They come back out and in record numbers they fail."

Some youths released from jail are sentenced to parole or to "after-care" programs that provide supervision and counseling. In both cases, the youths receive help getting into school and staying there. But in New York and elsewhere, a parole officer or after-care counselor may have dozens of cases to track and the contact ends when the sentence does, often after only a few months.

Correction officials, criminologists and educators all point to schooling as a possible solution, whether it's a traditional classroom, a vocational program or a path to a high school equivalency diploma.

Spurred by recidivism, jail crowding and the cost (up to $90,000 a year for a youth in jail), corrections and school officials have begun experimental programs to encourage the young criminals to return to school, although many schools are reluctant to accept them because of their criminal background, and behavioral and academic problems. New Jersey, Texas, Florida and California have gone further than New York has, opening residential schools for young offenders.

"School is obviously a critical ingredient," said Barry Krisberg, president of the National Council on Crime and Delinquency, in San Francisco. "If you fail in school or you drop out, you're not going to get a job except in the drug trade. But the vast majority of kids who exit the juvenile justice system never enter school and certainly never enter school successfully."

Public School
Out of Custody but Facing Hurdles

The television was flickering out of focus in the cramped East Harlem apartment where Herbert Carrasquillo was trying to figure out how to support his girlfriend Lili Centero, 21, and his daughters, Marelyn, 2, and Angela, 1.

His skills are limited. At 17, he did not have the high school credits needed to complete 10th grade, and his most recent accomplishment, heart stencils and cartoon-character cards he made in Rikers, were taped to the walls. He was waiting for replies to job applications he had filed at Macy's and Toys "R" Us. And he was avoiding neighborhood drug dealers and gang members.

When Herbert ricocheted out of Rikers four weeks ago, after serving 10 months on a drug charge, he wanted a high school diploma.

A Rikers psychologist, Karen Black, made an appointment for him with a high school administrator and even accompanied him there, going beyond her responsibilities. Seeing he needed two years to graduate and that he had a family to support, the administrator suggested a work program that included preparation for a high school equivalency diploma.

But when Herbert said no, the administrator made an appointment at the Murray Hill Borough Academy, an alternative high school for troubled youths. He did not show up.

Herbert gave several reasons, including that his mother, who supports some of her 12 children on welfare, did not want him in a "school for bad kids."

He said he planned to go back to his old school, the Martin Luther King Jr. High School on the Upper West Side. But even if he had shown up there, it would not have mattered.

"He cannot just decide to come here," said Stephanie D'Amore, the principal of King. "We would not let him in the building."

Herbert's roller-coaster ride is in many ways typical. Often, the school that youths want to go to will not take them back, especially if, like Herbert, they had truancy problems or got into trouble while they were there.

To the Board of Education, young offenders are officially off the rosters because they are in jail. While youths age 21 and under are entitled to free public education, offenders can return to school only if they request a placement. And placement may take time, leaving youths on their own during the precarious days just after release.

"Our kids are certainly not welcomed back into the school system," said Newell Eaton, director of planning for the State Division for Youth.

School and corrections officials say they have been trying to speed the process by finding school placements while the youths are still in jail. There are several hurdles, they say. Although incarcerated youths take classes, the courses are not always enough for high school credit or a spot in a grade that matches their age. Many also need extra help, like special education classes available only at certain schools.

School officials often prefer placing the released offenders in smaller alternative high schools for troubled youths. Or, if the teen-agers are older and have few credits, officials may recommend work programs or those geared for a high school equivalency diploma, or G.E.D.

But there is debate about this. Some experts suggest that some alternative schools only expose youths to more "bad kids." Others believe that offenders get lost in regular schools, shunned by good students, glamorized and goaded into bad behavior by delinquent ones. And many youths, parents and experts say the G.E.D. is second-rate or stigmatizing.

There is also the question of the school's location. Some experts believe the schools should be close to home to make it easier for youths to attend. But many say the schools should be far from the neighborhoods where the teen-agers got into trouble. One convicted teen-age drug dealer released from Rikers said that he fought with a teacher and started dealing again when he started school near his Brooklyn housing project. Transferred to a Manhattan school, he was able to keep his home life separate from classes: using his given name instead of his street name, leaving his gold teeth and chunky jewelry in Brooklyn, even betting on different World Series teams, the Yankees at school, the Braves at home.

From September 1995 to last August, about 1,500 ex-offenders age 21

and under were placed in city schools, a 13 percent increase from the year before. Abut 500 have been placed since school began in September. But Board of Education officials cannot say how successful these placements are because they do not monitor the students' progress. About 5,000 New York City youths serve several months in state and city correctional facilities each year, with thousands more spending shorter stints. In New York City, felony and misdemeanor arrests for youths age 15 to 19 climbed to 55,000 in 1995 from 46,000 in 1991.

Herbert, who finished his criminal sentence, is not on parole, so there is no parole officer or counselor prodding him to go to school. Rikers officials try to link youths with community aftercare groups, and Ms. Black even took him to visit one, but that contact is not required.

"We can make all the plans we want, but then they just don't show up," Ms. Black said. "I would like to see him get back into any kind of school, but that may not happen."

So far, Herbert has spent his days shopping for groceries with money borrowed from his brother, helping his 1-year-old try to take her first steps, watching television and trying fitfully to find work.

"I want the school, but right now, it's kind of hard, because I don't have money," he said. "I don't have nothing. I don't want to be on welfare. I want to work. What I always wanted was my diploma. But if I get this job and they

BY THE NUMBERS

Tracking Youth Crime

UNITED STATES

Arrests for violent crime per 100,000 youths ages 10 through 17.

NOTE: Criminologists predict an increased number of arrests in the next decade because of an increase in the teen-age population.

NEW YORK STATE

Youths, 16 through 20, in state prisons, not including those in juvenile programs or detention centers.

Sources: Federal Bureau of Investigation; New York State Department of Correctional Services

say full time . . . I don't know. I want to be so many things."

City Challenge
From Boot Camp to the Classroom

Before Tim got arrested at 16, he would get on the bus each day, usually only pretending to go to school. Later, he pretended to do homework, and he tore up the truancy postcards sent to his home.

But after spending six months in a Division for Youth boot camp for punching a high school dean and mugging people for gold chains, things were different. When he was released from the boot camp last year, he was immediately placed in City Challenge, an unusual school taught by public school teachers but supervised by the boot camp.

Youths go to City Challenge for five months as part of their criminal sentence and are then placed in other city public schools.

"They get out of here and the very next day they're in a school," said Col. Thomas Cornick, director of the boot camp, the Sgt. Henry Johnson Youth Leadership Academy in the Catskills. "In New York City, that's almost impossible to do."

City Challenge, a program started four years ago in a brownstone in Bedford-Stuyvesant, Brooklyn, tries to give youths the kind of individually tailored attention and supervision that experts have begun to consider crucial. It also saves money, state corrections officials argue, since it cuts boot camp to 6 months from the usual 10.

While teen-agers are in boot camp, staff members visit their homes, contact their old schools and talk to anyone important in their lives—a basketball coach, for example. They may place youths in foster homes. Once in City Challenge, the youths are monitored to make sure they attend school, go to job programs and get home before 10 P.M.

Experts say City Challenge is on the right track, but needs to last longer.

"Why do we think that normal kids need four years to receive a good education," Dr. Krisberg said, "and these kids need only a few months?"

With Tim, boot camp staff members decided he should live with his father, even though he had spent most of his life in a foster home in Queens.

"The place was neat," Colonel Cornick said of the father's apartment. "There was a lot of good furniture in the home. The father talked good."

But two weeks later, Colonel Cornick said, "He called me back and said 'Hey, my father's selling crack out of the living room.'" Tim went back to the foster family.

City Challenge also helped Tim deal with other problems, like his mother's health.

After finishing his City Challenge classes each day, Tim would go to East Harlem and pound on the door of a decrepit, drug-riddled building until his mother opened it. "I would help her wash up and stuff, get her food," Tim said. "A lot of times I'd be there late at night."

Because of the late nights, City Challenge allowed Tim to attend school part-time. And Hilton Cooper, City Challenge's top counselor, went with Tim to coax his mother to get AIDS treatment.

City Challenge also got Tim a part-time job, psychological counseling and engaged him in basketball. He achieved more than he ever had, finishing the 10th grade.

"It was like the best school," said Tim, a towering teen-ager slouched on a plastic-slipcovered couch in his living room. "They like working with you. And you can't leave once you got in."

But last spring, when Tim's City Challenge sentence ended, he went to a large public high school in Queens. Things began to unravel.

He cut classes and "got the attention of special ed department," said Sylvia Rowlands, a psychologist at the boot camp. "There was a lot of pressure and it just drove him right out of school altogether."

Over the summer, Tim was charged with a misdemeanor when the police found a gun in a car he was in. He has spent time putting up Sheetrock in the foster family's garage and playing with his pit bull puppy, Danger. He delivered food for a Chinese restaurant, whose regular delivery boys had been getting robbed.

"I wanted to get back in City Challenge," Tim said. Counselors there could not allow that, but encouraged him to keep in contact. Two weeks ago, he asked Colonel Cooper to help him get into a G.E.D. program.

"Mr. Cooper will help me," he said. "Colonel will help me."

Alternative Academy
A Smaller School with Daily Credit

Lisa Lovejoy was not the one actually wielding the eight-inch kitchen knife in the subway station, stabbing the young man in the back while the N and R trains thundered through. That was her best friend.

But Lisa, then 16, and another girl were helping, pummeling the young man, as their friend, who said the man had raped her, punctured his lung and nearly killed him.

Now, after a year in jail for attempted murder, Lisa is in high school and has earned enough credits to graduate in June. The school newspaper has published her poetry, "If I Must Die," and "Rage of Fear." And she is looking for colleges where she can learn to become a mortician.

The other day, in her favorite class, science, Lisa pulled on surgical gloves and picked up a blade and forceps, dissecting a frog.

"I'm about to cut and stab this thing," she said, chomping on gum.

Immediately after she got out of an upstate detention center last December, Lisa was placed in a large public school. But in February, school officials recommended the Murray Hill Borough Academy, which has only 135 students.

The school has strict attendance requirements, provides counseling and a jobs program. Students get no grades, but they are awarded partial credits for class work every day, allowing them to chart their own progress toward the 40 credits needed to graduate.

While other ex-offenders at the school have had setbacks, Lisa, who sees a parole officer every other week, has managed to do well, using the school as a partial escape from life's hardships: her brother's murder, the fatal shooting of her boyfriend, the pressures from "the fellas" on the block to sell drugs. After school, she visits a friend who was hospitalized after being shot in the head in a drug-related incident. At home in Washington Heights, she might be summoned by her father at midnight to help clean apartment buildings.

"It's been real hard," said Lisa, seeming callow yet street-smart in red silk pants, a red silk blouse, a red leather jacket and white satin pumps. "Just the other day someone said to me, 'Let's go make this money.' I could go on the corner, sell my little bit of stuff. It was tempting."

But, Lisa said, she resists.

"I see a lot of people, they come home from being incarcerated and do the same thing and go back," she said. "Or they come out and kill somebody. I don't want to be out there collecting cans. I don't want to have to sell drugs. I don't want to have to sell my body. I don't want that to be me."

CLINICAL ASSESSMENT OF ADOLESCENTS INVOLVED IN SATANISM

ABSTRACT

Satanism is a destructive religion that promises power, dominance, and gratification to its practitioners. Unfortunately, some adolescents are seduced by these promises, often because they feel alienated, alone, angry, and desperate. This article explores the psychosocial needs of adolescents that are often met by participation in Satanic worship. Gratification of these needs, when met, may make leaving the cult a difficult and lengthy process. Included is a method for determining the adolescents' level of involvement and an assessment strategy for the therapeutic evaluation process. A brief overview of clinical intervention is also discussed.

Cynthia M. Clark

An adolescent who practices Satanism recently said to the author, "I was a throwaway kid. Nobody wanted me and I needed a place to belong. I had a lust for power, and I needed to find a place where my violence was acceptable." This teenager is one of a growing number who feel empty and alienated, and may be searching for an identity and a place to belong. Unfortunately, some adolescents are fulfilling a number of their needs by aligning with deviant subcultures, one of which is Satanism.

Satanism is devil worship, a recognition of Satan as the charismatic being who is honored and exalted by his followers. Satan and his demons are considered to be all-powerful and will extend their power to those who choose them as their supreme deity. It is a religion that advocates violence, hatred, and revenge. In the adolescent culture, many teens learn about Satanism from peers, books, the media, and from heavy metal bands. Most teens initially lack sophistication when practicing Satanism and make it up as they go along (Magic, A Deadly Solution, 1985). Curran (1989) describes Satanism as "a hole in the ground that some adolescents stumble into because they have been wandering desperate, angry and alone . . . and we should wonder less about why the hole was there than why these young people are wandering alone in the dark" (p. 13). Therefore, it is impor-

tant to understand the needs of adolescents that frequently are met by Satanism.

Adolescent Needs Met by Satanic Involvement

When these psychosocial needs are met, teens' allegiance to the cult is often reinforced, thus making separation much more difficult.

Sense of belonging. Many adolescents who practice Satanism do so out of a need to belong and to address feelings of alienation and detachment from friends, family, and community. Bronfenbrenner (1986) describes social alienation as a serious threat to the successful resolution of an adolescent's identity crisis. Because a sense of belonging is crucial to identity formation, teens struggle to find a place to belong (Levine, 1979). Unfortunately, some young people turn to deviant subcultures. Teenage involvement in Satanism has been termed an immediate antidote for loneliness (Curran, 1989) and a possible solution to alienation and neglect.

Mastery and structure. Adolescents require structure, order, and limits, which Satanism provides. Satanism is based on nine Satanic statements which furnish tangible principles for practice (LaVey, 1969). Since a sense of mastery and efficacy are integral to identity formation and development of a healthy sense of self, an adolescent may derive these from practicing Satanic rituals.

Power and control. Satanism is purported by its users to be a source of great power, one that offers a "quick fix" to their problems. Some Satanic rituals are performed as a means of deriving that power. Satanists believe that there is power and energy within the souls and

Reprint requests to Cynthia M. Clark, M.S., R.H., Manager of Residential Psychiatric Adolescent Services, CPC Intermountain Hospital of Boise, Idaho, 303 N. Allumbaug Street, Boise, Idaho 83702.

bodies of animals and humans which is released through torture and death and subsequently absorbed by the practitioner (America's Best Kept Secret, 1986).

Rebellion. Adolescent rebellion is considered by many as a normal developmental process and many teenagers experiment with different values and lifestyles. Satanism represents a hostile and extreme form of rebellion. Curran (1989) describes it as an irreverent rebellion against the accepted order which provides a way to escape conformity and the values of the established society. For many adolescents, Satanism is a violent and passionate form of rebellion that is acted out through rituals, incantations, spells, and ceremonies that is most often directed at parents and society.

Curiosity and relief from boredom. Teenagers are fascinated with magic and the supernatural. Often, merely out of curiosity, teenagers will seek to learn about the occult and various forms of magic. Satanism also provides an escape from boredom and conformity since it is a belief system that is radically different from the social mainstream.

Self-esteem. It is generally believed that the achievement of a clear sense of identity is a critical task of adolescence (Lloyd, 1985). Thus, many adolescents join cults at a time when their self-esteem is low, and once involved, their self-esteem may be heightened by a sense of mastery and belonging. This rise in self-esteem provides positive reinforcement for their behavior, and is likely to motivate further involvement.

Validation of anger and violence. Since a sense of alienation may foster feelings of anger and hostility, Satanism, by advocating revenge, encourages rage and the attainment of power through violent means. Thus, some teen-

agers find Satanic involvement a safe refuge for their hostility because it is encouraged and condoned.

Continuum of Deviant Cultism

The author has developed a Continuum of Deviant Cultism based on the patterns of drug using behavior described in the second report of the National Commission on Marijuana and Drug Abuse (1973). The continuum covers a range of subjects from those who have never participated in Satanism to those who are seriously involved.

Experimental use. Here experimental use of Satanism is defined as "dabbling." Adolescents who dabble are often introduced to Satanism at a social gathering of friends. Case example: Eric was a dabbler who began experimenting with Satanism when he attended a Halloween party. His friends suggested they go to a graveyard and perform a seance to summon Satan and his minions.

Eric participated, but was so frightened, he did not continue to pursue this type of activity. Such dabbling usually does not lead to deep involvement. Thus, it does not adversely affect psychosocial development, or lead to further exploration.

Social/recreational use. Social/recreational use of Satanism is defined as a deeper fascination with magic and the occult. The adolescent begins to find time to practice magic and learn about rituals and ceremonies. Case example: Adam often loitered near a teen center where devil worshippers were known to frequent. He had been introduced to them a week earlier by a friend. After reading about demon possession and ritualized human dismemberment, Adam became more curious and ap-

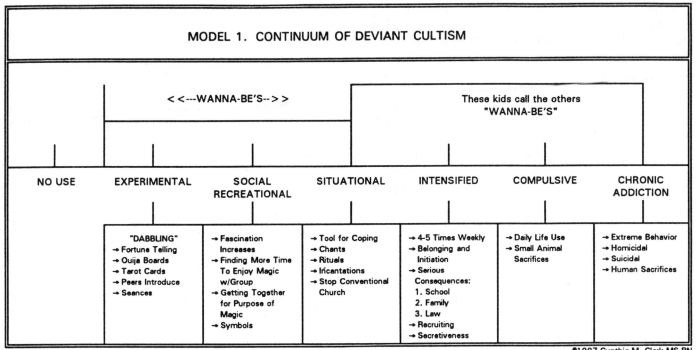

MODEL 1. CONTINUUM OF DEVIANT CULTISM

NO USE	EXPERIMENTAL	SOCIAL RECREATIONAL	SITUATIONAL	INTENSIFIED	COMPULSIVE	CHRONIC ADDICTION
	"DABBLING" → Fortune Telling → Ouija Boards → Tarot Cards → Peers Introduce → Seances	→ Fascination Increases → Finding More Time To Enjoy Magic w/Group → Getting Together for Purpose of Magic → Symbols	→ Tool for Coping → Chants → Rituals → Incantations → Stop Conventional Church	→ 4-5 Times Weekly → Belonging and Initiation → Serious Consequences: 1. School 2. Family 3. Law → Recruiting → Secretiveness	→ Daily Life Use → Small Animal Sacrifices	→ Extreme Behavior → Homicidal → Suicidal → Human Sacrifices

*1987 Cynthia M. Clark, MS, RN

proached the cult members to inquire about attending a ritual.

At this stage, adolescents begin to seek opportunities for practicing their craft. Although they remain in the category of "wanna-be's," they may develop psychosocial complications. However, most do not develop long-standing problems if the Satanic practice is discontinued.

Situational use. Satanic practice for the situational user has become a tool for coping with life's stressful situations. Adolescents at this stage are striving to learn more about Satanism and to rely on its practice to ease their discontent and to resolve specific conflicts. Case example: Nikki had been dabbling in the black arts for more than a year when she began using rituals and spells to seek revenge on her boyfriend for breaking up with her. Having lacked the skills necessary for asserting herself during the break-up, she resorted to Satanism to pursue reprisal.

Nikki used Satanism to deal with uncomfortable feelings and circumstances. If clinical intervention is implemented at this stage, the chances for successful recovery are usually good.

Intensified use. Once a teenager advances beyond situational use and moves into intensified use, treatment and recovery become more difficult. At this stage, adolescents are very deeply involved in Satanism, and formal cult initiation has almost always occurred. Case example: Allen was initiated by attending a ceremony that highlighted his own "debaptism," a rite performed to rid him of the Holy Spirit that had come into him during his Christian baptism. During the debaptism, he was forced to drink a mixture of blood, semen, and urine to force the "good spirits" out of him, thus allowing the demons to enter his body. He entered into a written contract swearing him to secrecy and pledging his allegiance to the cult. In addition, Allen committed a burglary that was witnessed by cult members, making it difficult for him to leave the group. He was told that if he tried to leave, the police would be notified of his crime.

By the time a teenager is this fully involved, other forms of delinquent behaviors such as truancy, petty theft, vandalism, and drug abuse become prevalent.

Compulsive use. At the compulsive stage, secretiveness increases as a direct result of the growing level of offensive activity. Case example: Cory was heavily involved with Satanism and performed rituals that summoned demons thought to enhance power and sexual energy. He would mutilate a small animal, make multiple superficial cuts all over his own body, and then lie in a bathtub of hot water. He would lie there for hours in his own blood while sexually manipulating the animal and chanting to Satan. Cory had dropped out of school following numerous suspensions and was seriously chemically dependent.

At this stage, psychosocial development may be severely compromised, treatment is extremely difficulty and lengthy, and the prognosis is often poor. It is important to understand that these patterns are descriptive in nature and do not necessarily imply that a youth will progress through these stages of deepening involvement. Some youths will remain in the lower stages, some may progress over a long period of time, while others may become deeply involved from the start and progress rapidly to the more serious stage.

Chronic addiction. While the term "chronic addiction" may not precisely define the level of Satanic involvement occurring at this final stage, it is used because it is consistent with the Drug Abuse Continuum (1973). At this stage, Satanism has clearly become a way of life, and leaving the cult is nearly impossible without therapeutic intervention. This level of involvement may include sacrificial human offerings (Weather, 1989; Young et al., 1991), or one's own suicide as a way of pledging unequivocal allegiance to Satan (Tenant-Clark, Fritz, & Beauvais, 1989). Young et al. (1991) notes an account of an adolescent who had been serially raped by male cult members when she was 13 years old, resulting in pregnancy. After premature induction of labor, she was forced to assist in her infant's sacrifice during a Satanic ritual. She also recalled two more pregnancies terminated by forced abortion where the fetuses were reportedly dismembered and consumed during subsequent rituals. While gruesome accounts like these are extreme, they continue to be reported (Snowden, 1988; VanBenschoten, 1990; Young et al., 1991). Obviously adolescents at this level of involvement are seriously compromised psychologically and require extensive treatment. Their prognosis for a full recovery is very poor.

Assessment of Adolescents Involved with Satanism

As an adolescent becomes more involved with Satanism, withdrawal from normative society increases, secretiveness intensifies, and antisocial behaviors become more prevalent. There is a change in peer group, activities, and vocabulary. Drug and alcohol abuse, truancy, violent acts, family conflicts, and legal problems escalate. Serious cult members are often from disengaged, chaotic family systems, and lack the capacity to establish and maintain intimate and flexible relationships with peers. Their outlook on life may be dismal as they are frequently preoccupied with darkness, evil, and violence. Many cult-involved teens appear hopeless and harbor negative feelings about the future.

Many lose their sense of humor and become deeply depressed. There are frequent episodes of suicidal ideation often accompanied by self-mutilation and/or blood-letting of themselves, animals, or both.

General Guidelines for Clinical Intervention

In order to treat an adolescent who is involved in Satanism, the clinician must be knowledgeable of precipitating factors. It is critical to focus therapy on the psychosocial needs being met rather than on attempting to understand the intricate details of the Satanic practice itself. Addressing the underlining motivators keeps therapy manageable and allows the clinician to address such fundamental issues as self-esteem, sense of belonging, and the need for structure (Clark, 1992).

It is useful to ask when the cult activity began because it is almost always preceded by a significant event. Involving the family is often effective, but this depends on the individual case. This author has had success in involving the family once a solid therapeutic alliance had been established with the adolescent and after he had demonstrated a desire to break loose from his cult activities. Therapy must include helping the teen develop reliable and healthy alternatives to both his participation in Satanism and probable substance abuse. Active involvement by the therapist is required to assist the adolescent with problem-solving and finding new ways of coping.

Occasionally an adolescent is so disturbed that hospitalization is required. Without the structure and safety of the inpatient therapeutic milieu, the adolescent may become increasingly self-destructive. Hospitalization provides resolution of a crisis, stabilization, and an opportunity to effect change. Many of these adolescents have long-standing problems that require continued outpatient therapy and follow-up long after hospitalization has ended.

CONCLUSIONS

While involvement in Satanism is a problem for teenagers, it is important to understand that the Satanic experience is usually an attempt to regain control, frequently in response to feelings of alienation, poor attachment, and lowered self-esteem. Adolescents who have been neglected, abused or unloved often act out violently. Thus they may be attracted to Satanism which is based on violence, power, and destruction. Clinicians dealing with these teens must be knowledgeable and empathic about these issues and sophisticated in the application of treatment methods.

REFERENCES

America's Best Kept Secret: A Special Report. (1986). *Passport,* Oct./Nov., 1–15.

Bronfenbrenner, U. (1986). Alienation and the four winds of childhood. *Phi Delta Kappan,* Feb., 430–436.

Clark, C. M. (1992). Deviant adolescent subcultures: Assessment strategies and clinical intervention. *Adolescence,* 27(106), 283–293.

Curran, D. K. (1989). Why troubled teens might turn to satanism. *The American School Board Journal,* August, 12–15.

LaVey, A. S. (1969). *The satanic bible.* New York: Avon.

Levine, S. V. (1979). Adolescents: Believing and belonging. *Adolescent Psychiatry, 1,* 41–53.

Lloyd, M. (1985). *Adolescence.* New York: Harper & Row.

Magic: A deadly solution. (1985). *Denver Magazine,* Feb., 23–28.

National Commission on Marijuana and Drug Abuse. (1973). Drug use in America: Problem in perspective (Second report of the National Commission on marijuana and drug abuse). Washington, DC: U.S. Government Printing Office.

Snowden, K. K. *(1988). Satanic cult ritual abuse.* Unpublished Manuscript.

Tennant-Clark, C. M., Fritz, J. J., & Beauvais, F. (1989). Occult participation: its impact on adolescent development. *Adolescence,* 24(96), 751–772.

VanBenschoten, S. C. (1990). Multiple personality disorder and satanic ritual abuse: The issue of credibility. *Dissociation, 1*(3), 13–20.

Wertheim, P. A. (1989). Investigation of ritualistic crime scenes. *Journal of Forensic Identification, 39*(2), 97–106.

Young, W. C., Sachs, B. G., Braun, B. G., & Wathins, R. T. (1991). Patients reporting ritual abuse in childhood: A clinical syndrome. Report of 37 Cases. *Child Abuse and Neglect, 15,* 181–189.

The A's and B's of Eating Disorders

Eating to Extremes

Sandra Arbetter, MSW

 7-year-old in Chicago cries herself to sleep because she thinks she has the fattest thighs in her class.

A couple of junior high boys in Los Angeles get together to eat pizza and make themselves vomit afterward.

Hundreds of 18- to 25-year-olds told *Esquire Magazine* they would rather get run over by a truck than gain a lot of weight.

Fear of food has become rampant among young people in the United States. Reports vary, but one estimate is that eating disorders affect 2 million girls ages 12 to 18 and half a million boys. The National Association of Anorexia Nervosa and Associated Disorders (ANAD) says there are 7 million females and 1 million males in the United States who have anorexia nervosa or bulimia nervosa—the two major eating disorders. Anorexia is self-starvation. Bulimia is eating and then getting rid of the food by vomiting or taking diuretics, laxatives, or purgatives.

Binge eating (compulsive overeating without purging) is considered by some experts to be a third eating disorder.

Anorexia Nervosa

Katie Maloney, now 14, was in third grade when she began anorexic behaviors. "I compared myself to others and to the commercials on losing weight. And my mom and my friends' moms are always talking about dieting.

"Then one day this boy and I were kidding around and he said, 'You're fat.'" That did it. Katie was determined to lose weight—by not eating.

"About that time my dad was told he had diabetes. My mother and father both went on diets. There was a lot of talk in the house about what to eat and what not to eat.

"I just stopped eating. I didn't know what was going on. My mom and dad began to worry and they'd try to make me eat. I refused.

"This went on through 4th, 5th, and 6th grades. The summer before 6th grade I weighed 42 pounds. I probably should have weighed about 70. I weighed myself all the time. Mom hid the scales and finally threw them out. We don't have scales in the house now."

The summer before 6th grade

Actress Tracey Gold—An Anorexic at Age 12

When Tracey Gold got down to 80 pounds, she looked in the mirror and said, "This is somebody who could die of anorexia." She decided not to be that somebody.

Tracey, who played Carol Seaver on "Growing Pains" for six seasons, is 5 feet 3½ inches tall and now weighs 92 pounds. That's still less than the minimum desirable weight set by the Department of Health and Human Services, and progress is slow.

Although she now has some color in her cheeks and no longer hides under oversize clothes, she still considers fatty foods to be a mortal enemy, and she weighs herself every day. "I'm still not a normal person about food," she says.

Tracey was first diagnosed with anorexia at age 12. After four months of therapy, the problem seemed to be under control. By the time she was 19, she weighed 133 pounds. She went on a diet of 500 calories—with the aid of a doctor—to get to 113 pounds.

She did that easily, but kept right on starving herself and losing more weight. In January 1992 she had to leave "Growing Pains" to enter a Los Angeles hospital. She entered outpatient therapy and got up to 95 pounds. Then she panicked. She was afraid that once she hit 100 pounds she would no longer have control over her weight.

Being in show biz puts people at extra risk of developing an eating disorder. That's true of other careers where weight and fitness are important. But then there's Anna Nicole Smith, model for Guess? jeans. She's 5 feet 11 inches and weighs 155 pounds. "Who wants to hug a skeleton?" she asks. Rumor has it she eats anything she wants and insists on chocolates at every shoot.

Katie was put in the hospital. "It didn't help. I had to go back to the hospital in October of 6th grade. The second time was my choice. I knew I wasn't doing well. Besides, I knew if I got worse they'd make me go.

"I missed most of 6th grade and was in the hospital for the summer before 7th grade. I haven't had to go back since, and I'm halfway through 8th grade."

Most anorexics are girls—about 90 percent. Some experts used to think there were no male anorexics, but ANAD says it's an increasing problem that's still often overlooked. One college senior who is 6 feet 2 inches tall and once was down to 100 pounds says his friends and family pretended the signs weren't there. "It's lonely being a male anorexic," he says. He was in the hospital several times for treatment of the physical effects of starvation. "I told my friends I was in the hospital for depression. It sounded more manly."

Social Stresses

The disorder is as painful for boys as it is for girls, but more girls succumb to the social pressures to be thin. That's true for bulimics, too. Girls are taught early on to be good and to please other people. One way to please is to be thin. Girls are trained to value their body for how it looks; boys see their body in terms of performance—what it can do.

Girls are especially vulnerable in early adolescence. According to psychologist Carol Gilligan, girls show a drop in self-esteem and an increase in depression and eating disorders at that time. Boys are most vulnerable to stress earlier in childhood.

As their breasts and hips get fuller with maturing, girls see that as getting fat. Since they have learned to judge themselves by what they think others want, they now try to shape themselves to what they think will please others. They are further pressured by the attention they get from boys.

Along with a changing body comes a feeling that something is taking place over which the young girl has no control. Self-starvation is a way to feel in control again. It's also a way to halt the growing-up process.

In adolescence, girls are beginning to find their own identity. There may be conflict with parents. It's not necessarily a rejection of family values, but rather a way for girls to say: I am not my mother. I am someone else. Katie Maloney expressed some of this in her anorexia. "My mom used to be overweight. I remember thinking I didn't want to be like her."

For many girls, refusing to eat is the first time they've expressed their own needs. These girls are masters at hiding unhappiness. One eating specialist put it this way: "The anorexic gets where she is because she has learned she is valued for needing nothing." They often are described as perfect children: obedient, high achievers in school, even though they actually may feel terrible.

They want to be "perfectly" thin—like the models. British model Kate Moss has made millions from her 5 foot 7 inch, 100-pound figure. Critics have taken to scrawling "Feed me" across her billboard image. They say her popularity is a perfect example of how we reward women for being thin.

That message gets across to girls at an early age. In a study by the University of South Carolina of more than 3,000 5th to 8th graders, more than 40 percent said they felt fat or wanted to lose weight. Only 20 percent actually were overweight.

In a survey of 11,000 high school students by the Centers for Disease Control and Prevention, almost half the girls reported they were on a diet although many didn't even think they were overweight.

Dieting can be harmful enough, but many teens use drugs to speed the process. Vivian Meehan, president of ANAD, says it's easy for teens to get over-the-counter drugs to cut their appetite, to get rid of fluids, and to purge what they have eaten.

Meehan says many diet pills contain phenylpropanolamine hydrochloride (PPA), which works like the amphetamine, speed. It may temporarily curb the appetite, but it may raise blood pressure and can cause kidney

Eating Disorders at a Glance

Anorexia
- deliberate self-starvation
- intense fear of being fat
- refusal to eat, except for tiny portions
- denial of hunger
- distorted body image
- abnormal weight loss
- hair loss (only after disorder has progressed to severe stage)
- sensitivity to cold
- cessation of menstruation

Bulimia
- preoccupation with food
- binge eating, usually in secret
- vomiting after bingeing
- abuse of laxatives, water pills, diet pills
- compulsive exercising
- swollen salivary glands
- broken blood vessels in eyes
- discolored teeth
- irritation of esophagus

damage and hallucinations, as well as fatal stroke.

Unreasonable Expectations

Over the past few decades, it's become politically correct for women to work toward gaining control over their lives. Being thin is a way of proving control of the body, and, by implication, of other things, too.

Eating disorders are especially common in certain professions in which weight and high achievement are important—entertainment, dance, athletics. It goes beyond fitness; it's kind of a status symbol of the discipline needed to achieve success. One survey found that 15 percent of female medical students had had an eating disorder at some time.

But Dr. Michael Strober, specialist in eating disorders at UCLA, says there's more to it than social pressures. "Just admiring super-thin models will not turn a person into an anorexic. A real anorexic suffers from self-doubt and self-esteem anxieties. Her world has been battered by the unreasonable expectation that…fat—any fat—equals failure."

Family Factors

Social pressures and self-esteem issues are not even the whole story. There also are family factors. Some experts say anorexics are trying to divert attention from family problems. As long as parents are focused on their starving child, they don't have to face their own problems—problems that might split apart the family.

"For me, it was a feeling that I should be able to solve all my family's problems," says 16-year-old Karen Mann. "I was in 8th grade and my family was going through a lot. My sister was looking at colleges. My mom was having eye surgery. There were things at home I was not in control of. I WAS in control of eating.

"It started at the end of 8th grade when we used to get weighed in gym. I was 5 feet tall and overweight. Someone screamed across the room, 'Oh, my God, you weigh 150.' I was so upset. Besides, I had relatives who made rude comments about my being fat. I began dieting to show them.

"By the end of the school year I was down to 135. People were saying I looked great. People who would never even talk to me were paying attention. By the end of the summer before high school I weighed 96 pounds.

"I wasn't happy. My face was drawn. I cried a lot. Before I went to sleep I'd crawl into bed with my mom and practically sit in her lap. My friends didn't understand and were kind of scared. My parents' friends said, 'Why don't you just make her eat?'

"I didn't have all the typical symptoms. When I was skinny, I knew it—I didn't see myself as still being fat. I wouldn't get dressed in front of the mirror—my bones showed. My parents didn't know how thin I was. I wore sweats. Then one day I was in my underwear trying on a dress and my mom almost fainted.

"She took me to a counseling group. The social worker said I was anorexic and sent me to an eating disorders specialist. Now I was 86 pounds. For one week I ate full meals, and I still lost two pounds. I was down to 84 pounds.

"The doctor gave me an EKG (electrocardiogram, measuring heart function), and I was close to being a flatliner. I was anemic and dehydrated and had a calcium deficiency. The doctor said I had to go into the hospital or I could die in a month.

"My dad wanted to go home and talk about it, but Mom knew I'd run away or talk them out of it, so I went right to the hospital. I was there for a month, on seven or eight medications to stabilize my body. Even now I have physi-

cal effects, like lots of cavities from the calcium deficiency.

"I had group and individual therapy. I learned to handle stress in other ways than through food. I learned not to isolate myself. I'm into softball and I'm in a leader's program at school. I take heavy gym courses and then I help teach the class.

"My advice is that if you like yourself you won't change for others—even to be thin. People who like you only because you're thin aren't worth it.

"I used to always apologize if I thought a friend didn't like something I said or did. Now I have more confidence. I stand up for myself.

"Listen to others when they tell you you have an eating disorder. Find a specialist. Girls die of eating disorders."

A Family Affair

Eating disorders may run in families. The rate of anorexia among sisters is much higher than in the general population. Katie Maloney's older sister, Beth, is also anorexic. "We were in competition for two years: Who can be thinner, who can eat less, who can exercise more. We have our own lives now."

Some studies show that in families where there are eating disorders, family members do not talk easily about feelings. Conflicts are not brought into the open where they can be resolved. Katie says one thing that has come out of her illness is that family members have learned to talk with one another. "I can talk to my mom about anything," she says.

Focusing on food can divert individual problems, too, and blot out painful feelings. What happens, though, is that good things are also blotted out. Anorexics become isolated. They stop seeing friends and having fun. Katie Maloney says, "I'd go to school, come home, fight with my parents about eating, and exercise. I didn't see anyone. Now I baby-sit. I love kids. And I play volleyball and swim."

Anorexia may involve genetic factors, also. Some studies show low levels of body chemicals such as serotonin and norepinephrine in those with anorexia. These chemicals affect appetite, weight, mood, and reactions to stress.

Bulimia Nervosa

Bulimia nervosa literally means "oxlike hunger of nervous origin." It's sometimes called binge-and-purge syndrome because many bulimics binge on thousands of calories and then purge by making themselves vomit or by taking laxatives, purgatives, or diuretics. According to ANAD, however, not all bulimics gorge themselves. Some eat moderate amounts and vomit up even that.

It's not uncommon for a person to alternate bulimic and anorexic behaviors. The medical explanation is that when weight drops below a certain point, the body tries to return it to normal. There's an almost irresistible urge to take in a lot of calories. What faster way than binging?

Starving can shrink organs, including the brain. The brain tries to get the body back to normal by creating thoughts of food. Maybe that's why anorexics often like to cook and feed others and why bulimics obsess about food.

That's how it started for Sari Burris. "I was on this diet of 800 calories a day, and I was losing lots of weight. One day I was home alone and I couldn't get out of my mind the chips in the kitchen cabinet. I ate the whole bag. And then half a package of chocolate-covered graham crackers. I was so sick, I threw up. The next time I went on a binge I felt disgusted with myself, but I didn't throw up. So I stuck my finger down my throat.

"It was easy to keep my behavior a secret. I'd eat normally in front of everyone and binge when my parents were working, so they never even heard me vomiting. And I worked out at least two hours every day."

Compulsive exercising is common with anorexics and bulimics. Karen Mann went through two exercise tapes every day—a total of two hours. Katie Maloney would run up and down stairs. "Once my mom was in New Mexico and I got lonely. My dad and I didn't talk, so I jogged. I'd get up at 12:30 in the morning and

Self-Image by Madison Avenue

Draw a picture of what you look like.

Draw a picture of what you'd like to look like.

If you're a girl, you've probably drawn your ideal as thinner than you think you are.

If you're a boy, your ideal is probably more muscular than you think you are.

jog until I had to go to school. I kept falling asleep in class."

Karen, too, had problems in school. "I fainted once because I was dehydrated. The school nurse figured it all out. She told my parents, and we all had to go for counseling. The nurse told me I was lucky that I wasn't sicker. She knew one girl whose esophagus had ruptured from all the acid from throwing up."

Purging can result in stomachaches, nausea, weakness, sore muscles, and rotting teeth. Even more serious is dehydration, which can cause a loss of potassium and trigger a heart attack.

Experts say bulimics are easier to treat than anorexics because they more often want to be helped. Antidepressants help, and so does education about nutrition. So does learning what situations trigger the binges. For Sari it was fighting—with her boyfriend, her mother, her sister. "I couldn't deal with anyone being mad at me. I'd go right for the cookies."

It's important to put food into the proper perspective. Vivian Meehan of ANAD says young people shouldn't think in terms of

Getting Help

If you or someone you care about has an eating disorder:
• face up to it. Talk about it. Don't pretend it doesn't exist.
• seek help from parents, teachers, school counselors
• contact these groups for information and help:

ANAD—National Association
   of Anorexia Nervosa and
   Associated Disorders
Box 7
Highland Park, IL 60035
(708) 831-3438

American Anorexia/Bulimia
   Association
418 E. 76th St.
New York, NY 10021
(212) 734-1114

Anorexia Nervosa and Related
   Eating Disorders (ANRED)
P.O. Box 5102
Eugene, OR 97405
(503) 344-1144

National Anorexic Aid Society
445 E. Greenville Road
Worthington, OH 43085
(614) 436-1112

dieting but of eating healthy foods that taste good.

That can help turn the A's and B's of eating disorders into the ABCs of physical and emotional health:

Approach food as a friend, not an enemy.

Believe in yourself, not in some phony social image.

Cope with stress by expressing your feelings verbally. Learn how to be assertive and communicate honestly with everyone in your life. ☐

For More Information

Consumer Information Center
Department 551A
Pueblo, CO 81009
Pamphlet: "Eating Disorders," single copy free.

American Academy of Child & Adolescent Psychiatry
Att: Public Information
3615 Wisconsin Avenue, NW
Washington, DC 20016
Fact Sheet: "Teenagers with Eating Disorders," single copy free with self-addressed, stamped business-size envelope.

National Institute of Child Health and Human Development
PO Box 29111
Washington, DC 20040
Pamphlet: "Facts About Anorexia Nervosa," single copy free.

American Psychiatric Association
Division of Public Affairs
1400 K St., NW
Washington, DC 20005
Booklet: "Let's Talk Facts About Eating Disorders," Code #GLC, single copy free with self-addressed, stamped business-size envelope.

National Mental Health Association
1021 Prince Street
Alexandria, VA 22314
Fact Sheet: "Anorexia and Bulimia," single copy free.

Biceps in a bottle

Teenagers turn to steroids to build muscles

He is the new man. His state-of-the-art physique is displayed on everything from billboards and television shows to dance-music videos and the fashion pages of men's magazines. He is young and muscular, but eschews the steel-belted-radial appearance of competitive body-builders. His is the lean and hungry "cut" look as exemplified by Markey Mark, the rapper turned Calvin Klein model. Bulging biceps, chiselled chest and washboard stomach are his fashion accessories, amply exposed over low-riding jeans. As portrayed in pop culture, the new man is Saturday night-primed, his hard body a turn-on to women and a threat to other men. And that is precisely what a lot of teenage boys want. But their bodies are still developing, so the only quick way to achieve that ideal look is by turning to anabolic steroids to get what nature did not supply. "You see anyone in high school who is big—has ripped mass, the curl in the bicep, the veins—and you know he's on it," says a teenage steroid user who asks to be called Joe. "He's juiced."

Steroids, once exclusive to elite athletes and hard-core body-builders, are now the elixirs of young males' vanity. The muscle-building substances, generally used by veterinarians on animals, are widely available to Canadian high-school students through networks of other athletes or at gyms. They are costly: a five-week cycle of use costs $600 or more. Yet according to a 1993 study commissioned by the Ottawa-based Canadian Centre for Drug-Free Sport, about 83,000 Canadians between the ages of 11 and 18 now use steroids, and nearly half of those are solely concerned with improving body image. Experts link the phenomenon to the recent exploitation of "beefcake" to sell everything from fragrances to floor cleaners. "These guys are out there with really distorted views of what they should look like," says Dr. Arthur Blouin, a psychologist at the Ottawa Civic Hospital who is studying the similarities between steroid abuse and eating disorders. "They are willing to risk the side-effects of steroids to avoid the negative perception that they are too small and weak."

Tom (not his real name) agrees. A decent student and good athlete, he began weight training to keep fit after breaking his leg. He liked how it made him look but, he says, "I wanted more size, faster." Last summer, encouraged by a training partner, he began taking steroids, both in pill form and by injections into the muscles of his buttocks. When school resumed in September, he says, "I got a huge response, from guys and girls. I was sort of shocked at first,

but after a while, I began to like it." He found, however, that when he went off the drugs he lost weight rapidly—much the way sprinter Ben Johnson did when he stopped his own steroid use. Deeply depressed, Tom would buy more and begin another cycle. "You might be able to dodge the physical side-effects for a long time if you know what you're doing," he says. "But you can't avoid what steroids do to your head."

Tom and others like him confirm that, in part, their body-image obsession is a response to the depiction of men as sex objects in mainstream media. "Kids see the well-built guys on TV, getting the girls and the respect from the guys," says Tom, "and they want that, too." But in their zeal to look great, steroid users risk a far worse fate than a skinny body. Steroid use commonly leads to prolific outbreaks of acne on the upper back, baldness, shrunken testicles, reduced sexual drive, heavier beards, a puffy face and depression. Prolonged abuse can cause heart and liver disorders, growth of tumors and damage to the endocrine system. Just as dangerous are what users call steroid rages. "Your whole mentality changes," says Joe. "You go from an intelligent, normal guy to someone who resorts to beating people up if they don't agree with you. It's a totally physical mentality, and very aggressive."

Furthermore, novice users don't realize that a large percentage of black-market steroids are cut with other substances to improve dealers' profits, says Vancouver-based RCMP Const. Keith Pearce. In a raid on a Vancouver dealer's home last March, members of Pearce's detachment seized liquid anabolic steroids that were mixed with Armor-All, a compound used to shine car dashboards. Metropolitan Toronto police Sgt. Savas Kyriacou says that the vast majority of users do not consult physicians, and instead rely on informa-tion from people in the gyms. "Like any type of street-level drug, ster-oids get cut every time they change hands," Kyriacou says. "A lot of these kids are injecting themselves with chemicals that are even worse than the steroids."

Starting out, of course, young users see only the benefits. "I'd be at a club or something and no one would mess with me," Tom says. "And girls were more friendly—I got more dates." But that high can be short-lived. Joe stopped taking the drugs because he could no longer work out after seriously injuring his shoulder. Now 19 and getting ready to begin university, he says he has gained perspective. "If I hadn't had the injury, I would probably still be taking them now," he says. "But that could just as easily have kept head-ing me down the road to self-de-struction. I mean, would they find me dead of a heart attack in my dorm room some day, with a needle sticking out of my ass? I don't know." He is glad, he says, that he never found out.

—**James Deacon**

Adolescent Suicide:
Risk Factors and Countermeasures

Raquel D. Norton

Raquel D. Norton is a Graduate Student in School Health at Brigham Young University, Provo, UT 84602.

Abstract

Suicide is the second leading cause of death for adolescents aged 15-to-24. The rate of completed and attempted suicides could be reduced by training teachers, counselors, and students to recognize those who are high risk and immediately responding by implementing both prevention and postvention strategies. Prevention strategies include identifying warning signs of suicidal behavior, referring to trained personnel, and teaching alternative coping techniques. Postvention strategies are directed toward sharing information, expressing feelings, and identifying those who are most vulnerable for suicidal actions.

Adolescent suicide, a major public health problem in the United States, is now the second leading cause of death among 15-to 24-year-olds, with the rate of suicides increasing for females by 250 percent, and 300 percent for males (Conrad, 1992).

The magnitude of the problem becomes even more apparent when statistics on suicide attempts are examined. In a study conducted by Moore et al., (1991), the rate of attempted suicide by those high school students who participated in state and local surveys was estimated to range from five percent to 12 percent. Data also revealed that although adolescent males die more often from suicide than do adolescent females, females attempt suicide more frequently than do males (Shaffer, Garland, Underwood, & Whittle, 1987).

Risk Factors

There is no single profile for the suicidal adolescent. However, suicidal behavior may be manifested in a variety of ways such as part of a psychotic process where hallucinatory voices tell one to perform self-destructive acts, or a personality disturbance in which feelings of anger and impulse get out of control, thus causing self-destruction to take over. Suicidal behavior may manifest itself in the adolescent who has a conduct disorder, finds himself constantly in trouble, and eventually comes to the conclusion that life is too difficult. The adolescent may feel like a loner and finds life isn't worth living if he or she cannot be identified with a certain peer group (Reynolds, 1985).

In general, youth at high risk are those who are depressed, isolated, and angry-impulsive. Over 50 percent of suicidal adolescents are considered depressed (Marttunen, Hillevi, & Lonnqvist, 1992). Most are isolated in that they are cut off either geographically or emotionally from friends and relatives. Most are angry-impulsive and tend to strike out without thinking. Usually, the more depressed the adolescent, the higher the risk that he or she will attempt suicide (Andrews & Lewinshon, 1992).

Garland, Whittle, and Shaffer (1989) assessed the risk factors for adolescent suicide and found that the strongest predictors were prior attempts and major depression. Up to 80 percent of those individuals who commit suicide have a history of previous suicide attempts (Wilson, 1991). Substance abuse, antisocial behavior (or the lack of friends), and a family history of suicide followed in importance (Sorenson, 1991). Other common factors among youth who attempt suicide are feelings of hopelessness, anger, fear, confusion, severe stress, and those who have poor problem-solving skills (Wagner & Calhoun, 1991).

Warning Signs

Very few suicides occur spontaneously. Usually the suicide is the final step of a progressive failure of the adolescent to adapt appropriately to his or her living situation. Because suicidal adolescents are ambivalent about dying and usually want to be rescued, two-thirds of the victims have given a cry for help by either communicating their wishes verbally or by suicidal acts. Seventy-five percent of the time, communication had taken place more than three months before the act (Marttunen et al., 1992). Therefore, school staff are in an opportune position to pick up the early warning signs given by a suicidal youth and may be able to prevent a suicide from happening.

While there are early warning signs which may indicate risk for suicide, it is very important to look for a constellation of behavioral, verbal, and situational signs. Suicidal gestures and attempts are the most obvious behavioral warnings (Marttunen et al., 1992). Talk about suicide, or even the most superficial attempts, should be taken seriously. Making special preparations such as settling all debts, writing a will, saying goodbye, obtaining the means to suicide (gun, poison), or giving away valued possessions, may be a sign that the adolescent is preparing for death (Reynolds, 1985; Andrews & Lewishon, 1992). Other behavioral warnings include sudden changes in behavior, such as a quiet student who becomes aggressive, a high achiever who suddenly begins failing, or an outgoing student who becomes withdrawn. Each may signal increased suicidal risk (Sorenson & Rutter, 1991). The adolescent who has appeared depressed over a long period of time and suddenly bounces back overnight may have decided upon total escape, thus signaling suicidal behavior (Wilson, 1991).

A second type of early warning sign consists of verbal warnings. The idea that people who talk about killing themselves never do is clearly a myth. Verbal statements often precede suicide attempts (Marttunen, et al., 1992). Some adolescents use vague phrases while others use more direct messages such as "I am thinking about committing suicide." Examples of possible verbal warnings include, "Everyone would be better off without me," or "I just want to end it all," or "I wish I'd never been born," (Barnes, 1986).

Some situations constitute the early warning signal, meaning that the adolescent need not say anything to indicate that it's a warning sign, but just by being in the situation means the adolescent is at high risk for suicide. Typical situations which can lead to suicidal thoughts and feelings include: (1) losses such as the loss of a family member, status, self-esteem, or health; (2) the perception of failure as in the adolescent who sets unrealistic goals, doesn't receive an expected grade, or tries to live up to his or her parents' expectations; and (3) family turmoil such as previous suicidal behavior by family members (Garland et al., 1989; Wilson, 1991; Brent et al., 1992).

Intervention

It has been suggested that suicide rates could be reduced by training persons to perform appropriate "psychological first aid" by identifying and responding to danger signals. Teachers are in an excellent position to take an active role in recognizing behaviors that are not adaptive because of their constant interaction with young people (Mulder, Methorst, & Diekstra, 1989).

However, before intervention strategies can be implemented by the teacher, he or she must be trained to recognize the signs and symptoms of suicidal behavior, where students can be referred to get help, and how to help youth find alternative

ways for solving their problems. According to the 1990 Wisconsin State Department of Public Instruction Bulletin No. 0500, titled "Suicide Prevention: A Guide to Curriculum Planning," there are five "tips" recommended in helping the suicidal adolescent.

Tip Number One: Should the teacher suspect that a student is suicidal, after having determined the student has certain risk factors or warning signs, the teacher should refer the suicidal student to a trained professional. This trained professional, whether he or she is the school counselor or a psychologist, should be available to help school personnel and students at the school at regularly scheduled times for risk assessment, family contact, intervention, and linking youth with the most appropriate care.

Tip Number Two: When a student is suspected to be suicidal, help should be sought from another adult for assistance, or from a trained professional.

Tip Number Three: Do not agree to "keep a secret" should it involve a potential victim of suicide. Explain to the informer that a break in confidence is better than having a dead friend, and that by their friend confiding in him or her about his or her suicidal intentions, the potential suicidal victim is really pleading for help.

Tip Number Four: A potential suicidal adolescent should never be left alone, but rather taken to a professional for counseling and risk assessment. Consultation should be sought from the school suicide prevention staff, a counselor, or a professional. Upon consultation, the adolescent's parents or guardian should be contacted.

Tip Number Five: It is important that the teacher listens, supports, gathers information, and refers the suicidal adolescent to the appropriate professional.

Even if the teacher does not approve of the student's perceptions of the problems or solutions, it is important that the teacher compassionately accepts those perceptions as his or hers at the moment, acknowledge his or her right to them, and be a good friend. Time also should be set aside to listen carefully to the student, to focus on the student's feelings, and to help the student understand his or her situation by paraphrasing the feelings just heard. The teacher should then help the student to define alternatives and find other sources of support. Thus, the teacher should gather

as much information as possible from the suicidal student by asking direct questions to help assess the individual's risk of suicide. The seriousness of self-destructive behavior can be classified as being immediate or long-range simply by determining the specificity, the availability, and the lethality of means the individual has chosen (Shneidman, 1987).

A student who has a well-thought-out plan which includes time, place, circumstances of how the suicide will be carried out, and by what method (specificity), is considered to be an immediate high risk for suicide. Is the means the individual has chosen easily assessable such as in the home, or can it be easily purchased (availability)? If so, the individual is in immediate danger of suicide. If the student has chosen a highly lethal method, in which death quickly follows the act, the student is again considered to be at an immediate high risk (Wisconsin Bulletin No. 0500, 1990). Such highly lethal methods include guns, jumping from a height, hanging, drowning, carbon monoxide poisoning, antidepressants, and the combination of barbiturates and prescription sleeping pills (Litman, 1987).

Peer Survivors

Exposure to a peer's suicide may render adolescents more likely to engage in subsequent attempted or completed suicide (Brent et al., 1992). The peer's death creates a loss of identity and a threat to self-esteem due to the mutual trust, openness, self-disclosure, and affection created within the friendship. Thus, the death of a friend is a "profound" loss (Gordon, 1986).

The death of peers also destroys the social network in which the individual is a member of and, since most friendship groups are dyads, the death of one means the termination or the ending of the group and thus, the absence of a social support system. Friendship is a unique type of relationship, with secrets and self-disclosure (Gordon, 1986). Thus, following the suicide of a friend, the feelings experienced by the peer left behind cannot be shared, and his or her coping strategies are challenged by the sudden loss for which the adolescent could not have been prepared (Wagner, 1991).

Adolescent suicide is a particularly

harmful form of death for peers who are left behind in that they suffer from a traumatic experience. They are not only grieving for their friend, but they are also potential victims of Post-Traumatic Stress Disorder (Brent et al., 1992), which can impede the normal grieving process, as can silence and the avoidance of discussion of the topic of suicide (Leenaars & Wenckstein, 1991).

Because the act of suicide and its implications can leave emotional scars on the survivors (Hazell, 1991), the death can be seen not as a crisis but as a unique opportunity for the school's involvement in postvention activities for peer survivors. With timely, appropriate assistance, individuals can be helped through the traumatic experience (Hetzel, Winn, & Tolstoshev, 1991).

Postvention

Postvention programs in the schools should incorporate both an immediate crisis response and a long term follow-up plan, in which students, teachers, administrators, counselors, parents, and community health personnel are involved. Long term postvention programs are geared toward following-up on the survivor and monitoring his or her adjustment back to normal activities, whereas immediate postvention programs are directed toward sharing information, expressing feelings, identifying those who are most vulnerable, and teaching students appropriate coping techniques.

It is important to have a method for getting the information out to all staff and students. School staff left unaware of the suicide are not in a position to be supportive of their peers or students. Many school districts will hold an emergency faculty meeting to discuss the facts of the event and the procedures for the day (Cultice, 1992).

All those who knew the person who has committed suicide will need some type of support. Allowing expression of such feelings as shock, panic, disbelief, anger, helplessness, and guilt (Wagner, 1991) is important for healing. These are just a few of the feelings experienced by both school staff and students following a suicide (Brent et al., 1992).

Through a supportive atmosphere where staff and students can express their feelings about the victim, students who are most vulnerable can be identified, referred for additional help, and assisted in using that help. Those students who are at an increased risk following a suicide are those who feel guilty about the things they have said or done to the victim (Hazell, 1991). This might include those who have a previous history of suicide attempts (Garland, 1989), those who were very close to the victim, and those who took part in the suicide act by providing the means, helping write the note, or keeping the event a secret (Ruof, Harris, & Robbie, 1987).

According to Wagner and Calhoun (1991), students need to know that suicide is a poor option for problem solving. It is a poor permanent solution to a temporary problem. It is important for students to know how to deal with difficult personal situations, how to use certain problem-solving techniques, how to deal with depression, and how to recognize when they or their friends need outside help. In dealing with these problems, coping strategies should be taught in the classroom setting.

Summary

Suicide by an adolescent is a psychosocially violent death, primarily because it is unanticipated by others and is unnatural. It is an act of aggression by the victim against himself, and against the survivors. For the majority of adolescents exposed to the suicide of a peer, healing will come from support and interaction with sensitive and caring people. Postvention in the school setting may serve several useful functions, including the alleviation of guilt among peer survivors, reduction of the scapegoating of parents, teachers, and peers, and most importantly, the reduction of imitative suicidal behavior. Thus, implementation of both prevention and postvention programs in the schools is essential in avoiding such precious losses.

Andrews, J.A., & Lewinsohn, P.M. (1992). Suicidal attempts among older adolescents: Prevalence and co-occurrence with psychiatric disorders. *Journal of the American Academy of Child Adolescent Psychiatry, 31*(4), 655-661.

Barnes, R.A. (1986). The recurrent self-harm patient. *Suicide and Life Threatening Behaviors, 16*(2), 399-408.

Brent, D.A. (1992). Psychiatric effects of exposure to suicide among the friends and acquaintances of adolescents suicide victims. *Journal of the American Academy of Child Adolescent Psychiatry, 31*(4), 629-639.

Conrad, N. (1992). Stress and knowledge of suicidal others as factors in suicidal behavior of high school adolescents. *Issues in Mental Health Nursing, 13*(2), 95-104.

Cultice, W.W. (1992). Establishing an effective crisis intervention program. *NASSP Bulletin, 76*(543), 68-72.

Garland, A., Whittle, B., & Shaffer, D. (1989). A survey of youth suicide prevention programs. *Journal of the American Academy of Child Adolescent Psychiatry, 28*, 931-934.

Gordon, A.K. (1986). The tattered cloak of immorality. In C.A. Corr & J.N. McNeil (Eds.), *Adolescence and Death*, 16-21.

Hazell, P. (1991). Postvention after teenage suicide: An Australian experience. *Journal of Adolescence, 14*(4), 333-342.

Hetzel, S., Winn, V., & Tolstoshev, H. (1991). Loss and change: New directions in death education for adolescents. *Journal of Adolescence, 14*(2), 323-334.

Leenaars, A.A., & Wenckstein, S. (1991). Post-traumatic stress disorder: A conceptual model for postvention. In A.A. Leenaars & S. Wenckstein (Eds.), *Suicide prevention in schools*, 173-180.

Litman, R.E. (1987). Mental disorders and suicidal intention. *Suicide and Life Threatening Behaviors, 17*(2), 85-92.

Marttunen, M.J., Hillevi, M.A., & Lonnqvist, J.K. (1992). Adolescent suicide: Endpoint of long-term difficulties. *Journal of the American Academy of Child Adolescent Psychiatry, 31*(4), 649-654.

Moore, J. (1991). Behaviors related to unintentional and intentional injuries among high school students:

United States. *Journal of School Health, 62*(9), 439-440.

Mulder, A.M., Methorst, G.J., & Diekstra, R.F. (1989). Prevention of suicidal behavior in adolescents: The role and training of teachers. *Crisis, 10*(1), 36-51.

Reynolds, D.E. (1985). How to recognize and cope with the suicidal teen. *Suicide Prevention: A special report.* Oregon State Department of Education, March.

Ruof, S., Harris, J., & Robbie, M. (1987). *Handbook: Suicide prevention in the schools.* Weld BOCES, LaSalle, CO.

Shaffer, D., Garland, A., Underwood, M., & Whittle, B. (1987). An evaluation of three youth suicide prevention programs in New Jersey. Report prepared for the New Jersey State Department of Health and Human Services.

Shneidman, E.S. (1987). At the point of no return. *Psychology Today, 21*(3), 54-58.

Sorenson, S.B., & Rutter, C.M. (1991). Transgenerational patterns of suicide attempt. *Journal of Consulting and Clinical Psychology, 59*(6), 861-866.

Wagner, K.G., & Calhoun, L.G. (1991). Perceptions of social support by suicide survivors and their social networks. *Omega, 24*(1), 61-73.

Wilson, G.L. (1991). Comment: Suicidal behavior: Clinical considerations and risk factors. *Journal of Consulting and Clinical Psychology, 59*(6), 869-872.

Index

Credits/Acknowledgments

Cover design by Charles Vitelli.

1. Perspectives on Adolescence
Facing overview—© 1997 by Cleo Freelance Photography.

2. Biological and Psychological Aspects of Puberty
Facing overview—© 1997 by Cleo Freelance Photography.

3. Cognitive Growth and Education
Facing overview—Dushkin/McGraw-Hill photo. 69—"Illustration of a Question" Test Sample from the Texas Assessment of Academic Skills.

4. Identity and Socioemotional Development
Facing overview—© 1997 by Cleo Freelance Photography.

5. Family Relationships
Facing overview—© 1997 by PhotoDisc, Inc. 106—*Philadelphia Inquirer* photo by Bonnie Weller.

6. Peers and Youth Culture
Facing overview—© 1997 by Cleo Freelance Photography.

7. Teenage Sexuality
Facing overview—Stock Boston photo by Michael Weisbrot.

8. Problem Behaviors and Interventions
Facing overview—© 1997 by Cleo Freelance Photography.

ANNUAL EDITIONS ARTICLE REVIEW FORM

■ NAME: _____ DATE: _____

■ TITLE AND NUMBER OF ARTICLE: _____

■ BRIEFLY STATE THE MAIN IDEA OF THIS ARTICLE: _____

_____

■ LIST THREE IMPORTANT FACTS THAT THE AUTHOR USES TO SUPPORT THE MAIN IDEA:

_____

_____

_____

_____

■ WHAT INFORMATION OR IDEAS DISCUSSED IN THIS ARTICLE ARE ALSO DISCUSSED IN YOUR
TEXTBOOK OR OTHER READINGS THAT YOU HAVE DONE? LIST THE TEXTBOOK CHAPTERS AND
PAGE NUMBERS:

_____

_____

_____

_____

_____

■ LIST ANY EXAMPLES OF BIAS OR FAULTY REASONING THAT YOU FOUND IN THE ARTICLE:

_____

_____

_____

_____

■ LIST ANY NEW TERMS/CONCEPTS THAT WERE DISCUSSED IN THE ARTICLE, AND WRITE A SHORT
DEFINITION:

_____

_____

_____

We Want Your Advice

ANNUAL EDITIONS revisions depend on two major opinion sources: one is our Advisory Board, listed in the front of this volume, which works with us in scanning the thousands of articles published in the public press each year; the other is you—the person actually using the book. Please help us and the users of the next edition by completing the prepaid article rating form on this page and returning it to us. Thank you for your help!

ANNUAL EDITIONS: ADOLESCENT PSYCHOLOGY 98/99
Article Rating Form

Here is an opportunity for you to have direct input into the next revision of this volume. We would like you to rate each of the 58 articles listed below, using the following scale:

1. **Excellent: should definitely be retained**
2. **Above average: should probably be retained**
3. **Below average: should probably be deleted**
4. **Poor: should definitely be deleted**

Your ratings will play a vital part in the next revision. So please mail this prepaid form to us just as soon as you complete it.
Thanks for your help!

Rating	Article	Rating	Article
	1. Teenage Wasteland?		28. Enjoying Your Child's Teenage Years
	2. The Way We Weren't: The Myth and Reality of the "Traditional" Family		29. "Don't Talk Back!"
			30. Gay Families Come Out
	3. WAAAH!! Why Kids Have a Lot to Cry About		31. Bringing Up Father
	4. The Age of Embarrassment		32. Longitudinal Studies of Effects of Divorce on Children in Great Britain and the United States
	5. "My Body Is So Ugly"		
	6. I'm Okay!		33. Football, Fast Cars, and Cheerleading: Adolescent Gender Norms, 1978–1989
	7. The Body of the Beholder		
	8. A Study of White Middle-Class Adolescent Boys' Responses to "Semenarche" (The First Ejaculation)		34. Friendship and Friends' Influence in Adolescence
			35. Too Old, Too Fast?
	9. A Dangerous Rite of Passage		36. Why Working Teens Get into Trouble
	10. The Long and Short of It: New Medications for Growth Disorders		37. Perils of Prohibition
			38. Surge in Teen-Age Smoking Left an Industry Vulnerable
	11. Developmentally Appropriate Middle Level Schools		
	12. Program Helps Kids Map Realistic Goals		39. The New Pot Culture
	13. Mommy, What's a Classroom?		40. Chips Ahoy
	14. Boys' Schools Reconsidered: Good News in Troubled Times		41. Too Young to Date?
			42. A Clack of Tiny Sparks
	15. At-Risk Students and Resiliency: Factors Contributing to Academic Success		43. Learning to Love
			44. Virgin Cool
	16. Good Mentoring Keeps At-Risk Youth in School		45. The Neglected Heart: The Emotional Danger of Premature Sexual Involvement
	17. Schools the Source of Rough Transitions		
	18. The Test of Their Lives		46. Sexual Correctness: Has It Gone Too Far?
	19. International Differences in Mathematical Achievement: Their Nature, Causes, and Consequences		47. In Defense of Teenaged Mothers
			48. How Should We Teach Our Children about Sex?
	20. Gender Gap in Math Scores Is Closing		49. Key Skill for Teen Parents: Having Realistic Expectations
	21. There's a First Time for Everything: Understanding Adolescence		
			50. Will Schools Risk Teaching about the Risk of AIDS?
	22. College Kids' Parents Should "Keep Cool"		51. Young Adults and AIDS: 'It Can't Happen to Me'
	23. Ethnicity, Identity Formation, and Risk Behavior among Adolescents of Mexican Descent		52. Programs Go beyond "Just Saying No"
			53. Seeking the Criminal Element
	24. "I'm Just Who I Am"		54. The Youngest Ex-Cons: Facing a Difficult Road Out of Crime
	25. The EQ Factor		
	26. Adolescence: Whose Hell Is It?		55. Clinical Assessment of Adolescents Involved in Satanism
	27. How Teens Strain the Family		56. The A's and B's of Eating Disorders: Eating to Extremes
			57. Biceps in a Bottle
			58. Adolescent Suicide: Risk Factors and Countermeasures

(Continued on next page)

ABOUT YOU

Name _____ Date _____

Are you a teacher? ❏ Or a student? ❏

Your school name _____

Department _____

Address _____

City _____ State _____ Zip _____

School telephone # _____

YOUR COMMENTS ARE IMPORTANT TO US!

Please fill in the following information:

For which course did you use this book? _____

Did you use a text with this *ANNUAL EDITION*? ❏ yes ❏ no

What was the title of the text? _____

What are your general reactions to the *Annual Editions* concept?

Have you read any particular articles recently that you think should be included in the next edition?

Are there any articles you feel should be replaced in the next edition? Why?

Are there any World Wide Web sites you feel should be included in the next edition? Please annotate.

May we contact you for editorial input?

May we quote your comments?

ANNUAL EDITIONS: ADOLESCENT PYSCHOLOGY 98/99